MTEL Math 03

Prepare for the Massachusetts General Curriculum Subtest

Mary DeSouza Stephens

Contents

Chapter 3:

Number Sense 99

Chapter 4:

Functions & Equations 139

Introduction

The mathematics subtest of the Massachusetts Tests for Educator Licensure (MTEL) General Curriculum (03) Exam requires educators to demonstrate mastery of the elementary mathematics material necessary to become an effective educator. It is one of the two subtests included in the MTEL General Curriculum test and may be taken independently or in conjunction with the Multi–subject subtest. The lessons and practice questions contained in the chapters of this book cover all of the material on the math subtest, and the included practice tests closely mirror the wording, style, tone, difficulty, and format of the questions. The test is only offered as a computer–based test, so please see www.mtel.nesinc.com for more information.

About the Test

The mathematics subtest is administered by appointment year–round at designated test centers. You are allowed up to four hours to complete both sections of the general curriculum exam, keeping in mind it is acceptable to pass each subtest in a different administration. In other words, you could choose to spend the entire four hours on the math subtest and take the multi–subject test on another day.

The subtest is divided into two sections: 45 multiple–choice questions and 1 open response assignment. Calculators are not permitted. Test content is broken down as follows:

Question Type	Subarea	Approximate Number of Questions	Percentage of Score
45 Multiple Choice Questions	⊙ Numbers and Operations ⊙ Functions and Algebra ⊙ Geometry and Measurement ⊙ Statistics and Probability	19 – 21 10 – 12 8 – 10 4 – 6	90%
Open Response Item	⊙ Integration of Knowledge and Understanding	1	10%

You must achieve a score of 240 or higher to pass the test. You will not be deducted points for incorrect answers; therefore, do not leave anything blank (even if that means guessing). For current information regarding test framework, registration, scheduling, and other pertinent notices, please visit www.mtel.nesinc.com.

How to Use this Book

This book is designed to help you successfully pass the mathematics subtest of the MTEL. It is recommended you work through each of the eight chapters, focusing on your areas of weakness. The material in each chapter is broken into categories. Each category consists of a lesson and practice questions. In addition, each chapter has a comprehensive quiz. After completing the lessons and practice questions, review the open response chapter.

Approximately two weeks before your scheduled test, take and score the two practice exams included at the end of the book. Spend time reviewing all the answer explanations and based on your results, go back and review any areas of weakness.

About the Author

Mary Stephens (nee DeSouza) graduated from MIT with a bachelor's degree and a master's degree in Computer Science and Electrical Engineering. She has over 20 years of teaching experience, including designing courses and teaching as an adjunct faculty member at UMass Boston; TAing discrete math at MIT; and developing curriculum for and teaching classes in high school computer science, LSAT, algebra, geometry, science, humanities, and K–12 math and computers. Outside of teaching, Mary worked in engineering, product management, and strategy for companies including Edusoft and Oracle. In the past few years, she has spoken at international education conferences and served as adjunct faculty teaching prospective teachers at UMASS and Elms college, professional math consultant at Merrimack College, founder of Omega Teaching, board member of Alpha Public Schools, and Research and Development Manager at Houghton Mifflin Harcourt. She currently serves as the CEO of PrepForward (www.prep-forward.com), a leading provider of teacher preparation materials. She can be contacted at mary@prepforward.com.

Please visit the PrepForward website to find out about other preparation materials for the MTEL 03 General Curriculum Math Subtest, including self–paced, online courses and diagnostic exams. In addition, PrepForward offers prospective teachers preparation for other MTEL exams and existing teachers professional development courses that are certified by the Massachusetts Department of Education for PDPs.

Testing Strategies

There are several things you can do to help yourself be successful on the mathematics subtest:

⊙ **Read all of the directions.**
Take the time to read, listen and carefully review all directions on each section of the test.

⊙ **Read through the entire question and all of the answers before making your final selection.**
Make sure to take the time to read through all of the possible choices — remember, you are asked to determine the "best answer". At a first glance, though choice A may appear to be a good answer, it is possible another choice will be better.

- ⊙ **When in doubt, take a guess.**
  Because unanswered questions are considered incorrect, it is important to answer every question even if you are unsure of the answer.

- ⊙ **Evaluate the problem**
  If you know how to solve the problem, go ahead and do it! But, don't waste time on problems that cover material you don't know or can't recall. Remember, you have four hours to complete the exam. While you should not race through the test, you should also take care not to spend too much time on any one question. Keep in mind you also need to leave time to answer one open response item. Should you find yourself struggling on a question, there will be an option to "Flag for Review". Make a selection, flag the question, and if you have time at the end of the exam, go back for further review.

- ⊙ **Guessing and eliminating answers**
  It's to your advantage to guess on this test — but, be clever about it. Eliminate any unreasonable answer choices before guessing. NEVER leave a question blank.

- ⊙ **Back solving**
  Since the majority of the questions are multiple–choice, you can plug the numbers from the answers into the question.

  ### Example – Which of the following values for N will make the statement true?

  $$N \times N = N + N$$

  A. 1
  B. 2
  C. 3
  D. 4

When you try each of the answers in the original problem, it becomes obvious choice B makes the statement true and is therefore correct.

⊙ Plugging In

Guess a number, plug into the original problem, and then plug it into each of the answers to see what works. This strategy is particular effective when you have variables in the question stem and in the answer choices. Make sure to plug in "good numbers". For example, if a problem is dealing with minutes, use 30 or 60, not 143. Whenever there is a problem with percents, always plug in 100.

Example – If N is an even number, which of the following products is an odd number?

A. $(N+1)(N-3)$
B. $(N+1)(N+2)$
C. $N(N+1)$
D. $N(N-3)$

For this problem, think of any even number, such as 4. Then plug that number into each answer choice to see which answer is odd. Again, it becomes obvious that one choice (choice A) is correct.

When answering the open response item, remember to address each of the directives and write from the perspective of a teacher reviewing a student's work. This portion of the test is worth 10% of your score, so answer the question thoroughly to receive as many points as possible.

1. Before test day, make sure you know where your test center and parking facilities are located.
2. The day before the test, make sure to review the test–taking strategies in the introduction of this book.
3. Check the official MTEL website for a list of items you may and may not bring to the test site.
   Note—use of calculators is not allowed on this test.
4. The night before the test, make sure to relax and sleep well. Performing well on this test requires critical thinking, which is simpler when you are fully alert.
5. Get to the test center early in case there are unforeseen issues with registration, parking, etc.
6. Make sure to bring one current, government–issued identification containing your photograph and signature. The identification must be in English and display the same name in which you registered. Acceptable forms include a valid driver's license, passport, military identification card, state or national identification or alien registration.

Cell phones, electronic devices, and printed material are prohibited at test sites. For additional information regarding acceptable identification and test center rules, visit www.mtel.nesinc.com.

Chapter 1:
Numbers & Operations

Lessons

1.1 Foundations

Sets of Numbers

Most likely, numbers and counting were the first things you learned about in math. You might have begun by learning about the set of **"natural" or counting numbers**: 1, 2, 3, 4... Later, your knowledge would have expanded to include all **whole numbers**, the set of natural numbers plus zero: 0, 1, 2, 3... Numbers are used to represent distances, measurements, and other quantities, both positive and negative. **Integers** include zero and all the positive and negative numbers that do not need to be represented with fractions or decimals. A number line is a great way to visualize integers.

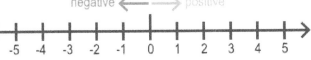

If a number can be written as a fraction, it is a **rational** number. Rational numbers include all decimals that either terminate or repeat, since those numbers can be expressed as fractions. Numbers, such as π, whose decimal does not terminate or repeat, are called **irrational** numbers. The **real** numbers include all rational and irrational numbers.

Reals
π, √2

Rationals
-3.46, 1/3, 74.222222...

Integers
... -4, -3, -2, -1

Whole
0

Natural (or Counting)
1, 2, 3, 4, 5, 6, ...

The diagram shows the relationship among the sets of numbers. For instance, the integers include the negatives and all the whole numbers, while the whole numbers include 0 and the counting numbers. Each of these sets is infinitely large. In other words, there is not a finite number of whole numbers. You can always keep adding 1 to the largest and get another whole number.

Other common number sets include the evens and odds. Even numbers include all numbers that equal 2 times an integer, for example -6, 0, 2, 10. Odd numbers are all integers that are not even, such as -5, 1, 9, or 17.

Ordering and Comparing Numbers

The number line helps to show the order of numbers. The further to the right a number is, the greater its value. For example, when comparing two negative numbers, the one closest to zero will be greater.

The following symbols are used to compare numbers:
= Equal to
> Greater than
< Less than
≥ Greater than or equal to
≤ Less than or equal to

Examples: 28 > 12   (28 is greater than 12)
-12 < -4   (-12 is less than -4)

NUMBERS & OPERATIONS PRACTICE

1. **What is the greatest integer smaller than 100?**

    A. 101
    B. 99.99
    C. 99 ½
    D. 99

2. **Which is a possible value for x if:**
    $12 > x > 8$

    A. 9
    B. 20
    C. 7
    D. not possible

3. What is a possible value for x if:

   $12 < x < 8$

   A. 9
   B. 20
   C. 7
   Ⓓ not possible

4. Choose all the answers that are true about 3.25:

   I. integer
   II. irrational
   III. real

   A. I and III
   Ⓑ III only
   C. II and III
   D. I, II, and III

5. Which of the following numbers are irrational?

   I. ⅓
   II. -12.451
   III. π

   A. none
   B. I and III
   Ⓒ III only
   D. all

6. Which answer is a list of negative integers ordered from least to greatest?

   A. -8, -9, -10, -11
   B. -8.5, -9.5, -10.5, -11.5
   C. 8, 9, 10, 11
   Ⓓ -11, -10, -9, -8

7. If you want to count all the integers that are greater than -3 and less than 4, how many numbers would you be counting?

   A. 5
   Ⓑ 6
   C. 7
   D. 8

8. If you wanted to count all the negative odd integers between -10 and 4, how many numbers would that include?

   Ⓐ 5
   B. 6
   C. 7
   D. 8

9. How many positive rational numbers are greater than -2 and less than 7?

   A. 6
   B. 7
   C. 9
   Ⓓ infinite

   -1, 0, 1, 2, 3, 4, 5, 6

10. The fraction ⅓ which equals 0.33333333... (repeats forever) belongs to which of the following number sets?

    I. Integers
    II. Rationals
    III. Reals

    A. III only
    Ⓑ II and III
    C. I and III
    D. I, II, and III

1. D   An integer is a whole number that can be positive, negative, or zero. Integers do not include decimals or fractions. The question asks for the greatest integer that is smaller than 100. Therefore, we need the closest integer that is less than 100. Answer choices A = 101 and D = 99 are the only integers. Answer choice D is the one that is the greatest integer that is smaller than 100.

2. A   Go through each answer choice and eliminate those that don't work. 12 is not greater than 20 (eliminate B). 7 is not greater than 8 (eliminate C). There are numbers that work (eliminate D). Answer choice A works. 12 is greater than 9 and 9 is greater than 8.

> $12 > x > 8$
> x must meet two different conditions.
> 12 must be greater than x.
> x must be greater than 8.

3. D   There are no numbers that are both bigger than 12 and less than 8. There are no possible values for x.

> $12 < x < 8$
> x must meet two different conditions.
> 12 must be less than x.
> x must be less than 8.

4. B   Let's examine each option:

     I.   **integer:** Integers do not include decimals or fractions. Therefore, 3.25 is not an integer.

     II.   **irrational:** Irrationals numbers are numbers that can not be expressed as fractions. Numbers with terminating decimals are rational. 3.25 is rational since the decimal terminates. Another way to think about it is that 3.25 can be expressed as 3 $\frac{1}{4}$, so it is rational. 3.25 is not irrational.

     III.   **real:** Real numbers include all rational and irrational numbers. 3.25 is a real number.

5. C Irrational numbers are numbers that can not be expressed as fractions.

     I. $\frac{1}{3}$: Since this number is a fraction, it is rational.

     II. -12.451: Any number with a terminating decimal can be expressed as a fraction. In this case, -12.451 = $\frac{-12451}{1000}$. Therefore, it is rational.

     III. π: If π is written in decimal form it goes on forever and does not repeat. π can not be written as a fraction, and therefore is irrational.

     III is the only irrational.

---

6. D Negative integers do not include any decimals or fractions. That eliminates answer choice B. Answer choice C only includes positive numbers, therefore, that is eliminated.

Now, let's examine answer choices A and D.

The greater a negative number is, the closer it is to zero. Therefore -10 is greater than -11. If we want to order the numbers from least to greatest, then answer choice D is the correct answer.

---

7. B List out all the integers that are greater than -3 and less than 4. Note that the question says greater than -3, not greater than or equal to -3. Therefore, we do not include -3. In the same way, the question asks for the integers less than 4, not less than or equal to 4. Therefore, we do not want to include 4.

> -2, -1, 0, 1, 2, 3
> 6 numbers

---

8. A You want only negative odd integers. List all those that are between -10 and 4.

> -9, -7, -5, -3, -1
> 5 numbers

---

9. D There are an infinite number of rational numbers. Rationals include any number that can be made into a fraction. For example, 1.1, 1.231, 1.42347824, etc.

---

10. B Integers do not include any fractions or decimals. Therefore, $\frac{1}{3}$ is not an integer. Rationals are any number which can be expressed as a fraction. Decimals that repeat forever are also rational numbers since they are equivalent to a fraction. $\frac{1}{3}$ is rational.

Real numbers include all rationals and irrationals, and therefore, $\frac{1}{3}$ is real.

1.2 Numbers & Place Value

Place Value

The number 9,876,543 could be viewed simply as a string of digits. But, with an understanding of place value you can break the number into its parts. In 9,876,543, the digit 7 stands for 70,000 and the 6 represents 6,000. Each digit is given a specific value by its place in the number. The chart above shows some of the place values.

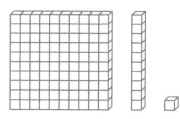

Numbers can be written in expanded form, which shows the value of each digit. For example: 9,876,543 = 9,000,000 + 800,000 + 70,000 + 6,000 + 500 + 40 + 3

 In the base 10 system, every place value is ten times larger than the place value to its right.

Illustrating Place Value

Pictures or blocks are often used to illustrate the concept of place value. A small block represents one unit. A group of ten small blocks makes a stick that is used to represent the tens place. This approach makes it easy to see, for instance, that 3 sticks actually represent 30 blocks or the number 30. The same concept applies to the hundreds and thousands of blocks.

These blocks can also be useful for visualizing redistribution, which is necessary for addition and subtraction. To imagine redistribution, think of a stick of ten blocks being broken into single units or vice versa.

Rounding and Estimation

Imagine that you drove 1297 miles on a road trip. You would most likely tell your friends you drove 1300 miles. Approximating numbers to the powers of ten in this way is called rounding. Rounding is useful for quickly estimating the outcome of various operations.

There are specific rules for rounding:
1. To round a number to a place value, you must look at the value of the digit to the right of the rounding digit. For example, look at the value of the digit in the tens place when rounding to the hundreds place.
2. If the digit is a number from 0 to 4, round down by keeping the rounded digit the same and making the digits to the right equal to zero. For example, to round 938 to the nearest hundred, look at the digit in the tens place. Because 3 is less than 5, round down to 900.
3. If the digit is a number from 5 to 9, round up by increasing the digit by 1 and then making all digits to the right equal to zero. For example, to round 217 to the tens place look at the digit in the ones place. It is 7, which is greater than 5, so you must round up to 220.

If the digit to be rounded up is a 9, then two digits of your number will be affected. For example, if you are rounding 1,296 to the nearest tens, you would first note that the 9 is in the tens place. You would then look to the right of that 9 and see that the 6 is between 5 and 9 and you must round up. First, make the 6 a zero and then round the 9 up by 1 digit to 10. This creates a problem as you can't put a two digit number into the tens place. So, you must redistribute, giving you 1300.

1296 = 1000 + 200 + 90 + 6
We rounded the 90 to 100 and made the 6 a zero.
= 1000 + 200 + 100 + 0
= 1300

NUMBERS & PLACE VALUE PRACTICE

1. **What digit is in the ten-thousands place in the following number:**

   5,609,823

   A. 6
   B. 0
   C. 9
   D. 5

2. **Which number has a 9 in the ones place and a 2 in the hundreds?**

   A. 9222
   B. 9292
   C. 9229
   D. 2999

3. **Round 72,349 to the nearest hundred.**

   A. 72,350
   B. 72,000
   C. 72,300
   D. 72,400

4. **What number is shown below?**

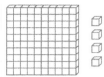

    A. 5
    B. 14
    C. 104
    D. 1004

5. **What is 800,000 + 3000 + 600 + 20 + 1?**

    A. 83,621
    B. 836,210
    C. 803,621
    D. 830,621

6. **Choose the best answer to replace the question mark.**

 ?

    A. >
    B. <
    C. =
    D. ≥

7. **Order the following from least to greatest:**
  I. 7000 + 6
  II. 800 + 90 + 9
  III. 7000 + 30

    A. I, III, II
    B. III, I, II
    C. II, I, III
    D. II, III, I

8. **Round 28,956 to the nearest hundred.**
    A. 28,900
    B. 28,960
    C. 29,000
    D. 29,100

9. **What number is equal to 40 + 1000 + 900 + 300000 ?**
    A. 4193
    B. 3194
    C. 31,940
    D. 301,940

10. **What number is eight hundred forty thousand three hundred six?**
    A. 84,306
    B. 840,306
    C. 840,360
    D. 80,040,306

1. B 5,609,823 Working from the right, the following are the place values:

> 3 is in the ones place.
> 2 is in the tens place.
> 8 is in the hundreds place.
> 9 is in the thousands place.
> 0 is in the ten-thousands place.
> 6 is in the hundred-thousands place.
> 5 is in the millions place.

Therefore, the answer is 0.

2. C Remember that the ones place is the digit that is on the far right. The next place, moving left, is the tens place, next is the hundreds place and then the thousands place.

If we want a 9 in the ones place and a 2 in the hundreds, then the number must follow this format: $x2x9$. The only number that meets this requirement is 9229.

3. C To round 72,349 to the hundreds place, first determine which digit is in the hundreds place. The 3 is in the hundreds place. Now, look at the digit to the right of that 3, which is the 4. If the number to the right is 5 or greater, you round the 3 up. In this case, since it is less than 5, you leave the 3 the same. Therefore, 72,349 rounded to the nearest hundred is 72,300.

4. C The larger box represents 100. Each of the smaller boxes represents 1. There is 1 large box and 4 small boxes. Therefore, we want 100 and 4 = 104.

5. C This question gives you the expanded form and asks you what number it is equal to.

$$800,000 + 3000 + 600 + 20 + 1 = 803,621$$

You can either add the numbers or look at the place values. The 8, must be in the hundred thousands place. The 3 in the thousands place. The 6 in the hundreds place. The 2 in the tens place. The 1 in the ones or unit place.

6. B   To determine which is larger, you must first figure out the value of each image.

There are 4 tens and 8 ones, which equals 48.
There are 5 tens and 1 one, which equals 51.
Therefore, since 48 is less than 51, the answer is B, <

---

7. C   Let's determine the value of each so that they can be ordered.

I. 7000 + 6 = 7006
II. 800 + 90 + 9 = 899
III. 7000 + 30 = 7030

Ordering from least to greatest: 899, 7006, 7030 or II, I, III

---

8. C   To round 28,956 to the nearest hundred, first identify what digit is in the hundreds place, and then look at the digit to the right.

The 9 is in the hundreds place. Look at the digit to the right, since it is a 5, which is ≥ 5, then you must round up.

Rounding 28,956 up to the next closest hundred would be to round it to 29,000. You can think about rounding the 9 up to the next number, which is 10, would change the digit to the left of the 9 up by 1 and change the 9 to a 0.

---

9. D   First, put the numbers in decreasing order.

40 + 1000 + 900 + 300000
= 300000 + 1000 + 900 + 40

Next, convert from expanded form to standard form.

300000 + 1000 + 900 + 40 = 301940

---

10. B   Take each number and put in the correct place value.

Let's take the first part: eight hundred forty thousand

This equals: 840,000

The second part: three hundred six

This equals: 306

Now, put them together:

840,000 + 306 = 840,306

1.3 Operations

Addition

Addition is the process of combining two or more numbers to get a total. To add large numbers, line the numbers up vertically by place value and add the digits of each column, beginning with the ones place.

Sometimes adding numbers will require redistribution (see place values module). Adding 50 + 70 involves redistribution. You have 5 tens and 7 tens, which adds up to 12 tens. 10 of those tens can be combined or redistributed to 1 hundred, with 2 tens remaining. Therefore, the sum of 50 and 70 is 100 + 20 or 120. Here is another sample problem with redistribution. In this question, the 9 ones and the 3 ones added to 12 ones. Those were redistributed to 1 ten, leaving 2 ones.

Example:

$$
\begin{array}{r}
7{,}325 \\
+\ 10{,}644 \\
\hline
17{,}969
\end{array}
$$

$$
\begin{array}{r}
1 \qquad\quad \\
4563 \quad \leftarrow\ 3+9=12 \\
+\ 1319 \\
\hline
5882
\end{array}
$$

Subtraction

Subtraction is the inverse of addition and the result of a subtraction problem is called the difference of the numbers subtracted. As with addition, line up big numbers by place value to subtract, beginning with the ones place. Redistribution is necessary when the number being subtracted for a certain place value is larger than the number it is being subtracted from. In such cases, 1 from the place value above is broken into 10 pieces.

Example:

$$
\begin{array}{r}
97{,}642 \\
-\ 23{,}120 \\
\hline
74{,}522
\end{array}
$$

$$
\begin{array}{r}
7\ 11 \\
728\!1 \\
-\ 5137 \\
\hline
2144
\end{array}
$$

In the ones place, 1 is smaller than 7, therefore you must redistribute.

From the tens place, you take 1 from the 8 to make it a 7, and you break that into ten ones. Those ten ones are added to the 1 to make 11.

Multiplication

Multiplication, which is repeated addition, results in the product of two or more numbers. Three multiplied by four is the same as adding four three times ($3 \times 4 = 4 + 4 + 4 = 12$) or three four times ($3 \times 4 = 3 + 3 + 3 + 3 = 12$). In order to multiply large numbers, multiply each digit of one number by each digit of the other number, and sum the results.

$$
\begin{array}{r}
2 \\
2014 \\
\times\ \ \ 756 \\
\hline
12084 \\
+\ 100700 \\
1409800 \\
\hline
1522584
\end{array}
$$

$6 \times 4 = 24$, put the 4 in the ones place and carry the 20 to be added in with the tens place.

Remember that the 5 in 756 is actually 50. Use a placeholder 0 to account for that fact.

Division

Division is the inverse of multiplication, and the result of a division problem is called a quotient. It asks how many groups of a given number can be made out of another number. For example, how many groups of 2 can be made out of 12? $12 \div 2 = 6$; six groups of 2 can be made out of 12.

Long division is division that shows out each step of the process. Unlike all other basic operations, long division starts with the greatest place value and works back to the ones.

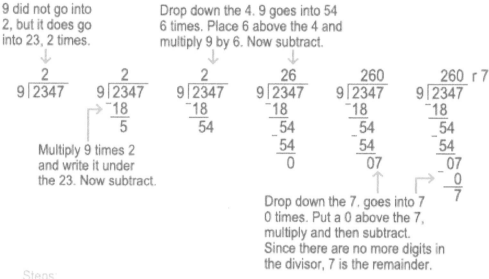

9 did not go into 2, but it does go into 23, 2 times.

Multiply 9 times 2 and write it under the 23. Now subtract.

Drop down the 4. 9 goes into 54 6 times. Place 6 above the 4 and multiply 9 by 6. Now subtract.

Drop down the 7. goes into 7 0 times. Put a 0 above the 7, multiply and then subtract. Since there are no more digits in the divisor, 7 is the remainder.

Steps:
1. Determine how many times the divisor (9) goes into the first part of the dividend.
2. Place that number abive the line. Multiply thr divisor by that number.
3. Subtract, and bring down the next digit of the divisor.
4. Determine how many times the divisor goes into that number. Repeat steps 1-3.

The problem above had a remainder of 7. It can also be thought of as $\frac{7}{9}$. Or, you can add a decimal place and zeros to the dividend, and continue the long division process. This will be covered in additional detail in the Fractions and Decimals chapter.

Order of Operations

For problems containing multiple operations, there is a standardized order in which these operations must be carried out. Without such an order, a single problem could generate multiple answers. The order is PEMDAS.

A common mnemonic device for remembering the order is "Please Excuse My Dear Aunt Sally"

Parentheses
Exponents
Multiplication and **D**ivision from left to right
Addition and **S**ubtraction from left to right

Example:

$200 - 7 + 6 \times (2 \times 3) \div 4 =$	• Parentheses first.
$200 - 7 + 6 \times 6 \div 4 =$	• No Exponents. Multiply and Divide from left to right.
$200 - 7 + 36 \div 4 =$	• Keep multiplying and dividing.
$200 - 7 + 9 =$	• Now Add and Subtract from left to right.
$193 + 9 =$	• The final addition step.

 Common mistake is that people perform multiplication always before division. It is multiplication or division from left to right, whichever comes first. $12 \div 2 \times 3 = 6 \times 3 = 18$.

Averages

The average of a set of numbers is equal to the sum of the numbers divided by the number of numbers.

> For example, find the average of 3, 4, and 8.
> Average $= (3 + 4 + 8) \div 3 = 5$

Averages will be covered in more detail in the Statistics & Probability Module.

OPERATIONS PRACTICE

1. **What is the sum of 327,516 and 4,890,471?**
   A. 4,117,987
   B. 4,217,987
   C. 5,217,987
   D. 8,165,631

2. **What is the difference between 84,763 and 27,888?**
   A. 56,875
   B. 56,975
   C. 64,985
   D. 64,976

3. **Nadine is totaling her accounts due and accounts payable for the month. She owes $496 to one creditor and $736 to another. She receives $1326 from one source of income and $139 from another. How much has she earned or lost this month?**
   A. lost $233
   B. lost $333
   C. gained $233
   D. gained $333

4. **7958 ÷ 25 = ?**
    A. 318
    B. 319
    C. 318 R8 ⟵
    D. 319 R8

5. **What number is 32 less than 8 times the quotient of 28 and 4?**
    A. 0
    B. 24 ⟵
    C. 88
    D. 160

6. **What is the product of 1408 and 321?**
    A. 422,400
    B. 450,560
    C. 423,808
    D. 451,968 ⟵

7. **Deidre went to the store and bought 5 notebooks, each cost \$2. Then, she purchased 2 bags for \$7 each. If she paid \$30, how much change should she receive?**
    A. \$6 ⟵
    B. \$16

    C. \$24
    D. \$54

8. **Barbara had the same lunch on Monday, Tuesday, and Friday that costs \$6 each. On Wednesday, she spent \$3 and Thursday \$4. What was her average cost for lunch for the week?**
    A. \$2.60
    B. \$4.33
    C. \$5 ⟵
    D. \$8.33

9. **$4 \times 9 - 6 \div (2 + 1) =$**
    A. 4
    B. 10
    C. 16
    D. 34 ⟵

10.
$$\frac{(12 + 6) \div 3 \times (18 - 16)}{16 - 5 \times 2}$$
    A. 2 ⟵
    B. ½
    C. ⁵/₁₁
    D. 18

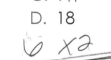

OPERATIONS EXPLANATIONS

1. C   In order to add large numbers, line them up vertically by place value and add the digits, remembering to redistribute as necessary.

$$\begin{array}{r} 327{,}516 \\ + 4{,}890{,}471 \\ \hline 5{,}217{,}987 \end{array}$$

2. A   To subtract large numbers, line up by place value. Don't forget to redistribute when nececssary.

$$\begin{array}{r} {\scriptstyle 13\ 16\ 15} \\ {\scriptstyle 7\ \ 3\ 6\ 5\ 13} \\ 84{,}763 \\ -\ 27{,}888 \\ \hline 56{,}875 \end{array}$$

3. C   Add the total amount she earned. She received \$1326 from one source of income and \$139 from another.
Now, find the total amount she owes. She owes one creditor \$496 and another \$736.

She owes \$1232 and earned \$1465. There-fore, she gained money this month. Sub-tract to find out how much she gained.

1326	496	1465
+ 139	+ 736	- 1232
1465	1232	233

4. C   Use long division to solve this problem. First, deter-mine how many times 25 divides into 79. Three times. When you multiply 25 by 3, you get 75. Subtract 75 from 79 and bring down the next number. Repeat these steps. You will see that the quotient is 318 with a remainder of 8.

$$\begin{array}{r} 318\ R8 \\ 25\overline{)7958} \\ 75 \\ \hline 45 \\ 25 \\ \hline 208 \\ 200 \\ \hline 8 \end{array}$$

5. B   Let's break up the problem. First, let's find the "quotient of 28 and 4". Remem-ber, the quotient is the result of a division problem. This means $28 \div 4$, which equals 7. Now, the new statement is:
You have a number that is 32 less than 8 times 7.

Next, let's find 8 times 7. Times means multiplication. $8 \times 7 = 56$
The statement is now, you have an number that is 32 less than 56.

Be careful - you don't want 32 minus 56, you want 32 less than 56. Therefore, subtract 32 from 56. $56 - 32 = 24$

6. D   The product is the result of a multiplication problem- Line the numbers up by place value and multiply each digit of one number by each digit of the other number. Remember placeholder zeros. Then add the results.

$$\begin{array}{r} 1408 \\ \times\ \ \ \ 321 \\ \hline 1408 \\ 28160 \\ +422400 \\ \hline 451968 \end{array}$$

7. A Let's first figure out the total cost of what she spent and then subtract that from what she paid to determine the change.

She bought 5 notebooks at $2 each. Therefore, multiply to find the total cost of the notebooks.

$$5 \times \$2 = \$10$$

She bought 2 bags at $7 each. Multiply to find total cost of bags.

$$2 \times \$7 = \$14$$

Now, add those two quantities to determine her total purchases.

$$\$10 + \$14 = \$24$$

Finally, subtract the total from $30 to figure out how much change she received.

$$\$30 - \$24 = \$6$$

8. C The average is found by finding the sum of the numbers and dividing by the number of numbers.
Let's list out the costs for lunch for each day of the week:
Monday - $6, Tuesday - $6, Wednesday - $3, Thursday - $4, Friday - $6

Now, find the sum. $6 + $6 + $3 + $4 + $6 = $25
Divide by the number of numbers. In this case, there are 5. $25 ÷ 5 = $5

9. D Use order of operations. PEMDAS.

Parentheses first.
$$4 \times 9 - 6 \div (2 + 1) =$$
$$4 \times 9 - 6 \div 3 =$$

Multiply and Divide from left to right.
$$4 \times 9 - 6 \div 3 =$$
$$36 - 6 \div 3 =$$
$$36 - 2 =$$

Finally, Add and Subtract from left to right.
$$36 - 2 = 34$$

10. A In the last step, you see that the fraction bar has the same meaning as divide. This will be explored further in the next module.

$$\frac{(12 + 6) \div 3 \times (18 - 16)}{16 - 5 \times 2} =$$

$$\frac{18 \div 3 \times 2}{16 - 5 \times 2} =$$

$$\frac{6 \times 2}{16 - 10} =$$

$$\frac{12}{16 - 10} =$$

$$\frac{12}{6} = 2$$

1.4 Factors, Multiples, Divisibility

Factors

A factor of a number is an integer that divides evenly into the number with no remainder. For example, 5 is a factor of 50, since 50 divided by 5 is 10 with no remainder. However, 6 is not a factor of 50, since 50 divided by 6 is 8 with a remainder of 2. A number that has only 1 and itself as factors is called a prime number. Examples of prime numbers include: 5, 17, and 23.

Fundamental Theorem of Arithmetic

The fundamental theorem of arithmetic states that every positive integer can be expressed as a product of prime numbers. The theorem also states that it can be expressed in only one way, other than rearrangement. This product of the prime numbers is known as the prime factorization of the number.

Finding the prime factorization of numbers is a critical first step to many arithmetic and algebraic concepts, such as simplifying and factoring numbers, all which are covered in later lessons. One way to find the prime factorization of a number is by using a factor tree. The "leaves" at the bottom of the two factor trees here are the prime factors of the number 200. It doesn't matter that each level is different, the final prime factorization will always be the same.

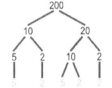 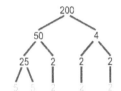

The prime factorization of 200 can be written as:

$$5 \times 2 \times 5 \times 2 \times 2 \ = \ 5 \times 5 \times 2 \times 2 \times 2 \ = \ 5^2 \times 2^3$$

Remember that the leaves at the bottom of a factor tree only show the prime factors of a number. If you needed to list out all the factors of 200, you would list out:

Factors of 200 = 1, 2, 4, 5, 8, 10, 20, 25, 40, 50, 100, 200

Greatest Common Factor

The **greatest common factor (GCF)** of two numbers is the largest factor that they both share. To explain, let's figure out the GCF of 24 and 18.

Factors of 24: 1, 2, 3, 4, **6**, 8, 12, 24
Factors of 18: 1, 2, 3, **6**, 9, 18
The largest factor they both share is 6.

Another way to find the GCF is from the prime factorization. If we list out all the factors that the numbers share and multiply them, then we will be left with the GCF. Let's look at the following example to illustrate the steps.
Find the GCF of 120 and 84.

$120 = 5 \times 3 \times 2 \times 2 \times 2 = 5 \times 3 \times 2^3$

$84 = 7 \times 3 \times 2 \times 2 = 7 \times 3 \times 2^2$

Start by finding the prime factorization of each number. You could do this using a factor tree if you find that easier. Now, let's see which factors they share. Both numbers have 3 and two 2s as factors. Therefore, multiply those common factors to find the GCF. GCF = $3 \times 2^2 = 12$

Divisibility

Divisibility is another way of stating factors of a number. There are a few tricks to easily determine the divisibility of certain numbers.

- ⊙ **2:** Only even numbers are divisible by 2. No odd numbers are divisible by 2.
- ⊙ **3:** If the sum of the digits of a number is divisible by 3, the number is also divisible by 3. For example, to determine if 4,158 is divisible by 3, add the digits: $4 + 1 + 5 + 8 = 18$. 18 is divisible by 3, so, 4,158 is divisible by 3.
- ⊙ **4:** If the last two digits of a number are divisible by 4, the whole number is divisible by 4. This works because 4 divides evenly into 100. For example, 23,924 is divisible by 4, since 24 is divisible by 4.
- ⊙ **5:** Any number that ends in 0 or 5 is divisible by 5.
- ⊙ **6:** Any number that is divisible by both 2 and 3 is divisible by 6.
- ⊙ **8:** If the last three digits of a number are divisible by 8, then the whole number is divisible by 8. For example, 984,840 is divisible by 8 since 840 is divisible by 8.
- ⊙ **9:** If the sum of the digits of a number is divisible by 9, then the number is also divisible by 9. Since its digits add up to 18, 4,158 is divisible by 9.
- ⊙ **10:** Any number that ends in 0 is divisible by 10.

Multiples

A multiple of a number is equal to that number times an integer. For example, all even numbers are multiples of 2.

$$2 \times 0 = 0, \ 2 \times 1 = 2, \ 2 \times 2 = 4, \ 2 \times 3 = 6, \ ...$$

It is often useful to find the **Least Common Multiple (LCM)** of two numbers, the smallest non–zero multiple that the numbers share. To find the LCM, list the multiples of each number until you find a common one.

Let's find the LCM of 8 and 6.
Multiples of 8: 8, 16, **24**
Multiples of 6: 6, 12, 18, **24**

24 is the smallest multiple that they share—in other words, 24 is the LCM.
If two numbers do not share any factors, the LCM is their product. For example, the LCM of 6 and 7 is 42.
The Least Common Multiple is used often in mathematics, especially when finding equivalent fractions, which will be reviewed in later lessons.

FACTORS, MULTIPLES, DIVISIBILITY PRACTICE

1. Which of the following is/are factors of 36?

   I. 12
   II. 24
   III. 72
   A. I only
   B. III only
   C. I and II
   D. I, II, and III

2. How many distinct factors does 24 have?

   A. 4
   B. 6
   C. 8
   D. 9

3. Write 234 as a product of its prime factors.

   A. 39 × 6
   B. 13 × 2 × 3
   C. $13 \times 2 \times 3^2$
   D. 13 × 23

4. Find the least common multiple of 12 and 48.

   A. 12
   B. 24
   C. 48
   D. 96

5. Find the least common multiple of 15, 25, and 6.

   A. 1
   B. 75
   C. 150
   D. 2250

6. Which of the following is divisible by 9?

   A. 3201
   B. 4050
   C. 3009
   D. 7127

7. Two teams are competing to split all the candy in a jar. If Team A wins, each member will get 6 pieces. If Team B wins, each member will get 5 pieces. Which of the following could be the total amount of candy in the jar?

    A. 65
    B. 36
    C. 11
    D. 60

8. If pn = 360 and 9 does not divide evenly into p, what could be the prime factorization of n?

    A. $3^3 \times 5$
    B. $2^3 \times 5$

    C. 2×3^2
    D. 4×9

9. What is the sum of the least common multiple and greatest common factor of 12 and 24?

    A. 30
    B. 36
    C. 54
    D. 60

10. What is the sum of the prime numbers greater than 1 and less than 20?

    A. 58
    B. 60
    C. 75
    D. 77

FACTORS, MULTIPLES, DIVISIBILITY EXPLANATIONS

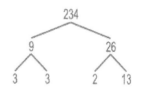

1. A   I only. If a number is a factor of 36, then it divides evenly into 36 with no remainder.

    I.   **12:** Since $36 \div 12 = 3$, then 12 is a factor of 36.
    II. **24:** Since $36 \div 24 = 1$ remainder 12, then 24 is not a factor of 36.
    III. **72:** 72 is a multiple of 36, not a factor. 72 does not divide evenly into 36.
    Factors are always less than or equal to the number.

2. C   The factors of 24 are: 1, 2, 3, 4, 6, 8, 12, 24. There are 8 factors.

3. C   One way to find the prime factors of a number are to create a factor tree.

    The prime factors of 234 are $3 \times 3 \times 2 \times 13$.
    Answer C is correct.
    Answer choice A: 39×6. Those are not prime numbers.
    Answer choice B: Does not multiply to 234.
    Answer choice D: Does not multiply to 234.

4. C Remember that the least common multiple is the smallest non-zero multiple that a set of numbers share. The LCM can be equal to one of the numbers.

> Multiples of 12: 12, 24, 36, 48, ...
> Multiples of 48: 48, ...
> 48 is the smallest multiple that they share. Answer choice C.

5. C To find the least common multiple of 25, 15, and 6, you can list out the multiples until you find the smallest multiple they share.

> Multiples of 25: 25, 50, 75, 100, 125, 150
> Multiples of 15: 15, 30, 45, 60, 75, 90, 105, 120, 135, 150
> Multiples of 6: 6, 12, 18, 24, 30, 36, 42, 48, 54, 60, 66, 72, 78, 84, 90, 96, 102, 108, 114, 120, 126, 132, 138, 144, 150

The LCM of 15, 25, and 6 is 150.

Another way to find the LCM is to find the prime factors of each number and then multiply the highest powers of each the prime factors together.

> 15 as product of prime factors = 3×5
> 25 as product of prime factors = 5^2
> 6 as product of prime factors = 2×3

The highest powers of the prime factors are: $2 \times 3 \times 5^2 = 150$

6. B One way to solve this problem is to divide each answer choice by 9 and see which does not give you a remainder. Another way is to remember the trick for determining whether a number is divisible by 9.

If you add the digits of a number and that sum is divisible by 9, then the original number is also divisible by 9.

Answer choice B satisfies this requirement: 4050, $4 + 0 + 5 + 0 = 9$, 9 is divisible by 9, therefore 4050 is divisible by 9.

7. D If all the candy can be split evenly into either 6 pieces if Team A wins or 5 pieces of Team B wins, then the total amount of candy must be divisible by both 5 and 6.

60 is the only answer that is evenly divisible by 5 and 6, therefore Answer D is correct.

8. C   First, let's figure out the prime factorization of 360. You can use a factor tree if that helps.

$$360 = 36 \times 10 = 6 \times 6 \times 5 \times 2 = 3 \times 2 \times 3 \times 2 \times 5 \times 2 = 2^3 \times 3^2 \times 5$$

We know that pn = 360 and therefore, $p \times n = 2^3 \times 3^2 \times 5$

We know that 9 does not divide evenly into p. As $9 = 3 \times 3$, that means that both factors of 3 are not factors of p. Therefore, at least one of those 3's must be a factor of n. If we want the prime factorization of n, we know it must include at least one 3 and then any other combination of factors that divides into 360, which equals $2^3 \times 3^2 \times 5$.

There are too many 3's in answer choice A. The prime factorization of n can not include three 3's as 360 does not include three 3's as factors.

Answer choice B does not include a 3 as a factor. Since 3 divides evenly into 360, but not into p, then it must be a factor of n.

Answer choice C works. It includes factors that are all factors of 360, including a 3.

The numbers in answer choice D are not prime.

---

9. B   The least common multiple is the smallest number that both 12 and 24 multiply evenly to. Since both 12 and 24 go evenly into 24, it is a common multiple. It is the least common multiple since 24 does not have any multiples that are smaller.

The greatest common factor is the biggest number that divides evenly into both 12 and 24. Since 12 divides evenly into both numbers and is the greatest factor of 12, it is the greatest common factor.

The sum of 12 and 24 is 12 + 24 = 36.

---

10. D   First, list out all the prime numbers that are greater than 1 and less than 20, and then add them.

2, 3, 5, 7, 11, 13, 17, 19

2 + 3 + 5 + 7 + 11 + 13 + 17 + 19 = 77

1.5 Signed Numbers & Absolute Value

As discussed in the "Foundations" module, all numbers greater than zero are positive and all numbers less than zero are negative. This can be represented on a number line.

Zero is neither positive nor negative.

To add and subtract positive and negative numbers, use the following techniques.

Add two positive numbers:

Add as normal.

Example: 23 + 74 = 97

Add two negative numbers:

Add as usual, but place a negative sign in front of the sum.

Example: -23 + -74 = -97

Add one positive and one negative number:

Subtract the smaller number from the larger and then assign the sign of the greater number to the result.

Example: -48 + 32; Subtract 48 − 32 = 16. Since 48 is greater and it was negative, the answer is negative. -48 + 32 = -16
Example: -32 + 48; Subtract 48 − 32 = 16. Since 48 is greater and it is positive, the answer is positive. -32 + 48 = 16

Subtraction of a positive number:

When dealing with a combination of positive and negative numbers, treat subtraction as the addition of a negative number.

Example: 25 − 75 is the same as 25 + -75. Now follow the rules you learned for adding signed numbers. 75 − 25 = 50; 75 is greater, and it is negative, so answer is negative. 25 + -75 = -50
Example: -25 − 75 is the same as -25 + -75.
Add the numbers as usual, but keep the negative sign since they are both negative. -25 + -75 = -100

Subtraction of a negative number:

Subtracting a negative number is equivalent to adding a positive number.

> Example: $32 - -45 = 32 + 45 = 77$
> Example: $-15 - -40 = -15 + 40 = 25$

Multiplication or Division of Signed Numbers:

To multiply or divide by negative or positive numbers, use the following rules.

A positive times a positive is positive.
A negative times a negative is positive.
A positive times a negative is negative.

> Example: $-2 \times -3 = 6$
> Example: $-1 \times -1 \times -1 = -1$

Another way to think about that, is if there are an even number of negative signs then you get a positive answer. If there are an odd number of negative signs, the result is negative.

Absolute Value:

The absolute value of a number is its magnitude or distance from zero. Absolute value is always expressed in positive terms.

> Example: $| 42 | = 42$
> Example: $| -13 | = 13$

SIGNED NUMBERS & ABSOLUTE VALUE PRACTICE

1. $-49 - 53 =$
   - A. -4
   - B. 4
   - C. 102
   - D. -102 *(circled)*

   (handwritten: 53, 49, =102)

2. **Choose the best answer to replace the question mark:**

   $20 - 70 \ ? \ -70 + 20$

   - A. ≥
   - B. >
   - C. <
   - D. = *(circled)*

3. $32 - 59 =$
   - A. 27
   - B. -27 *(circled)*
   - C. 91
   - D. -91

   (handwritten: 59, 32, 27)

4. $79 \times -1 \times -1 =$
   - A. -79
   - B. 97
   - C. 79 *(circled)*
   - D. 77

   (handwritten: -79 × -1 = 79)

5. Choose the best answer to replace the question mark:
   | -7 | **?** -7
   - A. ≤
   - B. > (circled)
   - C. <
   - D. =

6. Choose the best answer to replace the question mark:

   0 **?** All Positive Numbers
   - A. >
   - B. < (circled)
   - C. ≤
   - D. ≥

7. Which of the following is true?
   - A. The absolute value of a number is always greater than the number.
   - B. The absolute value of a number is sometimes negative.
   - C. The absolute value of a number is the same as the number times -1.
   - D. The absolute value of a number is its distance from zero. (circled)

8. $-3 \times 20 \div -4 - 40 =$
   - A. -55
   - B. -25 (circled)
   - C. 25
   - D. -104

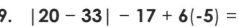

9. $|20 - 33| - 17 + 6(-5) =$
   - A. -60
   - B. -34 (circled)
   - C. -10
   - D. 34

$|-13| -17 +6(-5) =$
$13 - 17 + 6(-5)$
$-4 - 30 = \boxed{-34}$

10. A math teacher curves all the test scores so that the average is always a ⟨70⟩ on her tests. Sandra gets a 74 on her first test, and then on the next test gets a score 11 below that. She studies much harder for her 3rd test and gets 15 points higher than her 2nd test. Finally, for the 4th test which was extremely difficult, Sandra gets 22 points below her score on the 3rd test. How does Sandra's score on her 4th test compare to the class average?

   1.) $74 - 11 = 63$
   2.) $63 + 15 = 78$
   $78 - 22 = 56$
   $70 - 56 = 14$

   - A. 18 below
   - B. 14 below (circled)
   - C. 10 below
   - D. Class Average ⟨14⟩

SIGNED NUMBERS & ABSOLUTE VALUE EXPLANATIONS

1. D Subtraction is equivalent to adding a negative number.

$$-49 - 53 = -49 + \text{-}53$$

To add two negative numbers, add the two numbers and give the sum a negative sign since they are both negative.

$$-49 + \text{-}53 = -102$$

2. D These two expressions are identical. They are simply written in a different order.

$$20 - 70 = 20 + \text{-}70 = -50$$

You can solve each side to see:

$$-70 + 20 = -50$$

3. B First, change the subtraction problem into addition of a negative number.

$$32 - 59 =$$
$$32 + \text{-}59 =$$
$$-27$$

Then, since the signs of the two numbers are different, subtract the digits and then take the sign of the larger number.

$59 - 32 = 27$. Since $59 > 32$, take the sign of 59 which is negative.

4. C To multiply signed numbers, first multiply the numbers and the determine the signs.

Then count the negative signs. There are two, which is an even number, so the answer is positive.

$$79 \times \text{-}1 \times \text{-}1$$

Another way to think about it is multiply the first two numbers, and then multiply the result by the third number.

$$79 \times 1 \times 1 = 79$$

$79 \times \text{-}1 = \text{-}79$ (since positive times negative = negative)
$\text{-}79 \times \text{-}1 = 79$ (since negative times negative = positive) Answer: C = 79.

5. B Remember, the absolute value is the distance the number is from zero and is always expressed as a positive number.

$$|\text{-}7| = 7$$
$$7 > \text{-}7$$

6. B Positive numbers are all those greater than zero. Zero is neither positive nor negative. Therefore, zero is less than all positive numbers.

$$0 < \text{All Positive Numbers}$$

7. D To determine which is true, let's analyze each answer.

A: The absolute value of a number is always greater than the number. —This is false. The absolute value of a number could equal the number. Ex: $|3| = 3$

B: The absolute value of a number is sometimes negative.—This is false. The absolute value, which is the distance of a number from zero, is always positive.

C: The absolute value of a number is the same as the number times -1. This is false. This is only true if you are taking the absolute value of a negative number. If you are taking the absolute value of a positive number, the absolute value is the same as the number, not the same as the number multiplied by -1.

D: The absolute value of a number is its distance from zero.—This is true. This is the definition of absolute value.

---

8. B To solve this question, follow the order of operations and rules for signed numbers.

$-3 \times 20 \div -4 - 40 =$

The first step is to multiply $-3 \times 20 = -60$
Next, divide: $-60 \div -4 = 15$

$-60 \div -4 - 40 =$

$15 - 40 =$

To subtract, change the problem into the addition of a negative.

$15 - 40 = 15 + -40 = -25$

---

9. B Following the order of operations, first solve whats in parentheses.

You can treat what is in the absolute value symbols as parentheses.

Next, perform the multiplication. Finally, working from left to right add or subtract.

$|20 - 33| - 17 + 6(-5) =$

$|20 - 33| - 17 + 6(-5) =$
$|-13| - 17 + 6(-5) =$
$13 - 17 + 6(-5)$

$13 - 17 + 6(-5)$
$13 - 17 - 30$
$-4 - 30$
-34

---

10. B Sandra gets a 74 on her first test. The next test she scores 11 below that. That means the score on her 2nd test was $74 - 11 = 63$. On the third test she gets 15 points higher than that $= 63 + 15 = 78$. Her final test was 22 points below the third. Fourth test $= 78 - 22 = 56$.

Now, compare 56 to the class average of 70.
$70 - 56 = 14$. Therefore, Sandra scored 14 points below the average on her 4th test.

1.6   Roots, Powers, Scientific Notation

Powers or Exponents

The terms powers and exponents are interchangeable. The power or exponent represents how many times a number is multiplied by itself. In the expression 2^5, the base number 2 is raised to the 5th power. When a number is raised to a power, it is multiplied by itself the number of times equal to the power.

$$2^5 = 2 \times 2 \times 2 \times 2 \times 2 = 32$$
$$4^3 = 4 \times 4 \times 4 = 64$$

Multiplying and Dividing Exponents

When multiplying numbers with exponents, if their bases are the same, you can just add the exponents.

For example, $2^3 \times 2^4$ is equal to $(2 \times 2 \times 2) \times (2 \times 2 \times 2 \times 2) = 2^7$

or, since both numbers had a base of 2, you could just add the exponents. When dividing numbers with exponents, if their bases are the same, you can just subtract the exponents.

For example, $4^7 \div 4^5 = 4^2$

Negative Exponents

Numbers can also be raised to negative exponents, which indicates that the expression is a fraction with 1 as the numerator and the base raised to the power as the denominator. (See Fractions module for help)

$$2^{-5} = \frac{1}{(2 \times 2 \times 2 \times 2 \times 2)} = \frac{1}{32}$$
$$4^{-2} = \frac{1}{(4 \times 4)} = \frac{1}{16}$$

Scientific Notation

Scientific Notation is a way of writing numbers (usually very small or very large) as powers of ten. Numbers written in scientific notation take the form of coefficient $\times 10^{power}$. The coefficient must be greater than or equal to 1 and less than 10. As can be seen in the examples, first find the coefficient which will be a number between 1 and 10. To figure out the coefficient, place the decimal point after the digit in the greatest place value. Then, deter-

$$63{,}500{,}000 = 6.35 \times 10^7$$
$$470{,}000 = 4.7 \times 10^5$$
$$0.0000348 = 3.48 \times 10^{-5}$$
$$0.0023 = 2.3 \times 10^{-3}$$

mine how many times you moved the decimal places, either in the positive or negative direction.
When multiplying numbers in scientific notation, use the commutative property of multiplication to rearrange the terms and then multiply the coefficients and then the powers of ten.

$$(3 \times 10^8) \times (2 \times 10^{-5})$$
$$= (3 \times 2) \times (10^8 \times 10^{-5})$$
$$= 6 \times 10^3$$

Roots

A root is the opposite of an exponent. Since the square of a number is a number times itself, for example $9^2 = 81$, the square root of a number is what number times itself equals that number. The square root of 81 is 9.
To find the third root of 64, you need to figure out what number times itself 3 times gives you 64. Since, $4 \times 4 \times 4 = 64$, the third root of 64 is 4. The square root of $25 = 5$. The third root of $27 = 3$. There are two notations for writing roots.

Example:
the third root of 64 can be written:

$$\sqrt[3]{64} \qquad 64^{1/3}$$

Fractional Exponents

In the second notation of roots from above, you see that the root is written as a fractional exponent. The denominator is the root, and the numerator should be treated as any exponential power.

Example:
$81^{1/4}$ = fourth root of 81 = 3
$2^{4/2}$ = square root of 2^4
    = square root of 16 = 4.

Bases

A number system has a base to describe the digits. Our typical number system is base 10. For the first digit on the right, we multiply by 10^0. The second digit, we multiply by 10^1. The third digit, we multiply by 10^2…and so on.

In a base 2 number system, we multiply the first digit by 2^0. The second digit, we multiply by 2^1. The third digit, we multiply by 2^2…and so on.

In this fashion, we can use a number system of any integer base. For example, if the following number was in base 3, we could determine its value in base 10 by determining the value of each digit.
$$201_3 = 1(3^0) + 0(3^1) + 2(3^2) = 1 + 0 + 18 = 19$$

Note, that you start with the digit with the smallest place value. For example, note that above the 1 in the ones place was multiplied by 3^0 and then the 0 in the tens place was multiplied by 3^1 and the 2 in the hundreds place was multiplied by 3^2.

Here is another example from base 4 to base 10.
$1032_4 = 2(4^0) + 3(4^1) + 0(4^2) + 1(4^3) = 2 + 12 + 0 + 64 = 78$

ROOTS, POWERS, SCIENTIFIC NOTATION PRACTICE

1. $(-3)^4 =$
   A. -12
   B. 12
   C. -81
   D. 81

2. $100^{1/2} =$
   A. -100
   B. 10
   C. 50
   D. $1/100$

3. In the following base 10 number, which digit is multiplied by 10^3?
   5,241,837
   A. 1
   B. 2
   C. 4
   D. 8

4. Write 9,000,000.00 in scientific notation.
   A. 9×10^6
   B. 9×10^7
   C. 9×10^8
   D. 9×10^9

5. $(-4)^{-3} =$
   A. 64
   B. -64
   C. $1/64$
   D. $-1/64$

6. 2.3×10^{-4} is equal to what number?
   A. 0.0023
   B. 0.00023
   C. 2300
   D. 23000

7. What is the product of (2×10^3) and (4×10^{-7}) ?
   A. 8×10^{10}
   B. 8×10^{-21}
   C. 8×10^{-4}
   D. 8×10^4

8. $36^{3/2}$ is equal to
   I. $(36^{1/3})^2$
   II. $(36^{1/2})^3$
   III. 216
   A. I and II
   B. II and III
   C. I only
   D. III only

9. Translate the following number to base 10: 100101_2

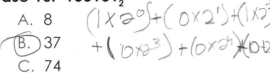

    A. 8

    B. 37

    C. 74

    D. 100,101

10. $2^5 \times 2^4 \div 2^2 =$

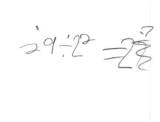

    A. 2^3

    B. 2^7

    C. 2^{10}

    D. 2^{11}

ROOTS, POWERS, SCIENTIFIC NOTATION EXPLANATIONS

1. D A number raised to a power is multiplied by itself the number of times indicated by the power.

Notice that there was an even number of negative signs (four), so the answer is positive.

$$(-3)^4 = (-3) \times (-3) \times (-3) \times (-3) = 81$$

2. B A number raised to a fractional power is equal to the corresponding root of the number. In this case, $100^{1/2}$ is the same as the second root or square root of 100. Therefore, you need to determine what number times itself equals 100. Since 10 times 10 equals 100, it is the square root of 100.

3. A $10^3 = 1000$. We need the digit in the thousands place. In this number, the 1 is in the thousands place.

$$5{,}241{,}837 = 7 \times 10^0 + 3 \times 10^1 + 8 \times 10^2 + 1 \times 10^3 + 4 \times 10^4 + 2 \times 10^5 + 5 \times 10^6$$

4. A When writing a number in scientific notation you need to figure out how many times you are moving the decimal point.

To go from 9 to 9,000,000.00, move the decimal point 6 places in the positive direction. Therefore, 6 is the exponent of the power of 10.

5. D A number raised to a negative power is the same as 1 over that number raised to the positive power.

$$(-4)^{-3} = \frac{1}{(-4)^3} = \frac{1}{-64} = \frac{-1}{64}$$

6. B This problem asks us to take the scientific notation of a number, and write the number in standard form. The exponent in the power of ten tells you what direction and how many places to move the decimal point. In this case, we want to move the decimal point 4 places in the negative direction. This will give you 0.00023.

7. C To multiply numbers in scientific notation, break the problem into two problems. First, multiply the coefficients, then multiply the powers of ten.

$2 \times 4 = 8$. Therefore, the new coefficient will be 8.

$10^3 \times 10^{-7}$: To multiply powers, add the exponents.

$$8 \times 10^{-4}$$

You can also think of this as moving the decimal 3 places in the positive direction and then moving the decimal 7 places in the negative direction, which is the same as moving the decimal 4 places in the negative direction. Now combine the two products.

8. B Remember with fractional exponents, the denominator is the root of the number and the numerator is what power the number is raised to. Therefore, we want the second root or square root of 36 and then we want to raise that to the third power.

  I. $(36^{1/3})^2$: This says take the third root of 36 and raise it to the second power. This is not the same thing.

  II. $(36^{1/2})^3$: This says take the square root of 36 and raise that to the third power. That is correct.

  III. **216:** Let's calculate and see if we get 216. The square root of 36 is 6. Then, 6 raised to the third power is $6 \times 6 \times 6 = 216$. This is correct.

9. B The subscript 2 denotes that the number is in base 2. To convert from base 2 to base 10, start from the right, take each digit, and multiply it by consecutive powers of 2, starting with zero.

$(1 \times 2^0) + (0 \times 2^1) + (1 \times 2^2) + (0 \times 2^3) + (0 \times 2^4) + (1 \times 2^5)$
$= 1 + 0 + 4 + 0 + 0 + 32 = 37$

10. B Let's break this problem into 2 separate problems. Let's first find the product and then take that result and find the quotient.

$2^5 \times 2^4$: When multiplying numbers with exponents, if the bases are the same, you can just add the exponents. Another way to think about it is that 2^5 is 2 times itself 5 times, and 2^4 is 2 times itself 4 times, therefore the product will be 2 times itself 9 times $= 2^9$.

Now, take the 2^9 and divide it be 2^2. To divide numbers with exponents, if the bases are the same, you can subtract the exponents.

$2^9 \div 2^2 = 2^7$

1.7 Chapter Review

1. Write 19,703 in expanded form.
   - A. $10,000 + 9,000 + 700 + 3$
   - B. $10,000 + 900 + 70 + 3$
   - C. $1000 + 900 + 70 + 3$
   - D. $10000 + 9000 + 700 + 30$

2. In a family, the oldest child is four times the sum of the younger children's ages. If the younger children are 1 and 3, what is the oldest child's age?
   - A. 10
   - B. 11
   - C. 13
   - D. 16

3. Choose which of the following are true about 21,936:

   I. It is divisible by 12.
   II. It is divisible by 8.
   III. It is divisible by 6.

   - A. I only
   - B. I and II
   - C. I and III
   - D. I, II, and III

4. On an extremely cold day in Chicago, the temperature at noon was 3°. By 6PM, the temperature had dropped another 5 degrees. If the wind chill factor reduces the temperature by another 10 degrees, what does it feel like outside at 6PM factoring in the wind chill?
   - A. -18°
   - B. -12°
   - C. -8°
   - D. 8°

5. Which of the following is a set of four consecutive odd integers?
   - A. 1, 2, 3, 4
   - B. 0, 1, 3, 5
   - C. -9, -11, -13, -17
   - D. -3, -1, 1, 3

6. $(-2)^4 - 3^2 =$
   - A. -25
   - B. -14
   - C. 7
   - D. 25

7. $1 + 6 \times (7 + 14) \div 2 - 8 =$
   - A. 31
   - B. 32
   - C. 48
   - D. 56

8. **Which of the following is true?**

~~I.~~ There are no even prime numbers.

II. The greatest common factor of 2 numbers will always be smaller than both numbers.

< III. The least common multiple of 2 numbers will always be greater than both numbers.

    A. I only

    B. II and III ⟵ (circled)

    C. I, II, and III

    D. None of the above.

9. **Could any of these operations change an irrational number into a rational number?**

    A. Add 1

    B. Multiply by 2

    C. Square it (circled)

    D. Any of the above could change an irrational number to a rational

10. **Order the following from least to greatest:**

    I. $300,000 + 80,000$

    II. $30,000 + 9000 + 900$

    III. $300,000 + 70,000 + 900 + 90$

    A. I, II, III

    B. II, I, III (circled)

    C. III, II, I

    D. II, III, I

11. **If the number 720 is written as a product of its prime factors in the form: ab^2c^4. Then what is the sum of a, b, and c?**

    A. 10

    B. 19

    C. 25

    D. 27

12. **$-12 + 3 \times -7 + |-4 + 6| \times 6 =$**

    A. -45

    B. -21

    C. 21

    D. 27

13. **$(-1)^6 - (-1)^5 - (-1)^4 =$**

    A. -3

    B. -1 $|+ = | - |$

    C. 1 (circled)

    D. 3 $1 + | = 2 - | = 1$

14. **Which of the following is/are false?**

    I. Adding a negative number is the same as subtracting the absolute value of that number.

    — II. Zero is a negative number.

    — III. Any multiplication problem containing a negative number will produce a negative answer.

    A. I and II

    B. II and III (circled)

    C. I and III

    D. III only

15. $(-3)^3 - 3(-2)^2 + 25^{\frac{1}{2}} =$

A. -34
B. -26.5
C. -16
D. -14

handwritten: PEMDAS → $\sqrt{25}$, $25^{\frac{1}{2}}$ → 4, $-27 - 12 + 5$, $-39 + 5 = \boxed{-34}$

16. What is the product of the least common multiple and greatest common factor of 12, 8, and 6?

A. 24
B. 36
C. 48
D. 96

handwritten: 12: 12, 24, 36, 48
8: 8, 16, 24
6: 6, 12, 18, 24, 36, 42, 48

17. There are four monkeys stealing bananas from the trees, monkeys A, B, C, and D. Monkey A steals 9 bananas. Monkey B steals 3 less than 4 times what A stole. C steals the difference of A and B. Monkey D steals 2 more than twice C. How many bananas total did the four monkeys steal?

A. 80
B. 82
C. 116
D. 118

handwritten: 9

18. What is the quotient of 3×10^{-4} and 6×10^7 in scientific notation?

A. 5×10^{-10}
B. 2×10^{10}
C. 5×10^{-12}
D. 1.8×10^4

handwritten: $\dfrac{3 \times 10^{-4}}{6 \times 10^7} =$
Division
$\frac{1}{2} \times$
0.5, $5 \times 10^{-4} \times 10^{-11}$
$\boxed{5 \times 10^{-12}}$

19. What is the sum of the following 2 numbers in proper expanded form?

First number: 200,000 + 30,000 + 8,000 + 70 + 6
Second number: 400,000 + 80,000 + 900 + 10

A. 700,000 + 10,000 + 8,000 + 900 + 80 + 6
B. 600,000 + 10,000 + 8000 + 900 + 80 + 6
C. 600,000 + 110,000 + 8000 + 900 + 80 + 6
D. 700,000 + 10,000 + 8,000 + 900 + 70 + 16

20. $\dfrac{-3 \times 10 \div 2 - 6 + 4^2}{12 - 8 \times 2}$

A. $\frac{5}{4}$
B. $-\frac{5}{8}$
C. $\frac{37}{4}$
D. $-\frac{5}{4}$

handwritten: PEMDAS
$-3 \times 10 \div 2 - 6 + 16$
$-30 \div 2$
$-15 - 6 + 16$
$-21 + 16$
$\boxed{-5}$
$12 - 8 \times 2$
$12 - 16 = \boxed{-4}$
$\dfrac{-5}{-4} = \boxed{\dfrac{5}{4}}$

1. A You can determine expanded form by figuring out the place value of each digit. In 19,703, let's start with the 1.

> $10{,}000 + 9{,}000 + 700 + 3 = 19{,}703$

> 1 is in the ten-thousands place. Therefore, it's value = 10,000.
> 9 is in the thousands place. It's value = 9,000.
> 7 is in the hundreds place. It's value = 700.
> 3 is in the ones place. It's value = 3.

Expanded form involves making an addition statement for the value of each digit.

---

2. D Translate the problem from words to numbers. Start with the ages they give you.

> $4 \times (1 + 3) =$
> $4 \times 4 =$
> 16

The question calls for the "sum of the younger children's ages" and the problem tells you that the "younger children are 1 and 3". Translated: $1 + 3$.

The question states that the oldest child is "four times the sum". Translated: $4 \times (1 + 3)$.

Now solve for the oldest child's age.

---

3. D To figure out whether or not a number is divisible by 12, you can divide by 12 and see if it goes in evenly. However, the easier way is to check if the number is divisible by both 3 and 4.

To determine divisibility for 3, remember you can add the digits and check if the sum is divisible by 3. $2 + 1 + 9 + 3 + 6 = 21$. 21 is divisible by 3, therefore, 21,936 is also divisible by 3.

To determine divisibilty for 4, you can check if the last two digits are divisible by 4. In this case, 36 is divisible by 4, therefore 21,936 is also divisible by 4.

Since, 21,936 is divisible by 3 and 4, it is divisible by 12. I is true.

To determine divisibility by 8, you can check if the last three digits are divisible by 8. In this case, $936 \div 8 = 117$. Therefore, 21,936 is divisible by 8. II is true.

Since we already determined that 21,936 is divisible by 12, we know that it must also be divisible by 6. III is true.

I, II, and III are all true. Answer D.

4. B If the temperature was originally 3° and then dropped 5 degrees, you must subtract to find the new temperature.

$$3° - 5° = -2°$$

Now, we must factor in the wind chill effect. This would drop the temperature another 10 degrees, so we must subtract.

$$-2° - 10° = -12°$$

5. D Integers are numbers that can be positive, negative, or zero, but not including decimals or fractions. Odd integers are not divisible by 2. We want a list of consecutive odd integers, thus each number in the list must be the next biggest odd integer. Let's examine each answer choice:

A: 1, 2, 3, 4 : These are not all odd integers. 2 and 4 are even.

B: 0, 1, 3, 5 : These are not all odd integers. 0 is not odd.

C: -9, -11, -13, -17 : These are all odd integers. However, they are not consecutive. Between -13 and -17 there is another odd integer, -15.

D: -3, -1, 1, 3 : These are consecutive odd integers. Answer D.

6. C Use order of operations. There is nothing to solve within parentheses, so solve the exponents and then finish solving by subtracting.

| $(-2)^4 - 3^2$ | $(-2)^4 = (-2) \times (-2) \times (-2) \times (-2) = 16$ | $3^2 = 3 \times 3 = 9$ | $16 - 9 = 7$ |

7. D Use order of operations.

Parentheses is first:

$$1 + 6 \times (7 + 14) \div 2 - 8 =$$
$$1 + 6 \times 21 \div 2 - 8 =$$

Multipy and divide, left to right:

$$1 + 126 \div 2 - 8 =$$
$$1 + 63 - 8 =$$

Add and subtract, left to right:

$$64 - 8 =$$
$$56$$

8. D Let's examine each option.

I. There are no even prime numbers.
This is not true. There is one even prime number, 2. The only factors of 2 are 2 and 1, and a prime number is a number whose only factors are itself and 1. I is false.

II. The greatest common factor of 2 numbers will always be smaller than both numbers.
The greatest common factor can equal one of the numbers. For instance, the GCF of 6 and 12 is 6, since 6 is a factor of both 12 and 6. Therefore, GCF is not always smaller since it can be equal. II is false.

III. The least common multiple of 2 numbers will always be greater than both numbers.
The least common multiple can equal one of the numbers. For instance, the LCM of 6 and 12 is 12, since 12 is a multiple of both 12 and 6. Therefore, LCM is not always bigger since it can be equal. III is false.

None of the above are true.

---

9. C Irrational numbers cannot be expressed as fractions. Decimals that do not repeat and do not terminate are irrational. Let's take each answer choice and see the affect of each operation.

A. If you think of a number that has a non-repeating and non-terminating decimal, such as 5.3181947142096…. Then, adding 1 wouldn't change the fact that the decimal does not terminate or repeat. For instance, in this case it would change the number to: 6.3181947142096…. This number is still irrational. Eliminate A.

B. If you multiply an endless non-repeating decimal by 2, it would still be endless and non-repeating. Eliminate B

C. Squaring an irrational number could make it rational. The square root of 2 is equal to 1.41421356… It does not repeat or terminate. Therefore, it is irrational. $(\sqrt{2})^2 = \sqrt{2} \times \sqrt{2} = 2$. This is your answer.

---

10. D First, change each number from expanded form to standard form.

I. $300,000 + 80,000 = 380,000$
II. $30,000 + 9000 + 900 = 39,900$
III. $300,000 + 70,000 + 900 + 90 = 370,990$

Now, compare the numbers and write them from least to greatest.

> 39,900 is the smallest
> 370,990 is next
> 380,000 is the biggest
> II, III, I

---

11. A 720 is written as a product of its prime factors in the form: ab^2c^4. The easiest way to solve this problem is to first make a factor tree.

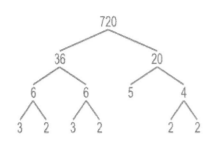

Then, take the bottom "leaves" of this factor tree.

Then, write the product of any repeated factors, as the factor to a power

$720 = 3 \times 2 \times 3 \times 2 \times 5 \times 2 \times 2$

$720 = 5 \times 3^2 \times 2^4$

We can now see that $a = 5$, $b = 3$, and $c = 2$.

$a + b + c = 5 + 3 + 2 = 10$

---

12. B Follow the order of operations. PEMDAS.
P – Parentheses. First, perform what is in the absolute value since the absolute value acts as parentheses for what is inside.

E – No exponents.

MD – Multiplication and Division from left to right.

AS – Addition and subtraction from left to right.

$-12 + 3 \times -7 + |-4 + 6| \times 6 =$
$-12 + 3 \times -7 + |2| \times 6 =$
$-12 + 3 \times -7 + 2 \times 6 =$
$-12 + -21 + 2 \times 6 =$
$-12 + -21 + 12 =$
$-33 + 12 =$
-21

---

13. C $-1 \times -1 = 1$. Therefore, -1 times itself an even number of times will always be positive 1. -1 times itself an odd number of times will always be negative.

$(-1)^6 - (-1)^5 - (-1)^4 =$
$1 - (-1) - 1 =$
$1 + 1 - 1 =$
$2 - 1 =$
1

---

14. B The question asks for which statements are false. Let's analyze each option.

I.   Adding a negative number is the same as subtracting the absolute value of that number. This statement is true.

For example:
$5 + -3 = 5 - 3 = 2$

II. Zero is a negative number. This statement is false. Zero is neither positive nor negative.

III. Any multiplication problem containing a negative number will produce a negative answer. This statement is false. Multiplication problems with an even number of negative numbers will give a positive answer.

For example:
$-3 \times -2 = 6.$

Therefore, II and III are false. Answer B.

15. A $(-3)^3 - 3(-2)^2 + 25^{1/2} =$

Let's break this problem up.

$(-3)^3 = (-3)(-3)(-3) = -27$
$3(-2)^2 = 3(-2)(-2) = 12$
$25^{1/2} = 5$

Now, let's solve the entire problem.

$(-3)^3 - 3(-2)^2 + 25^{1/2} =$
$-27 - 12 + 5 =$
$-39 + 5 =$
-34

---

16. C First, let's find the least common multiple of 12, 8, and 6. You can start listing out the multiples of each of them until you find a common one.
24 is the LCM of the three numbers.

12: 12, 24
8: 8, 16, 24
6: 6, 12, 18, 24

Now, let's find the greatest common factor. List out the factors of each number.

12: 1, 2, 3, 4, 6, 12
8: 1, 2, 4, 8
6: 1, 2, 3
The GCF is 2

The product of the LCM and the GCF is $2 \times 24 = 48$.

---

17. C Let's break this problem down to figure out how many bananas each monkey stole.

Monkey A steals 9 bananas.
The number A stole has been given.

Monkey B steals 3 less than 4 times what A stole.
First, find 4 times A and then subtract 3.

$4(9) - 3 = 36 - 3 = 33$

Monkey C steals the difference of A and B.

$33 - 9 = 24$

Monkey D steals 2 more than twice C.
Multiply 24 by 2 and then add 2.

$24 \times 2 + 2 = 48 + 2 = 50$

Now, find the sum.

$9 + 33 + 24 + 50 = 116$

---

18. C To find the quotient of two numbers in scientific notation, you should break it into smaller problems. First, divide the coefficients, then divide the powers of 10 by subtracting the exponents, and then put those results into scientific notation.

$(3 \times 10^{-4}) \div (6 \times 10^{7})$

$3 \div 6 = 0.5$
$-4 - 7 = -11$
0.5×10^{-11}

Unfortunately, 0.5×10^{-11} is not in proper scientific notation since 0.5 is not between 1 and 10.

$0.5 \times 10^{-11} =$
$5 \times 10^{-1} \times 10^{-11} =$
5×10^{-12}

19. A There are two ways to approach this problem. Leave the numbers in expanded form and add or convert to standard form, add, and then convert back to expanded form.

Method 1: Convert to standard form and then back.
First number: $200{,}000 + 30{,}000 + 8{,}000 + 70 + 6 = 238{,}076$
Second number: $400{,}000 + 80{,}000 + 900 + 10 = 480{,}910$

Now add: $238{,}076 + 480{,}910 = 718{,}986$
Convert back to standard form.

> $718{,}986 = 700{,}000 + 10{,}000$
> $+ 8{,}000 + 900 + 80 + 6$

Method 2: Leave in expanded form and add
When adding numbers in expanded form, it is easiest to start with the smallest place value and work up.
First number: $200{,}000 + 30{,}000 + 8{,}000 + 70 + 6$
Second number: $400{,}000 + 80{,}000 + 900 + 10$

The ten-thousands place went beyond the ten-thousands. Therefore, keep the 10,000 for the ten-thousands place, and bring the 100,000 to the next place.
Hundred-thousands Place: $100{,}000 + 200{,}000 + 400{,}000 = 700{,}000$

> Ones Place: 6
> Tens Place: $70 + 10 = 80$
> Hundreds Place: 900
> Thousands Place: 8,000
> Ten-Thousands Place:
> $30{,}000 + 80{,}000 = 110{,}000$

Now, write number in expanded form.

> $700{,}000 + 10{,}000 + 8{,}000 + 900 + 80 + 6$

---

20. A

$$\frac{-3 \times 10 \div 2 - 6 + 4^2}{12 - 8 \times 2} =$$

Exponents - take 4 squared.

$$\frac{-3 \times 10 \div 2 - 6 + 16}{12 - 8 \times 2} =$$

Multiply / divide from left to right on top and bottom.

$$\frac{-30 \div 2 - 6 + 16}{12 - 16} =$$

$$\frac{-15 - 6 + 16}{12 - 16} =$$

Add / subtract from left to right on top and bottom.

$$\frac{-21 + 16}{-4} =$$

$$\frac{-5}{-4} =$$

$$\frac{5}{4}$$

Chapter 2:
Fractions, Decimals, Percents

Lessons

2.1   Fractions Overview

Fraction Definition

A fraction is simply a number that expresses parts of a whole. The classic way of beginning to work with fractions is to use shapes.

In this example, you see four squares, three of which are shaded. If you think of all four squares as the "whole," then it makes sense to say that three out of four or three fourths of the squares are shaded.

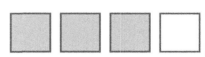

When you write in fractional notation, we use a numerator, the number on top of the bar or division sign (we'll return to the idea of fractions as division later in this lesson), and a denominator, the number on the bottom. Going back to the squares example, you would write three fourths as $\frac{3}{4}$. The denominator, a 4 in this case, gives the number of parts in the whole. The numerator states the number of parts that satisfy a certain requirement. With regard to the squares, 3 of the 4 total parts meet the requirement of being shaded, so, if asked what fraction of the squares is shaded, you would answer $\frac{3}{4}$.

Naming Fractions

Now that you understand the parts of a fraction, you need to be able to name them. The system is simple, use the normal word for the number in the numerator and, for the denominator, use the word for describing someone's place in a line. For example, $\frac{1}{7}$ is written as one seventh. If the number in the numerator is plural, add –ths to the end of the word for the number in the denominator. For example, $\frac{82}{95}$ is written as eighty–two ninety–fifths.

Equivalent Fractions

Since the denominator of a fraction describes the total number of parts in the whole and the numerator states the number of parts that you "have," when does a fraction equal one whole?

In this picture, all of the seven faces are smiling. This fraction is written as $\frac{7}{7}$, which equals one. Whenever the numerator of a fraction equals the denominator, the fraction

is equal to one. This property of fractions is very useful in mathematics because any number or variable can be multiplied or divided by one, or any fraction that equals one, without changing its value.

Here's an example of multiplying a fraction by a fraction equal to one without changing its value:

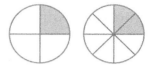

$$\tfrac{1}{4} \times \tfrac{2}{2} = \tfrac{2}{8}$$

If you look at the shaded areas of the circles, you will see that the fractions $\tfrac{1}{4}$ and $\tfrac{2}{8}$ are equal.

Simplifying Fractions

Manipulating numbers by multiplying and dividing by fractions equal to one is necessary to find the simplest form of a fraction. Simplest form is a way of writing a fraction so that the numerator and denominator have no common factors other than one. If asked to put $\tfrac{54}{72}$ into simplest form, you should recognize that 54 and 72 share the factor 9. Divide the numerator by 9, then divide the denominator by 9.

$$\tfrac{54}{72} \div \tfrac{9}{9} = \tfrac{6}{8}$$

Now that you have simplified the fraction, see if it can be simplified further. Both 6 and 8 share the factor of 2.

$$\tfrac{6}{8} \div \tfrac{2}{2} = \tfrac{3}{4}$$

Since 3 and 4 share no common factors, this fraction is in simplest form. It pays to simplify fractions after adding, subtracting, multiplying, and dividing. The correct answer to a multiple choice problem will almost always be in simplest form.

Comparing Fractions

Another time that you will need to manipulate fractions in this way is when you are comparing them. When comparing fractions, remember that the larger the denominator is, the more parts the whole is divided into. Since the whole is split into more parts, the parts are smaller. Look at the figure (right), which shows that $\tfrac{1}{4}$ is greater than $\tfrac{1}{8}$.

The numerator works in the opposite way. Since the numerator describes the parts of the whole that meet the requirements, a larger numerator includes more parts. Therefore, $\tfrac{3}{8}$ is smaller than $\tfrac{7}{8}$.

One easy way to compare fractions is to manipulate them so that they all have the same denominator. Since you know that you can multiply and divide any number by one, that's easy. Look at the following example:
Put the fractions $\frac{1}{4}$, $\frac{3}{32}$, $\frac{11}{64}$, and $\frac{9}{16}$ in order from least to greatest.
By multiplying by fractions equal to one, all of the numbers above can be converted to fractions with a denominator of 64.

$$\frac{1}{4} \times \frac{16}{16} = \frac{16}{64} \qquad \frac{3}{32} \times \frac{2}{2} = \frac{6}{64} \qquad \frac{9}{16} \times \frac{4}{4} = \frac{36}{64}$$

Now the problem is easy, with common denominators, the fractions can be ordered by their numerators from least to greatest: $\frac{6}{64} < \frac{11}{64} < \frac{16}{64} < \frac{36}{64}$.

Therefore, $\frac{3}{32} < \frac{11}{64} < \frac{1}{4} < \frac{9}{16}$

While many people find the concept of fractions intimidating, a deep understanding of the subject is necessary for understanding and expressing probabilities, which will be discussed in Lesson 8. Make sure that you are comfortable manipulating fractions before moving on.

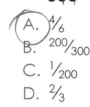

FRACTIONS OVERVIEW PRACTICE

1. **Write the following words as a mixed number in simplest form.**

    Five and Fifteen Twenty–Fifths

    A. $5\frac{1}{2}$
    B. $5\frac{3}{5}$ —
    C. $20\frac{3}{5}$
    D. $\frac{515}{25}$

    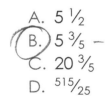

2. **What is the denominator of the fraction thirty-five fortieths when put in simplest form?**

    A. 7
    B. 8
    C. 35
    D. 40

3. **Put $\dfrac{400}{600}$ into simplest form.**

    A. $\frac{4}{6}$
    B. $\frac{200}{300}$
    C. $\frac{1}{200}$
    D. $\frac{2}{3}$

4. **The green triangle is equal to what fraction of the square?**

    A. $\frac{1}{4}$
    B. $\frac{1}{2}$
    C. $\frac{3}{4}$
    D. $\frac{1}{8}$

5. Which is the smallest number of this set?

$\frac{5}{9}$ $\frac{9}{17}$ $\frac{10}{20}$ $\frac{140}{300}$

    A. $\frac{5}{9}$

    B. $\frac{9}{17}$

    C. $\frac{10}{20}$

    (D.) $\frac{140}{300}$

$\frac{14}{3}$

6. Charles drew a picture of his family. The picture shows one man, one woman, two boys, and two girls. What fraction of Charles' family is female?

    (A.) $\frac{1}{2}$

    B. $\frac{4}{6}$

    C. $\frac{1}{3}$

    D. $\frac{3}{7}$

7. Which of the following fractions represents one whole?

$\frac{19}{30}$ $\frac{50}{50}$ $\frac{1}{0}$ $\frac{0}{1}$

    A. $\frac{19}{30}$

    (B.) $\frac{50}{50}$

    C. $\frac{1}{0}$

    D. $\frac{0}{1}$

8. $\frac{17}{20}$ can be expressed in words as:

    A. seventeen minus twenty

    B. seventeen plus twenty

    (C.) seventeen divided by twenty

    D. seventeen times twenty

9. Which of the following fractions is the greatest?

    (A.) $\frac{7}{8}$

    B. $\frac{8}{9}$

    C. $\frac{9}{10}$

    D. $\frac{10}{11}$

10. What fraction of the shapes below are parallelograms?

    A. $\frac{4}{5}$

    (B.) $\frac{2}{5}$

    C. $\frac{2}{10}$

    D. 1

FRACTIONS OVERVIEW EXPLANATIONS

1. B   First you must take the words and put them into a fraction, and then reduce.

The whole number will be everything before the "and". In this case, five = 5. Then, for the fraction, first is written the numerator and then the denominator.

Simplify. Since both the numerator and denominator of the fraction are divisible by 5, you should reduce.

Now put the whole number with the reduced fraction giving you:

> Fifteen Twenty–Fifths = $\frac{15}{25}$

> $\frac{15}{25} = \frac{3}{5}$

> $5\frac{3}{5}$

2. B   The easiest way to answer this question is to first write out the fraction. Remember that the term in the numerator comes first and is the normal word for the number, so 35 is the numerator here. Fortieths is the denominator term for 40. The fraction is $^{35}/_{40}$.

Now we must simplify the fraction. 5 divides evenly into both the numerator and denominator. The question asks for the denominator, which is 8.

$$^{35}/_{40} \div {}^{5}/_{5} = {}^{7}/_{8}$$

3. D   To simplify a fraction, you must find a number that divides evenly into the numerator and denominator. You could do this in several steps, such as dividing by $^{2}/_{2}$ and then by $^{100}/_{100}$.

You could also do it in one step by finding the greatest common factor, which is 200, and dividing the numerator and denominator by that.

$$^{400}/_{600} \div {}^{200}/_{200} = {}^{2}/_{3}$$

4. D   Approach this question using estimation. The fraction of the square covered by the triangle is clearly smaller than $^{1}/_{2}$, so $^{3}/_{4}$ can be ruled out as well. That leaves $^{1}/_{4}$ and $^{1}/_{8}$ as choices. Now it's time to draw on the diagram.

After dividing the square into four parts, it becomes obvious that the triangle is less than $^{1}/_{4}$ of the square, so it has to be $^{1}/_{8}$.

5. D   There are many ways to compare fractions. One way is to give them all the same denominator. But in this case, there is no easy common denominator. Another way is to convert them all to decimals and compare the decimals. But, in this problem, you can see that it will involve a lot of work to divide these numbers.

Therefore, let us see if there is a simpler solution. First, look at the third fraction: $^{10}/_{20}$. If you reduce this fraction, you get $^{1}/_{2}$. Now, let's compare the other fractions to $^{1}/_{2}$.

$^{5}/_{9}$ and $^{9}/_{17}$ are both greater than $^{1}/_{2}$.
$^{140}/_{300}$ is smaller than $^{1}/_{2}$ since $^{1}/_{2}$ of 300 is 150.

6. A   There are six people in Charles' family, so the denominator of our fraction is six. Three of the six people are females, making the numerator three. $^{3}/_{6}$

Remember to simplify. Divide both numerator and denominator by 3. $^{3}/_{6} = {}^{1}/_{2}$

7. B Because the numerator indicates the parts of the whole and the denominator indicates the total number of parts into which the whole has been divided, a fraction is equal to one whole when the numerator and denominator are equal. $^{50}\!/_{50}$

8. C The bar between the numerator and the denominator symbolizes division. This will be addressed again in the sub–lesson "Converting between Fractions, Decimals, and Percents."

> $^{17}\!/_{20} =$
> seventeen divided
> by twenty

9. D Comparing fractions can be done in many ways. One way is to find a common denominator for all the fractions and comparing the numerators. Another way is to convert all the fractions to decimals and then compare that way. But, in this case, let us think of what each fraction represents.

Remember that the larger the denominator, the greater the number of pieces into which the whole has been divided. Since each of the fractions above is missing one piece of the whole, $^{10}\!/_{11}$, the fraction missing the smallest piece, is the greatest.

10. B A parallelogram is a shape with four sides that has two sets of parallel lines. Four of the ten shapes satisfy that requirement, but don't forget to simplify.

> $^{4}\!/_{10} = ^{2}\!/_{5}$

2.2   Fractions – Adding/Subtracting

Process for Adding/Subtracting Fractions

The first step when adding or subtracting fractions is to convert them to a common denominator. To make things simple, use the least common denominator, which is the least common multiple of all of the denominators to be added or subtracted. After all of the fractions have been converted to the same denominator, they can be added and subtracted by adding and subtracting their numerators and keeping the denominator the same. Remember to simplify the result. Steps for adding or subtracting fractions:

- ⊙ Convert all fractions to same denominator
- ⊙ Add or subtract numerators, keep denominator the same
- ⊙ Simplify result

Example
$\dfrac{9}{17} - \dfrac{17}{51} + \dfrac{6}{34}$

The least common multiple for 17, 51, and 34 is 102, so that is the least common denominator for the fractions to the left. Convert each fraction into one with a denominator of 102 by multiplying by a fraction equal to one.

$$\frac{9}{17} \times \frac{6}{6} = \frac{54}{102} \qquad \frac{17}{51} \times \frac{2}{2} = \frac{34}{102} \qquad \frac{6}{34} \times \frac{3}{3} = \frac{18}{102}$$

Now that we have all fractions with the same denominator, we can add and subtract. Keep the denominator the same and add and subtract the numerators left to right. Finally, simplify the result.

$$\frac{54}{102} - \frac{34}{102} + \frac{18}{102} = \frac{54-34+18}{102} = \frac{38}{102} = \frac{19}{102}$$

FRACTIONS – ADDING/SUBTRACTING PRACTICE

1.

$$\frac{8}{34} + \frac{12}{34} =$$

$\frac{20}{34} \div 2 = \boxed{\frac{10}{17}}$

A. $^5/_{17}$
B. $^{20}/_{68}$
C. $^{16}/_{34}$
D. $^{10}/_{17}$

2. $\dfrac{51}{99} - \dfrac{33}{99} = \dfrac{18}{99}$

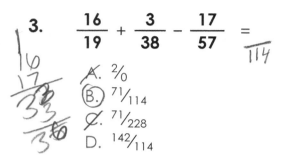

  A. $^{18}/_0$
  (B.) $^2/_{11}$
  C. $^2/_{99}$
  D. 18

$\dfrac{18 \div 9}{99 \div 9} = \boxed{\dfrac{2}{11}}$

3. $\dfrac{16}{19} + \dfrac{3}{38} - \dfrac{17}{57} = \dfrac{}{114}$

  A. $^2/_0$
  (B.) $^{71}/_{114}$
  C. $^{71}/_{228}$
  D. $^{142}/_{114}$

4. $\dfrac{1}{6} + \dfrac{3}{8} + \dfrac{1}{3} =$

  6: 6, 12, 18, 24, 30, 36, 41, 47
  8: 8, 16, 24, 32, 40
  3: 3, 9, 12, 15
  18, 24, (24)

  A. $^7/_{24}$
  B. $^5/_{17}$
  C. $^{21}/_{72}$
  (D.) $^7/_8$

$\dfrac{4}{24} + \dfrac{9}{24} + \dfrac{8}{24} = \dfrac{21 \div 3}{24}$ $\boxed{\dfrac{7}{8}}$

5. Robert mowed $\frac{1}{3}$ of his lawn and his sister Lisa mowed $\frac{1}{2}$ of it. In total, how much of the lawn did they mow?

  A. $^5/_{12}$
  B. $^1/_5$
  C. $^1/_6$
  (D.) $^5/_6$

$\dfrac{2}{3} + \dfrac{1}{2} = 3$

$\dfrac{2}{6} + \dfrac{3}{6} = \boxed{\dfrac{5}{6}}$

6. In a bag, $^{16}/_{30}$ of the marbles are blue and $^4/_{20}$ of the marbles are red. What fraction of the marbles are blue or red?

  A. $^{20}/_{50}$
  (B.) $^{11}/_{15}$

$\dfrac{16}{30} + \dfrac{4}{20}$

$\dfrac{32}{60} + \dfrac{12}{60} = \dfrac{44 \div 4}{60 \div 4}$

C. $^{12}/_{10}$
D. $^{16}/_{60}$

7. On her test, Joanne missed $\frac{1}{9}$ of the questions. What fraction of the questions did she answer correctly?

  A. $\frac{1}{9}$
  B. 8
  C. $^8/_0$
  (D.) $^8/_9$

$1 - \dfrac{1}{9}$

$\dfrac{9}{9} - \dfrac{1}{9} = \boxed{\dfrac{8}{9}}$

8. An elementary school teacher graded $\frac{4}{7}$ of her class' test papers before lunch and $\frac{2}{7}$ of the papers between lunch and dinner. If she plans to finish her grading by bedtime, what fraction of the papers will she need to grade between dinner and bedtime?

  A. $^6/_7$
  B. $^2/_0$
  (C.) $^1/_7$
  D. $^1/_6$

9. A couple is flying from Orlando, Florida to Honolulu, Hawaii for a vacation. The first leg of their trip is from Orlando to Atlanta, Georgia and it takes 2 hours. The next leg of their flight is from Atlanta to Los Angeles, California and it lasts 5 hours. If their total flight time is 13 hours, what fraction of their flight time is spent on the last leg, which is from Los Angeles to Honolulu?

2. Fractions, Decimals, Percents

A. $6/13$

B. $6/1$

C. $7/13$

D. $7/1$

13 - J - 2 = 6

$\frac{6}{13}$

13 = whole

10. At a county-wide orchestral competition, the only two ratings that earn ribbons are superior and excellent. June has scored a superior on three

of her solo violin performances. She has scored an excellent on five performances. If June has given 12 performances, what fraction of her performances have earned ribbons?

A. $8/24$

B. $2/12$

C. $1/3$

D. $2/3$

$12 - 3 - 5 = \frac{4}{12} \div 2$

$\frac{2}{6} \neq ? \; 7$

FRACTIONS – ADDING/SUBTRACTING EXPLANATIONS

1. D To add fractions with a common denominator: add the numerators, keep the denominator, and then simplify.

$$\frac{8}{34} + \frac{12}{34} = \frac{20}{34} \qquad \text{Simplify} \qquad \frac{20}{34} \div \frac{2}{2} = \frac{10}{17}$$

2. B To subtract fractions with a common denominator, subtract the numerators and then simplify.

$$\frac{51}{99} - \frac{33}{99} = \frac{18}{99} \qquad \text{Simplify} \qquad \frac{18}{99} \div \frac{9}{9} = \frac{2}{11}$$

3. B Before adding or subtracting fractions, you must give them a common denominator. The least common multiple (See Numbers and Properties: Factors, Multiples, and Divisibility for help) of 19, 38, and 57 is 114. You must convert each fraction so that it has a denominator of 114.

Add and subtract the numerators from left to right. Keep the denominator.

$6/19 \times 6/6 = 96/114$
$3/38 \times 3/3 = 9/114$
$17/57 \times 2/2 = 34/114$

$(96 + 9 - 34)/114 = 74/114$

Simplify. $71/114$

4. D Before adding fractions, you must convert them into fractions with a common denominator. The least common multiple (See Numbers and

Properties: Factors, Multiples, and Divisibility for help) of 6, 8, and 3 is 24.

Convert the fractions so that they all have a denominator of 24.

$$\frac{1}{6} \times \frac{4}{4} = \frac{4}{24}$$
$$\frac{3}{8} \times \frac{3}{3} = \frac{9}{24}$$
$$\frac{1}{3} \times \frac{8}{8} = \frac{8}{24}$$

Now add the numerators and keep the denominator the same.

$$\frac{4}{24} + \frac{9}{24} + \frac{8}{24} = \frac{4+9+8}{24} = \frac{21}{24}$$

Now simplify the fraction. 3 divides evenly into both 21 and 24.

$$\frac{21}{24} \div \frac{3}{3} = \frac{7}{8}$$

---

5. D Robert and Lisa each mowed part of the lawn, which means that you need to add to find the total amount mowed. Give the fractions a common denominator, in this case 6.

$$\frac{1}{3} = \frac{2}{6}$$
$$\frac{1}{2} = \frac{3}{6}$$

Add the numerators, keep the denominator.

$$\frac{2}{6} + \frac{3}{6} = \frac{5}{6}$$

---

6. B To add fractions, you need to find a common denominator. The least common multiple of 30 and 20 is 60. Convert the fractions so that they have a denominator of 60.

$$\frac{16}{30} = \frac{32}{60}$$
$$\frac{4}{20} = \frac{12}{60}$$

Add and simplify.

$$\frac{32}{60} + \frac{12}{60} = \frac{44}{60}$$
$$\frac{44}{60} = \frac{11}{15}$$

---

7. D To find out what fraction of the questions Joanne answered correctly, you need to subtract the fraction she missed from the total. The first step in this problem is to express the total as a fraction. The test is one whole.

$$1 - \frac{1}{9}$$

Write 1 as $\frac{9}{9}$ so that you can subtract with a common denominator.

$$\frac{9}{9} - \frac{1}{9} = \frac{8}{9}$$

---

8. C To solve this problem, you must understand that the whole, or all of the papers, can be represented as 1 which can also be written as $\frac{7}{7}$. Subtract the completed parts from the whole to find out how much grading the teacher has left to complete.

$$\frac{7}{7} - \frac{4}{7} - \frac{2}{7} = \frac{7-4-2}{7} = \frac{1}{7}$$

---

9. A   To solve this problem, you must understand that the whole, or total flight time, can be represented as 1 or $^{13}\!/_{13}$ hours.

That means that the Orlando to Atlanta leg of the flight is 5 out of the total 13 hours or is $^{5}\!/_{13}$ of the flight time and the Atlanta to Los Angeles leg is $^{2}\!/_{13}$ of the trip time. Now this is a simple subtraction problem.

$$\frac{13}{13} - \frac{5}{13} - \frac{2}{13} = \frac{13-5-2}{13} = \frac{6}{13}$$

10. D   Write the fraction of performances that earned a superior rating, which is 3 out of the 12: $^{3}\!/_{12}$.

Write the fraction that earned an excellent, which is 5 out of the 12: $^{5}\!/_{12}$ Add the two fractions.

$$\frac{3}{12} + \frac{5}{12} = \frac{8}{12} \qquad\qquad \text{Simplify} \quad \frac{8}{12} = \frac{2}{3}$$

2.3 Fractions – Multiplying/Dividing

Multiplying Fractions

To multiply fractions, simply multiply the numerators to get the new numerator and multiply the denominators to get the new denominator.

$$\frac{3}{4} \times \frac{7}{9} = \frac{3 \times 7}{4 \times 9} = \frac{21}{36}$$ Then simplify if applicable. $\frac{21}{36} = \frac{7}{12}$

Often, it is easier to simplify before multiplying. In the same example from above: There is a 3 in the numerator and a 9 in the denominator. Since 3 divides evenly into both of them, you can simplify those numbers by dividing both by 3. The 3 in the numerator becomes 1 and the 9 in the denominator becomes 3. Now write the simplified problem and multiply.

$$^3/_4 \times {}^7/_9$$

$$^1/_4 \times {}^7/_3 = {}^7/_{12}$$

Dividing Fractions

To divide fractions, invert the divisor and then multiply the fractions. Another way to think about it is to flip the second fraction and multiply. In the division problem to the right, we first turned the division problem into a multiplication. Now, below you see that the fractions were simplified before multiplication. Since 15 and 3 are both divisible by 3, and 32 and 2 are both divisible by 2.

$$^{15}/_{32} \div {}^3/_2 = {}^{15}/_{32} \times {}^2/_3$$

$$\frac{\overset{5}{\cancel{15}}}{32} \times \frac{2}{\cancel{3}_1} = \frac{5}{\cancel{32}_{16}} \times \frac{\cancel{2}^1}{1} = \frac{5}{16} \times \frac{1}{1} = \frac{5}{16}$$

FRACTIONS - MULTIPLYING/DIVIDING PRACTICE

1. $^3/_5 \times {}^8/_9 =$

$\frac{24}{45} =$ $\frac{8}{15}$

  A. $^8/_{15}$
  B. $^{11}/_{14}$
  C. $^{11}/_{45}$
  D. $^{24}/_{14}$

2. $^6/_7 \times {}^9/_{19} =$

$\frac{14}{7}$

  A. $^{54}/_{26}$
  B. $^{15}/_{133}$
  C. $^{15}/_{26}$
  D. $^{54}/_{133}$

3. $^3/_{10} \div {}^1/_2$

  A. $^2/_8$
  B. $^3/_5$
  C. $^4/_{12}$
  D. $^3/_{20}$

$\frac{3}{10} \times \frac{2}{1}$

$\frac{5}{} \quad \frac{3}{5}$

4. $^{19}/_{20} \div {}^4/_{10} \div {}^{19}/_{32} =$

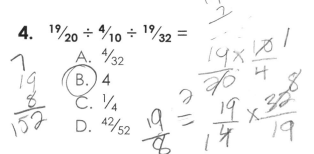

   A. $^4/_{32}$
   B. 4
   C. $^1/_4$
   D. $^{42}/_{52}$

5. In a 36 card deck, 12 are aces. In the same deck 9 are spades, 9 are diamonds, 9 are clubs, and 9 are hearts. If the aces are distributed evenly between all the suits, what fraction of the deck are aces of spades?

   A. 3
   B. 1
   C. $^1/_{12}$
   D. $^1/_{36}$

6. $^5/_7 \div {}^{25}/_{35} \times {}^4/_{12} =$

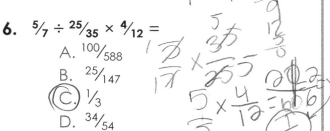

   A. $^{100}/_{588}$
   B. $^{25}/_{147}$
   C. $^1/_3$
   D. $^{34}/_{54}$

7. Which problem can be modeled with this diagram?

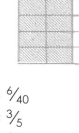

   A. $^3/_8 \times {}^2/_5 = {}^6/_{40}$
   B. $^2/_3 \times {}^5/_8 = {}^3/_5$
   C. $^2/_8 \times {}^3/_5 = {}^6/_{40}$
   D. $^2/_{16} \div {}^3/_{15} = {}^6/_{15}$

8. A woman is calculating the dividend that she will make from an investment. There are 100 investors, each of whom gets an equal share of the profits. If her share is $80, what were the total profits?

   A. $80
   B. $0.80
   C. $800
   D. $8000

9. A fifth grade club gets an extra large pizza with 16 slices. The teachers take 2 of the slices. If the students divide the remaining pizza equally, each child gets $^1/_8$ of the pizza. How many students are in the club?

   A. $^7/_{64}$
   B. 14
   C. 8
   D. 7

10. A group of pirates finds a chest of buried treasure containing 16 pounds of gold. The captain takes $^5/_8$ of the treasure as his share. How many pounds of treasure is remaining to be divided between the rest of the pirates?

   A. $^{11}/_8$
   B. $^{21}/_8$
   C. 6
   D. 10

1. A   *Method 1:* **Multiply and then Simplify:** Multiply the two numerators to get the new numerator—in this case, 8 × 3 = 24. Then multiply the two denominators to find the new denominator, 5 × 9 = 45. This gives the fraction $^{24}/_{45}$, which simplifies to $^{8}/_{15}$.

Method 2: **Simplify first:** You can see that 3 in the numerator and 9 in the denominator are both divisible by 3. Simplify by dividing both by 3.

$$^{3}/_{5} \times {}^{8}/_{9} = {}^{1}/_{5} \times {}^{8}/_{3}$$

Then multiply numerators to get 1 × 8 = 8. Then multiply denominators, 5 × 3 = 15. Giving you the fraction: $^{8}/_{15}$

2. D   Multiply the two numerators to get the new numerator, in this case, 6 × 9 = 54. Then multiply the two denominators to find the new denominator, 7 × 19 = 133. This gives the fraction $^{54}/_{133}$.

3. B   To divide one fraction by another, invert the divisor and then multiply the two fractions.

$$\frac{3}{10} \div \frac{1}{2} = \frac{3}{10} \times \frac{2}{1} = \frac{3 \times 2}{10 \times 1} = \frac{6}{10} = \frac{3}{5}$$

4. B   Break this problem into multiple steps. Divide the first two fractions, and then take that result and divide it by the last fraction.

Remember, to divide fractions, invert the divisor and multiply. The following problem shows the simplification before multiplying.

$$^{19}/_{20} \div {}^{4}/_{10} = {}^{19}/_{20} \times {}^{10}/_{4} = {}^{19}/_{2} \times {}^{1}/_{4} = {}^{19}/_{8}$$

Now take the result of that division problem and divide it by the last fraction.

$$^{19}/_{8} \div {}^{19}/_{32} = {}^{19}/_{8} \times {}^{32}/_{19} = {}^{1}/_{8} \times {}^{32}/_{1} = {}^{1}/_{1} \times {}^{4}/_{1} = {}^{4}/_{1} = 4$$

5. C   The first step is to write the fraction of the deck that consists of aces. There are 12 aces out of the total deck of 36: $^{12}/_{36}$.
That can be simplified to $^{1}/_{3}$.

Then write the fraction that represents the portion of the deck that is spades. There are 9 spades out of the total deck of 36: $^{9}/_{36}$, which equals $^{1}/_{4}$.

To find the portion of the deck that is both aces and spades, multiply the two fractions.

$$\tfrac{1}{3} \times \tfrac{1}{4} = \tfrac{1}{12}$$

---

6. C Following order of operations, multiply and divide from left to right. Therefore, do the division problem first, by inverting the divisor, simplifying, and then multiplying:

$$\tfrac{5}{7} \div \tfrac{25}{35} = \tfrac{5}{7} \times \tfrac{35}{25} = \tfrac{1}{7} \times \tfrac{35}{5} = \tfrac{1}{1} \times \tfrac{5}{5} = \tfrac{5}{5} = 1$$

Now multiply that result by $\tfrac{4}{12}$

$$1 \times \tfrac{4}{12} = \tfrac{4}{12} = \tfrac{1}{3}$$

---

7. A In the first image, we are looking at just the rows. There are 8 rows total and 3 rows are shaded. Therefore, 3/8 of the rows are shaded.

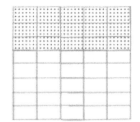 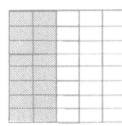 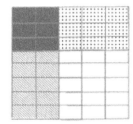

In the second image, we are looking at the columns. There are 2 out of 5 or 2/5 of columns shaded.

If we multiply the fraction of the shape of shaded rows by the fraction of the shape of shaded columns, we will get the fraction of the shape that has shaded rows and columns.

$$\tfrac{3}{8} \times \mathbf{\tfrac{2}{5}} = \tfrac{6}{40}$$

---

8. D Because the profits will be divided equally among 100 investors, the woman's $80 share of the profits is $\tfrac{1}{100}$ of the total. To find what the total profits are, divide her share by the fraction of the total.

$$\$80 \div \tfrac{1}{100} =$$
$$\$80 \times \tfrac{100}{1} =$$
$$\$80 \times 100 = \$8000$$

---

9. D Let's figure out what is remaining of the pizza. The pizza started with 16 slices and 2 were eaten, leaving 14. Therefore, the pizza that must be divided equally among the students includes 14 slices out of 16 slices or $^{14}/_{16}$ of the entire pizza.

$$^{14}/_{16} \div ^1/_8 =$$
$$^{14}/_{16} \times ^8/_1 =$$
$$7 \text{ students}$$

To find the number of students in the club, divide the fraction of the pizza that they have to share, $^{14}/_{16}$, by the fraction that each child receives, which is $^1/_8$.

---

10. C **Method 1: Determine Captain's share first.**
Multiply the total gold in the chest by the fraction that equals the captain's share.

$$\text{Gold in Chest} \times \text{Captain's Share} =$$
$$16 \times ^5/_8 =$$
$$^{16}/_1 \times ^5/_8 =$$
$$^2/_1 \times ^5/_1 =$$
$$^{10}/_1 = 10$$

The captain's share is 10 lbs and the total is 16 lbs. Therefore, there are 6 lbs remaining to be divided among the rest of the pirates.

Method 2: Determine fraction remaining first.
You know the total amount of treasure is 1, which is equivalent to $^8/_8$. We can subtract the captain's share to determine what fraction of the treasure is remaining for the rest of the pirates.

$$^8/_8 - ^5/_8 = ^3/_8$$

Now multiply this fraction by the total treasure to determine how much treasure the rest of the pirates will have.

$$\text{Gold in Chest} \times \text{Pirates' Share} =$$
$$16 \times ^3/_8 =$$
$$^{16}/_1 \times ^3/_8 =$$
$$^2/_1 \times ^3/_1 =$$
$$^6/_1 = 6$$
$$6 \text{ lbs remaining}$$

2.4 Mixed Numbers/Improper Fractions

Mixed Numbers

When a fraction is greater than one, it can be written as a mixed number—a number containing both a fraction and a whole number. In the following example, each square represents 1. We see two whole squares that are shaded, but there is a third square that has been divided into halves. Only one of those parts is shaded. To name the portion of the squares that are shaded, we use the fraction two and one half or $2\frac{1}{2}$.

Mixed numbers can be useful when adding or subtracting fractions and whole numbers, such as $4\frac{1}{2} - 1 = 3\frac{1}{2}$ or fractions with common denominators.

> **Example**
>
> $5\frac{3}{4} + 4\frac{1}{4} = 9\frac{4}{4} = 9 + 1 = 10$

Improper Fractions

> **Example**
>
> $\frac{7}{2} \times \frac{5}{4} = \frac{35}{8}$

Mixed numbers can also be written as improper fractions, or fractions with a numerator greater than the denominator. This is useful when multiplying and dividing fractions because improper fractions can be treated the same as proper fractions when performing those operations.

Converting from Mixed Number to Improper Fraction

Often you will need to convert mixed numbers into improper fractions. To do this, multiply the whole number by the denominator and then add the numerator to that number. This will give you your new numerator, and the denominator will remain the same.

> **Example**
>
> $5\frac{3}{4} = \frac{(5\times4+3)}{4} = \frac{23}{4}$

Another way to think of the conversion is that you need to turn the whole number into a fraction with the same denominator as its accompanying fraction and then add the two. To convert $5\frac{3}{4}$, first convert 5 to a fraction with a denominator of 4 and then add that to $\frac{3}{4}$.

> $5 \times \frac{4}{4} = \frac{20}{4}$
>
> $\frac{20}{4} + \frac{3}{4} = \frac{23}{4}$

Converting from an Improper Fraction to a Mixed Number

To convert an improper fraction into a mixed number, divide the numerator by the denominator. The quotient is the whole number and the remainder is the numerator of the fraction.

$^{23}/_4 = 23 \div 4 = 5$ remainder $3 = 5\,^3/_4$
$^{77}/_9 = 77 \div 9 = 8$ remainder $5 = 8\,^5/_9$

Remainders as Fractions

When dividing numbers, you can think of the problem as a fraction problem. For instance, $13 \div 5$ is the same as $^{13}/_5$, so you can convert the fraction into a mixed number.

$^{13}/_5 = 2\,^3/_5$

Another way to think of this step is to convert the remainder into a fraction. $13 \div 5 = 2$ remainder 3. That means there were only 3 out of the 5 needed to get to the next whole number. Therefore, you can write the remainder as a fraction with the remainder as the numerator and the divisor as the denominator.

$13 \div 5 = 2$ remainder $3 = 2\,^3/_5$

MIXED NUMBERS/IMPROPER FRACTIONS PRACTICE

1. **Which of the following is fourteen and seven eighths?**
   A. $^{21}/_8$
   B. $^{14}/_8$
   C. $14\,^7/_8$
   D. $14\,^8/_7$

2. **The shaded portion of the picture below can be represented by what mixed number?**
   A. $5\,^1/_3$
   B. $^{16}/_3$
   C. $^5/_3$
   D. $5\,^2/_3$

3. **Jorge is in the middle of doing laundry when a detergent bottle runs out. He needs to pour $1\,^3/_5$ cups of detergent into the washing machine for this load, and he poured $1\,^1/_5$ cups from the old bottle. How much detergent from the new bottle does Jorge need for washing this load?**
   A. $^1/_5$
   B. $^2/_5$
   C. $1\,^2/_5$
   D. $^4/_5$

4. Which of the following is fifty-seven ninths?

A. $^{57}/_9$ ⟵ *(circled)*

B. 57.9

C. $^1/_{579}$

D. 57 $^1/_9$

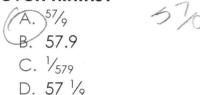

5. The Suarez family's pool was finished yesterday, and they started to fill it with water. The pool's capacity is 800 gallons, but they were only able to pump in 400 $^3/_7$ gallons. It rained overnight, which added another 3 $^4/_7$ gallons to the pool. How many gallons of water will the Suarez family need to finish filling their pool to capacity?

A. 404 gallons

B. 399 gallons

C. 396 gallons ⟵ *(circled)*

D. 393 gallons

6. What improper fraction describes the portion of the circles that is not shaded?

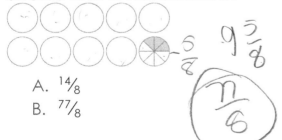

A. $^{14}/_8$

B. $^{77}/_8$

C. $^{72}/_8$

D. $^5/_8$

7. $^8/_9 \times 4^3/_4 =$

A. $^{38}/_9$ ⟵ *(circled)*

B. $^1/_6$

C. $^{14}/_9$

D. $4^2/_3$

8. $2^7/_9 - 1^3/_8 + ^2/_3 =$

A. $1^1/_{12}$

B. $2^5/_{72}$ ⟵ *(circled)*

C. $2^1/_2$

D. $4^{59}/_{72}$

9. Derek ate $^{18}/_8$ of a petite pizza, Cordelia ate $^5/_{12}$ of another, and Raul ate $^7/_{14}$ of a different pizza. Assuming that the three pizzas were equal in size, how much pizza did all three eat?

A. $^{42}/_{139}$

B. $3^{13}/_{42}$ ⟵ *(circled)*

C. $^{32}/_{34}$

D. $3^1/_2$

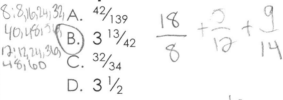

10. What is $27 \div 4$?

A. $3^6/_4$

B. $7^1/_4$

C. $6^3/_4$ ⟵ *(circled)*

D. $6^3/_{27}$

MIXED NUMBERS/IMPROPER FRACTIONS EXPLANATIONS

1. **C**   Which of the following is fourteen and seven eighths? When writing a mixed number, write the whole number, 14 in this case, followed by the fraction $^7/_8$.

$14^7/_8$

2. D To write a mixed number, write the number of wholes. There are five shaded squares, so you should write 5. Then write the fraction of the square that is partially shaded: $\frac{2}{3}$. As a mixed number, this is written $5\frac{2}{3}$.

Notice that answer choices B and C are improper fractions, and the question asks for a mixed number.

---

3. B To find the amount that he still needs to pour, subtract what Jorge has already poured into the machine from the total amount needed.

$1\frac{3}{5} - 1\frac{1}{5} = \frac{2}{5}$

---

4. A To translate an improper fraction from words to numerical form, remember that improper fractions use the same naming scheme as proper fractions. The term in the numerator comes first and is the normal word for the number, so 57 is the numerator here. Ninths is the denominator term for 9. The fraction is $\frac{57}{9}$.

---

5. C Begin by finding out how much water is in the pool. Do this by adding the volumes of water that were pumped in yesterday and deposited by rain.

$400\frac{3}{7} + 3\frac{4}{7}$

To add mixed numbers, add the whole numbers separately, add the fractions separately and then combine the results.

$400 + 3 = 403$
$\frac{3}{7} + \frac{4}{7} = \frac{7}{7} = 1$
$403 + 1 = 404$ gallons

Now subtract the amount of water in the pool from the pool's capacity of 800 gallons to find out how much more water is needed.

800 gallons − 404 gallons = 396 gallons

---

6. B First, look at the circle that is partially shaded and name the fraction of the circle that is not shaded. The circle is divided into 8 parts, 5 of which are not shaded. So the fraction is $\frac{5}{8}$, and there are 9 whole circles that are not shaded. Combining those two gives us the mixed number: $9\frac{5}{8}$.

The question asks for the improper fraction, so we must convert $9\frac{5}{8}$ to an improper fraction.

First, take the 9 and give it a common denominator with the fraction.

$9 \times \frac{8}{8} = \frac{72}{8}$

Now add the 9 wholes to the fraction.

$\frac{72}{8} + \frac{5}{8} = \frac{77}{8}$

Another way to think of converting the mixed number to an improper fraction is to take the whole number, multiply it by the denominator of the fraction, add it to the numerator, and put that all over the denominator of the fraction.

$$9 \frac{5}{8} = \frac{9 \times 8 + 5}{10} = \frac{77}{8}$$

7. A To multiply mixed numbers, you must first convert to improper fractions. You can NOT multiply the whole numbers and fractions separately. First, convert 4 ¾ to an improper fraction. Now, multiply as you would with proper fractions.

$$4 \tfrac{3}{4} = \tfrac{19}{4}$$

$$\tfrac{8}{9} \times \tfrac{19}{4} = \tfrac{38}{9}$$

8. B First, convert all of the numbers to fractions with a common denominator.

Then add and subtract from left to right, following order of operations.

Change from an improper fraction to a mixed number.

$$2 \tfrac{7}{9} = \tfrac{25}{9} \times \tfrac{8}{8} = \tfrac{200}{72}$$
$$1 \tfrac{3}{8} = \tfrac{11}{8} \times \tfrac{9}{9} = \tfrac{99}{72}$$
$$\tfrac{2}{3} \times \tfrac{24}{24} = \tfrac{48}{72}$$

$$\tfrac{200}{72} - \tfrac{99}{72} = \tfrac{101}{72}$$
$$\tfrac{101}{72} + \tfrac{48}{72} = \tfrac{149}{72}$$

$$\tfrac{149}{72} = 2 \tfrac{5}{72}$$

9. B To add improper fractions, give them a common denominator.

$$\tfrac{18}{8} \times \tfrac{21}{21} = \tfrac{378}{168}$$
$$\tfrac{5}{12} \times \tfrac{14}{14} = \tfrac{70}{168}$$
$$\tfrac{9}{14} \times \tfrac{12}{12} = \tfrac{108}{168}$$

Then add the fractions by adding the numerators and keeping the denominator.

$$\tfrac{378}{168} + \tfrac{70}{168} + \tfrac{108}{168} =$$
$$= \tfrac{556}{168}$$
$$= \tfrac{139}{42}$$
$$= 3 \tfrac{13}{42}$$

10. C You can approach this problem in two ways.

Think of $27 \div 4$ as $\tfrac{27}{4}$. Then convert the improper fraction to a mixed number.

Or divide 4 into 27 and turn the remainder into a fraction. 27 divided by 4 is 6 with a remainder of 3. The remainder is then converted to a fraction by placing the remainder as the numerator and the divisor as the denominator.

$$27 \div 4 = 6 \text{ R } 3 = 6 \tfrac{3}{4}$$

2.5 Decimals Overview

Fractions with denominators that are powers of 10 (100, 1000, etc.) can also be written as numbers called decimals. In a number with a decimal sign, all of the numbers to the left of the decimal sign are whole numbers, while all of the numbers to the right of it are fractions.

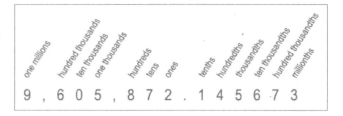

The digit 1 in the tenths place on this place-value chart literally means $\frac{1}{10}$. The digit 4 in the hundredths place means $\frac{4}{100}$ and the 3 in the millionths place symbolizes $\frac{3}{1000000}$. To the right are examples of decimals written as fractions.

Example:
.59 = $^{59}/_{100}$ = fifty–nine hundredths

.2222 = $^{2222}/_{10000}$ = two–thousand two-hundred twenty-two ten-thousandths

.30303 = $^{30303}/_{100000}$ = thirty–thousand three–hundred three one–hundred thousandths

DECIMALS OVERVIEW PRACTICE

1. **Write seven hundred thousand two hundred ninety and four thousand seventy five ten thousandths as a decimal.**
    - A. 7,290.475
    - B. 700,290.4075 *(circled)*   700,290,4
    - C. 700,294.75
    - D. 700,294.175

2. **Which decimal has a 6 in the hundreds place but not in the hundredths place?**
    - A. 632.165
    - B. 8642.165
    - C. 64.046
    - D. 8642.046 *(circled)*

3. **In words, 637.951 is**
    - A. Six hundred thirty-seven and nine hundred fifty one
    - B. six hundred thirty-seven and nine hundred fifty one hundredths
    - C. six hundred thirty seven and nine hundred fifty one thousandths *(circled)*
    - D. six hundred thirty seven and nine hundred fifty one ten thousandths

4. Write 5.3847 as a mixed number.

10000

$5\dfrac{3847}{10000}$

A. $\dfrac{53847}{10000}$

B. $\dfrac{53847}{100000}$

C. $5\dfrac{3847}{10000}$

D. $5\dfrac{3847}{100000}$

5. What number is represented by the M on the number line?

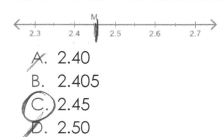

A. 2.40

B. 2.405

C. 2.45

D. 2.50

6. 12.50 × twenty ten thousandths

A. 0.00025

B. 0.250

C. 0.0025

D. 0.025

12.50

7. Order the following from greatest to least: 1.389, $\dfrac{14}{3}$, $1\dfrac{1}{3}$

A. $\dfrac{14}{3}$, $1\dfrac{1}{3}$, 1.389

B. $1\dfrac{1}{3}$, 1.389, $\dfrac{14}{3}$

C. $\dfrac{14}{3}$, 1.389, $1\dfrac{1}{3}$

D. 1.389, $\dfrac{14}{3}$, $1\dfrac{1}{3}$

8. There are 3 students in a club. If the students' GPAs are 4.02, 4.1, and 3.88, what is their average GPA?

A. 3.099

B. 4

C. 4.12

D. 4.2

$4.02 = \dfrac{402}{100}$

$\dfrac{402}{410}$ $\dfrac{410}{100}$ $\dfrac{388}{100}$
388
$\dfrac{1200}{100}$

$\dfrac{1200}{100} = 12 \cdot 3 = 1$

4

9. Four basketball players are comparing their free throw shooting records. These are the fractions of shots made.

Player 1: $\dfrac{42}{63}$
Player 2: $\dfrac{75}{94}$
Player 3: 0.324
Player 4: 0.846

Who has the worst free throw shooting record of the four?

A. Player 1

B. Player 2

C. Player 3

D. Player 4

10. Doreen has taken 4 different tests. Each of the tests was scored by a different person. These are the results:

Test A: $\dfrac{9}{10}$
Test B: .954
Test C: 0.9099
Test D: $\dfrac{5}{6}$

$\dfrac{954}{100}$ 9 $\dfrac{105}{}$
$\dfrac{30)10}$ $\dfrac{27}{30}$ $\dfrac{25}{30}$

On which test did Doreen score highest?

A. Test A

B. Test B

C. Test C

D. Test D

1. B The "and" in a written number always represents a fraction or a decimal sign. Everything to the left of the "and" is a whole number and should be written to the left of the decimal. Seven hundred thousand two hundred ninety is 700,290. Everything to the right of the "and" is a fraction and should be to the right of the decimal. Four thousand seventy five ten thousandths is written: 0.4075. Put it together to get 700,290.04075

2. D The hundreds place is three to the left of the decimal. Answers A, B, and D each have a six there. The hundredths place is two to the right of the decimal. Answers A and B each have a six in the hundredths place, making D the answer.

3. C Break the number into two pieces, what is to the left of the decimal point and what is to the right of the decimal point. The two pieces will be joined with "AND".

To the left of the decimal point is 637. This whole number is written as six hundred thirty seven.

To the right of the decimal point is .951. The last digit is in the thousandths place, so the fraction is nine hundred fifty one thousandths.

> six hundred thirty seven AND nine hundred fifty one thousandths
>
> 637.951

Now connect the two pieces.

4. C The number to the left of the decimal is a whole number, 5. The digits to the right of the decimal are a fraction and the last digit is in the ten thousandths place. Therefore, $5 \frac{3847}{10000}$.

5. C On the number line, the letter M is halfway between 2.4 and 2.5. Remembering, adding a zero to the end of a decimal doesn't change the value, therefore we can think of M being halfway between 2.40 and 2.50.

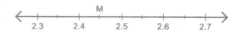

> 2.40 can be written as $2 \frac{40}{100}$
> 2.50 can be written as $2 \frac{50}{100}$

It can be seen that the number halfway between those would be $2 \frac{45}{100}$, which is written as 2.45.

6. D One way to solve this problem is to take each number, write them as fractions, multiply, and then convert back. You will learn another method in Multiplying/Dividing Decimals.

Write 12.50 and 20 ten thousandths as fractions and then multiply them. You can reduce to help multiply.

$$12.50 = \frac{1250}{100}$$
$$20 \text{ ten thousandths} = \frac{20}{10000}$$
$$\frac{1250}{100} \times \frac{20}{10000} = \frac{157250}{1000000}$$
$$\frac{125}{10} \times \frac{2}{1000} = \frac{250}{10000}$$

Now convert back from fraction to decimal. Remember that you want the last digit of the numerator to be in the place value of the denominator.

$$0.0250 = 0.025$$

7. C You could either convert them all to decimals or convert them all to fractions. In this problem, let's try converting each number to a fraction with the same denominator.

$$1.389 = \frac{1389}{1000} \times \frac{3}{3} = \frac{4167}{3000}$$
$$\frac{14}{3} \times \frac{1000}{1000} = \frac{14000}{3000}$$
$$1\,\frac{1}{3} = \frac{4}{3} \times \frac{1000}{1000} = \frac{4000}{3000}$$

Now we can easily compare the fractions since they have the same denominator. In order from greatest to least, the fractions are:

$$\frac{14000}{3000}, \ \frac{4167}{3000}, \ \frac{4000}{3000}$$

8. B We are asked to find the average of a set of numbers. Answer choice A is smaller than all the decimals and can not be the average. Answers C and D are both greater than all the decimals, and therefore, they can not be the average. This leaves answer B. You could also convert them to fractions, add them and divide by 3.

$$4.02 = \frac{402}{100}$$
$$4.1 = \frac{41}{10} = \frac{410}{100}$$
$$3.88 = \frac{388}{100}$$

$$\frac{402}{100} + \frac{410}{100} + \frac{388}{100}$$
$$= \frac{1200}{100} = 12$$
$$12 \div 3 = 4$$

9. C Use estimation here. Player 1 has made about $\frac{2}{3}$ of his free throws. Player 2 has made approximately $\frac{7}{8}$, and Player Four has made about $\frac{85}{100}$. These are all significantly greater than $\frac{1}{2}$. Player 3, however, has made about $\frac{1}{3}$ of his free throws. That's less than half, so Player 3 has the worst record.

10. B ❶ First find the greatest decimal.

❷ Then find the greatest fraction by giving them the same denominator and comparing.

❸ Finally, compare the greatest fraction, $\frac{9}{10}$, with the greatest decimal, .954, to find the highest test score.

❶ $0.954 > 0.9099$ Eliminate C.

❷
$$\frac{9}{10} = \frac{27}{30}$$
$$\frac{5}{6} = \frac{25}{30}$$
$$\frac{27}{30} > \frac{25}{30}$$
Eliminate D.

❸
$$0.954 = \frac{954}{1000}$$
$$\frac{9}{10} = \frac{900}{1000}$$
$$\frac{954}{1000} > \frac{900}{1000}$$
Answer B, 0.954

2.6 Decimals – Adding/Subtracting

Adding and Subtracting Decimals

Adding or subtracting decimal numbers is very similar to adding and subtracting whole numbers. The key is to line up the decimal points in a column. Even if the two numbers have a different number of digits after the decimal point, as long as the decimal places are lined up, you can add as you normally would.

Remember, if you are adding or subtracting a number with no decimal point, the decimal goes after the number.

$$\begin{array}{r} 3.425 \\ +\ 12.2 \\ \hline 15.625 \end{array}$$

└─ Line up the decimal places.

Placeholder Zeros

People often find it easier to add and subtract decimals by putting in placeholder zeros. This can be seen in the following problem.

$$\begin{array}{r} 7.243 \\ +\ 11.1 \\ 3 \\ 8.53 \end{array} \qquad \begin{array}{r} 7.243 \\ +\ 11.100 \\ 3.000 \\ 8.530 \\ \hline 29.873 \end{array}$$

←— Add placeholder zeros.

└─ Line up the decimal places.

ADDING/SUBTRACTING PRACTICE

1. You open a bank account and deposit $150. Over the next month you withdraw $12.50, $17, and $45.23. How much money is left in the account?
   A. $74.27
   B. $75.27
   C. $76.73
   D. $92.10

2. Jake stayed home from school because he had a fever. In the morning, his temperature was 100.8 degrees. By the afternoon, it was 103.4 degrees. How many degrees had his temperature gone up?
   A. 3.6 degrees
   B. 2.4 degrees
   C. 2.6 degrees
   D. 3.4 degrees

3. 0.695 – 0.0021 =
   A. 0.6939
   B. 0.6829
   C. 0.6929
   D. 0.6839

4. $49.627 + 321.395 - 10.001 =$
    - A. 371.022
    - B. 371.021
    - C. 361.021
    - D. 361.022

5. A woman has seven ten dollar bills, two nickels, seven quarters, and six pennies in her purse. How much will she have after buying groceries for $25.72 and lunch for $4.90?
    - A. $40.39
    - B. $41.29
    - C. $71.91
    - D. $30.62

6. Chris needs a plant to grow 12 inches before he can put it in his shop window. The first month it grew 5.47 inches, the next month it grew 3.94 inches, and in the last two weeks it has grown 1.13 inches. How many inches are left for it to grow before it can be displayed?
    - A. 2.35
    - B. 1.79
    - C. 1.46
    - D. 10.54

7. Three students are competing for a prize. In the first phase of the competition, Julie scored 93.67 points, Sophia scored 75.12, and Travis earned 82.53.

In the second phase, Julie and Sophia each scored 58.34 points. How many points must Travis score in the second phase to tie with Julie?
    - A. 144.6
    - B. 101.08
    - C. 70
    - D. 69.48

8. Frank deposits all of his extra income into savings. He earned $762.97 last week, $832.64 the week before, and $1000.74 this week. If Frank took a vacation for the rest of the month and his total expenses for the month were $2235.52, how much will he be able to save this month?
    - A. $360.83
    - B. $36.83
    - C. $2596.35
    - D. $258.64

9. $692.004 + 72.58 - 38.299 =$
    - A. 660.963
    - B. 726.285
    - C. 6609.63
    - D. 7262.85

10. $10 - 0.478 + 1.23 =$
    - A. 10.545
    - B. 10.752
    - C. 11.248
    - D. 11.708

ADDING/SUBTRACTING EXPLANATIONS

1. B To figure out how much money is left in the account, first find the total amount that was withdrawn. Then, subtract that from the original deposit.

The withdrawal amounts are $12.50, $17, and $45.23. To add, line up the decimal places and add as normal. For $17, put the decimal point after the number and use placeholder zeros so everything lines up.

$$\begin{array}{r} \$12.50 \\ \$17.00 \\ + \$45.23 \\ \hline \$74.73 \end{array}$$

Now, we must subtract the withdrawals from the original deposit.

$$\begin{array}{r} \$150.00 \\ - \$74.73 \\ \hline \$75.27 \end{array}$$

2. C To subtract decimals, make sure to line up the decimal places. Then subtract as you normally would.

$$\begin{array}{r} 103.4 \\ -100.8 \\ \hline 2.6 \end{array}$$

3. C To subtract decimals, line up the decimal points, add placeholder zeros, and subtract.

$$\begin{array}{r} 0.6950 \\ - 0.0021 \\ \hline 0.6929 \end{array}$$

4. C ❶ Split it into two problems. First, line up the decimal places and add 49.627 and 321.395.

❷ Now, subtract 10.001 from that sum.

❶ $$\begin{array}{r} 49.627 \\ + 321.395 \\ \hline 371.022 \end{array}$$ ❷ $$\begin{array}{r} 371.022 \\ - 10.001 \\ \hline 361.021 \end{array}$$

5. B ❶ Seven ten dollar bills is $70, two nickels is $0.10, seven quarters is $1.75, and six pennies can be written $0.06. Add them together to find out how much money she started with.

❷ Calculate the total amount that she spent.

❸ Subtract the amount she spent from what she started with.

❶ $$\begin{array}{r} 70.00 \\ 0.10 \\ 1.75 \\ + 0.06 \\ \hline 71.91 \end{array}$$ ❷ $$\begin{array}{r} 25.72 \\ + 4.90 \\ \hline 30.62 \end{array}$$ ❸ $$\begin{array}{r} 71.91 \\ - 30.62 \\ \hline 41.29 \end{array}$$

6. C ❶ Add up the amount that the plant has grown until now and subtract that from 12 to find how much is left to grow.

❷ Now subtract the height it grew from the total that Chris needs.

❶ $$\begin{array}{r} 5.47 \\ 3.94 \\ + 1.13 \\ \hline 10.54 \end{array}$$ ❷ $$\begin{array}{r} 12.00 \\ - 10.54 \\ \hline 1.46 \end{array}$$

7. D ❶ Travis wants to tie with Julie. So, let's figure out Julie's total. She scored 93.67 in the first round and the same as Sophie, 58.34 in the second phase. Add to find her total points.

❶
```
  93.67
+ 58.34
 152.01
```

❷
```
 152.01
- 82.53
  69.48
```

❷ Then subtract Travis' first round points from her total.

---

8. A ❶ First, add up Frank's earnings.

❷ Next, subtract his expenses.

❶
```
 1000.74
  762.97
+ 832.64
 2596.35
```

❷
```
  2596.35
- 2235.52
   360.83
```

---

9. B ❶ Line up the decimal places when adding and subtracting the number in order from left to right. Add first.

❷ Then subtract.

❶
```
 692.004
+ 72.580
 764.584
```

❷
```
 764.584
- 38.299
 726.285
```

---

10. B Order of operations states that you should do adding and subtracting from left to right. Therefore, first subtract 10 − 0.478.

When subtracting you have to line up the decimal places. Since 10 does not have a decimal point, it automatically goes after the 10. In addition, since 0.478 has 3 numbers following the decimal, it will be easier to subtract if both numbers have the same number of digits following the decimal, so add 3 placeholder zeroes to 10.

```
 10.000
- 0.478
  9.522
```

Now, add 9.522 to 1.23. Again, line up the decimal points and you can add a placeholder zero to 1.23 so both numbers have the same number of digits after the decimal.

```
  9.522
+ 1.230
 10.752
```

2.7 Decimals – Multiplying/Dividing

Multiplying Decimals

Like adding and subtracting decimals, multiplying decimals is similar to multiplying whole numbers. Simply multiply the digits as you would with whole numbers, and then count the digits to the right of the decimal in all of the multipliers. Place the decimal point so that the product has an equal number of digits to the right of the decimal point.

$$
\begin{array}{r}
49.83 \\
\times \quad 5.7 \\
\hline
34881 \\
+ 249150 \\
\hline
284.031
\end{array}
$$

⊠ two digits to the right of the decimal sign

⊠ one digit to the right of the decimal sign

⊠ three digits to the right of the decimal sign

Dividing Decimals

To divide a decimal by a whole number, simply transfer the decimal sign to the quotient directly above its position in the dividend; then divide as usual.

$$
\begin{array}{r}
7.05 \\
7\overline{)49.35}
\end{array}
$$

The divisor has no decimal places, so divide as you normally would. But in this case, bring the decimal point from the dividend up to the answer.

To divide any number by a decimal, multiply the divisor and the dividend by the power of ten necessary to turn the divisor into a whole number.
Then divide as usual.

$$
0.3\overline{)9.42}
$$

First multiply the divisor by a power of ten necessary to make it a whole number, in this case, 10.

$$
\begin{array}{r}
31.4 \\
3\overline{)94.2}
\end{array}
$$

Multiply the dividend by the same.

Then divide as normally would, bringing the decimal point up to the quotient.

DECIMALS – MULTIPLYING/DIVIDING PRACTICE

1. **7.004 × 5.3 =**
   A. 0.371212
   B. 3.71212
   C. 37.1212
   D. 371.212

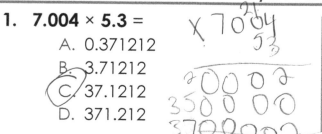

2. **What is one millionth of 12.97?**
   A. 12,970,000
   B. 12.97
   C. 0.000001297
   D. 0.00001297

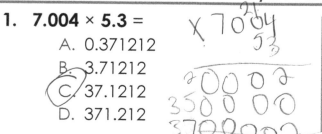

78   *2. Fractions, Decimals, Percents*

3. Sandra got up early and ran 7.8 km. Debra had more energy, and ran 1.5 times the distance that Sandra did. How far did Debra run?
   - A. 9.3
   - B. 10.6
   - C. 11.3
   - D. 11.7

4. Average 0.7, 0.11, and 0.75.
   - A. 0.52
   - B. 1.56
   - C. $^{156}/_{100}$
   - D. $^{156}/_{3}$

5. 395.84 ÷ 64 =
   - A. 618.5
   - B. 61.85
   - C. 6.185
   - D. 0.6185

6. A restaurant uses 1.5 pounds of flour every hour that it is open. It is open for 5.75 hours per day, 6 days per week. How many pounds of flour does the restaurant use each week?
   - A. 5.175

   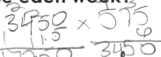

   - B. 13.25
   - C. 45.75
   - D. 51.75

7. Adam is 3.5 times the age of his son. If Adam is 42, how old is his son?
   - A. 7
   - B. 12
   - C. 14
   - D. 21

8. 72.4 ÷ 0.004 =
   - A. 0.0181
   - B. 1.81
   - C. 1810
   - D. 18100

9. 0.003 × 1.24 ÷ 0.05 =
   - A. 0.00744
   - B. 0.0744
   - C. 0.744
   - D. 7.44

10. 0.2 × 3.12 ÷ 0.1 =
   - A. 0.00624
   - B. 0.0624
   - C. 0.624
   - D. 6.24

DECIMALS – MULTIPLYING/DIVIDING EXPLANATIONS

1. C   Multiply as you normally would and add the number of decimal places.

$$
\begin{array}{r}
7.004 \\
\times\ \ 5.3 \\
\hline
21012 \\
+\ 350200 \\
\hline
37.1212
\end{array}
$$

three digits to the right of the decimal sign

one digit to the right of the decimal sign

four digits to the right of the decimal sign

2. D Write out one millionth as a decimal and then multiply the two numbers since of in math means multiply.

$$
\begin{array}{r}
12.97 \\
\times\ \ 0.000001 \\
\hline
0.00001297
\end{array}
$$

two digits to the right of the decimal sign

six digit to the right of the decimal sign

eight digits to the right of the decimal sign

---

3. D To find out how far Debra ran, we must multiply Sandra's distance by 1.5. Notice that 7.8 has one digit to the right of the decimal and 1.5 also has one digit, thus the product will have two digits to the right of decimal.

$$
\begin{array}{r}
7.8 \\
\times\ 1.5 \\
\hline
390 \\
+\ 780 \\
\hline
11.70
\end{array}
$$

---

4. A To average three numbers, add them up and divide by 3.

First, line the decimals up and add them.

Now, divide their sum by 3.

$$
\begin{array}{r}
0.70 \\
0.11 \\
+\ \ 0.75 \\
\hline
1.56
\end{array}
$$

$$1.56 \div 3 = 0.52$$

---

5. C Transfer the decimal point in the dividend directly above to the quotient, and divide. Note that you don't have to fully solve this problem, as you can scan the answer choices and eliminate quickly.

$$64\overline{)395.840}\quad 6.185$$

---

6. D First, calculate the number of hours the restaurant is open per week and then multiply that by the amount of flour used each hour.

To calculate the number of hours the restaurant is open, multiply the hours per day by the the days per week.

$$5.75 \times 6 = 34.50$$

Now, multiply that result by the amount of flour used per hour.

$$34.5 \times 1.5 = 51.75$$

---

7. B Since Adam is 3.5 times the age of his son, if we know Adams age we must divide to find his son's age.

Adam's age divided by 3.5 = Son's Age

$$
\begin{array}{l}
42 \div 3.5 = \\
420 \div 35 = \\
12
\end{array}
$$

You can also work backwards in problems like this. Take each answer choice and multiply it by 3.5 to see which one gets you to 42.

8. D To divide decimals, you need to move the decimal points and then divide as normal.

Move the decimal point 3 places.

---

9. B Following order of operations, multiply and divide from left to right. First, multiply 0.003 by 1.24 and then take that product and divide it by 0.05.

Since there were 3 digits to the right of the decimal point in 0.003 and 2 digits to the right of the decimal point in 1.24, you multiply the numbers as you normally would and then move the decimal point 5 places.

| 0.003 × 1.24 = 0.00372 |

Now, take the result and divide it by 0.05.

| 0.00372 ÷ 0.05 =
0.372 ÷ 5 = 0.0744 |

---

10. D First, multiply 0.2 × 3.12. Multiply the numbers as if there were no decimals, and then move the decimal point 3 places to left since there are 3 digits after the decimal place in the original question.

| 0.2 × 3.12 = 0.624 |

Now, divide 0.624 by 0.1. Move the decimal point the same number of times in both the dividend and divisor, in this case move it once.

| 0.624 ÷ 0.1
= 6.24 ÷ 1 = 6.24 |

for each /100 *(handwritten)*

2.8 Percents

Percent Definition

Percents are a way of expressing fractions, where the "whole" is 100%. Therefore, 1 is the same as 100%.
If you have a fraction with a denominator of 100, then the numerator of that fraction is equal to the percent and vice versa.

$$3/100 = 3\%$$
$$17\% = 17/100$$
$$50\% = 50/100 = 1/2$$

Finding Percents

To find the percent when given a fraction, convert the fraction to an equivalent fraction with a denominator of 100, then the numerator of that fraction is the percent.

$$7/25 = 28/100 = 28\%$$
$$1/20 = 5/100 = 5\%$$

Solving Percent Problems

Generally, convert the percent to a fraction or a decimal and then solve as you normally would.

What is 20% of 30?
$$= 20\% \times 30$$
$$= 20/100 \times 30$$
$$= 1/5 \times 30$$
$$= 6$$

PERCENTS PRACTICE

1. **Change 5 ¾ to a percent.**
   A. 5.75
   B. 575%
   C. 57.5%
   D. 5.75%

   5.75% (handwritten)

2. **What is 92% of 140?**
   A. 48
   B. 232
   C. 128⅘
   D. 12880

   ×.140 / 92 / 1288 / 12880 (handwritten)

3. **In how many of the categories in the figure below is the annual budget allotment less than $8,000?**

   A. One
   B. Two
   C. Three
   D. Four

   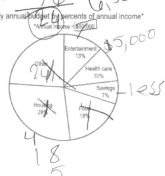

   Family annual budget by percents of annual income*
   *Annual income = $50,000

   Entertainment 13%
   Other
   Health care 10%
   Savings 7%
   Housing 28%
   Food 18%

   100 / 7% 6,500 / 5,000 / less (handwritten)

   50 000 / 18 (handwritten)

   4 / 18 / 5 (handwritten)

9009 / 90×10,0009 (handwritten)

4. If a bear that weighs 962 pounds in the autumn loses 20% of its weight while hibernating, what will the bear weigh in the spring?

    A. 769.6

    B. 76.96

    C. 192.4

    D. 942

5. Choose the best answer to replace the question mark:

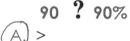

    90 **?** 90%

    (A.) >

    B. <

    C. =

    D. ≤

6. A group of 7 women bought a lottery ticket. If they win 84% of the million dollar jackpot and share their winnings equally, how much, will each woman receive?

    A. $120

    B. $1,200

    C. $12,000

    D. $120,000

7. What is 29% of 13%?

    A. $37 \frac{7}{10}$

    B. $\frac{377}{1000}$

    C. $\frac{377}{10000}$

    D. $\frac{377}{100000}$

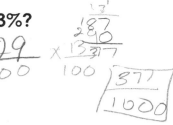

8. Two trees were hit by lightning. The sycamore is now 55% of its original 60 foot height. The elm is now 32% of its original 80 foot height. Which tree is taller now?

    A. The sycamore is taller.

    B. The elm is taller.

    C. They are equal.

    D. Not enough information.

9. Choose the best answer to replace the question mark:

    20% of 97 **?** 97% of 20

    A. >

    (B.) <

    C. =

    D. ≤

10. Order the following from least to greatest: 40% of 70, 45% of 70%, 70% of 60.

    A. 40% of 70, 45% of 70%, 70% of 60

    B. 40% of 70, 70% of 60, 45% of 70%

    C. 45% of 70%, 40% of 70, 70% of 60

    D. 45% of 70%, 70% of 60, 40% of 70

PERCENTS EXPLANATIONS

1. B   First, convert the mixed number to an improper fraction. $5 \frac{3}{4} = \frac{23}{4}$

    Now, write as a fraction with a denominator of 100. $\frac{23}{4} \times \frac{25}{25} = \frac{575}{100}$

    To write as a percent, take the numerator of the fraction. $\frac{575}{100} = 575\%$

2. C First, convert 92% to a fraction. Then "of" in math means multiply. Therefore, multiply the fraction by 140 to get your answer.

$$92\% = {}^{92}\!/_{100}$$
$${}^{92}\!/_{100} \times 140 = {}^{12880}\!/_{100} = 128\, {}^{80}\!/_{100} = 128\, {}^{4}\!/_{5}$$

---

3. C To determine how many categories are less than $8,000, we must first figure out the value of each category. To do this, we convert the percent to a fraction and multiply that by the annual budget of $50,000.

$$\text{Entertainment: } 13\% = {}^{13}\!/_{100}$$
$${}^{13}\!/_{100} \times \$50,000 = \$6500$$

Since Entertainment was 13% and that was below $8000, we know that Health Care and Savings will also be under $8000.

$$\text{Food: } 18\% = {}^{18}\!/_{100}$$
$${}^{18}\!/_{100} \times \$50,000 = \$9000$$

This is too high.

Housing will also be too high since it is 28% and Food was only 18%.

The percent for the Other category wasn't listed. Therefore, it must be calculated. All the percents will add up to 100%, so add up the other categories and subtract the sum from 100.

$$13\% + 10\% + 7\% + 18\% + 28\% = 76\%$$
$$100\% - 76\% = 24\%$$

The other category will also be more than $8000.

The only categories less than $8,000 are Entertainment, Health Care, and Savings.

Three – Answer C.

---

4. A You can estimate to solve. Otherwise, here are two ways to solve this problem.

Option 1: If the bear loses 20% of its bodyweight, then it keeps 80% of it. Multiply the original weight by 80% to find what it will weigh in spring.

$$962 \times 80\% = 962 \times {}^{80}\!/_{100} = {}^{76960}\!/_{100} = 769.6 \text{ pounds}$$

Option 2 : Calculate the amount of weight the bear will lose and subtract that amount from the original weight.

$$962 \times 20\% = 962 \times {}^{20}\!/_{100} = {}^{19240}\!/_{100} = 192.4 \text{ pounds}$$
$$962 - 192.4 = 769.6 \text{ pounds}$$

5. A $90\% = {}^{90}\!/_{100}$

This is less than 1, so it is definitely less than 90.

$90 > 90\%$

---

6. D   To find the amount that each woman receives, you need to calculate the amount that the entire group won and divide that amount by 7.

$$84\% \times \$1{,}000{,}000 = {}^{84}\!/_{100} \times \$1{,}000{,}000 = \$840{,}000$$
$$\$840{,}000 \div 7 = \$120{,}000$$

---

7. C   Convert each percent to a fraction and then multiply.

$$29\% = {}^{29}\!/_{100}$$
$$13\% = {}^{13}\!/_{100}$$
$${}^{29}\!/_{100} \times {}^{13}\!/_{100} = {}^{377}\!/_{10000}$$

---

8. A   To calculate their new heights, convert the percents to fractions and multiply their original heights by those fractions.

The sycamore is taller. Answer A.

Sycamore:	Elm:
55% of 60 feet	32% of 80 feet
$55\% \times 60 =$	$32\% \times 80 =$
${}^{55}\!/_{100} \times 60 =$	${}^{32}\!/_{100} \times 80 =$
${}^{3300}\!/_{100} = 33$	${}^{2560}\!/_{100} = 25.6$

---

9. C   Convert the percents to fractions and then multiply to compare.

They are equal. Answer C.

20% of 97 =	97% of 20 =
$20\% \times 97 =$	$97\% \times 20 =$
${}^{20}\!/_{100} \times 97 =$	${}^{97}\!/_{100} \times 20 =$
${}^{1940}\!/_{100}$	${}^{1940}\!/_{100}$

---

10. C   Let's examine each of the three expressions. Remember, that "of" means multiply and a percent could be made into a fraction with a denominator of 100.

$$40\% \text{ of } 70 = {}^{40}\!/_{100} \times 70 = 28$$
$$45\% \text{ of } 70\% = {}^{45}\!/_{100} \times {}^{70}\!/_{100} = {}^{3150}\!/_{10000}$$
$$70\% \text{ of } 60 = {}^{70}\!/_{100} \times 60 = 42$$

Therefore, ordering from least to greatest: 45% of 70%, 40% of 70, 70% of 60.

2.9 Conversions – Fractions/ Decimals/Percents

Decimals to Fractions

To convert a fraction to a decimal, simply write out the decimal as a fraction with a denominator that is a power of ten. Look at the place value of the last digit to determine what power of ten to use as the denominator. Then simplify.

> **Example:**
>
> $0.125 = {}^{125}/_{1000} = {}^{1}/_{8}$

Fractions to Decimals

Remember that the / symbol in a fraction is actually a division sign. To convert a fraction to a decimal, simply divide the numerator by the denominator.

> **Example:**
>
> ${}^{855}/_{4} = 855 \div 4 = 213.75$

Decimals to Percents

To convert a decimal to a percent, multiply the decimal by 100%. Another way to think about this process, is move the decimal point two places to the right and add a percent sign.

> **Example:**
>
> $0.7345 = 0.7345 \times 100\%$
> $= 73.45\%$

Percents to Decimals

To convert a percent to a decimal, divide the percent by 100%. Another way to think about it, is move the decimal point two places to the left and remove the percent sign.

> **Example:**
>
> $154.9\% = 154.9\% \div 100\%$
> $= 1.549$

Fractions to Percents

To convert a fraction to a percent, first convert the fraction to a decimal and then multiply the decimal by 100%.

> **Example:**
>
> ${}^{3}/_{4} = 0.75 = 75\%$

Percents to Fractions

To convert a percent to a fraction, convert the percent to a decimal by dividing by 100% and then write the decimal as a fraction with a denominator that is a power of 10. If possible, simplify the fraction.

> **Example:**
>
> $40\% = 0.40 = {}^{40}/_{100} = {}^{2}/_{5}$

CONVERSIONS –
FRACTIONS/DECIMALS/PERCENTS PRACTICE

1. Write the following words as a decimal.

   Eighteen and Thirty One Fiftieths

   A. 18.31
   B. 18.62
   C. 18.3150
   D. 49.50

2. Express $5/6$ as a percent that is rounded to the nearest whole number.

   A. 5
   B. 83
   C. 50
   D. 60

3. What decimal is equal to 89.75%?

   A. 890.75
   B. 89.75
   C. 8.975
   D. 0.8975

4. Write 504.30% as a fraction.

   A. $504\ ^3/_{10}$
   B. $5\ ^{43}/_{1000}$
   C. $^{5043}/_{100}$
   D. $50\ ^{43}/_{100}$

5. Express 0.0375 as a fraction.

   A. $^{375}/_{1000}$
   B. $^3/_{80}$
   C. $3\ ^{75}/_{100}$
   D. $^3/_8$

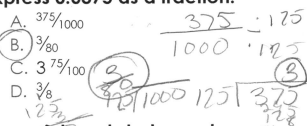

6. For an internet startup, sales increased this quarter by 716%. If their sales last quarter totaled $10,000, what was the sales total for this quarter?

   A. $10,716
   B. $17,160
   C. $71,600
   D. $81,600

7. Two teenagers go to a batting cage. One of them bats .287 and the other bats .345. If the decimal represents the fraction of balls thrown that each of them hit, what is the average percent of balls that the two players hit?

   A. 0.316%
   B. 0.632%
   C. 31.6%
   D. 63.2%

8. Drew answered all of the questions on a test correctly, and he also answered one extra credit question. If each of the test questions were counted equally, including the extra credit and his score was 112.5%, how many questions were on the test, including the extra credit?

    A. 8
    B. 9
    C. 10
    D. 12.5

9. Of the 216 employees at Tech Inc., 4 of them have private offices. What percent, rounded to the nearest tenth, of the employees have private offices?

    A. 1.9%
    B. 1.8%
    C. 0.019%
    D. .18%

10. Darlene washed 7 ⅖ loads of laundry, what percent of a full load did she wash?

    A. 37%
    B. 74%
    C. 370%
    D. 740%

CONVERSIONS – FRACTIONS/DECIMALS/PERCENTS EXPLANATIONS

1. B   It is easiest to first take the words and make them into a mixed number.

Eighteen and Thirty One Fiftieths

Eighteen is the whole number, and Thirty One Fiftieths is the fraction.

$$18\,{}^{31}\!/_{50}$$

Now we must take this fraction and convert it to a decimal. There are multiple ways to do this.

Method 1: Divide 31 by 50 and get a decimal and then put the whole number in front. 31 divided by 50 is 0.62. Therefore, the answer would be 18.62.

Method 2: Find an equivalent fraction whose denominator is a multiple of 10. In this case, ${}^{31}\!/_{50}$ can easily be converted to a fraction whose denominator is 100. Multiply numerator and denominator by 2, giving you ${}^{62}\!/_{100}$. Therefore, the equivalent mixed number is 18 ${}^{62}\!/_{100}$, which is 18 and 62 hundredths, which is written as 18.62

2. B   To convert a fraction to a percent, the easiest way is to first convert the fraction to a decimal and then convert the decimal to a percent.

To convert a fraction to a decimal, divide the numerator by the denominator.

$5 \div 6 = 0.83333...$

To convert the decimal to a percent, multiply by 100%. Rounded to a whole number: 83%

$0.8333... \times 100\% = 83.3333...\%$

---

3. D   To convert a percent to a decimal, divide by 100%.

$89.75\% \div 100\% = 0.8975$

---

4. B   First convert the percent to a decimal and then convert the decimal to a fraction.

To convert a percent to a decimal, divide by 100%.

$504.30\% \div 100\% = 5.043$

To convert a decimal to a fraction, look at the place value of the last digit, and put the number over that power of 10. In this case, the 3 is in the thousandths place so put the number over 1000.

$5.043 = \frac{5043}{1000}$

Now make the fraction a mixed number and reduce if possible.

$\frac{5043}{1000} = 5\frac{43}{1000}$

---

5. B   To convert a decimal to a fraction, look at the place value of the last digit and make the denominator a power of 10 corresponding to that place.

In 0.0375, the last digit is in the ten thousandths place.

$0.0375 = \frac{375}{10000}$

Now simplify.

$\frac{375}{10000} \div \frac{125}{125} = \frac{3}{80}$

---

6. D   Convert the percent to a decimal.

$716\% \div 100\% = 7.16$

Multiply the decimal by which the sales have increased by the sales total from last quarter.

$7.16 \times \$10,000 = \$71,600$

Therefore, the sales have increased by $71,600.

Add this to the sales total from last quarter to find out the sales total for this quarter.

$\$71,600 + \$10,000 = \$81,600$

---

7. C Average the decimals by adding them and dividing by two.

$$0.287 + 0.345 = 0.632$$
$$0.632 \div 2 = 0.316$$

Convert the decimal to a percent by multiplying by 100%.

$$0.316 \times 100\% = 31.6\%$$

---

8. B Answering the regular questions correctly earned Drew 100%. Subtract 100% from his total score to calculate the value of the extra credit question.

$$112.5\% - 100\% = 12.5\%$$

Since the extra credit counted equally with a regular test question, convert the percent of the test that consists of extra credit to a fraction with one in the numerator to find the number of regular test questions. Begin by converting the percent to a decimal.

$$12.5\% \div 100\% = 0.125$$

Convert the decimal to a fraction.

$$0.125 = {}^{125}/_{1000} = {}^{1}/_{8}$$

There were 8 regular test questions, plus 1 extra credit, so there were 9 questions total.

---

9. A At Tech Inc., 4 out of the 216 of the employees have private offices. Divide 4 by 216 to determine as a decimal what part of the employees have private offices.

$$4 \div 216 = 0.0185185...$$

Now, convert the decimal to a percent.

$$0.0185185 \times 100\% = 1.85185\%$$

Now round to the nearest tenth.

$$1.9\%$$

---

10. D Write the mixed number of loads that she washed as an improper fraction.

$$7\,{}^{2}/_{5} = {}^{37}/_{5}$$

Convert the fraction of loads to a decimal.

$${}^{37}/_{5} = 37 \div 5 = 7.4$$

Now, convert the decimal to a percent.

$$7.4 \times 100\% = 740\%$$

2.10 Chapter Review

1. Order the numbers from least to greatest.

   0.81, $^9/_{100}$, 0.819, $^4/_5$

   A. $^9/_{100}$, $^4/_5$, 0.81, 0.819
   B. 0.81, $^4/_5$, $^9/_{100}$, 0.819
   C. $^9/_{100}$, 0.819, 0.81, $^4/_5$
   D. $^4/_5$, 0.81, 0.819, $^9/_{100}$

2. Doug worked 3 $\frac{1}{2}$ hours on Monday and 1 $\frac{3}{4}$ hours on Tuesday. If Susanna worked 4 hours on Monday and 2 $\frac{3}{7}$ hours on Tuesday. How many more hours did Susanna work than Doug on those two days?

   A. 1 $^2/_3$
   B. 1 $^5/_{28}$
   C. 2 $^1/_4$
   D. 2 $^2/_5$

3. In a speed–eating contest, Bart ate $^3/_4$ of a pizza and Darlene ate $^7/_8$ of another the same size. Who won, and how much more pizza did he or she eat?

   A. Darlene won by $^4/_4$ of a pizza.
   B. Bart won by $^4/_4$ of a pizza.
   C. Darlene won by $^1/_8$ of a pizza.
   D. Bart won by $^1/_8$ of a pizza.

4. $^6/_9 - ^2/_4 - ^1/_7 =$
   A. $^{12}/_{252}$
   B. $^3/_2$
   C. $^1/_{42}$
   D. $^3/_{20}$

5. Juana made two–dozen snowmen this afternoon. One–twelfth of them melted by sunset. How many of Juana's melted by sunset?

   A. 2
   B. 12
   C. 22
   D. 24

6. A cake recipe calls for 2 cups of powdered sugar. It says to use $\frac{1}{4}$ of the sugar in the cake batter and the remainder in the frosting. How much sugar, in cups, is needed for the frosting?

   A. 1 $\frac{1}{2}$
   B. $^3/_4$
   C. $^3/_8$
   D. $\frac{1}{2}$

7. The electronics store is holding a sale where everything in the store is 20% off. If the sale price of the stereo is $47.00, what was the original price?

A. $37.60
B. $47.20
C. $56.40
D. $58.75 *(circled)*

8. Hannah's cat eats pet food that is 2.9% protein. What fraction of her cat's food is not protein?

   A. $^{971}/_{1000}$ *(circled)*
   B. $^{9971}/_{10000}$
   C. $97^{1}/_{10}$
   D. $^{71}/_{100}$

9. A yardwork company cut down a tree that was 98 ¼ feet tall. They must divide the tree into segments no larger than $^{13}/_{16}$ feet for disposal. What is the minimum number of segments into which they can cut the tree for disposal?

   A. 119
   B. 120 *(circled)*
   C. 121
   D. 122

10. Convert $^{5692}/_{10}$ to a decimal.

    A. 569.2
    B. 56.92 *(circled)*
    C. 5.692
    D. 0.5692

11. Kate is budgeting out her expenses for the next month. She has allotted ⅖ of her salary for food, ⅕ for clothing, $^{7}/_{18}$ for rent, and $^{1}/_{10}$ for entertainment.

Assuming that she sticks to her budget and saves what is left over from her salary, what fraction of her salary will Kate save next month?

    A. $^{11}/_{42}$
    B. $^{4}/_{45}$
    C. $^{31}/_{42}$
    D. $^{41}/_{45}$

12. Louise's shoe is $^{17}/_{24}$ feet long, and Andrew's shoe is $^{55}/_{120}$ feet long. What is the average length of their shoes?

    A. 7 inches *(circled)*
    B. $^{7}/_{6}$ feet
    C. 1 foot
    D. 6 inches

13. Julian is 6 feet 3 inches tall. Barbara is 5 ¼ feet tall, and Sandra is 70 inches tall. Order them from shortest to tallest.

    A. Julian, Sandra, Barbara
    B. Julian, Barbara, Sandra
    C. Barbara, Julian, Sandra
    D. Barbara, Sandra, Julian

14. Aaron works 7.5 hours per day, 6 days per week. If he makes $9.35 per hour, how much does he make each week?

    A. $42.75
    B. $70.13
    C. $374
    D. $420.75

15. Order the following from least to greatest:

I. $3 \div \frac{1}{2}$

II. $3 \times \frac{1}{2}$

III. $\frac{1}{2} \div 3$

   A. I, II, III
   B. III, II, I
   C. III, I, II
   D. II, III, I

16. Debra worked 4.25 hours on Monday, 5.6 hours on Tuesday, 8 hours on Wednesday, and she took off both Thursday and Friday. What was the average number of hours she worked over the 5 days?

   A. 3.462 hours
   B. 3.57 hours
   C. 5.95 hours ·
   D. 6.85 hours

17. One liter of a solution is 0.723 water and 0.178 hydrochloric acid. What part of the solution's composition is unstated?

   A. 0.901
   B. 9.01
   C. 0.99
   D. 0.099

18. Susanna runs her own jewelery shop. For each necklace, it costs her $2.21 for materials, $1.24 for overhead, and $0.47 for marketing. She charges $19.60 per necklace. What percentage of the selling price of the necklace is Susanna's profit? (hint: Profit = Revenue − Cost)

   A. 16%
   B. 20%
   C. 80%
   D. 83%

19. Which answer choice is the smallest?

   A. $^{21}\!/_5$
   B. 215%
   C. 2.5
   D. $^{12}\!/_5$

20. Matthew was offered 2 possible salaries for the month. Option 1: $10,000 plus 10% of whatever he sold. Option 2: $8,000 plus 15% of whatever he sold. If Matthew sold $35,000 worth of goods, which option should he choose?

   A. Option 1
   B. Option 2
   C. Either, they are the same
   D. Not enough information.

1. A   The easiest way to compare numbers is to make them all decimals. So, first convert $\frac{9}{100}$ and $\frac{4}{5}$ to decimals.

> $\frac{9}{100}$ = nine hundredths = 0.09
> $\frac{4}{5} = \frac{8}{10}$ = eight tenths = 0.8

Now your task is to order: 0.81, 0.09, 0.819, 0.8

There are two methods for ordering decimals.

Method 1: Line up the decimal places and compare one digit at a time. So, comparing the first digit of each of those numbers, you see 8, 0, 8, 8. The smallest is 0, so that number (0.09) is the smallest. Now compare the next digit for the remaining numbers (0.81, 0.819, 0.8). The next digit is 1, 1, and no digit, which can be thought of as 0. Thus, the 0 is the smallest and 0.8 is the next smallest number. Then compare the third digit, nothing (or zero) and 9. The smallest is again 0, so that is the next smallest number.

> Final order:
> 0.09, 0.8, 0.81, 0.819

Method 2: You can also add zeros so that every number has the same number of decimal places, which may make it easier to compare.

Add zeros so each has 3 decimal places: 0.810, 0.090, 0.819, 0.800 Now order by comparing the numbers after the decimal place. 90 is the smallest, then 800, then 810, then 819.

Therefore, the decimal order is 0.090, 0.800, 0.810, 0.819

---

2. B   We first should find Doug's total, then Susanna's total, and then find the difference.

> Doug's Total: $3\frac{1}{2} + 1\frac{3}{4}$

You can convert the mixed numbers to improper fractions, give them the same denominator, and then add.

> $3\frac{1}{2} = \frac{7}{2} = \frac{14}{4}$
> $1\frac{3}{4} = \frac{7}{4}$
> $\frac{14}{4} + \frac{7}{4} = \frac{21}{4}$

Find Susanna's total: $4 + 2\frac{3}{7}$. You can add the whole numbers and fractions separately.

> Susanna's total = $6\frac{3}{7}$

Now, we must find the difference.

> $6\frac{3}{7} - \frac{21}{4}$

Give the fractions the same denominator.

> $6\frac{3}{7} = \frac{45}{7} = \frac{180}{28}$
> $\frac{21}{4} = \frac{147}{28}$
> $\frac{180}{28} - \frac{147}{28} = \frac{33}{28} = 1\frac{5}{28}$

3. C   This problem includes two tasks. The first thing you must do is compare the fractions to find the one that is greater. This can be accomplished by converting to a common denominator. The least common multiple of 4 and 8 is 8.

$$\tfrac{3}{4} = \tfrac{6}{8}$$

Now compare the fractions.

$$\tfrac{7}{8} > \tfrac{6}{8}$$

Therefore, Darlene won the contest. Now subtract the lesser number from the greater.

$$\tfrac{7}{8} - \tfrac{6}{8} = \tfrac{1}{8}$$

4. C   Before subtracting fractions, you must give them a common denominator. First, reduce. The least common multiple (See Numbers and Properties: Factors, Multiples, and Divisibility for help) of 3, 2, and 7 is 42. You must convert each fraction so that it has a denominator of 42.

$$\tfrac{6}{9} = \tfrac{2}{3}$$
$$\tfrac{2}{4} = \tfrac{1}{2}$$

$$\tfrac{2}{3} \times \tfrac{14}{14} = \tfrac{28}{42}$$
$$\tfrac{1}{2} \times \tfrac{21}{21} = \tfrac{21}{42}$$
$$\tfrac{1}{7} \times \tfrac{6}{6} = \tfrac{6}{42}$$

Subtract the numerators.

$$\tfrac{28-21-6}{42} = \tfrac{1}{42}$$

5. A   The first step in this problem is to write out the information. Juana made two-dozen snowmen, which means she made 24. You also know that $\tfrac{1}{12}$ of the snowmen melted. Multiply the number of snowmen by the fraction that melted to find the number that melted.

$$\tfrac{1}{12} \times 24 =$$
$$\tfrac{1}{12} \times \tfrac{24}{1} =$$
$$2$$

Therefore, 2 of the 24 snowmen melted, Answer A.

6. A   To determine how much sugar is needed for the frosting, first figure out the fraction of sugar for the frosting. If $\tfrac{1}{4}$ is needed for the cake batter, then $\tfrac{3}{4}$ is needed for the frosting.

Then multiply the fraction that is needed for the frosting by the total amount of sugar the recipe calls for.

$$\tfrac{3}{4} \times 2 \text{ cups} =$$
$$\tfrac{3}{4} \times \tfrac{2}{1} = \tfrac{6}{4} =$$
$$\tfrac{3}{2} = 1\,\tfrac{1}{2}$$

7. D   There are two ways to approach this problem, either solve or work backwards using the answer choices.

Method 1: To solve the equation, we must first take the word problem and translate it into an equation. If \$47.00 is 20% off the original price, that means that \$47 is 80% of the original price.

$47 = 80\% \times P$ - translate into an equation with P as the original price

$47 = 0.80 \times P$ - convert percent to decimal, 80% is the same as 0.80

$\dfrac{\$47}{0.80} = \dfrac{0.80 \times P}{0.80}$ - divide both sides by 0.80

$58.75 = P$

Method 2: Work backwards. Try each answer choice and take 20% of each of them and subtract it from the price to see which gives you $47.00.

$58.75 \times 20\%$ - Try answer choice D.

58.75×0.20 - convert from percent to a decimal

11.75 - this was the savings

$58.75 - \$11.75$ - subtract the savings from the price

47.00 - this would give you the correct sale price.
                 Answer D. $58.75

---

8. A Convert the percent that is protein to a decimal and then to a fraction. To convert to a decimal, divide by 100%. To convert to a fraction, look at the place value of the last digit and make a denominator that is a power of 10.

Subtract the fraction of her cat's food that is protein from 1 (use $\frac{1000}{1000}$ to give the two fractions a common denominator).

$2.9\% \div 100\% = 0.029 = \frac{29}{1000}$

$\frac{1000}{1000} - \frac{29}{1000} = \frac{971}{1000}$

---

9. C Convert the tree height into an improper fraction so that it can be divided by the maximum segment length.

$98\,\frac{1}{4} = \frac{393}{4}$ feet

Now, divide the total tree height by the length of each segment.

$\frac{393}{4} \div \frac{13}{16} =$
$\frac{393}{4} \times \frac{16}{13} =$
$\frac{393}{1} \times \frac{4}{13} =$
$\frac{1572}{13} =$
$120\,\frac{12}{13}$

That means 120 segments with $\frac{12}{13}$ of a segment left over. Round up to the nearest whole to find the minimum number of segments the yardwork company will need to cut.

---

10. A The fraction is over 10, so the last digit of the numerator should be in the tenths place. Remember that the tenths place is the first place after the decimal point. 569.2

---

11. B In order to find out how much of Kate's salary will go into savings, add up her expenses. First, convert to a common denominator, in this case use 90.

$\frac{2}{9} = \frac{20}{90}$
$\frac{1}{5} = \frac{18}{90}$
$\frac{7}{18} = \frac{35}{90}$
$\frac{1}{10} = \frac{9}{90}$

and then add the numerators.

$$\frac{20}{90} + \frac{18}{90} + \frac{35}{90} + \frac{9}{90} =$$
$$\frac{20+18+35+9}{90} = \frac{82}{90}$$

Therefore, she spent $\frac{82}{90}$. This must be subtracted from what she earned, which is 1 or $\frac{90}{90}$.

$$\frac{90}{90} - \frac{82}{90} = \frac{8}{90}$$

Simplify

$$\frac{8}{90} = \frac{4}{45}$$

12. A To find the average of numbers, you find their sum and divide by the number of numbers. Therefore, we must add the two fractions and then divide by 2.

$$\frac{17}{24} \times \frac{5}{5} = \frac{85}{120}$$
$$\frac{85}{120} + \frac{55}{120} = \frac{140}{120}$$
$$\frac{140}{120} = \frac{7}{6}$$

To add the fractions, we must first find the common denominator, in this case, 120.

Now that we found the sum, we must divide it by 2 to find the average.

$$\frac{7}{6} \div 2 =$$
$$\frac{7}{6} \times \frac{1}{2} =$$
$$\frac{7}{12} \text{ feet}$$

Since that isn't in the answer choices, lets convert that to inches. $\frac{7}{12}$ feet = 7 inches

13. D Convert all of the heights to mixed numbers with a common denominator. Remember that 1 foot equals 12 inches.

Julian: 6 feet 3 inches = $6\frac{3}{12}$ feet
Barbara: $5\frac{1}{4}$ feet = $5\frac{3}{12}$ feet
Sandra: 70 inches = $\frac{70}{12}$ feet = $5\frac{10}{12}$ feet

From shortest to tallest: Barbara, Sandra, Julian

14. D To calculate how much Aaron makes per week, multiply the dollars per hour by the number of hours per day by the days per week.

$$\$9.35 \times 7.5 = 70.125$$
$$70.125 \times 6 = \$420.75$$

15. B Let's solve each equation and then determine the order.

Order from least to greatest: $\frac{1}{6}$, $1\frac{1}{2}$, 6 (III, II, I)

I. $3 \div \frac{1}{2} = 3 \times \frac{2}{1} = 6$
II. $3 \times \frac{1}{2} = \frac{3}{2} = 1\frac{1}{2}$
III. $\frac{1}{2} \div 3 = \frac{1}{2} \times \frac{1}{3} = \frac{1}{6}$

16. B To find the average, add up all the numbers and divide by the total number of numbers.

❶ When adding, line up the decimal places.

❷ Now, divide by 5 to find the average.

❶
```
  4.25
  5.6
  8
  0
+ 0
─────
 17.85
```

❷ $17.85 \div 5$
$= 3.57$

17. D ❶ Add the known or stated fractions of the solution.

❷ Then subtract the fraction of the solution that is known from the total.

❶
$$\begin{array}{r} 0.723 \\ + 0.178 \\ \hline 0.901 \end{array}$$

❷
$$\begin{array}{r} 1.000 \\ - 0.901 \\ \hline 0.099 \end{array}$$

---

18. C You must first determine Susanna's profit. This can be found by adding her costs and subtracting that from her revenue or what she charges.

$$\begin{array}{r} 2.21 \\ 1.24 \\ + 0.47 \\ \hline 3.92 \end{array}$$

Total costs = \$3.92
Profit = Revenue − Costs
Profit = 19.6 − 3.92 = \$15.68

Remember, when adding or subtracting decimals, make sure to line up the decimal places.

$$\begin{array}{r} 19.60 \\ - 3.92 \\ \hline 15.68 \end{array}$$

To find out what percentage of the selling price Susanna's profit was, you divide the profit by the selling price.

$^{15.68}/_{19.60}$

You can get rid of the decimal places in both the dividend and divisor by multiplying each of them by 100. This will move the decimal place to the right for both values.

$^{1568}/_{1960}$

Then divide as you normally would.

0.80

To convert from a decimal to a percent, you move the decimal point two places to the right.

0.80 = 80%

---

19. B Convert each answer choice to a decimal and compare.

The smallest is 2.15, answer choice B.

A: $2^1/_5 = {}^{220}/_{100} = 2.20$
B: 215% = 2.15
C: 2.5
D: $^{12}/_5 = 2\,^2/_5 = 2\,^{40}/_{100} = 2.40$

---

20. A **Option 1:** \$10,000 plus 10% of what he sold. Matthew sold \$35,000, so find 10% of that.

\$10,000 + \$3,500 = \$13,500

Option 2: \$8,000 plus 15% of what he sold.

\$8,000 + \$5,250 = \$13,250

Option 1 will give Matthew more money.

\$35,000 × 10% =
\$35,000 × 0.10 =
\$3,500

\$35,000 × 15% =
\$35,000 × 0.15 =
\$5,250

Lessons

3.1 Number Line & Coordinate Plane

Number Line

When studying the fundamental concepts of math, particularly signed numbers, you were introduced to the concept of the number line, a straight line used for representing positive and negative numbers.

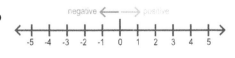

x–axis and *y*–axis

Graphs are useful for showing the relationships between variables. The coordinate plane on which graphs are shown is simply a two–dimensional variation of the number line.

The horizontal number line, labeled the *x*–axis, represents all possible values of the *x* variable. The vertical number line, called the *y*–axis, serves the same function for the *y* values. Any pair of possible *x* and *y*–coordinates is called a coordinate pair (also know as an ordered pair). Coordinate pairs are always written in the order (*x*, *y*). The point at which the *x*–axis and *y*–axis intersect (0,0) is called the origin.

Quadrants

The Roman numerals on the graph show the four quadrants of the coordinate plane.

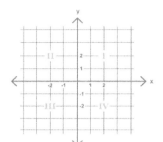

Quadrant I: all *x* and *y* values are positive
Quadrant II: *x* is negative, *y* is positive
Quadrant III: *x* and *y* are negative
Quadrant IV: *x* is positive, *y* is negative

Plotting Coordinate Pairs

The graph shows a few points and their coordinate pairs. The coordinate pair for point A is (1,2). To plot point A, you start at the origin (0,0) and move 1 space to the right along the *x*–axis. From there, move 2 spaces upwards along the *y*–axis.

Now check to see that you understand how to plot the rest of the coordinate pairs shown.

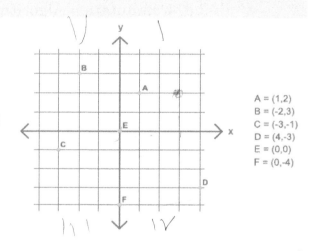

A = (1,2)
B = (-2,3)
C = (-3,-1)
D = (4,-3)
E = (0,0)
F = (0,-4)

NUMBER LINE & COORDINATE PLANE PRACTICE

1. **If you graphed the point (-3, 2), it would be in which quadrant?**
    A. I
    B. II
    C. III
    D. IV

2. What is the distance between points A and B on the number line below?

A. -6

B. 5

C. 6

D. 7

3. Name the coordinate pair which represents the point on the graph.

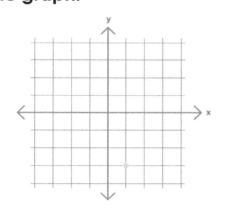

A. (-3, 1)

B. (1, -3)

C. (1, -4)

D. (-1, -3)

4. All of the points in quadrant III:

I. Have negative x–values.
II. Have negative y–values.
III. Can be described by a coordinate pair.

A. I and III

B. I and II

C. II and III

D. I, II, and III

5. If the graph below shows a circle with center at the origin, and the coordinates of the point shown is (3,0) , what are the coordinates of point A?

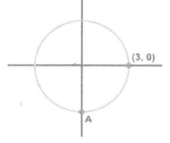

A. (-3, 0)

B. (0, -3)

C. (0, 3)

D. (3, 0)

6. What is the distance between point A and point B in the graph below?

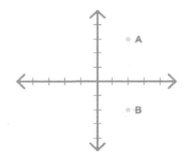

A. 3

B. 4

C. 5

D. 6

7. What is the coordinate pair for the last corner of a rectangle if the first 3 corners are at (-2, -3), (-2, 4), and (4, 4)?

    A. (-2, -2)
    B. (-2, 3)
    C. (4, -3)
    D. (-4, -3)

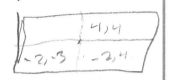

8. The coordinate plane is:

    A. unrelated to the number line
    B. the opposite of the number line
    C. made up of 4 number lines
    D. made of 2 perpendicular

9. What values does the number line represent?

Dots indicate that value not in-bet.

    A. whole numbers
    B. real numbers greater than -1
    C. positive integers
    D. integers greater than -2

10. Which axis runs vertically on the coordinate plane?

    A. x
    B. y
    C. number line
    D. coordinate pair

NUMBER LINE & COORDINATE PLANE EXPLANATIONS

1. B As can be seen in the graph, (-3, 2) is in the second quadrant, which is written as quadrant II. Remember, you start with the first coordinate, -3, which refers to the x or horizontal direction. Next, you go 2 up on the y-axis.

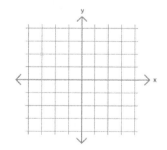

2. D Point B is at 6, point A is at -1. Find the difference between them to find the distance.

$$6 - (-1) = 6 + 1 = 7.$$

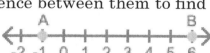

3. B When naming a coordinate pair, the x value is always first. The x values are horizontal and this point is 1 away in the positive horizontal direction. The y–value is second. The y–values are vertical and this point is 3 points below the y–axis, therefore, the y–value is -3.

Coordinate pair = (1, -3)

4. D Any point in the coordinate plane can be described by a coordinate pair, therefore III is true.
Any point in quadrant III will have negative x and y values. Therefore, I and II are also true.

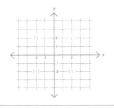

5. B All points on a circle are the same distance from the center, therefore each point is 3 away from the origin.
In a coordinate pair, the first element listed is the x–coordinate. In this case, point A is on the y–axis and did not move horizontally at all. Therefore, the x–coordinate is 0.
The y–coordinate of point A is -3 since it is 3 away from the origin in the negative direction.

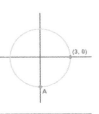

(0, -3), Answer B.

6. C Points A and B have the same x–coordinate, they only differ in y–coordinates.

Point A is 3 units above the x–axis, and Point B is 2 units below. That makes a total of 5 units separating the two points.

You could also do this by determining the coordinate pair of each point and then subtracting. Point A = (2, 3) and Point B = (2, -2). Therefore, the difference between the y–coordinates is $3 - (-2) = 3 + 2 = 5$.

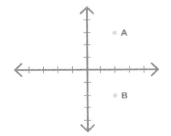

7. C Graphing the coordinate pairs will help you find the last corner of the rectangle.
The coordinates: (-2, -3), (-2, 4), and (4, 4) are graphed, and the last corner to complete the rectangle has been included in a darker grey.
Answer C : The last corner is at (4, -3).

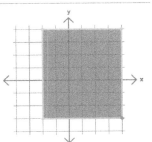

8. D The coordinate plane consists of two axes, the x–axis and the y–axis. Each of those axes is a number line, and the two number lines are perpendicular to each other. This allows any point in a two–dimensional plane to be labeled using two coordinates.

Answer D: The coordinate plane is made of 2 perpendicular number lines.

9. D

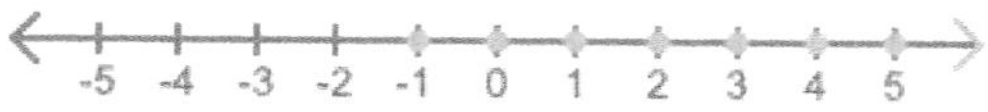

As you can see in the number line, only the values greater than -2 are marked. In addition, only the integers are marked, all the fractions or decimals in between are not highlighted. Therefore, the number line only represents integers.

Answer D: integers greater than -2

---

10. B There are two axes that make up the coordinate plane. The x–axis runs horizontally and the y–axis runs vertically. Each axis is a number line and any point on the coordinate plane can be represented by a coordinate pair.

Answer B: y–axis runs vertically

3.2 Unit Conversions

Conversion Methods

To convert measurements from one type of unit into another type of unit, multiply the number by the appropriate conversion factor. You can determine which is the appropriate conversion factor when the units you want to change are cancelled and the units you want are the only ones left. For example, to convert 17 yards into feet, you know that you want to find a conversion factor where the units of yards cancel and you are left with only feet. We know that 1 yard equals 3 feet, and the conversion factor is a fraction with different units in the numerator and denominator. Since we want the yards to cancel and be left with feet, we put the yards in denominator and feet in numerator.

$$17 \text{ yards} \times \frac{3 \text{ feet}}{1 \text{ yard}} = 51 \text{ feet}$$

Try converting 64 ounces into pounds (1 pound = 16 ounces).

$$64 \text{ ounces} \times \frac{1 \text{ pound}}{16 \text{ ounces}} = 4 \text{ pounds}$$

There are some common unit conversions that will appear time and again in word and other types of problems. Some of these should appear familiar from everyday life, and you should commit some of them to memory.

Weight and Mass
- 16 ounces (oz) = 1 pound (lb.)
- 1 kilogram (kg) = 2.20 pounds (lb.)
- 1000 grams (g) = 1 kilogram (kg)
- 1 ton = 2000 pounds (lb.)

Volume
- 2 cups (cp.) = 1 pint (pt.)
- 2 pints (pt.) = 1 quart (qt.)
- 4 quarts (qt.) = 1 gallon (gal.)
- 1 gallon (gal.) = 3.79 liters (L)
- 1 Liter (L) = 1000 milliliters (mL)
- 1 milliliter (mL) = 1 centimeter cubed (cm^3)

Length
- 1 inch (in.) = 2.54 centimeters (cm)
- 1 meter (m) = 3.28 feet (ft.)
- 100 centimeters (cm) = 1 meter (m)
- 1000 millimeters (mm) = 1 meter (m)
- 1000 meters (m) = 1 kilometer (km)
- 1 kilometer (km) = 0.62 miles
- 1 foot (ft.) = 12 inches (in.)
- 5280 feet (ft.) = 1 mile
- 3 feet (ft.) = 1 yard (yd.)

Temperature
- Degrees Fahrenheit = 32+ $\frac{5}{9}$ × Degrees Celsius
- Degrees Celsius = $\frac{5}{9}$ × (Degrees Fahrenheit – 32)

Metric System

Looking at the units above, a pattern is evident among the meters, grams, and liters. That is because they are the base units of the metric system. They all follow the following pattern of prefixes.

Examples of metric system conversions.

Convert 1.2 kilometers to meters

$$1.2 \text{ km} \quad \times \quad \frac{1000 \text{ m}}{1 \text{ km}} \quad = \quad 1200 \text{ m}$$

Convert 340 meters to kilometers

$$340 \text{ m} \quad \times \quad \frac{1 \text{ km}}{1000 \text{ m}} \quad = \quad 0.34 \text{ km}$$

1000	= kilo–
100	= hecto–
10	= deka–
.1	= deci–
.01	= centi–
.001	= milli–

Multiple Unit Conversions

If required to perform multiple conversions in the same problem, you could either do one at a time or multiply all the conversion factors at once. For example, if you are required to convert from 3 gallons to cups, you could perform either steps to get the correct answer:

$$3 \text{ gallons} = 3 \text{ gallons} \times \frac{4 \text{ quarts}}{1 \text{ gallon}} \times \frac{2 \text{ pints}}{1 \text{ quart}} \times \frac{2 \text{ cups}}{1 \text{ pint}} = 48 \text{ cups}$$

$$3 \text{ gallons} = 3 \text{ gallons} \times \frac{4 \text{ quarts}}{1 \text{ gallon}} = 12 \text{ quarts}$$

$$12 \text{ quarts} = 12 \text{ quarts} \times \frac{2 \text{ pints}}{1 \text{ quart}} = 24 \text{ pints}$$

$$24 \text{ pints} = 24 \text{ pints} \times \frac{2 \text{ cups}}{1 \text{ pint}} = 48 \text{ cups}$$

Another instance when you may have to use multiple unit conversions is if you are dealing with square or cubic units. For instance, you may be asked to convert 18 square feet to square yards.

$$18 \text{ square feet} = 18 \text{ feet} \times \text{feet} =$$
$$18 \text{ feet} \times \text{feet} \times \frac{1 \text{ yard}}{3 \text{ feet}} \times \frac{1 \text{ yard}}{3 \text{ feet}} =$$
$$2 \text{ yards} \times \text{yards} = 2 \text{ square yards}$$

UNIT CONVERSIONS PRACTICE

1. **Convert 78 inches into feet.**
   - A. 6.5 feet
   - B. 7 feet
   - C. 936 inches
   - D. 936 feet

2. **Convert 212 degrees Fahrenheit into degrees Celsius.**
   C = ⁵⁄₉ (F - 32)
   - A. 100° C
   - B. 324° C
   - C. 136° C
   - D. 439° C

3. **What is 27 grams in kilograms?**
   - A. 0.00027 kilograms
   - B. 0.027 kilograms   1000g=1kg
   - C. 0.27 kilograms
   - D. 27000 kilograms

4. **If there are 5280 feet in 1 mile, which of the following is the longest?**
   - A. 3 miles
   - B. 4000 yards
   - C. 15500 feet
   - D. 180,000 inches

5. **How many square inches is equal to 10 square yards?**

   - A. 360 sq in
   - B. 720 sq in
   - C. 1080 sq in
   - D. 12960 sq in

   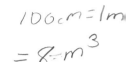

6. **If the volume of a box is 8 cubic meters, what is the volume in cubic centimeters?**
   - A. 0.08 cubic cm
   - B. 800 cubic cm
   - C. 80,000 cubic cm
   - D. 8,000,000 cubic cm

7. **A man is painting one of the walls in his dining room. He uses 1 gallon of paint to cover 14 square yards of wall space. If the wall is 12 feet high and 21 feet long, how many gallons of paint will he need?**
   - A. 1 gallons
   - B. 2 gallons
   - C. 6 gallons
   - D. 18 gallons

   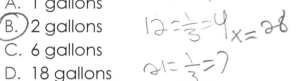

8. **70 centimeters is equal to how many kilometers?**
   - A. 0.0007 km
   - B. 0.7 km
   - C. 7000 km
   - D. 7,000,000 km

9. Baking a chocolate cake requires 2 cups of flour. If you have 3 quarts of flour, how many cakes can you make?

    A. 3 cakes
    B. 6 cakes
    C. 12 cakes
    D. 24 cakes

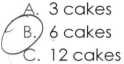

10. If 1 inch = 2.54 centimeters, 200 inches is equal to how many meters?

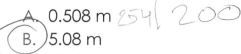

    A. 0.508 m
    B. 5.08 m
    C. 50.8 m
    D. 50,800 m

UNIT CONVERSIONS EXPLANATIONS

1. A   Multiply the original number, 78 inches, by the conversion factor, 1 foot is 12 inches, so that the inches cancel out, leaving an answer in feet.

$$78 \text{ inches} \quad \times \quad \frac{1 \text{ foot}}{12 \text{ inches}} \quad = \quad 6.5 \text{ feet}$$

2. A   The formula for converting from Fahrenheit to Celsius is:

Degrees Celsius = $\frac{5}{9}$ × (Degrees Fahrenheit – 32)

Plug 212 degrees F into the formula.
Then solve for degrees C.

> Degrees Celsius
> = $\frac{5}{9}$ × (212 – 32)
> = $\frac{5}{9}$ × 180
> = 100

3. B   To convert grams to kilograms, first note that 1000 grams = 1 kilogram. Now, multiply by the appropriate unit conversion. You want to make sure that the grams cancel and you are left with kilograms in the numerator.

$$27 \text{ grams} \quad \times \quad \frac{1 \text{ kilogram}}{1000 \text{ grams}} \quad = \quad \frac{27 \text{ kg}}{1000} \quad = \quad 0.027 \text{ kg}$$

4. A   Convert each answer choice to the same dimensions and then compare. Let's choose to convert each answer to feet.

$$\text{A:} \quad 3 \text{ miles} \quad \times \quad \frac{5280 \text{ ft}}{1 \text{ mile}} \quad = \quad 15,840 \text{ feet}$$

$$\text{B:} \quad 4000 \text{ yards} \quad \times \quad \frac{3 \text{ feet}}{1 \text{ yard}} \quad = \quad 12,000 \text{ feet}$$

$$\text{C:} \quad 15,500 \text{ feet}$$

$$\text{D:} \quad 180,000 \text{ in} \quad \times \quad \frac{1 \text{ foot}}{12 \text{ inches}} \quad = \quad 15,000 \text{ feet}$$

5. D   First, convert square yards to square feet then from square feet to square inches.

To convert from square yards to square feet, you will need to use two unit conversions since the units are each squared.

$$10 \text{ sq yds} \quad \times \quad \frac{3 \text{ feet}}{1 \text{ yard}} \quad \times \quad \frac{3 \text{ feet}}{1 \text{ yard}} \quad = \quad 90 \text{ sq feet}$$

Now, use 2 unit conversions to convert from square feet to square inches.

$$90 \text{ sq feet} \quad \times \quad \frac{12 \text{ inches}}{1 \text{ foot}} \quad \times \quad \frac{12 \text{ inches}}{1 \text{ foot}} \quad = \quad 12960 \text{ sq in}$$

Another way to solve this problem is to note that 1 yard = 3 feet = 36 inches, and then convert from square yards directly to square inches.

$$10 \text{ sq yds} \quad \times \quad \frac{36 \text{ inches}}{1 \text{ yard}} \quad \times \quad \frac{36 \text{ inches}}{1 \text{ yard}} \quad = \quad 12960 \text{ sq in}$$

---

6. D   Use three unit conversions to convert each dimension of meters to centimeters.

$$8 \text{ meters}^3 \quad \times \quad \frac{100 \text{ cm}}{1 \text{ m}} \quad \times \quad \frac{100 \text{ cm}}{1 \text{ m}} \quad \times \quad \frac{100 \text{ cm}}{1 \text{ m}}$$
$$= 8{,}000{,}000 \text{ cubic centimeters}$$

---

7. B   This problem has many steps: ❶ Convert wall dimensions from feet to yards. ❷ Find the area of the wall. ❸ Determine how many gallons of paint are needed to cover that wall.

❶ Convert wall dimensions from feet to yards.

$$12 \text{ feet} \quad \times \quad \frac{1 \text{ yard}}{3 \text{ feet}} \quad = \quad 4 \text{ yards}$$

$$21 \text{ feet} \quad \times \quad \frac{1 \text{ yard}}{3 \text{ feet}} \quad = \quad 7 \text{ yards}$$

❷ Find area of the wall.

$$4 \text{ yards} \times 7 \text{ yards} = 28 \text{ square yards}$$

❸ Find number of gallons of paint needed.

$$28 \text{ sq yards} \quad \times \quad \frac{1 \text{ gallon}}{14 \text{ sq.yds}} \quad = \quad 2 \text{ gallons}$$

8. A First convert centimeters to meters. Then from meters convert to kilometers.

$$70 \text{ centimeters} \quad \times \quad \frac{1 \text{ meter}}{100 \text{ cm}} \quad = \quad 0.7 \text{ meters}$$

$$0.7 \text{ meters} \quad \times \quad \frac{1 \text{ km}}{1000 \text{ m}} \quad = \quad 0.0007 \text{ km}$$

---

9. B Convert 3 quarts to pints to cups and then figure out how many cakes can be made.

$$3 \text{ quarts} \quad \times \quad \frac{2 \text{ pints}}{1 \text{ quart}} \quad = \quad 6 \text{ pints}$$

$$6 \text{ pints} \quad \times \quad \frac{2 \text{ cups}}{1 \text{ pint}} \quad = \quad 12 \text{ cups}$$

$$12 \text{ cups} \quad \times \quad \frac{1 \text{ cake}}{2 \text{ cups}} \quad = \quad 6 \text{ cakes}$$

---

10. B First, convert from inches to centimeters, then from centimeters to meters.

$$200 \text{ inches} \quad \times \quad \frac{2.54 \text{ cm}}{1 \text{ inch}} \quad = \quad 508 \text{ cm}$$

$$508 \text{ cm} \quad \times \quad \frac{1 \text{ m}}{100 \text{ cm}} \quad = \quad 5.08 \text{m}$$

3.3 Properties of Arithmetic

There are several properties of numbers, most of which you will already be aware of — even if you are unfamiliar with the names.

Associative

The associative property says that for problems containing only addition or only multiplication, grouping of numbers does not affect the result. In the cases below, it does not matter whether a and b or b and c are multiplied or added first, the result will always be the same.

$$a + (b + c) = (a + b) + c$$
$$a(bc) = (ab)c$$

For example, $3 + (4 + 5) = (3 + 4) + 5$ and $2(5 \times 4) = (2 \times 5) \times 4$

Commutative

The commutative property states that for problems containing only multiplication or only addition, order does not matter.

$$a + b = b + a$$
$$ab = ba$$

For example, $3 + 5 = 5 + 3$ and $2 \times 6 = 6 \times 2$.

Distributive

The distributive property states:

$$a(b + c) = ab + ac$$

On the left hand side of the equation above, a is multiplied by the sum of b and c, and this is equivalent to the sum of a multiplied by b and a multiplied by c.

Example: $5(2 + 3 + 4) = 5(2) + 5(3) + 5(4) = 10 + 15 + 20 = 45$

Zero

The identity of addition is 0. Therefore, any number plus zero will equal itself. $17 + 0 = 17$
The product of any number and zero is 0. $17 \times 0 = 0$
Zero divided by any number is 0. $0 \div 17 = 0$
No number can be divided by 0. $17 \div 0$ can not be done.
Any number raised to the power of zero is 1. $17^0 = 1$

One

The identity of multiplication is 1. Therefore, any number times 1 will equal itself. $17 \times 1 = 17$.

Any number divided by 1 is itself. $17 \div 1 = 17$.

Any number raised to the power of 1 is itself. $17^1 = 17$

PROPERTIES OF ARITHMETIC PRACTICE

1. **Which property could you use to more easily calculate the following product?**

   $$815 \times 100.1$$

   A. associative
   B. commutative
   C. distributive
   D. identity

2. **How would you estimate the sum of 9,178,476 and 97?** $= 100$

   A. $9,178,500 + 100$
   B. $9,178,400 + 100$
   C. $9,178,000 + 0$
   D. $9,178,500 + 95$

3. **Which of the following is/are false?**

   I. $0 \div 7 = 0$
   II. $7 \div 0 = 7$ $0 =$
   III. $7 \div 0 = 0$

   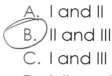
   A. I and II
   B. II and III
   C. I and III
   D. I, II, and III

4. **Simplify the following expression using the distributive property.**

   $$\frac{12x + 4y - 16}{4}$$

   A. $3x + 4y - 16$
   B. $3x + y - 16$
   C. $12x + 4y - 4$
   D. $3x + y - 4$

5. **The associative and commutative properties apply to which of the following operations?**

   A. Addition only
   B. Addition and Multiplication
   C. Adding and Subtraction
   D. Addition, Subtraction, Multiplication, and Division

6. **What is the value of: $99^1 - 99^0$?**

   A. 0
   B. 1
    $99 - 1 = 98$
   C. 98
   D. 99

7. Choose the best answer to replace the question mark.

$p(r - s)$ **?** $pr - ps$

A. >

B. <

C. = *(circled)*

D. Not enough information.

(handwritten: pr − ps)

8. $(30 + 17) \div 2 =$ *(handwritten: 47 ÷ 2)*

I. $47 \div 2$ *(check mark)*

II. $15 + 8\frac{1}{2}$

III. $(30 \div 2) + (17 \div 2)$

A. I only

B. I and III

C. II and III

D. I, II, and III *(circled)*

9. What is $8(9 + 6)7$? *(handwritten: Can switch Both multiplication)*

I. $7(9 + 6)8$

II. $8 \times 9 + 6 \times 7$

III. $8 \times 9 \times 7 + 8 \times 6 \times 7$

A. I only

B. II only

C. I and III *(circled)*

D. I and II

(handwritten notes: have to do everything Distribute)

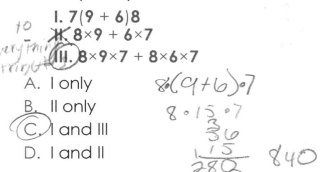

10. Which property would you use to help you solve the following problem quickly in your head?

$5 \times 73 \times 2$

A. Associative

B. Commutative *(circled)*

C. Inverse

D. Identity

PROPERTIES OF ARITHMETIC EXPLANATIONS

1. C The distributive property would be extremely useful in calculating the product.

The property states that $a(b + c) = ab + ac$.

Let's see how that could be applied in this problem.

❶ The number 100.1 can be broken into the sum of two numbers.

❷ The distributive property could then be used.

❸ Both of these products can be calculated in your head.

❶ $815 \times 100.1 =$
$815 \times (100 + .1)$

❷ $815(100 + .1) =$
$815(100) + 815(.1)$

❸ $815(100) + 815(.1)$
$= 81500 + 81.5$
$= 81581.5$

2. A When estimating a sum, first look at the smaller of the two numbers. In this case, 97 is very close to 100. Therefore, you should round both numbers to the nearest hundred.

9,178,476 to the nearest hundred is 9,178,500

97 to the nearest hundred is 100

Now you would add them: 9,178,500 + 100. Answer A.

3. B   You can never divide by 0 in math. The reason is that division is the inverse of multiplication. For example, if you said that $7 \div 0 = n$, that would mean that n multiplied by 0 would result in 7. Nothing times zero will ever give you 7. Therefore, you can never divide by 0.

$0 \div 7 = 0$, This is true. You can see this by turning it into a multiplication and finding the product of the denominator and the other side of the equation and see if the result is the numerator. $7 \times 0 = 0$. True.

II and III are false. Answer B

---

4. D   First, use the distributive property on the numerator to factor out any like terms.
Numerator: $12x + 4y - 16 = 4(3x + y - 4)$

$$\frac{(12x + 4y - 16)}{4} = \frac{4(3x + y - 4)}{4}$$

Now, you can divide both the numerator and denominator by 4. Dividing the denominator by 4 results in 1. Dividing the numerator by 4, leaves $(3x + y - 4)$.

$$\frac{4(3x + y - 4)}{4} = 3x + y - 4$$

---

5. B   The associative and commutative properties only hold true for addition and multiplication. Here are some examples:

Associative
   Addition: $9 + (4 + 5) = (9 + 4) + 5$, Both equal 18.
   Subtraction: $9 - (4 + 5) \neq (9 - 4) + 5$, Left side = 0, Right side = 10
   Multiplication: $6 \times (2 \times 5) = (6 \times 2) \times 5$, Both equal 60
   Division: $(12 \div 4) \div 2 \neq 12 \div (4 \div 2)$, The left side equals 1.5, right side equals 6

Commutative
   Addition: $9 + 4 + 5 = 5 + 4 + 9$, Both equal 18.
   Subtraction: $9 - 4 - 5 \neq 5 - 4 - 9$, Left side = 0, Right side=−8
   Multiplication: $6 \times 2 \times 5 = 2 \times 6 \times 5$, Both equal 60
   Division: $40 \div 4 \div 2 \neq 4 \div 40 \div 2$, The left side equals 5, right side equals 0.05

Associative and Commutative are only true for addition and multiplication.

6. C Any number raised to the power of 1 is itself. Any number raised to the power of 0 is 1.

$$99^1 = 99$$
$$99^0 = 1$$
$$99^1 - 99^0 = 99 - 1 = 98$$

7. C This is an example of the distributive property, with just different variables. Also, do not get thrown off by the minus sign. Remember, that the original definition of the distributive property has addition, but subtraction is the same as the addition of the opposite.

$$p(r - s)$$

The distributive property states that you multiply each term on the outside by each term on the inside.

$$p(r - s) = pr - ps$$

8. D $(30 + 17) \div 2 =$ Let's examine each answer.

   I.   **$47 \div 2$**

      This is definitely true. Order of operations state that you do what is in parentheses first, which in this case is adding 30 and 17 to get 47.

   II. **$15 + 8 \frac{1}{2}$**

      This is an example of the use of the distributive property with division. To solve the original problem without first doing the operation in parentheses, you have to divide each term in the parentheses and then find their sum.

$$(30 + 17) \div 2 = (30 \div 2) + (17 \div 2) = 15 + 8\frac{1}{2}$$

   III. **$(30 \div 2) + (17 \div 2)$**

      This is true and was a step that was used to calculate II. See above.

   I, II, and III are all true. Answer D.

9. C $8(9 + 6)7$: To solve this problem, you would use both the commutative and distributive properties. Let's examine each option.

   I.   **$7(9 + 6)8$**

      This option is only different from the original because the positions of 7 and 8 are moved. The original problem is the multiplication of 3 expressions 8, 9+6, and 7. The commutative property states that you can multiply in any order and the result will still be the same. Option I is just the multiplication of those expressions in a different order. I is the same.

II. $8 \times 9 + 6 \times 7$

This answer is not the same. Use the distributive property on the first two expressions: 8 and (9 + 6). To expand this, you multiply the 8 by every term inside the parentheses. $8(9+6) = 8 \times 9 + 8 \times 6$. Then, you would multiply this result by 7. Even before multiplying by 7, you see that option II is different.

III. $8 \times 9 \times 7 + 8 \times 6 \times 7$

To see if this one is true, perform the distributive property twice. First, with 8 and (9+6) and then take that result and multiply it by 7 by using the distributive property.

$8(9+6)7 = (8 \times 9 + 8 \times 6)7 = 8 \times 9 \times 7 + 8 \times 6 \times 7$

III is also true.

I and III, Answer C

---

10. B $5 \times 73 \times 2$

Multiplying 5 by 73 in your head would be quite difficult. However, multiplying 5 by 2 first would give you 10. Then, you could multiply 10 by 73 in your head to give you 730.

Instead of multiplying 5×73 and then that result by 2, you would multiply 5×2 and that result by 73.

$$5 \times 73 \times 2 = 5 \times 2 \times 73$$

Changing the order that you multiply is the commutative property.

3.4   Computation Algorithms

This lesson is meant to serve as a review of the different ways of looking at the four basic operations and to highlight the connections among those operations. It also introduces a few additional methods of performing these operations.

Addition and Subtraction

Addition and subtraction are a pair of inverse or opposite operations, meaning that either operation can be undone by the other.

For example, $12 - 5 = 7$, $7 + 5 = 12$. Subtracting 5 from a number and then adding 5 to the result will lead back to the original number.

Adding is sometimes taught as "counting forward" from a particular number. For example, $29 + 3$ would be counting forward 3 times: 30, 31, 32. Subtraction can be thought of as counting backwards: $32 - 3$: 31, 30, 29.

Multiplication and Division

Multiplication and division make up the other set of inverse operations. Each of them can be represented in many ways, here are a few:

- ⊙ Multiplication is generally introduced as repeated addition: adding a number to itself the number of times indicated by the multiplier.

$$4 \times 5 =$$
$$4 + 4 + 4 + 4 + 4$$

- ⊙ Division is often shown as repeated subtraction — subtracting the divisor from the dividend until reaching zero. For repeated subtraction, the number of times the divisor is subtracted the dividend is equal to the quotient.

$$12 \div 3 = ?$$
$$12 - 3 - 3 - 3 - 3 = 0$$
$$12 \div 3 = 4$$

Rules for Evens and Odds

- ⊙ Any time that two even numbers are added or subtracted, the result will be an even number.

Examples:
$4 + 8 = 12, 22 - 6 = 16.$

- ⊙ Any time that two odd numbers are added or subtracted, the result will be an even number.

Examples:
$13 + 5 = 18, 21 - 7 = 14.$

- When one even and one odd number are added or subtracted, the result will always be odd.

- Whenever an even number is multiplied by an even number or an odd number, the result will be even.

- When an odd number is multiplied by an odd number, the result will be odd.

For division, you may get remainders when dividing even and odd numbers.

Arrays

Arrays are great ways to visually represent both multiplication and division. For multiplication 6×2 could be translated into 6 groups of 2 and drawn as:
To calculate the result, you would count up the total number of elements. For a division problem, such as $12 \div 2$, could be solved by drawing 12 objects and then circling groups of 2 (as in the image above). The number of groups would be the quotient. $12 \div 2 = 6$.

Partial Products Method for Multiplication

The concept behind the partial products method is to take the base ten factor of each number and then multiply all the terms, and then find their sum. This is easier to illustrate with an example which is done below.

Multiply 32 × 65:

❶
32 breaks into 30 and 2
65 breaks into 60 and 5

❷
Now, multiply all the possible combinations:

$30 \times 60 = 1800$
$30 \times 5 = 150$
$2 \times 60 = 120$
$2 \times 5 = 10$

❸
Find the sum:

$1800 + 150 + 120 + 10 = 2080$

$32 \times 65 = 2080$

Lattice Method for Multiplication

To understand this method, review the example below which shows the multiplication of 32 and 65.

- ⊙ You put the two numbers that you are multiplying on the outside, one along the top, one along the right hand side. These are circled.
- ⊙ Then, for each box, you multiply the two integers and put the tens digit above the diagonal, and the ones digit below the diagonal. For instance, in the top right box, you multiply 2 by 6 and you get 12. In the top left box, the result is from multiplying 3 and 6.
- ⊙ Finally, you add along the diagonals, from the right to the left. First diagonal adds to 0, then next is 5 + 1 + 2 which gives you 8. The next diagonal is 1 + 8 + 1 = 10. Therefore, put the 0 down and carry the 1. Finally, 1 and 1 = 2.
- ⊙ Now, the product can be read out, see the underlined numbers: 2080.

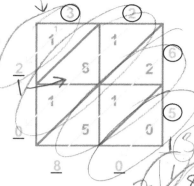

32 x 65 = 2080

COMPUTATION ALGORITHMS PRACTICE

1. **How many positive integers less than 200 are divisible by both 7 and 3?**
   - A. 9
   - B. 10
   - C. 20
   - D. 28

2. **This array would be used to solve which problem?**

   - A. 20 ÷ 5
   - B. 10 × 2
   - C. 4 + 5
   - D. 15 + 5

3. **An even integer divided by an an even integer could be:**
   - I. even
   - II. odd
   - III. fraction

   - A. I only
   - B. II only
   - C. I and III
   - D. I, II, and III

4. **8 + 8 + 8 + 8 + 8 + 8 =**
   - A. 86
   - B. 68
   - C. 6 × 8
   - D. 6 + 8

5. If you add 17 to a number and then divide the sum by 3, how can you manipulate the result to return to the original number?
    A. subtract 17 and then multiply by 3
    B. add 17 and then divide by 3
    C. multiply by 3 and then subtract 17
    D. subtract 17 and then divide by 3

6. $\dfrac{(6x + 21)}{3} =$
    A. $2x + 21$
    B. $2x + 7$
    C. $6x + 7$
    D. $18x + 63$

7. What is one method that can be used to solve $200 \div 50$?
    A. $200 \div 5 \times 10$
    B. $200 - 50 - 50 - 50 - 50$
    C. $200 \times 10 \div 5$
    D. 20050

200 ÷ 50

8. Which number line shows how to solve $-3 - 4$?
    -3-4
    A.
    B.
    C.
    D.

9. If you needed to solve 101×73 using mental math, which method would you use to help you solve it quickly?
    A. repeated addition
    B. an array
    C. distributive property
    D. counting forward

10. The sum of an even and an odd is:
    A. always odd
    B. always even
    C. sometimes odd and sometimes even
    D. no way to tell without actual numbers

COMPUTATION ALGORITHMS EXPLANATIONS

1. A   If a number is divisible by both 7 and 3, the number is divisible by the lowest common multiple of those numbers. The lowest common multiple of 7 and 3 is 21, since that is the smallest number that both divide evenly into.

We need to figure out how many integers less than 200 are divisible by 21. If you divide 200 by 21 you get $9\,^{11}\!/_{21}$. That means that there are 9 different numbers that are multiples of 21 and less than 200.

2. A There are 20 objects which are divided into groups of 5 in rows, or groups of 4 in columns. Therefore, this array can help you divide 20 by 5, answer A.

3. D An even integer divided by an even could be even. For example: $20 \div 2 = 10$. An even divided by an even can be odd. For example: $12 \div 4 = 3$. An even divided by an even can be a fraction. For example: $6 \div 8 = \frac{3}{4}$

4. C Multiplication is repeated addition. 8 added to itself 6 times is the same as 8 times 6.

5. C To "undo" an operation, apply its inverse. Addition is the inverse of subtraction. Multiplication is the inverse of division.

Since division was the last operation performed, you must first do the opposite of this operation. The inverse of divide by 3 is multiply by 3.

The next operation to undo is adding 17, so you must subtract 17. Multiply by 3 and then subtract 17.

6. B $\frac{6x + 21}{3}$ Use the distributive property to factor 3 out of the numerator. $6x + 21 = 3(2x + 7)$

Put the fraction back together and divide by 3.
$\frac{3(2x + 7)}{3} = 2x + 7$

7. B Repeated subtraction is one way to solve a division problem. Subtract the divisor from the dividend and keep subtracting until you reach zero. The number of times you subtract will be the quotient, or result of the division problem.

$$200 - 50 - 50 - 50 - 50 = 0$$
50 is subtracted 4 times, therefore, $200 \div 50 = 4$

8. B To use a number line to solve a problem, start at the first number, in this case -3. Then, the problem asks you to subtract 4. When subtracting, you move to the left on the number line. Therefore, you want to start at -3 and move 4 spaces to the left and then you arrive at -7, which is the answer to $-3 - 4$.

9. C   The distributive property is extremely useful when solving complex multiplication problems with mental math. In this case, the way to solve this question using distributive property would be:

$$101 \times 73 =$$
$$= (100 + 1) \times 73$$
$$= 73 \times 100 + 1 \times 73$$
$$= 7300 + 73$$
$$= 7373$$

10. A   Whenever you add an even and an odd number you will get an odd number. Here are some examples and then we will prove why this is true.

Examples: $4 + 3 = 7$, $12 + 5 = 17$, $12 + 11 = 23$, $2 + 7 = 9$

An even number is divisible by 2. If you add two even numbers together, you will be adding numbers which are both divisible by 2 and thus the result will also be divisible by 2. Thus, an even plus an even is an even.

An odd number is always 1 bigger than an even number. Therefore, if you add an even and an odd, it is the same as adding an even and an even and 1. Even + even is even. Therefore, it is like adding 1 to an even number, which will always be odd.

Even + Odd = Odd

3.5 Word Problems

Solving mathematical word problems is a great way to demonstrate your deep understanding of mathematical concepts and practice applying them to real–world situations. There is no single way to approach or solve word problems, but there are several strategies you may find helpful.

Understand What the Question is Asking

Read the problem carefully a few times to make sure you understand exactly what the question is asking.

Focus on Relevant Info

Once you know what you are looking for, recognize extraneous information and disregard it. For example, try to find out the relevant information from the following scenario:

> **Anna, Ralph, and Susan were sharing a pizza that cost $12.50. Ralph ate $\frac{1}{7}$, Susan ate $\frac{3}{8}$, and Anna ate $\frac{4}{9}$. How much pizza did the two girls eat?**

The price of the pizza and the amount Ralph ate are extraneous and can be ignored. To solve this question, simply add the fractions Susan and Anna ate.

Clue Words

Translate words into mathematical operations. For example, the word "of" often indicates multiplication. Examples: Fifteen percent of 20. $\frac{1}{3}$ of the 60 students are seniors. There is no guarantee that a certain word will always translate to the same operation; you must read the problem and think about what is actually happening. Still, the following chart provides a basic list of useful operation clue words.

Clue Words	Operation/Symbol
is, are, was, were, equals, totals	equals, =
of, by, times, product	multiplication, ×
difference, less than, reduced	subtraction, −

Clue Words	Operation/Symbol
together, more than, sum, all, total	addition, +
ratio, groups of, separated into	division, ÷

Diagrams

Another strategy for approaching word problems is to draw a picture or diagram to make the situation easier to comprehend and to help yourself see what information is missing.

> Carmen walked 3 miles due North and Sam walked 4 miles due East. if they started at the same point, how far apart were they when they stopped walking?

In this case, drawing a diagram helps to see that the distance between Carmen and Sam is the hypotenuse of a right triangle. (See Measurement – Triangles lesson for help)

Multiple Steps

For complex word problems, it is often necessary to break a problem into multiple steps to reach the answer. Many people become confused when they do not plan out those steps before beginning calculations and when they do not separate a problem into manageable pieces.

> Sandra went shopping for school supplies. She bought 3 notebooks which cost $0.75 each and 2 packs of pens for $2.50 each. If she paid with a $10 bill, how much change did Sandra get?

This is a simple example of a multiple step problem. First, you should find out the price of all 3 notebooks by multiplying 3 by $0.75. Next, figure out the total cost of the pens by multiplying 2 by $2.50. Then add the cost of the notebooks and the pens to final the total cost of the items Sandra purchased. Finally, subtract the total cost from $10 to determine the change she received.

Write down Information

If you have no idea how to begin a particular problem, it often helps to write down the information contained in the problem in an organized way. This may bring forward connections between pieces of information.

1. A company's sales revenue was $1,000,000 last year. This year its expected revenue is $25,000,000. What percentage of last year's sales revenue is this year's projected revenue?

   A. 2.5%
   B. 25%
   C. 250%
   D. 2500%

2. My cat eats ⅗ cups of food every day. How many cups of food does she eat in two weeks?

   A. 2 ⅕ cups
   B. 8 ⅖ cups
   C. 10 cups
   D. 10 ⅖ cups

3. Steven owns 17,000 shares of stock in a company with 51,000 equal shares. If the annual profits for the company are $270,000 and each stockholder gets a share proportionate to the amount of stock he or she owns, how much should Steven get for the year?

   A. $90,000
   B. $180,000
   C. $200,000
   D. $287,000

4. Jennifer gave Vanessa half of her candy. Vanessa gave David half of the candy she received from Jennifer. David ate 6 pieces and gave the remaining 4 pieces to John. How many pieces of candy did Jennifer start with?

   A. 5
   B. 20
   C. 40
   D. 60

5. Two thirds of the students at Sequoia Junior High are female. If 200 students are male, how many females attend Sequoia Junior High?

   A. 100
   B. 200
   C. 400
   D. 600

   200 ♀

   male =

   $1 - \frac{2}{3} = \frac{3}{3} - \frac{2}{3} = \frac{1}{3}$

6. If Jane's brother is five years older than twice her age when she is eight, how many years older is her brother?

   A. 5
   B. 10
   C. 13
   D. 21

7. A sweater is originally $80. It was marked down 10% and still didn't sell, so the store marked it down an additional 25%.

What percentage of the original price does the sweater cost?

    A. 35%

    B. 45%

    C. 65%

    D. 67.5%

8. **A car's gas tank holds 14 gallons. If the car had a full tank before being driven 250 miles and then was filled again, how many gallons were needed to refill the tank? If you wanted to answer the question above, what additional piece of information is needed?**

    A. Amount of time it took to drive the 250 miles.

    B. The car's average fuel consumption in miles per gallon.

    C. The price of gas when the tank was refilled.

    D. The average speed the car is driven in miles per hour.

9. **If you have an average of 82 after 4 math tests, what do you need on the 5th test to increase your average to an 85?**

    A. 88

    B. 92

    C. 95

    D. 97

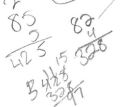

10. **Victoria and Jerry are running for Student Council. Victoria has 273 votes and Jerry has 289 votes. If the first to reach 350 votes wins, how many more votes does Victoria need than Jerry?**

    A. 16

    B. 61

    C. 77

    D. 212

WORD PROBLEMS EXPLANATIONS

1. **D**   This year's projected revenue is $25,000,000, which is 25 times last year's revenue. Multiply by 100% to find its percent of last year's revenue.

$$25 \times 100\% = 2500\%$$

Another way to think about this word problem is to take the words and translate them into an equation. "What percentage of last year's sales revenue is this year's projected revenue?"

"What percentage"	=	n
" of "	=	multiplication
"last year's sales revenue"	=	$1,000,000

$n \times \$1,000,000 = \$25,000,000$

$n = 25$

$n = 2500\%$

---

2. B There are 14 days in two weeks (7 days per week times 2 weeks).

Multiply the amount she eats each day by the total number of days to find out the total amount of food the cat eats.

$\frac{3}{5}$ cups per day × 14 days = $\frac{42}{5}$ cups = $8\frac{2}{5}$ cups

---

3. A Break the problem into multiple steps. First determine what fraction of the total shares Steven owns. Then determine how much Steven should get.

Steven owns 17,000 shares out of a total of 51,000 shares. Therefore, Steven owns: $\frac{17000}{51000}$ which equals $\frac{1}{3}$ of the shares.

To find out how much Steven should get, multiply the fraction he owns by the total annual profits.

$\frac{1}{3} \times \$270,000 = \$90,000$

---

4. C This problem is best solved by working backwards.

John: Got 4 pieces.

David: Ate 6 pieces and gave 4 to John. 6 + 4 = 10. Got 10 pieces.

Vanessa: Half for herself and half for David. Gave David 10 pieces. If 10 is half, then Vanessa must have received 20. Got 20 pieces.

Jennifer: Half for herself and half for Vanessa. Gave Vanessa 20 pieces. If 20 is half, then Jennifer must have started with 40.

You can check your work by going through the problem in order. Jennifer started with 40 pieces.

---

5. C If $\frac{2}{3}$ of the students are female, then subtract $\frac{2}{3}$ from 1 to determine the fraction of males.

Therefore, $\frac{1}{3}$ of the students are males.

$1 - \frac{2}{3} = \frac{1}{3}$

Thus, if $\frac{1}{3}$ are males and $\frac{2}{3}$ are females, there are twice as many females as males. Therefore, if 200 are male, then 400 are female.

Another way to think of the problem, is that if ⅓ of the students are male and that is 200 students, then the total number of students must be 600. Therefore, subtract the number of males from total to find number of females.

600 − 200 = 400. 400 females. Answer C.

6. C   Translate words into numbers.

Jane's age × 2 + 5 = Jane's brother's age when Jane is 8.

8 × 2 + 5 = 16 + 5 = 21

When Jane is 8, her brother is 21. Therefore, find the difference between their ages to find out how many years older the brother is.

21 − 8 = 13. Answer C.

7. D   This problem has many steps.

First, determine the price of the sweater after the first markdown.

$80 × 10% =
$80 × 0.10 =
$8

Now subtract that discount from the original price.

$80 − $8 = $72

Second, determine the price of the sweater after the second markdown.

$72 × 25% = $72 × 0.25 = $18

Now, subtract to find the new price.

$72 − $18 = $54

Finally, to find the percentage of the original, you must divide 54 by 80.

54 ÷ 80 = 0.675 = 67.5%

8. B   The question asks how many gallons are needed to refill the tank. Therefore, we must figure out how many gallons were used when driving the 250 miles. If you know how much gas is consumed for every mile driven, you can calculate the amount of gas used.

The time it takes (answer A), the price (answer C), and the speed (answer D), will not help you determine the number of gallons used which is needed to figure out how many gallons are needed to refill the tank.

9. D   To calculate the average, you find the sum and then divide by the number of terms. In average problems, it is often easier to think of the problem in terms of sums.

Average = Sum ÷ Number of numbers
Sum = Average × Number of numbers

In this problem, first find the sum of the scores on the first 4 math tests:

$$82 \times 4 = 328$$

Then, if you want an average of 85 on all 5 tests, the sum of your scores must be:

$$85 \times 5 = 425$$

If you know the sum on 4 tests and you know the sum that you want on 5 tests, if you subtract, you will find the score that you need on the 5th test.

$$425 - 328 = 97$$

---

10. A There are a few steps to this problem. First, determine the number of votes that Victoria needs to win. Next, determine the number of votes that Jerry needs to win. Finally, determine how many additional votes Victoria needs.

Victoria: She has 273 votes and needs 350 votes. Subtract to find the number she needs.

$$350 - 273 = 77$$

Jerry: He has 289 votes and needs 350 votes. Subtract to find the number he needs.

$$350 - 289 = 61$$

Difference between them:

$$77 - 61 = 16$$

Victoria needs 16 more votes than Jerry.

Another way to think of this problem is to see by how much Victoria trails and that will be the number of additional votes she needs to win.

Jerry has 289, Victoria has 273
$$289 - 273 = 16$$

3.6   Chapter Review

1. You need to paint a huge outside wall that is 36 feet by 25 feet. If every 2 gallons of paint covers 50 square yards, how many gallons of paint do you need?

   A. 2
   B. 4
   C. 12
   D. 36

2. What is the distance between point A with coordinates (-1,-2) and point B with coordinates (6, -2)?

   A. 5
   B. 6
   C. 7
   D. 8

3. If you wanted to solve 31 × 101 + 10 quickly in your head, what would you do?

   A. Commutative Property
   B. Associative Property
   C. Distributive Property
   D. Identity Property

4. If 1 kilogram is equal to approximately 2.2 pounds, how many ounces are there in 20 kilograms?

   A. 44 ounces
   B. 11/4 ounces
   C. 96.8 ounces
   D. 704 ounces

5. Carol bought 6 books for $6.95 each. She was charged an additional $3.34 total on her purchases. She was left with $5.96. How much money did Carol start with?

   A. $39.08
   B. $50.00
   C. $51.00
   D. $67.70

6. In the following problem, what properties were used from step 1 to 2 and step 2 to 3, respectively?

   1. 4(16 + 23) + 36 =
   2. 64 + 92 + 36 =
   3. 64 + 36 + 92 =
   4. 100 + 92 = 192

   A. Distributive, Associative
   B. Associative, Commutative
   C. Distributive, Commutative
   D. Commutative, Associative

7. If a rectangle has corners at the origin, (0,4), and (2,4), where is the fourth corner of the rectangle?

   A. (0, 2)
   B. (2, 0)

C. (4, 4)

D. (4, 0)

8. **Which of the following is the largest?**

   A. 1 sq yard

   B. 9 sq feet

   C. 1296 sq inches

   D. All of the above are the same.

9. **If you subtract 6 from a number and then multiply the difference by 8, how can you manipulate the result to return to the original number?**

   A. Add 6. Then, divide by 8.

   B. Subtract 6. Multiply by 8.

   C. Divide by 8. Then, add 6.

   D. Multiply by 8. Subtract 6.

10. **The average precipitation for the first 3 months of the year was 12.5mm. If the precipitation for each month had been 1.5mm greater, what would the average have been?**

   A. 13mm

   B. 14mm

   C. 17mm

   D. 39mm

11. **If you were on a trip when the exchange rate between Euros and dollars was 1 Euro = \$1.54 and wanted to purchase a book that cost \$10.78, approximately how many Euros would the book cost you?**

   A. 7 Euros

   B. 9.24 Euros

   C. 12.32 Euros

   D. 16.60 Euros

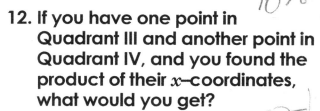

12. **If you have one point in Quadrant III and another point in Quadrant IV, and you found the product of their x–coordinates, what would you get?**

   A. Positive Number

   B. Negative Number

   C. Zero

   D. Not enough information.

13. **How many integers between 600 and 700, inclusive, are divisible by both 5 and 3?**

   A. 7

   B. 15

   C. 33

   D. 53

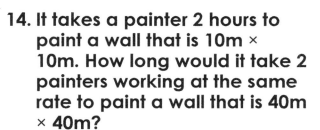

14. **It takes a painter 2 hours to paint a wall that is 10m × 10m. How long would it take 2 painters working at the same rate to paint a wall that is 40m × 40m?**

   A. 2 hours

   B. 4 hours

   C. 8 hours

   D. 16 hours

15. $12^0 - 12^1 =$
    A. -12
    B. -11
    C. -1 (circled)
    D. 0

16. If an even number is multiplied by an odd number and then added to an odd number, the result will be:
    A. Even (circled)
    B. Odd
    C. Zero
    D. Not enough information.

    $2 \times 7 + 9 =$

17. What is the midpoint of the line segment that connects point R at (-4, 6) and point S at (2, -1)?
    A. (-2, 3.5)
    B. (-2, 5)
    C. (-1, 2.5)
    D. (-1, 3)

18. Which of the following problems could be solved by finding the product of 3.5 and 6?
    A. You have a string that is 6 feet long and you need pieces that are each 3.5 feet. How many pieces can you make from the string?
    B. There are 6 documentaries whose average length is 3.5 hours. How many total hours of film are there?

    C. You have $6 and go to a store and buy $3.50 worth of supplies. How much change do you have?
    D. You are making cookies and put in 6 tablespoons of sugar. The recipe calls for an additional 3.5 tablespoons, how many total tablespoons have you put in?

19. You have a string of beads that starts with the following beads: Red, Yellow, Blue, and Green. This sequence continues throughout the entire string. What color is the 49th bead?
    A. Red
    B. Yellow
    C. Blue
    D. Green

20. Patricia drove the first 120 miles of her trip at 40mph and the remaining 120 miles at 60mph, what was her average speed for the entire trip?
    A. 45 mph
    B. 48 mph
    C. 50 mph
    D. 52 mph

1. B This problem involves many steps. First, find the area of the wall. Second, convert the units to square yards. Then, determine the gallons of paints needed.

Area of a rectangular wall is length × width = 36 ft × 25 ft = 900 sq. ft.

To convert from square feet to square yards, two unit conversions are necessary.

$$900 \text{ sq feet} \quad \times \quad \frac{1 \text{ yard}}{3 \text{ feet}} \quad \times \quad \frac{1 \text{ yard}}{3 \text{ feet}} \quad = \quad 100 \text{ sq yds}$$

You could also convert the dimensions from feet to yards first, and then find the area. Either way, you would end up with 100 square yards.

$$\frac{2 \text{ gallons}}{50 \text{ sq yds}} = \frac{x \text{ gallons}}{100 \text{ sq yds}}$$ - set up a ratio to find gallons

$50x = 2\,(100)$ - cross multiply and set them equal

$50x = 200$ - multiply

$x = 4$ - divide both sides by 50

Answer: B. 4 gallons

---

2. C Points A and B are graphed on the coordinate plane above. As you can see from the graph and their coordinates, points A and B have the same y coordinate. Therefore, we must find the difference in their x–coordinates to figure out the distance between the points.

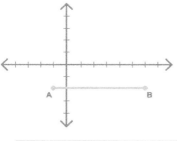

Point A's x–coordinate is at -1 and point B's x–coordinate is at 6. Subtract to find the difference or distance between them.

$$6 - (-1) = 6 + 1 = 7$$

---

3. C To solve the problem: 31 × 101 + 10 in your head, you would want to make the multiplication easier. The way to accomplish this is to separate the multiplication into 2 easier multiplication problems. This can be done with the distributive property.

$$31 \times 101 + 10 =$$
$$31(100 + 1) + 10 =$$
$$31(100) + 31(1) + 10 =$$
$$3100 + 31 + 10 =$$
$$3141$$

The commutative property would not work since you can't commute across different operations. The same is true for the associative property. Following the order of operations, you must multiply and then add.

4. D The question asks you to convert from kilograms to ounces. First, convert from kilograms to pounds and then convert that result to ounces.

$$20 \text{ kilograms} \quad \times \quad \frac{2.2 \text{ pounds}}{1 \text{ kilogram}} \quad = \quad 44 \text{ pounds}$$

Note that the kilogram units canceled and you were left with pounds. Now, convert from pounds to ounces. There are 16 ounces in 1 pound.

$$44 \text{ pounds} \quad \times \quad \frac{16 \text{ ounces}}{1 \text{ pound}} \quad = \quad 704 \text{ ounces}$$

5. C Break the problem into steps. First, figure out the total cost of the books. Now, add the sales tax.

6 books × $6.95 each = $41.70

$41.70 + $3.34 = $45.04

Then, if Carol left with $4.96, add that back to the $45.04 to see how much she started with.

$45.04 + $5.96 = $51.00

6. C From Step 1 to Step 2:

1.	4(16 + 23) + 36 =
2.	64 + 92 + 36 =

In the above steps, the property that was used was the distributive property. The distributive states that multiplication distributes to each term over addition.

From Step 2 to Step 3:

2.	64 + 92 + 36 =
3.	64 + 36 + 92 =

In the above steps, the 92 and 36 changed their order for addition. Commutative property states that you can change the order without changing the result.

Distributive, Commutative

7. B This problem gives you 3 of the coordinates of the rectangle and asks you to find the fourth. It is easy to see the solution to this problem when you graph the coordinates. The last corner is at (2,0).

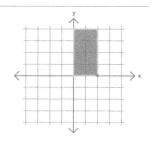

8. D Convert each answer choice to the same units and compare. Since the units are squared, use two unit conversions.

A: 1 square yard $\times \dfrac{3 \text{ feet}}{1 \text{ yard}} \times \dfrac{3 \text{ feet}}{1 \text{ yard}} = 9$ square feet

B: 9 square feet

C: 1296 sq inches $\times \dfrac{1 \text{ foot}}{12 \text{ in}} \times \dfrac{1 \text{ foot}}{12 \text{ in}} = 9$ square feet

Answer D: All same

---

9. C To "undo" an operation, apply its inverse. Addition is the inverse of subtraction. Multiplication is the inverse of division.

Since multiplication was the last operation performed, you must first undo this operation. The inverse of multiply by 8 is divide by 8.

The next operation to undo is subtracting 6, so you must add 6.

Divide by 8. Then, add 6.

---

10. B There are two ways to approach this problem.

Method 1: **Convert to totals.** Instead of dealing with averages, deal with total amount of precipitation. If the average as 12.5mm for 3 months, the total precipitation during those 3 months can be found by multiplying average by number of months.

> Total Precipitation =
> 12.5 × 3 = 37.5mm

If the precipitation increased by 1.5mm each month, multiply by 3 to find total precipitation increase.

> Precipitation increase =
> 1.5 × 3 = 4.5mm
> New total prec. =
> 37.5mm + 4.5mm = 42mm

To find new average, divide new total by 3 months.

> Average =
> 42mm ÷ 3 = 14mm

Method 2: **Keep everything in averages.** If the average was 12.5mm, you can think of each month as having 12.5mm of precipitation. If each month it increased by 1.5mm, you can add 1.5mm to each month to figure out new amount of precipitation.

If you think of each month as 14mm, then the average across all 3 months is 14mm.

> 12.5mm + 1.5mm =
> 14mm

11. A You are given a quantity in dollars and you want to convert it to Euros. Multiply by a unit conversion of Euros to dollars so that the dollars cancels and you are left with Euros.

$$\$10.78 \quad \times \quad \frac{1 \text{ Euro}}{\$1.54} \quad = \quad 7 \text{ Euros}$$

12. B If a point is in Quadrant III, then it's x–coordinate is negative. If a point is in Quadrant IV, it's x–coordinate is positive.

If you multiply a negative and a positive, you get a negative. Therefore, the product of their x–coordinates will be negative.

13. A If a number is divisible by both 5 and 3, then it must be divisible by 15. Now, we need to find out how many integers between 600 and 700 are divisible by 15.

Starting with 600, since 15 divides evenly into that, count the numbers divisible by 15:

> 600, 615, 630, 645, 660, 675, 690
> 7 integers

14. D Let's figure out the rate of each painter. The painter can paint a wall 10m × 10m in 2 hours. Therefore, he can paint 100 sq m in 2 hours, or to reduce that, 50 sq m in 1 hour.

Now, we have 2 painters.
The rate of one painter is 50 sq m in 1 hour, if you have 2 painters working at the same rate, then they can paint 100 sq m in 1 hour.

The wall is 40m × 40m.
The area of the new wall is 40m × 40m = 1600 sq m.
The two painters rate is 100 sq m in 1 hour, therefore, to paint 1600 sq m, it will take 16 hours.

15. B ❶ Anything raised to the power of 0 is 1.

❷ Anything raised to the power of 1 is itself.

> ❶ $12^0 = 1$ ❷ $12^1 = 12$
> $12^0 - 12^1 = 1 - 12 = -11$

16. B An even number multiplied by an odd number will always be even. The reason is that an even number has 2 as a factor, and if you multiply a number with 2 as a factor, the product will also have 2 as a factor. There-fore, the product will be even.

Now, we will take the even number and add it to an odd number. An odd number is just one more than any even number. Therefore, even + odd = even + even + 1.
Two even numbers added will always give you an even number since both numbers have 2 as a factor, their sum will also have 2 as a factor.

So, even + even = even.
even + odd = even + even + 1
= even + 1
= odd
Result will always be odd.

17. C To find the midpoint of a line segment between (-4, 6) and (2, -1), find the average of the x–coordinates and the average of the y–coordinates.

The x–coordinates are -4 and 2. The average can be found by adding and dividing by 2.

Average of x–coordinates = $^{-4\,+\,2}/_2$ = -1
The y coordinates are 6 and -1. The average can be found by adding and dividing by 2.

Average of y–coordinates = $^{6\,+\,-1}/_2$ = 2.5
The midpoint's coordinates are (-1, 2.5)

18. B Let's figure out how to solve each answer choice.

A: You have a string that is 6 feet long and you need pieces that are each 3.5 feet. How many pieces can you make from the string?
This problem would be found by dividing the total amount of string by the length of each piece. 6 ÷ 3.5. Eliminate A.

B: There are 6 documentaries whose average length is 3.5 hours. How many total hours of film are there?
The average 3.5 is found by dividing the total by 6. Therefore, you can find the total by finding the product of 3.5 and 6. This is the correct answer.

C: You have $6 and go to a store and buy $3.50 worth of supplies. How much change do you have?
To find the change, subtract what you spent from what you had. 6 − 3.5. Eliminate C.

D: You are making cookies and put in 6 tablespoons of sugar. The recipe calls for an additional 3.5 tablespoons, how many total tablespoons have you put in?

To find the total amount of sugar you put in, add the 6 tablespoons to the additional 3.5 tablespoons. 6 + 3.5. Eliminate D.

---

19. A Every four beads, the pattern "Red, Yellow, Blue, Green" repeats. Therefore, the bead in any position that is divisible by 4 will be Green.

Since 48 is divisible by 4, the 48th bead will be green. The 49th bead must be red, since a red bead always comes after a green bead.

---

20. B To find the average speed, divide the total number of miles by the total time.

Patricia drove the first 120 miles at 40 mph. Therefore, divide the distance by the speed to find the time it took.

120 miles ÷ 40 mph = 3 hours

She drove the remaining 120 miles at 60 mph. Divide to find the time this part of the trip took.

120 miles ÷ 60 mph = 2 hours

The total number of miles driven = 120 miles + 120 miles = 240 miles.

The total time for the trip = 3 hours + 2 hours = 5 hours.

Average speed = Total miles ÷ Total time

240 miles ÷ 5 hours = 48 mph

Chapter 4:
Functions & Equations

Lessons

4.1   Patterns & Variables

Variables

A variable is a letter that represents a value. If you are solving a problem and you have an unknown value, you could use a variable to represent that value. For example, if you knew that Sam was 5 years older than Andrew, but you were unsure of how old Andrew was, you could use a variable to represent Andrew's age, let's use "a" and then Sam's age could be expressed as: $a + 5$.

Once the value for the variable is determined, it can replace the variable in an expression. For instance, in the above expression, we know that Sam's age is $a + 5$, where a represents Andrew's age. If we found out that Andrew was 10, then we could substitute 10 in for a, and solve for Sam's age. $a + 5 = 10 + 5 = 15$. Therefore, if we knew that Andrew was 10, we would know that Sam was 15.

Algebraic Expressions

An algebraic expression is a phrase (no equality sign) that contains terms with numbers or variables and one or more operations. For example, $4 + y$ is an algebraic expression. If there is an equality sign, then it becomes a full statement or equation. For instance, $4 + y = 10$ is an algebraic equation. When expressing relationships between numbers or variables, algebraic expressions are used. Algebraic expressions are also conveniently a shorter way to write a long statement.

Add three to a number and then multiply the sum by six and take the result and subtract seven can be written as $6(n+3) - 7$

Patterns

A pattern is a predictable set of elements. The two basic types of patterns are those that repeat and those that are generated based on a model or template. We will briefly examine repeating patterns, but the focus of the lesson is on the second type of pattern, which is one of the more basic forms of algebra. Algebraic expressions are used to represent these patterns.

Repeating Patterns

A repeating pattern is one in which a sequence of elements, called a core, is repeated two or more times. The elements can be anything from shapes to letters to numbers. For instance, the patterns (right) show several examples of repeated cores. The cores are underlined.

OO□▽OO□▽OO□▽OO□▽

12345123451234512345123451234512345

●□○●□○●□○●□○●□○

Patterns based on models

The second type of pattern is a much broader category, but it is one that is vital to mathematics. A non–repeating pattern is any predictable set of elements, so anything that uses a template or model to create output for a given input generates a pattern. For mathematical purposes, the input is generally the element number (1st, 2nd, 3rd, 4th, etc) and the output is the element itself.

Example: 3, 6, 9, 12, 15, ...

For the input 1, there is an output of 3. For the input 2, there is an output of 6. This data is exhibiting a pattern $y = 3x$, where x is the input, and y is the output. On a multiple choice test, determining which pattern is exhibited by a set of data is often as simple as plugging in element numbers into the answer choices to find the expression that generates the appropriate outputs.

Example: Which pattern is exhibited by the data below?
-2, -4, -8, -16, -32, -64, -128, ...

A. $y = 2x$
B. $y = -2x$
C. $y = x - 3$
D. $y = 4x$

You can see in the pattern that the 1st input gives you a value of -2. Let's plug in 1 for x in each of the answer choices to see which gives a -2. Only answer choices B and C work, eliminate A and D. Now, try plugging in a 2 for x in the remaining equations to see which outputs a 4.

Answer choice C: $y = x - 3$, when $x = 2$, $y = 2 - 3 = -1$.
This does not work.
Answer choice B: $y = -2x$, when $x = 2$, $y = -2(2) = -4$.
This works. This is your answer.

Dependent and Independent Variables

The independent variable is the variable that is being manipulated or changed and the dependent variable is the observed result of the changes in the independent variable. For example, the number of layers of clothing you wear would be the dependent variable, while the temperature outside would be the independent variable. Also, in the case of standard equations, x is the independent variable and y is the dependent variable. Tables are often used to show how one variable relates to another variable. For example, the table (left) shows the relation of $y = x + 3$.

x	y
0	3
1	4
4	7
6	9

1. **What is the next element in the pattern?**

    -125, 25, -5, 1, ... ?

    A. 0.5

    B. -0.5

    C. ⅕

    D. -⅕

2. **Which pattern is exhibited by the data in the table below?**

    A. $x = y^3$

    B. $y = x^3$

    C. $y = x \div 4$

    D. $x = y^2 + 4$

x	y
1	1
8	2
27	3
125	5

3. **Sandra is 5 inches shorter than Melissa, whose height is m inches. Write an expression to represent Sandra's height.**

    A. $m + 5$

    B. $m - 5$

    C. $m \div 5$

    D. $5m$

4. **Identify the pattern exhibited by:**

    10.5, 20.5, 30.5, 40.5, ...

    A. $y = 10.5x$

    B. $y = 10x + 0.5$

    C. $y = 0.5x + 10$

    D. $y = x + 10.5$

5. **Which of the following patterns does the following data fit?**

    1, 4, 9, 16, 25, ...

    A. $y = 2x$

    B. $y = x^2$

    C. $y = x + 3$

    D. $y = x$

6. **Write "the product of 6 and the sum of 3 and a number n" as an expression.**

    A. $6 + 3n$

    B. $6(3n)$

    C. $6(3 + n)$

    D. $6 + 3 + n$

7. **Which equation represents the relationship between a and b in the table?**

a	b
2	1
5	-8
7	-14
12	-29

    A. $b = a - 1$

    B. $b = 2a - 3$

    C. $b = -3a + 7$

    D. $b = -4a + 7$

8. **What comes next in the series: 0, 1, 3, 6, 10, ...?**

    A. 14

    B. 15

    C. 16

    D. 17

9. Jenna makes a salary of $1000 per month plus 10% commission on whatever she sells. If Jenna sold y dollars worth of goods one month, how much did she make that month?

    A. $1010y$
    B. $1000 \div 10y$
    C. $1000 \times (0.1y)$
    (D.) $1000 + 0.1y$

10. If n represents an odd integer, what represents the sum of the next two consecutive odd integers?

    A. n + 3
    (B.) 2n + 6
    C. 3n + 1
    D. 4n + 4

PATTERNS & VARIABLES EXPLANATIONS

1. D   **-125, 25, -5, 1, ...**

In the above pattern, to get from one element to the next divide by -5. Therefore, the next number will be 1 divided by -5, which is $^{-}\frac{1}{5}$.

---

2. A   Plug in the values in the table into each equation and see which equation is true for every set of values.

This is true for all the data in the table. Answer A is correct.

x	y
1	1
8	2
27	3
125	5

$$x = y^3$$

Answer B switches x and y.
Answer C only works for one set of values.
Answer D only works for one set of values.

---

3. B   This question asks you to translate the words into an expression. In this case, the unknown quantity is Melissa's height which is represented with the variable m. Now, take the rest of the words in the sentence to write an expression.

Since Sandra is 5 inches shorter than Melissa, subtract 5 from Melissa's height to get Sandra's.

    Sandra's height = Melissa's height − 5
    = $m - 5$

4. B   Solve this problem by plugging in the element number for x into each equation. In other words, when x = 1, then y = 10.5 and when x = 2, then y = 20.5.

$$10.5, 20.5, 30.5, 40.5, ...$$

A: $y = 10.5x$; This works for the first element but not the other elements.

B: $y = 10x + 0.5$; This works for all the elements.

C: $y = 0.5x + 10$; This only works for the first element.

D: $y = x + 10.5$; This doesn't work for any elements.

---

5. B   **1, 4, 9, 16, 25, ...**

To determine which of the patterns does the data fit, try each answer.

A: $y = 2x$, The first input of 1 should give you a 1 as a result. If you plug in 1 into $y = 2x$, you get a 2. This does not work.

B: $y = x^2$, An input of 1 should give you a 1. An input of 2 should give you a 4. An input of 3 should give you a 9. All those are true for the equation $y = x^2$.

C: $y = x+3$, An input of 1 should give you a 1. This does not work.

D: $y = x$, An input of 1 should give you a 1. That works. Try the next element. An input of 2 should output a 4. It does not.

---

6. C   A product is the result of a multiplication problem. A sum is the result of an addition problem.

The problem states: the product of 6 and the sum of 3 and a number. Break it into two parts. The product of "6" and "the sum of 3 and a number" is the same as 6 multiplied by the "sum of 3 and a number."

Let's translate: "the sum of 3 and a number" into an expression. Since we don't know the number, we are using n to represent it.
$3 + n$

Now, going back to the product:
6 multiplied by "the sum of 3 and a number" equals 6 multiplied by $(3 + n)$, or $6(3 + n)$.

---

7. C   The easiest way to solve this problem is to try each answer choice to see which makes all the equations true.
A only works for the first pair of values. B also works for just the first pair of values. D does not work for any pair. C works for everything.

$b = -3a + 7$
$a = 2, b = 1: 1 = -3(2) + 7 = -6 + 7 = 1$
$a = 5, b = -8: -8 = -3(5) + 7 = -15 + 7 = -8$
$a = 7, b = -14: -14 = -3(7) + 7 = -21 + 7 = -14$
$a = 12, b = -29: -29 = -3(12) + 7 = -36 + 7 = -29$

a	b
2	1
5	-8
7	-14
12	-29

8. B **0, 1, 3, 6, 10, …?**

From the first element to the second element, add 1.

From the second to the third, add 2.

Then add 3.

Then add 4.

Therefore, to get to the next element add 5. $10 + 5 = 15$.

9. D Jenna makes a salary of $1000 per month plus 10% commission on what she sells. Therefore, there are two parts to Jenna's salary: the base salary and the commission. The base salary is $1000. Now, let's figure out the commission.

Her commission is 10% on what she sells. If she sells y dollars, multiply by ten percent to figure out how much she makes on commission.

Commission = $10\%(y) = 0.1y$

Total Salary = Base plus Commission
= $1000 + 0.1y$

10. B If n is an odd integer, the next consecutive odd integer would be two larger than n. For example, if $n = 3$, the next consecutive odd integer would be $3 + 2 = 5$. Therefore, the next consecutive odd integer is n + 2.

If you want the consecutive odd integer greater than n + 2, you would add another 2. The second consecutive odd integer is $n + 2 + 2 = n + 4$.

The sum is $(n + 2) + (n + 4) = 2n + 6$

4.2   Relations & Functions

Relations

Relations and functions are closely related to the topics covered in the previous lesson. A relation is simply a patterned relationship between two variables: by applying an independent variable to a model, it is possible to generate the corresponding dependent variable. Relations are often shown in †–charts, with the input listed in a column on the left side of the "†" and the corresponding output listed on the right.

x	y
2	5
3	7
4	9
5	?
?	15

From a set of data you might be asked to derive the relationship. In the case above, $y = 2x + 1$.

You might also be asked to use the relationship to fill in missing information. To find the y value that corresponds with $x = 5$, plug 5 into the equation:

$$y = 2(5) + 1 = 11.$$

To find the x–value that pairs with $y = 15$, plug 15 into the equation for y, solve for x:

$$15 = 2x + 1, \ x = 7$$

Functions

A function is a specific type of relation for which each independent variable produces exactly one dependent variable. So, for each value of x inputted into the function, there can be only one corresponding y–value. However, multiple x values can produce the same y value.

For example, the following are functions since each instance of x will produce only one y value:

$$y = 2x + 1$$
$$y = x^2$$

The following relation is not a function: $x = |y|$. In this case, if $x = 2$, y can be 2 or -2.

Function Notation

Functions are sometimes written using f(x), g(x), or other similar notation. The notation does not change the function in any way. Whether the dependent variable is labeled f(x) or y, and whether the independent variable is labeled x or another variable, treat the functions the same. For example, the notations $h(r)=r^2$, $y=x^2$, or $f(x)=x^2$ can all represent the same function.

Vertical Line Test

Functions can be verified graphically through the vertical line test. Since any function will have only one y–value for every x–value, a vertical line drawn through any x value should hit exactly one y–value and no more. If the vertical line hits more than one point on the graph, then it does not represent a function.

In the two graphs, the relations are shown in grey. The dashed lines are used as part of the vertical line test. In the first graph, no matter what vertical line is drawn, it will only cross the grey line once. Therefore, it is a function. In the second graph, the dashed vertical line crosses the grey line twice. Therefore, for that x–value there are two y–values, making this graph not a function.

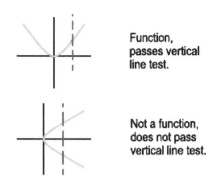

Function, passes vertical line test.

Not a function, does not pass vertical line test.

Domain and Range

The domain is a description of all the inputs or x–values for which the function has a valid output. For example, if we define a function $f = \{(1, 2), (3, 5), (6, 8), (7, 8)\}$; the domain is all valid values of x, which are $\{1, 3, 6, 7\}$.
While the domain covers all valid values of x, the range covers all valid values of y. Using our same example, the range of f is $\{2, 5, 8\}$. Note that we do not repeat any values in the domain or range.

Here is an example graph. As in all graphs, the domain represents all possible x–values. As you look at the curved line in the graph, notice that there will never be a value on the line where x is less than -3. The line keeps curving upwards and approaches the -3, but will never cross it. Therefore, when x is less than -3, the graph will have no outputs. Thus, the domain is $x > -3$.

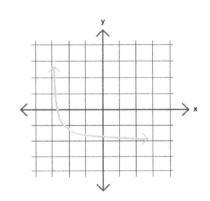

Now, let's look at the range, or all the possible y–values. As x increases, the y–value approaches -2, but it will never reach it. Therefore, the range is anything greater than -2, which can be written as $y > -2$. Another way to write the same thing is that $-2 < y < \infty$. The ∞ symbol is used to represent infinity. So, if you read the statement it says that y is greater than -2 and less than infinity.

Piecewise–Defined Functions

A piecewise–defined function is continuous over certain defined intervals of x. For example, the following is a piecewise–defined function:

$$f(x) = x \qquad \text{if } x < 1$$
$$f(x) = 2x^2 \qquad \text{if } x \geq 1$$

Continuous Functions

A continuous function is one that has no sudden breaks from one value of x to another. For example, $y = 2x$ is a continuous function because there are no breaks as the graph is a straight line. A function that is not continuous is said to be discontinuous. For example, a step function is discontinuous due to the sharp breaks at each step.

Inverses

An inverse function is one that reverses another function. For example, a function $f(x)$ transforms the value $x = 2$ to $f(2) = 5$; then, another function $g(x)$ transforms $x = 5$ back to $g(5) = 2$. Then, $f(x)$ and $g(x)$ are inverses. The inverse of the function $f(x)$ can be written $f^{-1}(x)$.

relation: $\{(0,3), (2,7), (8,9)\}$;
inverse: $\{(3,0), (7,2), (9,8)\}$

A more formal way of denoting inverse functions is: $f(g(x)) = x$ and $g(f(x)) = x$.
To find the inverse of a relation, you switch the inputs and the outputs. You can also think of it as switching the x and y values in each pair.

relation: $y = x + 3$;
inverse: $x = y + 3$,
rearrange $y = x - 3$

RELATIONS & FUNCTIONS PRACTICE

1. **Which function can be used to represent the following situation? A machine takes as an input the length of the side of a square and outputs the perimeter of the square.**

    A. $f(x) = 4x$
    B. $f(x) = x^2$
    C. $f(x) = x + 4$
    D. $f(x) = 2x$

2. **A particular function is defined as follows: Take any negative integer and multiply it by -2. What is the range of the function?**

    A. Negative integers
    B. Positive integers
    C. All real numbers
    D. Positive even integers

3. A particular function is defined as follows: Take any integer greater than zero. If the integer is odd, multiply it by 2. If the integer is even, add 1 and then multiply the result by 2. What is the domain of the function?

   A. the number 2
   B. set of even integers
   C. set of odd integers
   D. set of positive integers

4. Which of the following is not a function?

   A. $y = x^2$
   B. $y = |x|$
   C. $y > x$
   D. $x = y$

5. What is the function shown below?

   A. $x = -1$
   B. $f(x) = -x - 1$
   C. $f(x) = -1$
   D. $x = - f(x)$

x	f(x)
1	-1
2	-1
5	-1
23	-1

6. Which of the following is not a function?

   A.

   B.

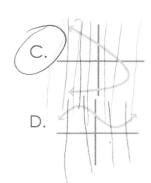

C.

D.

7. What is the function shown to the right?

   A. $f(x) = x \div 2$
   B. $f(x) = 2x$
   C. $f(x) = x - 2$
   D. $f(x) = x + 2$

x	f(x)
4	2
12	10
14	12
36	34

8. Which of the following best represents the data in the table?

x	f(x)
1	1
4	2
9	3
16	4

   A.

   B.

   C.

   D.

9. Why is the horizontal line test not used to determine whether a relation is a function?

    A. It could also be used, we just generally use vertical line test.

    B. All relations are functions, so no test is needed.

    C. Horizontal lines have an undefined slope.

    D. A function can have the same y–value for different x values.

10. What is the range of the function below?

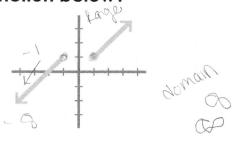

    A. $-\infty < x < \infty$

    B. $-\infty < x < -1$ and $1 \leq x < \infty$

    C. $-\infty < y < \infty$

    D. $-\infty < y < 1$ and $1 < y < \infty$

RELATIONS & FUNCTIONS EXPLANATIONS

1. A   A function takes an input and gives an output. In this case, the input is the length of a side of a square. As you can see in all the answer choices, this input is being represented by x.

Now, the machine is taking the input x, the length of the side of a square, and giving an output of the perimeter of the square.
x represents the input, the side of the length of a square f(x) represents the output, or the perimeter of the square

The perimeter of a square is found by adding the length of all the equal sides. The perimeter of a square with side length x is x+x+x+x = 4x.
f(x) = 4x

2. D   The range of a function is the output, or all possible y values. Let's try a few inputs to see what this function does.

Function: Take any negative integer and multiply it by -2.

x = -1, y = -1(-2) = 2
x = -2, y = -2(-2) = 4
x = -3, y = -3(-2) = 6

Multiplying a negative integer by a negative will always result in a positive. Multiplying any number by an even will always result in an even number. Therefore, multiplying a negative integer by -2 will result in a positive even integer.

Range = Positive Even Integers

3. D   The domain of the function is the set of inputs. The definition of this particular function states: "Take any integer greater than zero."

Therefore, the domain is the set of all positive integers.

4. C   A function is a set of ordered pairs for which every input x has exactly one output y.

Every time you put a value for x in the equations to the right, you get out exactly one y. It does not matter that for different inputs you may get the same output.

$$y = x^2, y = \mid x \mid, \text{ and } x = y$$

In this expression, a single value for x gives a range of y values. Therefore, this is not a function.

$$y > x$$

C is not a function.

5. C   As can be seen in the †–chart, no matter what x value you put in, the function will output -1. This function is written as: $f(x) = -1$.

6. C   From a graph, you can use the vertical line test to determine if the graph represents a function. If you can draw a vertical line through the graph and it crosses more than one point, then it is not a function.

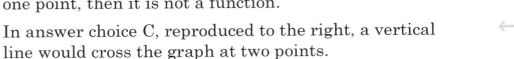

In answer choice C, reproduced to the right, a vertical line would cross the graph at two points.

7. C   The function must work for all possible inputs and outputs. For instance, when x is 4, $f(x)$ is 2 is true for the function $f(x) = x \div 2$ and $f(x) = x - 2$. However, when x is 12 and $f(x)$ is 10, this only works in the function $f(x) = x - 2$.

x	f(x)
4	2
12	10
14	12
36	34

$$f(x) = x - 2, \text{ Answer C}$$

---

8. B   In this table, you see as x increases, the y values also increase but at a slower rate.

x	f(x)
1	1
4	2
9	3
16	4

A: In this graph, x and y increase at a steady rate. This is not represented in the table.

B: In this graph, x and y increase and x increases faster than y. This is represented in the table and is the answer.

C: y increases much faster than x in this graph.

D: this graph has negative values and rises too quickly.

---

9. D   Let's go through each answer.

A: It could also be used, we just generally use vertical line test.
   This is not true. Only the vertical line test is used to determine whether a relation is a function.

B: All relations are functions, so no test is needed.
   This is not true. All functions are relations, but not all relations are functions. Therefore, a test is needed.

C: Horizontal lines have an undefined slope.
   This is not true. A horizontal line has a zero slope. Also, this is irrelevant to testing for functions.

D: A function can have the same y–value for different x values.
   This is true. A function is a set of ordered pairs where for each x value, there is only one y value. Therefore, the vertical line test would find any x value that has two y values. However, it is permissible that different x values produce the same y–value, so a horizontal line test would demonstrate nothing.

---

10. C   The range of a function is all the possible y–values. This graph shows that the function is continuous for all y–values. Therefore, the range is all real numbers from $-\infty$ to ∞.

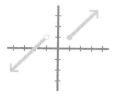

$$-\infty < y < \infty$$

4.3 Solving Equations

Solving for a Variable

Solving an equation means finding the set of values for the variable in the equation that makes the equation true. For example: $x^2 = 25$ is true when $x = 5$ or $x = -5$.

Plugging In

You can see if a number is a solution to an equation by plugging in the value for the variable and seeing if the equation is true. For example, to check if $x = 5$ is a solution to $x^2 = 25$, plug in 5 for x: $5^2 = 25$. This is true, therefore 5 is a solution.

Isolate the Variable

To solve for a variable in an equation, you need to isolate the variable on one side of the equal sign, with all of the numbers on the other side. This can be done by performing the inverse of whatever operations are performed on the variable on both sides of the equation. In the example above, x was squared in the equation. Taking the square root of both sides gives the two possible x values of 5 and -5. Let's go through a few examples.

You want the y to be alone, so perform the inverse to both sides of what is happening to the y. Since 5 is being added to y, subtract 5 from both sides. Simplify and solve for y.

$$y + 5 = 12$$
$$y + 5 - 5 = 12 - 5$$
$$y = 7$$

You want the n to be alone, so perform the inverse operation to both sides of the equation. Since n is being divided by 6, multiply both sides of the equation by 6. Simplify.

$$n/6 = 10$$
$$n/6 \times 6 = 10 \times 6$$
$$n = 60$$

You must perform the inverse operations in the reverse of the order of operations. Perform the inverse operation of the subtraction of 12 which is the addition of 12 to both sides. Next, do the inverse operation of the multiplication of 6, which is the division of 6 on both sides.

$$6x - 12 = 24$$
$$6x - 12 + 12 = 24 + 12$$
$$6x = 36$$
$$6x \div 6 = 36 \div 6$$
$$x = 6$$

After you solve for each variable, you can plug your answer back into the original problem to check your work.

Absolute Value Equations

To solve for variables inside an absolute value sign, remember that the contents could be positive or negative. Therefore, assign both positive and negative values to the other side of the equal sign and solve both equations to get all possible values of the variable. $x = 5$ OR -9, and you can check both in the equation to show that this is true.

> **Example:**
> $| x + 2 | = 7$
> $x + 2 = 7, x = 5$
> OR $x + 2 = -7, x = -9$

SOLVING EQUATIONS PRACTICE

1. **What is the value of n in the following equation?**

   $-3n + 6 = 12$ -6

   $-3n = 6$

   $\frac{-3n}{-3} = \frac{6}{3}$

   $n = -2$

   A. -6
   B. -2
   C. 2
   D. 4

2. **What would you do to both sides of the following equation to solve for y?**

   $\frac{4}{3} \cdot {}^{-3}/_4 \, y = 12 \cdot \frac{4}{3}$

   $y = -16$

   A. Add ¾
   B. Multiply by $^{-3}/_4$
   C. Multiply by $^{-4}/_3$
   D. Divide by $^4/_3$

3. **Which of the following is a possible value for c in the following equation:**

   $| c + 6 | = 14$

   A. 8
   B. -8
   C. 20
   D. -18

4. **Solve for y.**

   $14y + 27 = 6 \; -27$

   -27

   $\begin{array}{r} 27 \\ 6 \\ \hline 21 \end{array}$

   $\frac{14y}{14} = \frac{21}{14}$

   $y =$

   A. $^{33}/_{14}$
   B. $^{-3}/_2$
   C. 3
   D. $26\,^4/_7$

5. **What would you do to both sides of the following equation to solve for m?**

   $^m/_4 - 6 = 10$ $+6$

   $+6$

   $m/4 = 10$

   A. Add 6. Then, divide by 4.
   B. Subract 6. Then, divide by 4.
   C. Multiply by 4. Then, add 6.
   D. Add 6. Then, multiply by 4.

6. **Solve for m.**

   $3\sqrt{} \; m = m^3$

   $\left(1000m^3\right) = 1$

   $\frac{1000}{1000} \quad \frac{1}{1000}$

   $\sqrt[3]{m^3} = \sqrt[3]{\frac{1}{1000}}$

   $m = \frac{1}{10}$

   A. $^1/_{100}$
   B. $^1/_{10}$
   C. 10
   D. 100

   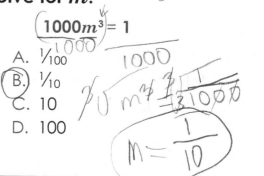

7. $|2y| - 1 = y^2$ $\quad$ *(handwritten: +1, y=1)*

$\quad$ *(handwritten: $|2y| = y^2 + 1$)*

A. -3

B. -1 *(circled)*

C. 0

D. 2

(handwritten work: $2y = y^2 + 1 - 2y$, $\frac{2y}{2y} = y^2 + 1$)

8. Solve for n in the following equation:

$$3n + 4 = 5n + 8$$

A. -2 *(circled)*

B. $\frac{4}{3}$

C. 2

D. -4

9. What is the value of m in the following equation?

$$\frac{(6m + 3)}{3} = 11$$

A. $\frac{5}{3}$

B. 4

C. 5 *(circled)*

D. 6

10. What does r equal in the following equation?

$$8p - 17 = -2r + 7$$

A. -4p + 12 *(circled)*

B. -4p - 24

C. 10p - 24

D. 6p - 10

SOLVING EQUATIONS EXPLANATIONS

1. B $\quad$ Isolate the variable by performing inverse operations to both sides of the equation.

$\qquad$ First subtract 6 from both sides.

$\qquad$ Next, divide both sides by -3

$-3n + 6 = 12$
$-3n + 6 - 6 = 12 - 6$ $-3n = 6$
$-3n \div -3 = 6 \div -3$ $n = -2$

2. C $\quad$ To solve for a variable, you must get that variable alone. In this case, you are multiplying the variable y by $-\frac{3}{4}$. Therefore, you must perform the inverse operation to get y alone.

$-\frac{3}{4} y = 12$

$\qquad$ The inverse operation of multiplying by $-\frac{3}{4}$ is dividing by $-\frac{3}{4}$. Since this isn't one of the answer choices, we have to determine if there is another way that this operation can be written.

$-\frac{3}{4} y = 12$ $-\frac{3}{4} y \times -\frac{4}{3} = 12 \times -\frac{4}{3}$ $y = -16$

$\qquad$ Dividing by $-\frac{3}{4}$ is the same as multiplying by its reciprocal.

$\qquad$ Therefore, multiplying both sides by $-\frac{4}{3}$ will solve for y.

3. A   To solve for a variable inside of an absolute value sign, you have to set up two new equations. The equations will set the contents of the absolute value sign equal to the positive and negative values of the contents of the other side.

$$| c + 6 | = 14$$

Equation 1: $c + 6 = 14$. In this case, $c = 8$
Equation 2: $c + 6 = -14$. In this case, $c = -20$

Answer choice A is one possible value for c.
You could also just plug in each answer choice to see which works.

---

4. B $14y + 27 = 6$

To isolate the variable, first subtract 27 from both sides and then divide by 14.

$$\begin{aligned}
14y + 27 &= 6 \\
14y + 27 - 27 &= 6 - 27 \\
14y &= -21 \\
14y \div 14 &= -21 \div 14 \\
y &= {-21}/{14} \\
y &= {-3}/{2}
\end{aligned}$$

---

5. D   To solve for m, you must isolate the variable.

Addition is the inverse of subtraction; add 6 to both sides of the equation.

$$\begin{aligned}
m/4 - 6 &= 10 \\
m/4 - 6 + 6 &= 10 + 6 \\
m/4 &= 16
\end{aligned}$$

Multiplication is the inverse of division; multiply both sides of the equation by 4.

$$\begin{aligned}
m/4 \times 4 &= 16 \times 4 \\
m &= 64
\end{aligned}$$

Add 6. Then, multiply by 4.

---

6. B   You must isolate m.
First, divide both sides by 1000.

Next, take the cube root of both sides.

$$\begin{aligned}
1000m^3 &= 1 \\
1000m^3 \div 1000 &= 1 \div 1000 \\
m^3 &= 1/1000 \\
m &= 1/10
\end{aligned}$$

---

7. B $|2y| - 1 = y^2$
This equation is difficult to solve directly, therefore plug in the answer choices to see which makes the equation true.

A: -3

$$\begin{aligned}
|2y| - 1 &= y^2 \\
|2(-3)| - 1 &= (-3)^2 \\
|-6| - 1 &= 9 \\
6 - 1 &= 9
\end{aligned}$$

Not true.

B: -1

$$\begin{aligned}
|2y| - 1 &= y^2 \\
|2(-1)| - 1 &= (-1)^2 \\
|-2| - 1 &= 1 \\
2 - 1 &= 1
\end{aligned}$$

True. Answer B.

C: 0	**D:** 2
$\lvert 2y \rvert - 1 = y^2$	$\lvert 2y \rvert - 1 = y^2$
$\lvert 2(0) \rvert - 1 = 0^2$	$\lvert 2(2) \rvert - 1 = 2^2$
$\lvert 0 \rvert - 1 = 0$	$\lvert 4 \rvert - 1 = 4$
$0 - 1 = 0$	$4 - 1 = 4$
Not true.	Not true.

8. A In this case, there are variables on both sides of the equation. Move all terms with the variable to one side of the equation, and then isolate n.

$$3n + 4 = 5n + 8$$

$$3n + 4 - 3n = 5n + 8 - 3n$$
$$4 = 2n + 8$$

Subtract $3n$ from both sides.

Subtract 8 from both sides to isolate n.

$$4 - 8 = 2n + 8 - 8$$
$$-4 = 2n$$

Divide both sides by 2.

$$-4 \div 2 = 2n \div 2$$
$$-2 = n$$

You could also plug in each answer choice.

9. C Isolate the variable by performing inverse operations to both sides of the equation.

$$\frac{6m + 3}{3} \times 3 = 11 \times 3$$
$$6m + 3 = 33$$

Multiply both sides by 3.

Subtract 3 from both sides.

$$6m + 3 - 3 = 33 - 3$$
$$6m = 30$$

Divide both sides by 6.

$$6m \div 6 = 30 \div 6$$
$$m = 5$$

10. A Get the variable r by itself on one side of the equation It may be easier to first rearrange the equation. We are used to seeing the variable we are solving for on the left hand side of the equation.

$$8p - 17 = -2r + 7$$
$$-2r + 7 = 8p - 17$$

Now, let's isolate the variable. Subtract 7 from both sides.

$$-2r + 7 = 8p - 17$$
$$-2r + 7 - 7 = 8p - 17 - 7$$
$$-2r = 8p - 24$$

Now, divide both sides by -2. Remember, you are dividing all terms on both sides.

$$-2r = 8p - 24$$
$$-2r \div -2 = (8p - 24) \div -2$$
$$r = -4p + 12$$

4.4 Inequalities

Definition of Inequalities

An inequality is a statement about the relationship between two values. The greater than >, the less than <, the greater than or equal to ≥, and less than or equal to ≤ signs are used to define the relationship in an inequality. For example, $y \geq 2$ means that the value of y is greater than or equal to 2.

Simplifying Inequalities

It is possible to solve for variables in inequalities in a way that is similar to solving for variables in an equation. Essentially, it is possible to simplify an inequality to generate a range of possible values for a variable. Simplify the inequality in the same way that you would approach an equation. You want to isolate the variable on one side of the inequality symbol.

Example:

$$3x - 6 > 12$$
$$3x - 6 + 6 > 12 + 6$$
$$3x > 18$$
$$3x \div 3 > 18 \div 3$$
$$x > 6$$

Some inequalities are compound, or contain two separate statements. To solve these, follow the same steps of isolating the variable, but make sure to perform the operations on all sides of the inequalities.

Example:

$$-4 \leq x + 8 < 3$$
$$-4 - 8 \leq x + 8 - 8 < 3 - 8$$
$$-12 \leq x < -5$$

Multiplying/Dividing by Negative Numbers

When multiplying or dividing an inequality by a negative number, switch the signs. Therefore, < becomes > and ≤ becomes ≥.

Example:

$-2x > 8$, divide both sides by -2 and flip the sign
$x < -4$

Example:

$$13 \geq -3x + 4 > -2$$
$$9 \geq -3x > -6$$
$$-3 \leq x < 2$$

Graphing Inequalities

The range of values for x can be shown graphically.

$$-4 \leq x < 3$$

A closed circle is used to represent $\leq$ or $\geq$ to show that the end value is included, and an open circle is used for $>$ or $<$ to show that the value is not included.

Absolute Value Inequalities

Just as an equation containing the absolute value of a variable generates two possible values, an inequality with an absolute value generates two ranges of possible values.

$|x| > 2$, Since the absolute value of the variable is greater than a value, this becomes a divergent inequality and can be split into two inequalities with an "or".

$$|x| > 2$$

$|x| > 2$ can be split into: $x > 2$ or $x < -2$. You can try possible values to show that this is true.

$|x| < 2$, Since the absolute value of the variable is less than a value, this becomes a convergent inequality and can be split into two inequalities with an "and"

$$|x| < 2$$

$|x| < 2$ can be made into $x < 2$ and $x > -2$. You can also combine these two statements into one compound inequality: $-2 < x < 2$. Therefore, all values between -2 and 2 will make this statement true.

INEQUALITIES PRACTICE

1. **Write $7 > y$ in words.**

   A. y is greater than 7
   B. 7 is greater than or equal to y
   C. 7 is less than y
   D. 7 is greater than y

2. **Simplify the inequality**

   $3r + 4 > 19$ -4
   $\quad \rightarrow 4$ $3r > 19 - 4$

   A. $r < 5$
   B. $r < 3$ $\dfrac{3r > 15 \div 3}{3}$
   C. $r > 3$ $r > 5$
   D. $r > 5$

3. Which of the following are possible solutions to the following inequality?

$$|y| \leq 3$$

A. -4, 0
B. -2, 4
C. -3, -5
D. 1, -3

4. Which answer shows $x \leq 90$ in light grey on a number line?

A.

B.

C.

D.

5. Solve the inequality:

$$\frac{16 < -2w}{} \quad -8 < w$$

A. $w > -32$
B. $w < -8$
C. $w > -8$
D. $w < 8$

6. Separate $|x| > 19$ into two expressions.

A. $|x| > 19$ and $|x| > -19$
B. $|x| > 19$ or $|x| < -19$
C. $x > 19$ or $x < -19$
D. $x > 19$ and $x < -19$

7. Show $|r| \leq 35$ on a number line.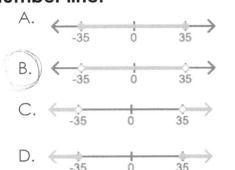

A.
-35 0 35

B.
-35 0 35

C.
-35 0 35

D.
-35 0 35

8. Give a range of possible values for n if:

$$1 + 9n > 100 \quad \text{and}$$
$$210 > (½)\, n$$

A. $100 < n < 210$
B. $11 > n > 420$
C. $11 < n < 105$
D. $11 < n < 420$

9. Solve for n in the following inequality.

$$-(^3/_5)n + 2 \leq 11$$

A. $n \geq -15$
B. $n \geq {}^{-27}/_5$
C. $n \leq {}^{-27}/_5$
D. $n \leq -15$

10. Give a range of possible values for d if $-48 < -3(12d - 4) < 48$.

A. $-1 < d < 1$
B. $^{-5}/_3 < d < ^5/_3$
C. $^5/_3 < d < -1$
D. $-1 < d < ^5/_3$

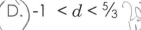

160   *4. Functions & Equations*

INEQUALITIES EXPLANATIONS

1. D > is the greater than sign. The wider side of the sign always points to the larger number. Therefore, 7 is greater than y.

$$7 > y$$

---

2. D ❶ To isolate the variable, the first step is to subtract 4 from all sides.

❷ Then, divide both sides by 3 to solve for r.

❶ $3r + 4 - 4 > 19 - 4$
$3r > 15$

❷ $3r > 15$
$3r \div 3 > 15 \div 3$
$r > 5$

---

3. D Let's examine each answer to determine which answers are possible solutions to the above equation.

$$|y| \leq 3$$

A: -4, 0	**B: -2, 4**	**C: -3, -5**	**D: 1, -3**
Plug in -4 for y, $|-4| \leq 3$, $4 \leq 3$, this is not true.	Plug in 4 for y, $|4| \leq 3$, $4 \leq 3$, this is not true.	Plug in -5 for y, $|-5| \leq 3$, $5 \leq 3$, this is not true.	Plug in 1 for y, $|1| \leq 3$, $1 \leq 3$, this is true. Plug in -3 for y, $|-3| \leq 3$, $3 \leq 3$, this is true.

---

4. A If x is less than or equal to 90, you need to include 90 (by using a closed circle) and an arrow pointing left towards all smaller numbers.

---

5. B You need to get w by itself. You must remember that when dividing or multiplying sides of an inequality by a negative, then the inequality sign must be flipped.

From the original equation: $16 < -2w$, you need to divide both sides by -2 and thus flip the inequality sign:

$$\frac{16}{(-2)} > \frac{-2w}{(-2)}$$

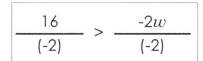

$-8 > w$
Rearranging
$w < -8$.

---

6. C An absolute value inequality statement can be separated into two inequality statements. In this case, $|x| > 19$, since the absolute value is greater than a number, it is split into two divergent inequalities joined by an or statement.

$|x| > 19$
$x > 19$ or $x < -19$

You can pick a few numbers to test out the answer. Make sure that the numbers work in both the original and the newly separated statements.

Example: 20, $|20| > 19$ = True
  20 > 19 or 20 < -19 = True, since it works for the first statement.

Example: -33, $|-33| > 19$ = True, since $|-33| = 33$
  -33 > 19 or -33 < -19 = True, since it works for the second statement.

$$x > 19 \text{ or } x < -19$$

---

7. A Since the absolute value is ≤ 35, this is a convergent inequality. The two statements that the inequality can be broken into are:

$$r \leq 35 \text{ and } r \geq -35$$

The circles should be closed since it is ≤ not <.

Answer A shows this on a number line.

---

8. D Solve both inequalities and then combine them.

Now we must combine the two inequalities. The first one, $n > 11$, states that n is greater than 11. The second one, $420 > n$, states that n is less than 420. We can combine this into one statement. $11 < n < 420$

$$1 + 9n > 100$$
$$9n > 99$$
$$n > 11$$

$$210 > (\tfrac{1}{2})n$$
$$420 > n$$

---

9. A Isolate the variable, just as you would if the equation was an equality.

$$-(\tfrac{3}{5})n + 2 \leq 11$$

Subtract 2 from both sides.

$$-(\tfrac{3}{5})n + 2 - 2 \leq 11 - 2$$
$$-(\tfrac{3}{5})n \leq 9$$

Now, multiply both sides by $-\tfrac{5}{3}$. When you multiply both sides of an inequality by a negative, you must flip the inequality sign.

$$-(\tfrac{3}{5})n \leq 9$$
$$-(\tfrac{3}{5})n \times -\tfrac{5}{3} \geq 9 \times -\tfrac{5}{3}$$
$$n \geq -15$$

---

10. D Solve for d by isolating the variable. Make sure what is done to the middle is done to all three sides of the inequality. Also, remember that when you multiply or divide by a negative, all signs flip.

$$-48 < -3(12d - 4) < 48$$

Divide all sides by -3 and flip the signs.

$$16 > 12d - 4 > -16$$

Add 4 to all sides.

$$20 > 12d > -12$$

Divide by 12 on all sides.

$$\tfrac{20}{12} > d > -1$$

Reduce the fraction and rearrange the inequality.

$$-1 < d < \tfrac{5}{3}$$

4.5   Ratios, Proportions, Variations

Written Forms of Ratios

A ratio is a means of comparing one expression containing numbers or variables to another. In words, ratios are written using "to". For example, in a group of animals containing 3 fish and 2 parakeets, the ratio of fish to parakeets is 3 to 2. This same ratio can be written as 3:2 or $\frac{3}{2}$. Mathematically, the most useful expression of a ratio is a fraction.

Ratios as rates of change

In most practical applications, ratios are used to indicate rates of change — the rate at which one variable changes with respect to another. For example, if a student reads 2 pages per minute, then every minute that goes by will increase the number of pages by 2. This can be written: $\frac{2 \text{ pages}}{1 \text{ min}}$.

Cross Multiplication

You can use cross–multiplication to easily solve for variables. When cross–multiplying, you create a new equation. Take the numerator of one side and multiply it by the denominator of the other side and set that equal to the denominator of the first side times the numerator of the second side.

For example, solve $\frac{3}{5} = \frac{x}{20}$

First, cross-multiply and get a new equation: $3(20) = 5x$.

Then, solve for x.

$$\frac{a}{b} = \frac{c}{d}$$
$$\frac{a}{b} \diagdown \frac{c}{d}$$
$$ad = bc$$

$$\frac{3}{5} = \frac{x}{20}$$
$$3(20) = 5(x)$$
$$60 = 5x$$
$$12 = x$$

Direct Variation

If two variables are in direct variation, as one increases the other increases. Rate of change is a case of direct variation, where the value of a variable is equal to a constant multiplied by another variable. The constant is the rate of change. Variable = constant times another variable, $y = kx$, where k is the constant.

In the above example, number of pages = 2 × number of minutes. Therefore, as the number of minutes increases, the number of pages goes up by a factor of 2.

Indirect Variation

If two variables vary indirectly, as one increases the other decreases. If two variables vary indirectly, then they are inversely proportional. If y and x vary indirectly, then:

$$y = \text{constant}/x \quad \text{or} \quad y = k/x, \text{ where } k \text{ is the constant}$$

For example, volume and pressure vary indirectly for a gas. What happens to the pressure of gas when you double its volume?
If you double the volume then V becomes 2V and $k/2V = P/2$, so the pressure is halved.

$$\text{pressure} = \text{constant}/\text{volume}$$
$$P = k/V$$

Proportions

By looking at indirect and direct variation as two possible variable relationships, you have been introduced to the concept of proportionality. Generally, a proportion is two equal ratios. For example, if the ratio of red to blue marbles in a bag is $3/5$ and the bag has 20 blue marbles, you can determine the number of red marbles.

$$\frac{\text{red}}{\text{blue}} = \frac{3}{5} = \frac{x}{20}$$

x must equal 12 for the ratios to be equal, therefore there are 12 red marbles.

RATIOS, PROPORTIONS, VARIATIONS PRACTICE

1. **If a bag contains only red and blue marbles and the ratio of red marbles to blue marbles is 3 to 5, what fraction of the bag is blue marbles?**
   A. $3/5$
   B. $5/3$
   C. $5/8$
   D. $3/8$

2. **What would 2 to 3 represent for a bag containing only 12 blue marbles and 8 red marbles?**

   A. Fraction of blue marbles in bag
   B. Fraction of red marbles in bag
   C. Ratio of red to blue marbles
   D. Ratio of blue to red marbles

3. **If Georgia bakes 8 cakes for every 4 hour shift she works, how many hours will it take her to bake 96 cakes?**
   A. 24 hours
   B. 48 hours
   C. 96 hours
   D. 192 hours

4. If the pressure and volume of a gas vary indirectly, what will happen to the pressure when the volume quadruples?
    A. Quadruples
    B. Remain same
    C. Decrease by a factor of 4
    D. Not enough information

5. If the height of Plant A is always $\frac{4}{3}$ the height of Plant B, how tall is Plant A when Plant B is 9 feet tall?
    A. $^{27}/_4$ feet
    B. 9 feet
    C. 10 feet
    D. 12 feet

6. For every 25 pairs of shoes he has, Gary has 60 complete outfits. Assuming this proportion stays the same, how many outfits could he make with only 10 pairs of shoes?
    A. 18
    B. 20
    C. 22
    D. 24

7. In which of the following does y vary inversely with x?
    I. $xy = 6$
    II. $y = (\frac{1}{2})x$
    III. $y = \frac{4}{x}$
    A. III only
    B. I and III
    C. II and III
    D. I, II, and III

8. If Anita needs 24 lbs of mix for every 120 gallons of concrete she mixes, how many pounds of mix will she need for a driveway that will require 35 gallons of concrete?
    A. 5
    B. 7
    C. 131
    D. 175

9. If y is directly proportional to x, and is y is 20 when x is 10, what is x when y is 5?
    A. 2.5
    B. 10
    C. 20
    D. 40

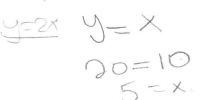

10. The ratio of engineering majors to humanities majors at a small community college is 4 to 7. If 10 more students join in the middle of the year and they are all engineering majors, then the ratio of engineering to total students will then be 5 to 12. If e represents the number of engineering majors at the start of the year and h the number of humanities majors, what equation represents the new ratio?
    A. $^{(e + 10)}/_h = \frac{4}{7}$
    B. $^{(e + 10)}/_{(h + 10)} = \frac{5}{12}$
    C. $^{(e + 10)}/_h = \frac{9}{19}$
    D. $^{(e + 10)}/_{(e + h + 10)} = \frac{5}{12}$

RATIOS, PROPORTIONS, VARIATIONS EXPLANATIONS

1. C If the ratio of red to blue is 3 to 5, that means for every 3 red in the bag there are 5 blue, making a total of 8 marbles for each of those groups. Therefore, the ratio of blue to total is 5 to 8. So, the fraction of blue marbles in the bag is: ⅝.

2. C The ratio of red to blue marbles is 8 to 12. You can reduce this since both are divisible by 4, so that the ratio of red to blue marbles is 2 to 3.

3. B Set up the ratio between cakes and hours it takes to build.

$$\frac{8 \text{ cakes}}{4 \text{ hours}} = \frac{96 \text{ cakes}}{n \text{ hours}}$$

Cross multiply to solve for n

$$8n = 96(4)$$
$$n = 48$$
48 hours to make 96 cakes.

4. C If pressure and volume vary indirectly, that means that as one increases the other will decrease. To relate them as an equation:
Pressure = k/volume where k is a constant
Therefore, if volume quadruples, then pressure will decrease by a factor of 4, as can be seen in the following.

$$\frac{\text{New}}{\text{Pressure}} = \frac{k}{4 \times \text{volume}} = \frac{1}{4} \times \frac{k}{\text{volume}} = \frac{1}{4} \times \frac{\text{Old}}{\text{Pressure}}$$

Therefore, new pressure is one fourth of old pressure which means it decreases by a factor of 4.

5. D This is a case of direct variation with a proportionality constant of ⅓.

Plant A's height = ⅓ × Plant B's height
If Plant B is 9 feet, plug it into above formula to find Plant A's height.

Plant A = ⅓ × 9 feet = 12 feet

6. D Set up a proportion between pairs of shoes and complete outfits.

$$\frac{25 \text{ pairs}}{60 \text{ outfits}} = \frac{10 \text{ pairs}}{n \text{ outfits}}$$

Cross multiply and then solve.

$$25n = 60(10)$$
$$n = {}^{600}\!/_{25} = 24 \text{ outfits}$$

7. B Let's look at each option to see which ones y varies inversely with x.

I. $xy = 6$

Let's rearrange the equation to isolate y. Divide both sides by x.

$$xy \div x = 6 \div x$$
$$y = \frac{6}{x}$$

As you can see from the equation, as x increases, y decreases. y varies inversely with x in I.

You could also try plugging in numbers and see what happens.

Try plugging in $x = 1$. When $x = 1$, $y = 6$.
Try plugging in $x = 3$. When $x = 3$, $y = 2$.
Try plugging in $x = 6$. When $x = 6$, $y = 1$.

Note, when x got bigger, y got smaller. So, inverse relationship.

II. $y = (\frac{1}{2})x$

As x increases, so does y. For instance, when $x = 2$, $y = 1$.
When $x = 4$, $y = 2$. Therefore, x and y are directly proportional.

Try plugging in $x = 4$. When $x = 4$, $y = 2$.
Try plugging in $x = 10$. When $x = 10$, $y = 5$.
Try plugging in $x = 100$. When $x = 100$, $y = 50$.

As x gets bigger, y gets bigger. So they are directly proportional.

III. $y = \frac{4}{x}$

This is already in the form of an equation where the two variables vary inversely. As x increases, y decreases.

Try plugging in $x = 1$. When $x = 1$, $y = 4$.
Try plugging in $x = 4$. When $x = 4$, $y = 1$.
Try plugging in $x = 8$. When $x = 8$, $y = \frac{1}{2}$.

So, as x gets bigger, y gets smaller. Inverse relationship.

I and III vary inversely. Answer B

---

8. B Set up the proportion between mix and concrete.

$$\frac{24 \text{ lbs mix}}{120 \text{ gal concrete}} = \frac{n \text{ lbs}}{35 \text{ gal}}$$

Cross multiply and then solve for n.

$$120n = 24(35)$$
$$120n = 840$$
$$n = 7$$

9. A   Set up an equation between x and y. If y is directly proportional to x, the equation can be written:

$$y = kx, \text{ where } k \text{ is the proportionality constant}$$

❶ Given the fact that y is 20 when x is 10, let's solve for k. Plug in x and y into the equation.

❷ Now, plug in $y = 5$, to solve for x.

❶
$$y = kx$$
$$20 = 10\,k$$
$$k = 2$$

❷
$$y = 2x$$
$$5 = 2x$$
$$x = 2.5$$

---

10. D   The question asks you to set up the ratio for the current situation. The problem states: "the ratio of engineering to total students will then be 5 to 12."

Alright, so let's look at each piece of this ratio problem.

The first thing we must determine is the engineering students. We know that we started with e students that were in the engineering majors. Then, 10 students joined. Therefore, the engineering students is equal to e + 10.

Next part of this ratio is the total students. We started with e engineering students and h humaniities students and then added 10 more students. Therefore, the total becomes e + h + 10.

We know that the ratio of engineering students to total students is now 5 to 12.

$$(e + 10)/(e + h + 10) = 5/12$$

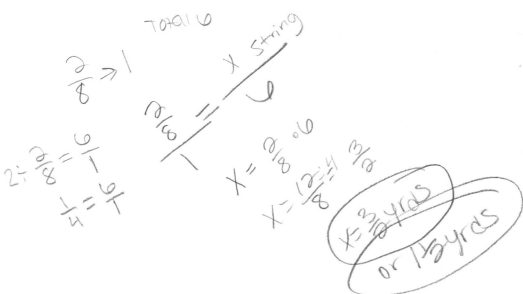

4.6 Chapter Review

1. A tree that is 18 feet tall casts a shadow that is 8 feet long. If the height of an object and the length of its shadow is proportionate, how long of a shadow will a man that is 6 feet tall cast?
   - A. 2 ft
   - B. 2 ⅓ ft
   - C. 2 ⅔ ft
   - D. 3 ft

2. Roger's age is 2 less than 5 times Luke's age. If Luke's age equals n, what expression represents Roger's age?
   - A. $2 - 5n$
   - B. $5n \div 2$
   - C. $3n$
   - D. $5n - 2$

   $= n$

   $2 - 5n$

3. The sum of 4 times a number y and 21 is greater than 45 and less than 73. What are all possible values for that number?
   - A. $6 < y < 13$
   - B. $y > 6$ or $y < 13$
   - C. 8, 9, and 10
   - D. $y > 6$

4. What does r equal in the following equation?

   $$\frac{(2r - 12)}{6} = 4$$

   - A. 3
   - B. 12
   - C. 18
   - D. 48

5. If $3y - 2 = 7$, what does $(⅔) y + 5$ equal?
   - A. $11⅓$
   - B. 11
   - C. 7
   - D. $8 ⅔$

6. Jennifer types at an average rate of 12 pages per hour. At that rate, how long will it take Jennifer to type 100 pages?
   - A. 8 hours and 3 minutes
   - B. 8 hours and 4 minutes
   - C. 8 hours and 20 minutes
   - D. 8 hours and 33 ⅓ minutes

7. What is the sum of the two missing values in the table?
   - A. 31
   - B. 32
   - C. 33
   - D. 34

x	y
5	8
7	10
?	13
12	15
17	20
21	?

8. If the temperature in degrees Fahrenheit is F, then the temperature in degrees Celsius is $(⅝)(F - 32)$. If the Fahrenheit

temperature increases from 50° to 68°, then what is the corresponding increase in the Celsius temperature?

    A. 8°
    B. 10°
    C. 18°
    D. 20°

9. The length of a rectangle is 5 feet less than 3 times the width. If the perimeter must be less than 86 feet, and the dimensions of the rectangle are all whole numbers of feet, what is the largest possible width for the rectangle?

    A. 10 ft
    B. 11 ft
    C. 12 ft
    D. 13 ft

10. Write the following equation with variables.

    The sum of the opposite of a number and 7 is equal to the quotient of the number and 3.

    A. $-7n = n - 3$
    B. $-n + 7 = n/3$
    C. $1/n + 7 = n/3$
    D. $-7 + n = 3n$

11. What is the domain of the function below?

$$y = \sqrt{x}$$

    A. All reals.
    B. $x \geq 0$
    C. $x > 0$
    D. Positive Integers

12. Identify the pattern shown by the following numbers:

    -2.1, -3.2, -4.3, -5.4, -6.5

    A. $y = 0.1x - 2$
    B. $y = -2.1x + 1$
    C. $y = -x^2 - 1.1$
    D. $y = -1.1x - 1$

13. The ratio of the number of marbles Mike has to the number David has is 5 to 8. If David has 12 more marbles than Mike, how many marbles does Mike have?

    A. 7 marbles
    B. 9 marbles
    C. 20 marbles
    D. 28 marbles

14. What are all possible values for y in the following equation:

$$| y - 12 | = | -15 |$$

    A. -3
    B. 27
    C. 30
    D. -3 or 27

15. Here is part of Pascal's triangle, a famous mathematical pattern. Every number is the sum of the numbers directly above it. What equation equals the sum of the numbers in row, r?

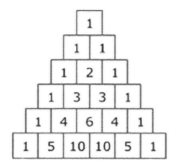

- A. 2(r - 1)
- B. $r^2 - r$
- C. $2^{(r-1)}$
- D. r^2

16. If a is inversely proportional to b and a is 16 when b is 4, what does b equal when a is 8?

- A. 2
- B. 8
- C. 16
- D. 64

17. What is the range of possible values for m if
$-14 \leq 2(-3m + 5) < 28$?

- A. $-3 < m \leq 4$
- B. $-3 > m \geq 4$
- C. $3 \leq m < -4$
- D. $-3 \geq m > 4$

18. Phone plan T costs \$25/month plus \$0.10/minute and plan R is \$10/month plus \$0.25/minute. How many minutes of talking in one month would cost the same on either plan?

- A. 10 minutes
- B. 25 minutes
- C. 100 minutes
- D. 250 minutes

19. Which of the following graphs represents the inequality:

$$-3n + 5 < -4$$

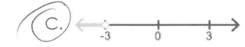

- A.
- B.
- C.
- D.

20. In the local college, the ratio of engineering majors to non–engineering majors is 2 to 7. If there are 1260 students in the whole school and all students fall under one of those categories, how many non–engineering majors are at the school?

- A. 140
- B. 180
- C. 630
- D. 980

CHAPTER REVIEW EXPLANATIONS

1. C Draw a picture to help you understand the problem.

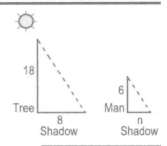

The sun shines on both the tree and the man at the same angle. This means that the triangles formed by the tree, the shadow, and the light will be similar to the triangle formed with the man, his shadow, and the light.

Use a proportion to solve for the shadow length.

$$^6\!/_{18} = {}^n\!/_8$$

Cross multiply to solve.

$$18n = 6(8)$$
$$n = {}^{48}\!/_{18}$$
$$n = 2\,{}^2\!/_3 \text{ feet}$$

2. D Take the words and translate them into an expression.
Roger's age is 2 less than 5 times Luke's age
Roger's age = 2 less than 5 times Luke's age
Roger's age = 2 less than 5 times n
Roger's age = 2 less than $5n$
Roger's age = $5n - 2$

3. A Take the words and translate them into an inequality.

The sum of 4 times a number and 21 is greater than 45 | $4y + 21 > 45$

The sum of 4 times a number and 21... less than 73 | $4y + 21 < 73$

Combine the two inequalities into one statement. | $4y + 21 > 45$ and $4y + 21 < 73$
$45 < 4y + 21 < 73$

Now, solve by isolating the variable. | $45 < 4y + 21 < 73$

Subtract 21 from all sides. | $24 < 4y < 52$

Divide by 4 on all sides | $6 < y < 13$

4. C **❶** Isolate the variable.

❷ Multiply both sides by 6.

❸ Add 12 to both sides.

❹ Divide both sides by 2.

❶ $\dfrac{(2r - 12)}{6} = 4$

❷ $\dfrac{(2r - 12)}{6} \times 6 = 4 \times 6$
$2r - 12 = 24$

❸ $2r - 12 + 12 = 24 + 12$
$2r = 36$

❹ $2r \div 2 = 36 \div 2$
$r = 18$

5. C This problem has multiple steps.

❶ First, solve the first equation for y.

❷ Plug into the second expression.

$$\begin{array}{l} ❶\ 3y - 2 = 7 \\ 3y - 2 + 2 = 7 + 2 \\ 3y = 9 \\ 3y \div 3 = 9 \div 3 \\ y = 3 \end{array}$$

$$\begin{array}{l} ❷\ (\tfrac{2}{3})y + 5 \\ = (\tfrac{2}{3})(3) + 5 \\ = 2 + 5 \\ = 7 \end{array}$$

---

6. C If Jennifer types 12 pages per hour, set up a proportion to find out how long it will take her to type 100 pages.

$$\frac{12 \text{ pages}}{1 \text{ hour}} = \frac{100 \text{ pages}}{y \text{ hours}}$$

$$\begin{array}{l} 12y = 100 \\ y = {}^{100}\!/_{12} = 8\tfrac{1}{3} \\ 8\tfrac{1}{3} \text{ hours} \end{array}$$

Now, cross multiply to solve this proportion.

All the answer choices have minutes, so let's convert the $\tfrac{1}{3}$ hour to minutes.

$$\frac{1}{3} \text{ hour} \times \frac{60 \text{ minutes}}{1 \text{ hour}} = 20 \text{ minutes}$$

8 hours 20 minutes, Answer C

---

7. D First, figure out the pattern between x and y. Then, determine the missing values, and find their sum.

The y value is always 3 greater than the x value; you can write this as:

$$y = x + 3$$

x	y
5	8
7	10
?	13
12	15
17	20
21	?

The first question mark represents 3 less than 13, which is 10.
The second question mark represents 3 more than 21, which is 24.

$$\text{Sum} = 10 + 24 = 34$$

---

8. B The problem gave you the formula for converting temperatures in Fahrenheit to Celsius.

$$C = (\tfrac{5}{9})(F - 32)$$

To solve this problem, find the corresponding Celsius temperatures, and then subtract.

50° Fahrenheit:
$C = (\tfrac{5}{9})(50 - 32)$
$= (\tfrac{5}{9})(18)$
$= 10$

68° Fahrenheit:
$C = (\tfrac{5}{9})(68 - 32)$
$= (\tfrac{5}{9})(36)$
$= 20$

Therefore, the corresponding increase in Celsius temperature is from 10 to 20, which is an increase of 10 degrees. Answer B.

---

9. B Let the width of the rectangle be w. Then, set up an equation for the length. "The length of a rectangle is 5 feet less than 3 times the width"

length = $3w - 5$

The perimeter is the length + length + width + width

Perimeter = $3w - 5 + 3w - 5 + w + w$
Perimeter = $8w - 10$

The perimeter must be less than 86 feet

If the width must be a whole number and is less than 12 ft, than the largest possible width is 11 ft.

$8w - 10 < 86$
$8w < 96$
$w < 12$

10. B Take the words and translate the expression into an equation.

❶ "The sum of the opposite of a number and 7"
Sum is the result of addition. Opposite of a number is -1 times that number; for example, the opposite of 3 is -3.
Let n represent the number

❶ $-n + 7$

❷ "is equal to the quotient of the number and 3."
Quotient is the result of division which can be written as a fraction.

❷ $= {}^n/_3$
$-n + 7 = {}^n/_3$

11. B The domain of a function is all the possible inputs or all possible x values. You can not take the square root of a negative number; therefore, x cannot be negative. Eliminate Answer choice A.

x does not have to be just an integer. For example, if $x = \frac{1}{4}$, then $y = \frac{1}{2}$. Eliminate Answer D.

x could equal 0. If so, $y = 0$. Therefore, eliminate answer C.

$x \geq 0$

x can be any real number, greater than or equal to 0.

12. D Plug in values for each answer choice, and see which exhibits the pattern:

-2.1, -3.2, -4.3, -5.4, -6.5
For $x = 1$, $y = -2.1$
For $x = 2$, $y = -3.2$
etc.

A: $y = 0.1x - 2$ $x = 1$ $y = 0.1(1) - 2 = -1.9$ Not true.	**B:** $y = -2.1x + 1$ $x = 1$ $y = -2.1(1) + 1 = -3.1$ Not true.
C: $y = -x^2 - 1.1$ $x = 1$ $y = -1^2 - 1.1 = -2.1$ $x = 2$ $y = -2^2 - 1.1 = -5.1$ Not true.	**D:** $y = -1.1x - 1$ $x = 1$ $y = -1.1(1) - 1 = -2.1$ $x = 2$ $y = -1.1(2) - 1 = -3.2$ True

13. C *Method 1:* The ratio of marbles that Mike has to marbles that David has is 5 to 8. Therefore, the ratio of the difference in the number of marbles to the marbles that Mike has is 3 to 5.

Set up a proportion knowing that the difference in the number of marbles is 12. Also, let m represent the number of marbles that Mike has.

Difference in number of marbles to Marbles Mike has

$$= 3 \text{ to } 5 = 12 \text{ to } m$$
$$= \tfrac{3}{5} = \tfrac{12}{m}$$

Cross multiply and solve.

$$3m = 60$$
$$m = 20$$

Mike has 20 marbles.

Method 2: Another way to solve this problem is to write out the possible numbers of marbles that each person has until you find a set of values with a difference of twelve. Assuming that each person can only have a whole number of marbles, the first few possibilities are:

5 & 8, 10 & 16, 15 & 24, and 20 & 32.

When David has 32 marbles and Mike has 20, David will have 12 more marbles than Mike.

Method 3: You can always plug in the answers to solve problems of this type.

A: If Mike has 7, David has 7+12 = 19.
   Ratio of 7 to 19 does not equal 5 to 8.
B: If Mike has 9, David has 9+12 = 21.
   Ratio of 7 to 19 does not equal 5 to 8.
C: If Mike has 20, David has 20+12 = 32.
   Ratio of 20 to 32 equals 5 to 8.
D: If Mike has 28, David has 28+12 = 40.
   Ratio of 28 to 40 does not equal 5 to 8.

14. D Simplifying the right side of the equation, $| y - 12 | = | \text{-}15 |$ is the same as $| y - 12 | = 15$.

To solve $| y - 12 | = 15$, set up two equations.

Equation 1: $y - 12 = 15$. In this case, $y = 27$

Equation 2: $y - 12 = \text{-}15$. In this case, $y = \text{-}3$.

For questions like this one, you can also plug in each answer choice to see which is true.

15. C Let's figure out the sum for the rows and determine the pattern.
Row 1, r = 1, sum = 1
Row 2, r = 2, sum = 1 + 1 = 2
Row 3, r = 3, sum = 1 + 2 + 1 = 4
Row 4, r = 4, sum = 1 + 3 + 3 + 1 = 8
Row 5, r = 5, sum = 1 + 4 + 6 + 4 + 1 = 16

We can see a pattern developing. For each new row, the sum is multiplied by 2. Let' confirm by checking if row 6 has a sum of 16 x 2 = 32.
Row 6, r = 6, sum = 1 + 5 + 10 + 10 + 5 + 1 = 32

Now that we know the pattern, we have to figure out the equation that represents the pattern. We know as r goes up by 1, the sum is multiplied by 2. Therefore, we want 2 raised to a certain power. When r = 1, the sum is 1, which is 20. The pattern is $2^{(r-1)}$. You can confirm by checking a different row. When r = 5, $2^{(5-1)} = 2^4 = 16$.

If you were stuck in figuring out the pattern, you could always plug in the values for the different rows into the equations and eliminate any choices that don't work for all the rows.

---

16. B Remember that if a and b are inversely proportional, if a decreases b increases and vice versa. So, we know that a is going from 16 to 8, so b must be increasing.

If a is inversely proportional to b, then you can set up an equation between them:

$a = {}^k/_b$ where k is a constant.

❶ We know that $a = 16$ when $b = 4$, and so we can solve for k.

❷ Now, plug in $a = 8$, to solve for b.

❶
$$a = {}^k/_b$$
$$16 = {}^k/_4$$
$$k = 64$$
$$a = {}^{64}/_b$$

❷
$$a = {}^{64}/_b$$
$$8 = {}^{64}/_b$$
$$b = {}^{64}/_8$$
$$b = 8$$

---

17. A Isolate the variable by performing inverse operations to all sides of the inequality.

$$-14 \leq 2(-3m + 5) < 28$$

Distribute

$$-14 \leq -6m + 10 < 28$$

Subtract 10 from all sides

$$-24 \leq -6m < 18$$

Divide all sides by -6. When dividing by a negative, you must flip all the inequality signs.

$$4 \geq m > -3$$

Rearrange

$$-3 < m \leq 4$$

18. C The unknown variable in this is case is the number of minutes of talking. Let's call that m.

Set the costs equal to solve for m, the number of minutes.

Cost for Plan T: $\$25 + 0.10m$
Cost for Plan R: $\$10 + 0.25m$

$25 + 0.10m = 10 + 0.25m$
$15 + 0.10m = 0.25m$
$15 = 0.15m$
$100 = m$
100 minutes

---

19. A $-3n + 5 < -4$

Subtract 5 from both sides.

Divide by -3. When dividing by a negative, flip the inequality sign.

$-3n + 5 < -4$
$-3n < -9$
$n > 3$

To determine which graph correctly represents the equation, note that the inequality is >, so the circle on the 3 should be open. Also, n is greater than 3, so all values that are larger than 3 should be shaded.

---

20. D The ratio of engineering majors to non–engineering majors is 2 to 7. Therefore, the ratio of engineering to non–engineering to total students is 2 to 7 to 9. Thus, the ratio of non-engineering majors to total students is 7 to 9.

If there are 1260 students in the school, set up a proportion with n representing the number of non–engineering majors at the school.

non–eng majors to total = 7 to 9 = n to 1260

Cross multiply to solve.

$7/9 = n/1260$

$1260(7) = 9n$
$8820 = 9n$
$n = 980$

Chapter 5:
Measurement

Lessons

5.1   Circles

Points and Circles

A circle is a set of points equidistant (the same distance) from a center point. Imagine picking a point on the *x–y* coordinate plane. If you were to mark every possible point 4 units away from the center point, you would create a continuous line around that point called a circle.

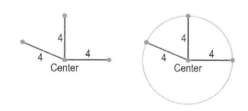

Circle Measurements

An important measurement for a circle is its radius (r). The radius is the distance between the center of a circle and any point on the circle itself. In the previous example, each point was 4 units from the center. Therefore, the circle's radius is 4.

The diameter of a circle is any line beginning at one point on a circle, passing through the center, and ending at another point on the circle. The diameter of a circle is always twice as long as its radius. When working with circles, you will often need to use the diameter to find the radius so that you can calculate perimeter, arc length, or area.

In the diagram, the radius is 4 and the diameter is 8.

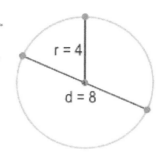

Circumference and Area

The number pi, also represented by the Greek letter π, equals approximately 3.14. Pi is an irrational number (an unending decimal), but 3.14 is accurate enough for most purposes. Pi gives the ratio of a circle's perimeter, which is the distance around the outside of the circle, to its diameter (d). The perimeter of a circle is also called its circumference (c). The equation can be expressed as ❶. The last of these equations probably looks most familiar to you, but keep in mind that it can be manipulated to generate the other two.

❶
$$\pi = {}^{c}/_{d}$$
$$c = \pi d$$
$$c = 2\pi r$$

The area of a circle is also calculated using pi. The formula is ❷. So, for a circle of radius 7 yards, the area is 49π square yards.

❷ $\text{Area} = \pi \times r \times r = \pi r^2$

Arcs and Wedges

There are 360 degrees in a circle. You can use this information to calculate the distance around a section of the circle, known as arc length. Formulate the angle of the arc as a fraction of 360, and then multiply that fraction by the perimeter of the whole circle. The equation is ❶.

❶ $\text{arc length} = \left({}^{\text{degrees}}/_{360}\right) \times 2\pi r$

For example, suppose you want to find the arc length around 30 degrees of a circle with a radius of 3 inches. $^{30}/_{360}$ is equal to $^{1}/_{12}$, so plug this into the formula to simplify your calculations ❷.

❷ $\text{arc length} = \left(^{1}/_{12}\right) 2\pi \times 3 = {}^{\pi}/_{2} \approx 1.57 \text{ inches}$

Just as arc length is a fraction of the perimeter of a circle, a wedge is a fraction of the area of a circle. The formula is analogous to that for arc length— it involves multiplying the angle of the arc in fractional form by the area of the entire circle. The formula is ❸.

❸ Area of a wedge = $(\text{degrees}/360) \times \pi \times r^2$

❹ $(50/360) \times \pi \times 16 = 20/9 \times \pi$ = 6.98 square meters

To find the area of 50 degrees of a circle with a 4–meter radius, plug the values into the formula ❹.

Tangents and Chords

Two other types of lines are commonly seen in problems involving circles.

Chords are lines that begin at one point on the circle and end at another but do not necessarily pass through the center. The diameter is the longest possible chord in a circle.

Tangents are lines on the outside of a circle that touch the circle at only one point.

Tangents and chords are useful for calculating radii of circles when they are part of a known shape (such as a triangle) or for finding the measure of angles within the circle (see "Angles and Parallel Lines"). When chords are present in a test problem, look for a familiar shape that might help you calculate the length of the radius.

CIRCLES PRACTICE

1. **Find the radius of the following circle:**

   A. 30
   B. 15
   C. 7.5
   D. 225

2. **Find the perimeter of the following circle:**

   A. 46π
   B. 23π
   C. 46
   D. 529π

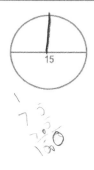

3. In the circle, which is the longest?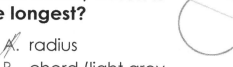

    A. radius

    B. chord (light grey line in image)

    C. diameter

    D. Not enough information

4. What is the area of a circle with a diameter of 20?

    A. 20π

    B. 40π

    C. 100π

    D. 400π

5. The perimeter of Circle A below is how many times the perimeter of Circle B below?

    A. ½

    B. 2

    C. 4

    D. ¹⁵⁄₄

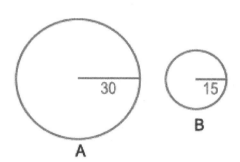

6. The area of Circle A above is how many times the area of Circle B above?

A. 2

B. 4

C. 8

D. 15

7. A dart board has a red bull's eye that is 6 inches in diameter. No other part of the dartboard is red. If the dart board is 30 inches in diameter, what area of the dartboard is not red?

    A. 576π sq. in.

    B. 396π sq. in.

    C. 216π sq. in.

    D. 144π sq. in.

8. What is the length of the light grey line that outlines the wedge of the circle below <u>if its radius is 4 meters</u>?

    A. 8 + π

    B. 2π

    C. 4 + 2π

    D. 8 + 8π

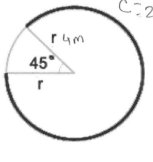

9. If the radius of the circle is 4 meters, what is the area of the wedge outlined in light grey?

    A. 2π sq. m

    B. 4π sq. m

    C. 8π sq. m

    D. 16π sq. m

10. A circular track is 63 meters long. Approximately how long is the diameter of the circle formed by the track?

A. 8m
B. 15m
C. 20m
D. 30m

CIRCLES EXPLANATIONS

1. C   The circle has a diameter of length 15. The radius is one half of that, or 7.5 units.

2. A   Remember that the perimeter of the circle is the same as the circumference of the circle.
Circumference = 2 × pi × r

Circumference =
2 × π × 23 = 46π

3. C   The radius of a circle is half the length of the diameter. Therefore, eliminate answer A.

A chord is a line that goes from one point on a circle to another point. The diameter of a circle is the longest possible chord since it goes from a point to the farthest point from it. Therefore, the diameter will be longer than the chord in the image.

4. C   Area of a circle is found by multiplying π × radius². Radius = half of diameter = 10

Area = π × radius²
= π × 10²
= 100π

5. B   The radius of Circle A is 30 and the radius of Circle B is 15. Let's find the perimeter of each and then create a ratio.

Perimeter or circumference of Circle A = 2 × π × r = 2 × π × 30 = 60π
Perimeter or circumference of Circle B = 2 × π × r = 2 × π × 15 = 30π

Now create a ratio with the perimeter of Circle A over the perimeter of Circle B.

$60π/30π = 2$

6. B   The radius of Circle A is 30 and the radius of Circle B is 15. Let's find the area of each and then create a ratio.

Area of Circle A = π × r² = π × 30² = 900π
Area of Circle B = π × r² = π × 15² = 225π

Now divide the area of Circle A by the area of Circle B.

900π ÷ 225π = 4

7. C Find the area of the dartboard and subtract the area of the bullseye to find the area that is not red.

Area of dartboard = $\pi 15^2 = 225\pi$
Area of bullseye = $\pi 3^2 = 9\pi$
Area of dartboard – area of bullseye = $(225 - 9)\pi = 216\pi$

---

8. A The question asks to find the length of the light grey line. There are 3 pieces to this line, 2 radii and a fraction of the circumference.

The fraction of the circumference: The wedge is 45 degrees and the entire circle has 360 degrees.
The entire circumference is = $2\pi r = 2\pi \times 4 = 8\pi$
The fraction of the circumference = $\frac{45}{360} \times 8\pi = \frac{1}{8} \times 8\pi = \pi$

Length of Light Grey Line = radius + radius + fraction of circumference

$= 4 + 4 + \pi$
$= 8 + \pi$

---

9. A To find the area of the light grey outlined part of the circle, first find the area of the entire circle. Area is calculated by multiplying $\pi \times radius^2$.

Area of circle = $\pi \times 4^2 = 16\pi$

A circle has 360 degrees and the wedge has 45 degrees. Determine what fraction of the circle the wedge is and multiply that by the area of the whole circle to find the area of the wedge.

$\frac{45}{360} \times 16\pi =$
$\frac{1}{8} \times 16\pi =$
2π

---

10. C If the distance around the track is 63m, that means the circumference or perimeter of the circle is 63m.

The circumference is equal to $2 \times \pi \times radius = \pi \times diameter$
The diameter is approximately 20 meters.

$63 = \pi \times diameter$
$63 = 3.14 \times diameter$
$63/3.14 = diameter$
$diameter \approx 20$

5.2 Triangles

Properties of Triangles

A triangle is a closed polygon with three sides. In a triangle, all angles **must add up to 180 degrees**. The angles of a triangle are always proportionate to the sides opposite them, meaning that the longest side of a triangle will be opposite the largest angle, and the shortest side will be opposite the smallest angle. The relationship between sides and angles is shown by using a letter for an angle and the same letter for the corresponding side, with either all the angles with lower–case letters and sides with upper–case letters, or vice versa.

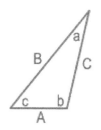

When any two sides of a triangle are added together, their sum is always greater than the third side. In the image, A + B > C, A + C > B, and B + C > A.

Types of Triangles

A triangle with two equal sides is called an **isosceles triangle**. Because angles are proportionate to the sides opposite them, the two angles opposite the two equal sides are also equal.
In the isosceles triangle shown here, A = B and $a = b$.

An equilateral triangle has three equal sides and three equal angles. Because $^{180}/_3 = 60$, the angles of an equilateral triangle will always equal 60 degrees. In the equilateral triangle to the left, A = B = C and $a = b = c$.

A right triangle is any triangle with a 90-degree angle, which is usually represented by a small square. In a right triangle, the side opposite the 90-degree angle, which will always be the longest side, is called the hypotenuse (C). The other two sides are labeled A and B, interchangeably.

Pythagorean Theorem

Right triangles are the only triangles for which The Pythagorean Theorem can be used to calculate missing side lengths. The Pythagorean Theorem states that the square of the hypotenuse is equal to the sum of the square of the other two sides. Or, $A^2 + B^2 = C^2$

If you have a right triangle and you know two sides, you can use the Pythagorean Theorem to calculate the missing side. Remember, make sure you are dealing with a right triangle and when using the formula for calculating the missing side, be sure that the C is the hypotenuse, or the side opposite the right angle.

TRIANGLES PRACTICE

1. **Angle b is how many degrees in the following triangle?**
    - A. 242
    - B. 180
    - C. 142
    - D. 62

2. **In degrees, what are the measures of the three angles in an isosceles right triangle?**
    - A. 30, 60, 90
    - B. 45, 45, 90
    - C. 45, 90, 90
    - D. 60, 60, 60

3. **In the diagram, Side A ? Side B?**
    - A. >
    - B. <
    - C. ≥
    - D. =

4. **Which of the following CANNOT be the length of side C in the triangle?**
    - A. 10
    - B. 12
    - C. 15
    - D. 19

    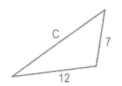

5. **Ken takes a 13–foot ladder to lean up against the side of a building. If the base of the ladder is 5 feet from the building, how high up the building does the ladder reach?**
    - A. 9 feet
    - B. 10 feet
    - C. 11 feet
    - D. 12 feet

6. What is the area of the circle shown?

A. 13π

B. 144π

(C.) 169π

D. 225π

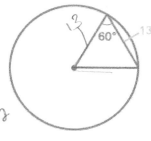

A = πr²

7. What is the perimeter of the triangle in meters?

A. 26

B. 72

C. 144

D. 288

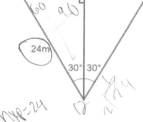

8. Todd and Anne were standing together and talking after school. Todd walked 2 miles due north to get home. Anne walked 1.5 miles due east to get home. How far apart are their houses?

A. 1 mile

B. 2.5 miles

C. 3.5 miles

D. 5 miles

9. If the hypotenuse of a right triangle is 25 meters, and one side of the triangle is 20m, what is the length of the third side?

A. 15m

B. 20m

C. 22.5m

D. 25m

10. What is the measure in degrees of angle b, one interior angle of the hexagon, if the hexagon is made up of 6 equilateral triangles?

A. 60

B. 120

C. 180

D. 360

TRIANGLES EXPLANATIONS

1. D   The angles of a triangle must add up to 180 degrees. Add the other two
angles, and subtract their sum
from 180 to find the measure of angle b.

180 − (75 + 43) =
180 − 118 = 62

2. B   You will need to use all the following facts about triangles to solve this question.

⊙ An isosceles triangle has two sides and two angles that are equal.

⊙ A right triangle has a 90 degree angle.

⊙ The angles in a triangle add up to 180 degrees.

Now, if you have two angles that are equal in an isosceles right triangle, then it must be the two smaller angles, otherwise the sum would be greater than 180.

Therefore, each of the smaller angles is 45°.

45-45-90 triangle, Answer B.

| Angle y + Angle y + 90° = 180° |
| 2 × Angle y = 90° |
| Angle y = 45° |

---

3. B The angle opposite side A is smaller than the angle opposite side B. Therefore, side A is smaller than side B. Answer B.

---

4. D Remember that the sum of any two sides of a triangle must be greater than the length of the third side.

Therefore, C has to be less than 19 and can not equal 19.

| 12 + 7 > C |
| 19 > C |

---

5. D The easiest way to solve this problem is to first draw a picture. The building, the ground, and the ladder create a right triangle as in the diagram.

To find how high up the building the ladder goes, use the Pythagorean Theorem. ❶

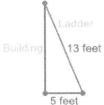

❶ $5^2 + x^2 = 13^2$
$25 + x^2 = 169$
$x^2 = 144$
$x = 12$

---

6. C Two sides of the triangle are radii of the circle. Therefore, they are equal. One of those sides is opposite a 60 degree angle, so the other side must also be opposite a 60 degree angle. Since the angles of a triangle must add up to 180 degrees and two of the angles add up to 120, the third angle must also be 60 degrees, making this an equilateral triangle. Equilateral triangles have three equal sides, so each side of this triangle is 13 units long.

Now that we know the sides of the triangle, we must determine the area of the circle. We know that the radius is 13, so we can calculate the area by squaring radius and multiplying by pi.

| Area of circle = πr^2 = |
| $\pi \times 13^2 = 169\pi$ |

7. B One angle of the large triangle was cut in half to create two 30-60-90 triangles. If you add the halves of that angle together, it equals 60 degrees. Therefore, each of the angles of the large triangle is 60 degrees, making the triangle equilateral.

Since it is equilateral, all the sides are equal. To find the perimeter, add the lengths of the three sides.

$$24m + 24m + 24m$$
$$= 72m$$

---

8. B Draw a picture to help solve the problem. If Todd and Anne both began walking at school, and Todd went north while Anne went east, their trips would look like the right triangle.

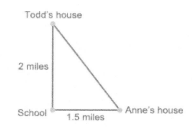

Use the Pythagorean Theorem to find the distance between their houses, which will be the hypotenuse of the right triangle.

$$(1.5)^2 + 2^2 = c^2$$
$$c^2 = 6.25$$
$$c = 2.5 \text{ miles}$$

---

9. A If you know two sides of a right triangle, you can always calculate the third side of the triangle using the Pythagorean Theorem. In this case, they have given you the hypotenuse (or the longest side) and one of the sides. Plug those values into the Pythagorean Theorem to calculate the third side. The third side is 15m.

$$a^2 + b^2 = \text{hypotenuse}^2$$
$$20^2 + b^2 = 25^2$$
$$400 + b^2 = 625$$
$$b^2 = 225$$
$$b = 15$$

---

10. B Each angle inside an equilateral triangle is 60 degrees. If you forget this value, you can easily calculate it as the total measure of the angles in a triangle is 180 and there are 3 equal angles in an equilateral triangle.

Each interior angle of the hexagon is made up of 2 angles of an equilateral triangle. You can add them together to find the total measure of angle b.

$$60 + 60 = 120$$

5.3 Perimeter

Perimeter

The perimeter of an object is the distance around its edge. Calculating the perimeter of any polygon simply requires finding the length of each side and then adding the lengths of all sides together.

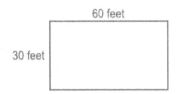

For example, the perimeter of the rectangle (left) is

30 + 30 + 60 + 60 = 180 feet.

Since all sides of a square are of equal length, the perimeter of a square is the length of 1 side times 4. The perimeter of the square shown here is 20 yards × 4, or 80 yards.

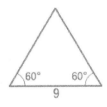

Finding the perimeter of a triangle sometimes requires you to use what you know about the properties of triangles. For example, based on the information shown, you should recognize that the triangle to the left is equilateral — in other words, all sides are the same length (see the lesson "Triangles" in this module). The perimeter is therefore 9 + 9 + 9, or 27 units.

PERIMETER PRACTICE

1. Calculate the perimeter of a square with sides of length 12.5 inches.

> A. 40 in
> B. 50 in
> C. 60 in
> D. 70 in

2. If x = 3 inches, what is the perimeter of the rectangle?

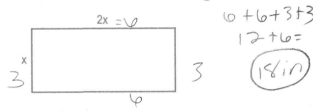

6 + 6 + 3 + 3
12 + 6 =
18 in

> A. 6 inches
> B. 1 foot
> C. 18 inches
> D. 2 feet

3. Find the perimeter of triangle ABC.

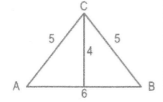

   A. 12
   B. 16
   C. 20
   D. 24

4. If the perimeter of the rectangle is 78, what is the value of x?

   A. 14.5
   B. 17
   C. 24.5
   D. 34

5. Find the perimeter of the following shape.

   A. 28 m
   B. 30 m
   C. 32 m
   D. 34 m

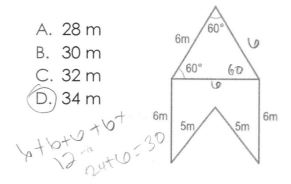

6. Choose the best answer to replace the question mark:

   Perimeter of Circle A **?**
   Perimeter of Square B

Circle A

Square B

A. >
B. <
C. =
D. Not enough information.

7. Jordan took a short cut when walking around her circular neighborhood. She walked halfway around the circumference and then cut straight across the middle to return to her starting point. If the distance around the circular path of the neighborhood is 7 kilometers, approximately how much walking did she save by taking the shortcut?

   A. 1.26 km
   B. 2.52 km
   C. 3.5 km
   D. 5.73 km

8. The field below is made up of two half circles on either end with a straight line of 50m connecting them. If the height of the field is 20m, what is the perimeter of the entire field?

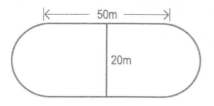

   A. 120m
   B. 140m
   C. 162.8m
   D. 414m

9. What is the perimeter of the figure below?

A. 40
B. 42
C. 44
D. 46

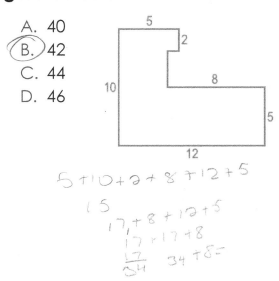

5 + 10 + 2 + 8 + 12 + 5
15
17 + 8 + 12 + 5
17 + 17 + 8
17   34 + 8 =
24

10. What is the perimeter of the figure, which shows a quarter of a circle, if the entire circle had a diameter of 10m?

A. 2.5π meters
B. 10π meters
C. 10 + 6.25π meters
D. 10 + 2.5π meters

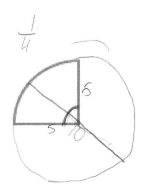

PERIMETER EXPLANATIONS

1. B   Since a square has four sides all of the same length, then the formula for the perimeter of a square is side length times 4.

> 12.5 inches × 4
> = 50 inches

2. C   The width of the rectangle is x, which is 3 inches. The length of the rectangle is $2x$, which is two times 3 inches or 6 inches.

To find the perimeter of the rectangle, add the lengths of all the sides. There are two widths and two lengths.

> Perimeter =
> (2 × width) + (2 × length)
> = (2 × 3 in) + (2 × 6 in)
> = 6 in + 12 in
> = 18 in

3. B   To find the perimeter, add the length of the three sides of the triangle. Be careful, the line with length 4 is not a side of the triangle.

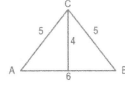

> 5 + 5 + 6 = 16

4. A

> ❶
> = 2x + 2(x + 10)
> = 2x + 2x + 20
> = 4x + 20

> ❷
> 4x + 20 = 78
> 4x = 58
> x = 14.5

❶ Perimeter = width + width + length + length = 2(width) + 2(length)

❷ The perimeter equals 78, so set the equation equal to 78 and solve for x.

5. D For any shape, the perimeter is simply adding the lengths of all the outside edges. You must first fill in the length of all the sides, in this shape there are 6 outside edges total.

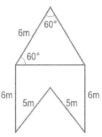

Perimeter = 6m
+ 6m + 6m + 6m
+ 5m + 5m
= 34m

Since two of the angles of the triangle are 60 degrees that means that the third angle is also 60 degrees, making it an equilateral triangle. An equilateral triangle has all sides of equal length, so the missing side of the shape is 6m.

---

6. B Don't forget to first convert the units so that they are the same.

Square B: First, convert the units from yards to feet. There are 3 feet in each yard, therefore the length of the side is 6 feet. To find the perimeter of the square, multiply the length of the side times 4. Therefore, the perimeter is 4 × 6 feet = 24 feet.

Circle A: The formula for calculating the perimeter or circumference of a circle is π × diameter. The diameter is 4.5 feet and pi is a little more than 3. A quick estimate will show that this is definitely less than the perimeter of the square.

Perimeter of Circle A < Perimeter of Square B

---

7. A To calculate the distance she walked, find the diameter of her neighborhood and add it to half of the circumference.

Circumference = 7 km, Therefore, half the circumference is: 7 km ÷ 2 = 3.5km

To find the diameter, use the circumference. The circumference can be found by multiplying the diameter times π. Therefore, divide the circumference by π to find the diameter. We want to find 7÷ π which is about 7 km ÷ 3.14, which is about 2km.

Therefore, Jordan walked a total of approximately 3.5km + 2km = 5.5km.

Subtract the distance she walked from the circumference to find the amount of walking she saved. 7km - 5.5km = 1.5km. This is closest to answer A.

8. C   The perimeter of the field is the total distance around the outside. First, let's find the perimeter around the two half–circles and then we can add in the two straight lines.

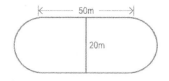

Since the two half–circles will equal one total circle, we need to find the perimeter of one circle. Perimeter of a circle, often called circumference, is found by multiplying π by the diameter. In this case, you can see that the height of the field, 20m, is equal to the diameter of the circle.

Perimeter of Circle = π × 20m = 62.8m

Now, there are two straight edges, the top and bottom. Each is 50m.

Total Perimeter = 62.8m + 50m + 50m = 162.8m

---

9. D   To determine the perimeter, you first need to find the lengths of the missing sides.

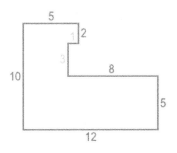

Let's first find the missing vertical side. Since the total height of the shape is 10, and you know that the three vertical edges make up the height and two of them are 5 and 2, and thus total to 7. The missing vertical side must be 10 − 7 = 3.

Now to find the missing horizontal side. The total width of the shape is 12, and two of the sides are 8 and 5, which total to 13. Therefore, they overlap by 13 − 12 = 1 unit.

To find the perimeter, add the lengths of all the sides:

5 + 2 + 1 + 3 + 8 + 5 + 12 + 10 = 46

---

10. D   If the circle had a diameter of 10m, then its radius must be 5m. Therefore, fill in the lengths of 2 of the sides of the figure.

To figure out the length around the curve, realize it is ¼ the circumference of the entire circle. The circumference of a circle is found by multiplying π by the diameter. Circumference = 10π.

Length of the Curve =

$$\frac{1}{4} \times 10\pi = \frac{10}{4\pi} = 2.5\pi$$

The total perimeter is found by adding the lengths of all the sides:
5m + 5m + 2.5 π m = 10 + 2.5 π m

5.4   Area

Area – Rectangles

Area is the two–dimensional space inside a figure. Its units are always a length measurement squared.

To find the area of a rectangle, multiply the length by the width.

For example, if a rectangular yard is 30 feet wide and 60 feet long, the area is 30 ft × 60 ft = 1800 sq ft.

Since all sides of a square are of equal length, the area of a square is the length of one side squared. The area of the square shown here is 20 yards × 20 yards, or 400 square yards.

20 yards

Area – Triangles

The formula for the area of a triangle is:
The height of a triangle is the length of a line from the base, or bottom, of the triangle to the opposite angle.

$\frac{1}{2}$ × **base** × **height**

The line representing the height will always be perpendicular to the base. For example, in the triangle to the right, the base length is 14, and the height is 6. Therefore, the area is $\frac{1}{2}$ × 14 × 6 = 42 sq. units.

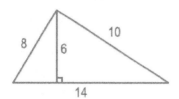

At times, you will have to use what you know about the angles and side lengths of triangles to calculate their heights. The equilateral triangle to the right has sides of length 18, so the base is 18. To find the height, draw a line down from the topmost angle to the base.

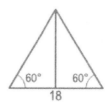

You can also use the Pythagorean Theorem to calculate the height because you already know two sides of the right triangle (the hypotenuse is 18, and half the base is 9). You can calculate the height by plugging these values into the theorem:

$18^2 = 9^2 + \text{height}^2$
$324 = 81 + \text{height}^2$
$324 - 81 = \text{height}^2$
$243 = \text{height}^2$
$\sqrt{243} = \text{height}$
$15.59 = \text{height}$

Then, use the formula to calculate the area:

$$\frac{1}{2} \times 18 \times 15.59 = 140.31 \text{ square units}$$

1. Find the area of a rectangle that is 7 centimeters long and 4 centimeters wide.

   A. 28 cm
   B. 28 sq cm
   C. 14 cm
   D. 14 sq cm

2. A backdrop for a play is a triangle 9 meters tall. If the total area of the backdrop is 45 square meters, then how wide is the base?

   A. 4.5 m
   B. 5 m
   C. 9 m
   D. 10 m

3. Daniel is painting a square wall with 9 foot sides. If he uses ⅓ gallon per square foot, how many gallons of paint will he need?

   A. 14 gal
   B. 27 gal
   C. 54 gal
   D. 81 gal

4. Calculate the area of the triangle.

   A. 15 sq. m.
   B. 21 sq. m.
   C. 54 sq. m.
   D. 108 sq. m.

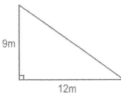

5. The area of Triangle T is how many times larger than the area of Triangle S?

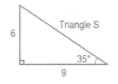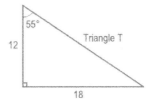

   A. 2
   B. 4
   C. 6
   D. 8

6. What is the area of the figure?

   A. 34
   B. 74
   C. 90
   D. 98

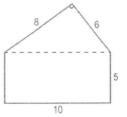

7. Choose the best answer to replace the question mark.

   The area of Square L is **?** the area of Circle M.

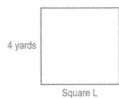

   A. >
   B. <
   C. =
   D. ≤

8. The field below is made up of two half circles on either end with a straight line of 50m connecting them. If the height of the field is 20m, what is the area of the entire field?

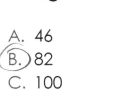

50×20
1000

$A = \pi r^2$

$\pi(10)^2 = 100\pi$

100×3.14=
314

A. 3140 sq. m.
B. 1000 sq. m.
C. 1062.8 sq. m.
D. 1314 sq. m.

314+1000

100π

9. What is the area of the figure:

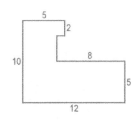

A. 46
B. 82
C. 100
D. 120

10. If you double all the sides of a rectangle, by how much does the area change?

A. doubles
B. increases by 2
C. quadruples
D. increases by 8

AREA EXPLANATIONS

1. B The formula for area of a rectangle is length times width. The units for area are a length measurement squared.

7 cm × 4 cm = 28 sq cm

2. D Use the area of a triangle formula to calculate the length of the base.

Area = ½ × base × height

$45 = \frac{1}{2} \times b \times 9$
$45 = 4.5 \times b$
$b = 10$ m

3. B Calculate the area of the wall.

Then multiply by the ratio of gallons to square feet.

9 ft. × 9 ft. = 81 sq. ft

81 sq. ft. × ^{1}gal$/_3$ sq ft = 27 gal.

4. C To find the area of a triangle, use the following formula:
Area = ½ × base × height

= ½ × 12m × 9m
= 54 sq. m.

5. B Let's calculate the area of each triangle using the formula = ½ × base × height

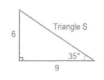 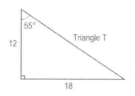

Triangle T's Area = ½ × 12 × 18 = 108

Triangle S's Area = ½ × 6 × 9 = 27

Divide to find how many times larger is Triangle T.

$$108 \div 27 = 4$$

6. B To find the area of the entire shape, find the area of the triangle and add that to the area of the rectangle.

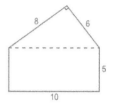

❶ Area of triangle = ½ × base × height = ½ × 6 × 8 = 24

❷ Area of rectangle = length × width = 5 × 10 = 50

❸ Area of shape. 50 + 24 = 74

7. A Calculate the areas, then compare them. Area of a square = side². Area of a circle = π × r²

Area of Square L = 4 yd. × 4 yd. = 16 yd. sq.

Area of Circle M = 2 yd. × 2 yd. × 3.14 = 12.56 yd. sq.

Area of Square L > Area of Circle M

8. D To find area of the entire field, first find area of the two half–circles and add in the area of the rectangular middle of the field.

The two half–circles add up to one whole circle. The area of a circle = π × radius². The diameter is the same as the height of the field, 20m. Therefore, the radius = 10m.

Area of Circle = π × 10² = 314 sq. m.

The area of the middle rectangular portion can be found by multiplying the base by the height. The base is 50m and height is 20m.

Area of Rectangle = 50m × 20m = 1000 sq. m.

Total Area = 1000 + 314 = 1314 sq. m.

9. B First, the lengths of the missing sides need to be filled in. The missing vertical side must be 3, since the total vertical height is 10 and you know two of the sides add up to 7. The missing horizontal side is 1, since the total horizontal width is 12 and the two sides that overlap add up to 13, therefore the missing side is 1.

Now, you know how to find the area of rectangles, so you must divide up the figure into shapes you can take the area of. In this case, let's divide it into 3 rectangles.

The top rectangle has a length of 5 and a width of 2, therefore area = 5 × 2 = 10.

The second rectangle has a width of 4 and a height of 3, area = 12.

The third rectangle's dimensions are 12 by 5 for an area of 60.

Total area = 12 + 10 + 60 = 82.

---

10. C Let's say that the original rectangle has a width of w and a height of h. Therefore, the area of the original rectangle is wh.

If all the sides are doubled, the new rectangle has a width of $2w$ and a height of $2h$. Therefore, the area of the new rectangle is $(2w)(2h) = 4wh$

Divide the new area by the original area to see how many times bigger the new area is:
Area goes up 4 times, or quadruples

$$4wh \div wh = 4$$

5.5 3D Objects & Volume

Properties of 3D Objects

The solid shapes that you see everyday are three-dimensional shapes. These 3D objects are also called geometric solids.

Each flat side of a 3D object is called a face. For instance, in the rectangular prism you will see that it has 6 faces: bottom, top, front, back, right side, and left side.
The line segment where two faces meet is called the edge of the object. The rectangular prism has 12 edges.
Each corner where the edges meet is called a vertex. The rectangular prism has 8 vertices.

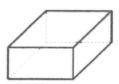

Nets

When analyzing 3D shapes, it is helpful to note the 2D shapes that make up each of the faces. For example, we learned about rectangular prisms that have 6 faces that are all rectangles.

A net is a pattern in two dimensions of the faces of an object that can be used to generate a 3-dimensional object. Let's look at the triangular prism and think about "unfolding it". It has 5 faces, including 3 rectangles and 2 triangles. If we started at the top edge and "opened" up the prism so that it would lay flat, we would create the following net.

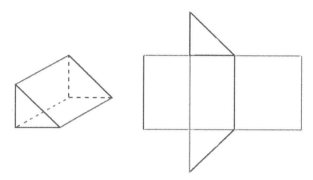

Volume

Volume is the three dimensional space filled by a figure. Its units are equal to a cubed length measurement. In general, volume can be calculated by finding the area of the base and multiplying that by the height.

> **Volume =
> Area of Base × Height**

Rectangular Prism or Box

Multiply the area of the base by the height. Therefore, multiply length × width × height.

Cube

To find the volume of a cube, find the area of the base and multiply it by the height. In the case of a cube, all the dimensions are the same length.

Therefore, volume = area × height = side × side × side = $side^3$

Triangular Prism

Volume is area × height = ½ × length × width × height.

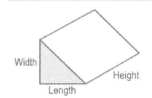

Cylinder

Again, to find the volume, multiply the area of the base by the height. In this case, the area of the base is a circle with area of $\pi \times radius^2$. Therefore, the volume $= \pi \times r^2 \times height$.

Sphere

The volume of a sphere can be calculated by multiplying $\frac{4}{3} \times \pi \times r^3$.

3D OBJECTS & VOLUME PRACTICE

1. **Find the volume of a box 7 inches wide, 10 inches tall, and 20 inches long.**
   - A. 140 in. sq.
   - B. 140 in. cubed
   - C. 1400 in. sq.
   - D. 1400 in. cubed

2. **Calculate the volume of a 9 foot tall cylinder with a base with a radius of 3 feet.**
   - A. 81π ft. cubed
   - B. 270 ft cubed
   - C. 40.5 ft. cubed
   - D. 54 ft. cubed

   3²=9π
   9π × 9=81π

3. **Which 3D object can be generated with the net?**
   - A. Triangular Prism
   - B. Square Pyramid
   - C. Triangular Pyramid
   - D. Cone

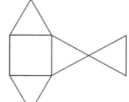

4. **What is the volume of the right triangular prism in units cubed?**
   - A. 48
   - B. 60
   - C. 96
   - D. 120

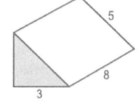

5. **Which can hold more water, a plastic cube with 2 inch sides or a plastic box that is 4 inches long, 3 inches wide, and ¾ of an inch tall?**
   - A. Cube
   - B. Box
   - C. Same
   - D. Not enough information.

6. **How many times bigger is the volume of a cube with sides of length 8m than the volume of a cube with sides of length 4m?**
   - A. 2
   - B. 4
   - C. 8
   - D. 16

7. If the width of a rectangular prism is w, and the length is twice the width, and the height is 4 more than than the length, what is the volume of the prism in terms of w?

    A. $5w + 4$

    B. w^3

    C. $2w^3 + 8w^2$

    D. $4w^3 + 8w^2$

8. You have a pool that is a rectangular prism. How many liters of water can fill the pool if its dimensions are 20m by 15m by 8m? (hint: 1 cubic meter = 1000 Liters)

    A. 2.4 Liters

    B. 43,000 Liters

    C. 1,200,000 Liters

    D. 2,400,000 Liters

9. If the volume of a right triangular prism is 400 cubic meters, and the perpendicular sides of the triangle are 8m and 5m, how long is the prism?

    A. 5m

    B. 10m

    C. 20m

    D. 40m

10. If the volume of a sphere is 288π, what is the diameter? (hint: sphere volume = $\frac{4}{3}\pi r^3$)

    A. 6m

    B. 12m

    C. 24m

    D. 144m

3D OBJECTS & VOLUME EXPLANATIONS

1. D   To find volume, multiply length × width × height. The units are always a length measurement cubed.

    | 7 in × 10 in × 20 in = 1400 in. cubed |

2. A   First, find the area of the circle on the base of the cylinder. Area of circle = π × radius²

    | Area of Base = π × 3² = 9π ft. sq. |

     Then multiply that area by the height of the cylinder.

    | 9π ft. sq × 9 ft. = 81π ft. cubed |

3. B   When given a question involving nets, you can try to visualize how to fold it to make a three-dimensional object, or you can start by analyzing the faces. In the net, there are 5 faces total: 1 square and 4 triangles. Now, let's go through each choice to see what faces those objects have.

     A. Triangular prism. Remember, a triangular prism has a triangle on either end, and it is connected by three rectangles. Therefore, 2 triangles and 3 rectangles. Different faces - eliminate answer.

B. Square pyramid. This object is a pyramid that has a base as a square. A triangle off of each side of the square connects up to a point. Therefore, 1 square and 4 triangles. Correct faces. Now, let's think about whether it would fold correctly. If you folded the top and bottom triangles together so they met at a point in the middle and then folded the triangles on the right to connect up to the left-hand side of the square, then it would create a square pyramid. This is your answer.

C. Triangular pyramid. This pyramid has a base as a triangle and connects up to a point with each of those faces as triangles. Therefore, 4 triangles total. Different faces - eliminate answer.

D. Cone. Eliminate as a cone has a circle, so different faces than the net.

---

4. A To find the volume of the triangular prism, you first need to find the missing side of the triangle. Since the base makes a right triangle and you know one side is 3 and the hypotenuse is 5, you can use the Pythagorean theorem to solve for the height of the triangle ❶.

❶
$3^2 + \text{height}^2 = 5^2$
$9 + \text{height}^2 = 25$
$\text{height}^2 = 16$
$\text{height} = 4$

To find volume, find the area of the base and multiply it by the length of prism. The base is a triangle and the area of a triangle can be found by multiplying $\frac{1}{2}$ by height by width.

❷ Area of Base = $\frac{1}{2}$ x height × width = $\frac{1}{2} \times 4 \times 3 = 6$
❸ Volume = Area of Base × Prism Length = 6 x 8 = 48

---

5. B Find the volume of each to see how much water they can hold.

Plastic Cube:	Plastic Box:
2 in × 2 in × 2 in	4 in × 3 in × $\frac{3}{4}$ in
8 cubic inches	9 cubic inches

Plastic Box can hold more.

---

6. C The volume of a cube is side^3.
Volume of cube with sides of length 8m = $8^3 = 512$
Volume of cube with sides of length 4m = $4^3 = 64$
$512 \div 64 = 8$

---

7. D Let's first put each dimension in terms of w.
Then multiply to find the volume of the prism.

Width = w
Length = twice the width = $2w$
Height = four more than length = $2w + 4$

Volume
= width x length x height
= $w \times (2w) \times (2w + 4)$
= $2w^2(2w + 4)$
= $4w^3 + 8w^2$

8. D Since the question asks how many liters of water can fill a pool, you must find the volume of the pool.

❶ = 20m × 15m × 8m = 2400 m³

❶ Volume = length × width × height

❷ Convert from cubic meters to Liters.

❷ 2400 cubic meters × $^{1000}L/_1$ cubic m = 2,400,000 Liters

---

9. C The volume of a triangular prism equals the area of the base times the length of the prism. Since we know the perpendicular sides of the triangle, we can find the area of the base and then we can solve for the length of the prism.

❶ $^1/_2$ × 8m × 5m = 20 sq meters

❶ Area of triangular base = $^1/_2$ × base × height

❷ Volume = Area of base × Length

❷ 400 cubic meters
= 20 sq meters × Length
400 ÷ 20 = Length
20 m = Length

---

10. B ❶ The formula for the volume of a sphere is $^4/_3$πradius³.
❷ Divide both sides by π
❸ Multiply both sides by $^3/_4$
❹ Take the cube root of both sides.
If 6m is the radius, then double that to find the diameter. Diameter = 12m

❶ 288π = $^4/_3$πradius³

❷ 288 = $^4/_3$ × radius³

❸ 216 = radius³

❹ 6 = radius

5.6   Surface Area

Surface Area

Surface area is the sum of the areas of all of the faces of an object. Its units are the same as those for area, a length measurement squared.

Rectangular Prism or Box

The surface area of a box is calculated by finding the area of each rectangle on the face of the box. There are 6 different faces, two with an area of length × width, two with an area of length × height, and two with an area of width × height. This can be written using the formula:

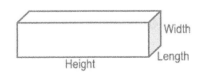

$$(2 × \textbf{length} × \textbf{width}) + (2 × \textbf{length} × \textbf{height}) + (2 × \textbf{width} × \textbf{height}).$$

Cube

Since a cube has 6 sides, all with the same area of side^2, the surface area of a cube = **6 × side^2**.

Triangular Prism

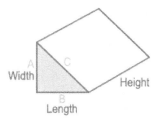

A triangular prism has 5 faces. To find the total surface area, add the areas of each of the base triangles and the rectangles that form the sides of the prism. The length of each rectangle is equal to the height of the prism and the widths are each equal to the length of one side of the triangular base. For the prism on the left, the surface area would be:

$$\tfrac{1}{2}(A \times B) + \tfrac{1}{2}(A \times B) + (A \times \textbf{height}) + (B \times \textbf{height}) + (C \times \textbf{height})$$

Cylinder

To find the surface area of a cylinder, add the areas of three different faces, the top, the bottom, and the side. The top and bottom of the cylinder are circles, each with an area of π × r^2. If you think about unrolling a cylinder, the side makes a rectangle with a width equal to the circumference of the base and a length equal to the height of the cylinder. Therefore, the area of the side = π × diameter × height. The total surface area of a cylinder is = **2πr^2 + 2πrh**.

Sphere

The formula for the surface area of a sphere is: **4 × π × r^2**.

SURFACE AREA PRACTICE

1. **Find the surface area of a cube with a side of length 7 m.**
    - A. 15 m sq.
    - B. 49 m sq.
    - C. 294 m. sq.
    - D. 343 m sq.

2. **A box is 9 m tall, 7 m long, and 3 m wide. What is its surface area?**
    - A. 189 square meters
    - B. 189 cubed meters
    - C. 222 square meters
    - D. 222 cubed meters

3. **What is the surface area of the cylinder in the diagram?**

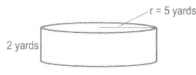
r = 5 yards

2 yards

    A. 10π
    B. 50π
    C. 70π
    D. 100π

4. **Calculate the surface area of a sphere with a radius of 6.**
    (hint: surface area of sphere = $4\pi r^2$)

    A. 36π
    B. 144π
    C. 288π
    D. 864π

5. **A family is wallpapering their living room. If the room is 26 ft. by 19 ft. with 10 foot ceilings and they are only covering the walls, how much wallpaper will they need in square feet?**

    A. 700
    B. 800
    C. 900
    D. 1000

6. **What is the surface area of the triangular prism if the units are all in meters?**

    A. 48 sq m
    B. 76 sq m
    C. 108 sq m
    D. 120 sq m

5
4
8
3

4 x 3 x 8 x 3

4 √180
48
608
12

7. **If the surface area of a cube is 150 square meters, what is the length of one side of the cube?**

    A. 5m
    B. 10m
    C. 25m
    D. 50m

8. **If a rectangular prism has a width of y, length of $2y$, and height of $3y$, what is its surface area?**

    A. $6y^3$
    B. $12y^2$
    C. $22y^2$
    D. $36y^2$

9. **If the surface area of a cylinder is 320π and the radius is 10, what is the height of the cylinder?**

    A. 6
    B. 12
    C. 16
    D. 32

10. **Which has a greater surface area: a cube with sides of length 8m or a rectangular prism which is 7m × 8m × 9m?**

    A. Cube
    B. Rectangular Prism
    C. Equal
    D. Not enough information.

1. C To find the surface area, add the areas of each of the faces. A cube has 6 faces each with an area of side × side.

Surface Area = Area of each Face × 6 faces = 7 x 7 x 6 = 294 m sq

---

2. C To find the surface area of a box, add the areas of each of the 6 faces.

Plug the height, length, and width into the formula.

> (2 × length × width) + (2 × length × height) + (2 × width × height)
> = (2 × 9 × 7) + (2 × 9 × 3) + (2 × 3 × 7)
> = 126 + 54+ 42
> = 222 sq meters

---

3. C To find the surface area of the cylinder, you must calculate the area of each of the faces.

Face 1: Top − The top of the cylinder is a circle with an area of πr^2.

> $\pi r^2 = \pi 5^2 = 25\pi$

Face 2: Bottom − The top and the bottom have the same area. $= 25\pi$

Face 3: Side − The side of the cylinder can be thought of as a rolled up rectangle with one side equal to the cylinder height and the other side equal to the circumference of the base, which can be found by multiplying $2\pi r$.

> height × $2\pi r$
> = 2 × 2π × 5
> = 20π

> Total Surface Area = 25π + 25π + 20π = 70π

---

4. B Use the formula for surface area of a sphere.

Surface Area of a Sphere = $4\pi \times r^2$

> = 4 × π × r^2
> = 4 × π × 6^2
> = 144 π

---

5. C The two shortest walls will be 19 feet long and 10 feet tall, find the area by multiplying and then multiply by 2 since there are 2 walls.

> 19 × 10 × 2 = 380 ft. sq.

The two longest walls will be 26 feet long and 10 feet tall, find the area by multiplying.

> 26 × 10 × 2 = 520 ft. sq.

Find the sum.

> 520 + 380 = 900 ft. sq.

6. C There are 5 surfaces on the triangular prism, so find the sum of all the areas of the surfaces.

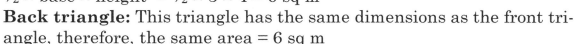

Bottom: This is a rectangle with dimensions 8m by 3m.
Area = $8 \times 3 = 24$ sq m
Front triangle: The area of a triangle is
$\frac{1}{2} \times$ base $\times$ height $= \frac{1}{2} \times 3 \times 4 = 6$ sq m
Back triangle: This triangle has the same dimensions as the front triangle, therefore, the same area = 6 sq m
Top: This is a rectangle with dimensions of 8m by 5m.
Area = $8 \times 5 = 40$ sq m
Left side: This is a rectangle with dimensions 8m by 4m.
Area = $8 \times 4 = 32$ sq m

Sum all the sides to find the total surface area.
Surface Area = 24 sq m + 6 sq m + 6 sq m + 40 sq m + 32 sq m = 108 sq m

---

7. A A cube has 6 faces, all with the same area. The area of each face is side $\times$ side or side^2.
So, surface area of a cube = $6 \times$ side^2

Length of one side = 5m

$$150 = 6 \times \text{side}^2$$
$$25 = \text{side}^2$$
$$5 = \text{side}$$

---

8. C A rectangular prism has 6 faces.

Two faces with dimensions: width $\times$ length
Two faces with dimensions: width $\times$ height
Two faces with dimensions: length $\times$ height

Total surface area = $4y^2 + 6y^2 + 12y^2 = 22y^2$

$$2 \times \text{width} \times \text{length} = 2 \times y \times 2y = 4y^2$$

$$2 \times \text{width} \times \text{height} = 2 \times y \times 3y = 6y^2$$

$$2 \times \text{length} \times \text{height} = 2 \times 2y \times 3y = 12y^2$$

---

9. A A cylinder has 3 faces.

❶ Top Circular Base: Area = πradius^2
❷ Bottom Circular Base: Same Area as top base

❸ Around side of Cylinder: can be thought of as a rolled up rectangle
Area of the rectangle = Circumference of base $\times$ height

❹ Total surface Area = Area of top base + Area of bottom base + Area of side

Height = 6

❶
$$= \pi 10^2$$
$$= 100\pi$$

❷
$$= 100\pi$$

❸
$$= 2\pi\text{radius} \times \text{height}$$
$$= 2\pi 10 \times \text{height}$$
$$= 20\pi\text{height}$$

❹
$$320\pi = 100\pi + 100\pi + 20\pi\text{height}$$
$$320\pi = 200\pi + 20\pi\text{height}$$
$$120\pi = 20\pi\text{height}$$
$$120 = 20 \times \text{height}$$
$$6 = \text{height}$$

10. **A** **Cube:** A cube has 6 equal faces, therefore the surface area is found by multiplying 6 by the area of one face.
Surface Area = 6 × side²

= 6 × 8²
= 6 × 64
= 384

Rectangular Prism: There are 6 faces. Two with area of length × width; two with area of width × height; two with area of length × height.
Surface Area = 2(length × width) + 2(width × height) + 2(length × height)

= 2(7 × 8) + 2(8 × 9) + 2(7 × 9)
= 2(56) + 2(72) + 2(63)
= 112 + 144 + 126
= 382

5.7   Chapter Review

1. If you have a circle with radius r, then the area of the circle is equal to how many times the circle's circumference?

   A. $2r$
   B. $4r$
   C. $^1/_2$
   D. $^1/_4$

   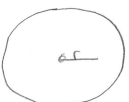

2. Victor ran around 30 degrees of a circular park. If the diameter of the park is 12 miles, how many miles did he run?

   A. 10π
   B. 6π
   C. 3π
   D. π

3. Selena wants to draw a line around the edge of the triangle. If the triangle has two sides of 4 centimeters each, then approximately how many centimeters will she need to color to draw a line that

   goes completely around the triangle?

   A. 8 cm
   B. 12 cm
   C. 5.66 cm
   D. 13.66 cm

   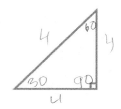

4. Triangle PQR is an isosceles triangle. If angle P = 70°, which of the following is not a possible measure for angle Q?

   A. 20°
   B. 40°
   C. 55°
   D. 70°

5. What is the volume and surface area of a cylinder with radius 5m and height 8m?

   A. 200π m³, 130π m²
   B. 200π m³, 105π m²
   C. 80π m³, 50π m²
   D. 80π m³, 130π m²

6. If a quilting club uses rolls of fabric measuring 6 feet by 3 feet to construct a quilt out of 4 inch squares, how many squares of fabric will it take to create a quilt measuring 3 yards by 3 yards?
    A. 729
    B. 162
    C. 27
    D. 11664

7. A gym teacher is painting a line around the outside of the rectangular basketball court. If he uses 2 gallons of paint for every 50 feet he paints, and the court is 50 feet wide and 100 feet long, how many gallons of paint will he need?
    A. 10
    B. 12
    C. 14
    D. 16

8. Find the perimeter of the triangle.
    A. 20
    B. 40
    C. 55
    D. 60

    25

    15

9. Which of the following is/are true?
    I. Surface area always has units of a length measurement squared.
    II. The surface area of a cube can never equal that of a cylinder.

    III. Surface area is the amount of space taken up by an object.
    A. I only
    B. II only
    C. III only
    D. I and III only

10. You have a picture that is 8 inches by 10 inches. You place it in a frame that is 2 inches wide all around. How much wall space will be covered up by the entire frame and picture?
    A. 96 sq in
    B. 100 sq in
    C. 120 sq in
    D. 168 sq in

11. Choose the best answer to replace the question mark.

surface area of a sphere with a radius of 9m	?	surface area of a cylinder with radius of 9m and height of 9m

    A. <
    B. >
    C. =
    D. Not Enough Information

12. What is the sum of the number of faces, edges, and vertices of the 3D object that is made from this net?
    A. 14
    B. 18
    C. 21
    D. 25

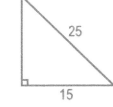

13. Point M is the midpoint of the line PQ. If the coordinates of P are (9, 11) and M is at (4, 7.5), find the coordinates of Q.

    A. (-1, 4)
    B. (5, 3.5)
    C. (6.5, 9)
    D. (-1, 3)

14. George is a kindergartener coloring in wedges of circles for a project on fractions. If the diameter of a circle is 6 inches, and the circle is divided evenly into 6 wedges, what is the area that George colored if he carefully colors in 1 wedge?

    A. π
    B. 1.5π
    C. 2π
    D. 3π

15. If the width of a rectangle is w and the length is 4 less than 3 times the width, what is the perimeter of the rectangle in terms of w?

    A. $8 - 4w$
    B. $3w^2 - 4w$
    C. $4w - 4$
    D. $8w - 8$

16. The area of the circle is how many times that of the triangle inscribed in it?

    A. π
    B. 2π
    C. 5π
    D. 10π

 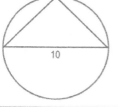

17. What is the volume of the triangular prism?

    A. 288
    B. 360
    C. 576
    D. 720

 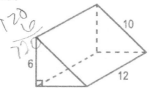

18. What is the surface area of the triangular prism?

    A. 60
    B. 94
    C. 108
    D. 120

 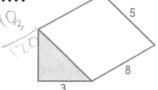

19. Which has the largest volume? (hint: sphere volume = $\frac{4}{3} \times \pi \times r^3$)

    A. Cube with sides length 6m
    B. Sphere with diameter 6m
    C. Cylinder with height 6m and diameter 6m
    D. Rectangular prism with sides length 5m, 6m, 7m

20. What is the distance between (-3,4) and (3,-4)? (hint: draw a right triangle on the coordinate plane)

    A. 7
    B. 8
    C. 10
    D. 14

1. C   The area of the circle = πr². The circumference of the circle = 2πr.

Now you must use algebra to solve this question. Let y represent the answer to this question which states that the area is how many times the circumference. This can be set up as:

Area = y × Circumference
Divide both sides by π
Divide both sides by r
Divide both sides by 2

$πr^2 = y × 2πr$
$r^2 = y × 2r$
$r = y × 2$
$r/2 = y$

2. D   To find the arc length, multiply the fraction of the circle that Victor ran around by the circumference of the circle.

Since there are 360 degrees in a circle, Victor ran $^{30}\!/_{360} = ^1\!/_{12}$ of the circle.

The total circumference of the circle is π × diameter = 12 π

Therefore, multiply the fraction of the circle times the total circumference.

$$(^1\!/_{12}) × 12π = π \text{ miles}$$

3. D   The triangle has a right angle and two equal sides, therefore it must be a right isosceles triangle. The side that remains to be figured out is the hypotenuse. You can use the Pythagorean Theorem to find the length of the hypotenuse.

Pythagorean Theorem says: one side squared plus second side squared = hypotenuse squared, or more commonly written as: $a^2 + b^2 = c^2$

$4^2 + 4^2 = \text{hypotenuse}^2$
$32 = \text{hypotenuse}^2$

If you take the square root of both sides, you find that the hypotenuse is approximately 5.66cm.

The question asks for the perimeter of the triangle.

4cm + 4cm + 5.66cm
= 13.66cm

4. A   If Triangle PQR is an isosceles triangle, then two angles must be equal. The question tells you one of the angles. Therefore, that angle is equal to a second angle, or it is the one different angle. Remember, that in a triangle, all the angles add up to 180°.

One possible triangle: angle P equals another angle. Therefore, two angles equal 70°. To find the third angle, subtract the sum of the two angles from 180. 180 − (70 + 70) = 180 − 140 = 40.

Another possible triangle: angle P is the different angle. Therefore, the other two angles, Q and R, must be equal. Let the variable y represent the measure of angle Q, which equals the measure of angle R.

$$70 + y + y = 180$$
$$70 + 2y = 180$$
$$2y = 110$$
$$y = 55$$

The diagram shows the two possible isosceles triangles. Angle Q can not equal 20°. Answer A.

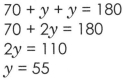

5. A

❶ Volume of a cylinder can be found by multiplying the area of the base by the height of the cylinder. Volume = Area of Base × Height

❶ = πr² × height
= π5² × 8
= 25π × 8 = 200
Volume = 200π m³

❷ The surface area of a cylinder can be found by adding the areas of the top base, bottom base, and side. Surface Area = area of top base + area of bottom base + area of side

❷ = πr² + πr² + πdh
= π5² + π5² + π(10)(8)
= 25π + 25π + 80π
= 130π
Surface Area = 130π m²

Volume = 200π m³, Surface Area = 130π m²

6. A To calculate the number of squares needed to create the quilt, find the length of one side of the quilt, which is 3 yards, in inches

3 yards × $^{3\ feet}/_{yard}$ = 9 feet   9 feet × $^{12\ inches}/_{foot}$ = 108 inches

Now, let us convert the number of inches to quilt squares.

108 inches × $^{1\ square}/_{4\ inches}$
= 27 squares long

Since the quilt is 3 yards by 3 yards, it is 27 squares by 27 squares. Therefore, to find the number of squares needed, find the area by multiplying the length of the two sides.

27 × 27 = 729

Notice that the information about the rolls of fabric is not important for solving the problem.

7. B Since the teacher is painting a line around the outside, you need to find the perimeter of the rectangular court.

Perimeter = 50 ft + 50 ft + 100 ft + 100 ft = 300 ft

Now, we can multiply it by the ratio of gallons of paint to feet, to find the amount of paint needed.

300 ft. × $^{2\ gal.}/_{50ft.}$
= 12 gal.

8. D To find the perimeter, you need to add the length of all the sides. Unfortunately, only two sides of the triangle were given. But, since the triangle is a right triangle, you can use the Pythagorean Theorem to find the length of the other side.

Now, add up all the sides.

$$15^2 + B^2 = 25^2$$
$$225 + B^2 = 625$$
$$B^2 = 400$$
$$B = 20$$

$$15 + 20 + 25 = 60$$

9. A Consider each statement individually to determine whether each is true or false.

Statement I: Surface area always has units of a length measurement squared. is true (see tutorial). To find surface area, you are adding the areas of each face. Area is expressed in units of length squared, therefore surface area will be the same units.

Statement II: The surface area of a cube can never equal that of a cylinder. is false; There is no reason that a cube and a cylinder could not have the same surface area, despite the fact that their formulas are different.

Statement III: Surface area is the amount of space taken up by an object. is false because it gives the definition of volume instead of that of surface area.

10. D Let's figure out the dimensions of the frame and picture.

Width of picture was 8 inches and the frame is 2 inches wide. That adds 2 inches to the left side of the picture and 2 inches to the right side. The total width is now $8 + 2 + 2 = 12$ inches

Length of picture is 10 inches and frame adds 2 inches to top and bottom. Total length = $10 + 2 + 2 = 14$ inches

Area = 12 inches × 14 inches = 168 sq in.

11. C Let's calculate the surface area of each shape.

Sphere: To calculate the surface area of a sphere, you can use the following formula: $4 \times \pi \times r^2$.

In this case, sphere's surface area = $4 \times \pi \times 9^2 = 324\pi$

Cylinder: To calculate the surface area of a cylinder, you must find the area of all the surfaces. The top and bottom are circles with an area of πr^2. The side of a cylinder can be found by taking the circumference of the base and multiplying by the height = $2\pi rh$

2 × area of base + area of side
$$= 2\pi r^2 + 2\pi rh$$
$$= 2\pi 9^2 + 2\pi \times 9 \times 9$$
$$= 162\pi + 162\pi$$
$$= 324\pi$$

Their surface areas are equal. Answer C.

12. B When solving problems related to 3D objects, the first step is to draw it out. Therefore, we must figure out what 3D object is made from this net. If you fold the four triangles up towards each other, they will meet at a single vertex at the top. This will create a pyramid with a square base.

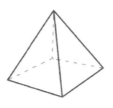

Now, let's examine the properties of this square pyramid. Faces = 1 Square, 4 Triangles = 5 Faces
Edges = 4 around the square at the bottom and 4 around the triangles = 8 Edges
Vertices = 4 at each corner of the square and 1 where the triangles meet = 5 Vertices

Sum = 5 + 8 + 5 = 18

---

13. A To find the coordinates of a midpoint, you find the average of the x–coordinates of the endpoints and the average of the y coordinates of the endpoints.

In this problem, they have given you the midpoint and you need to find the other endpoint. Let's first look at the x–coordinates. The x–coordinate of the end point is 9 and the x–coordinate of the midpoint is 4. Therefore, 4 equals the average of 9 and Q's x–coordinate. ❶
❷ Now, do the same thing for the y coordinate.
Therefore, the coordinates of Q are (-1, 4)

❶
$$4 = (9 + x)/2$$
$$8 = 9 + x$$
$$-1 = x$$

❷
$$7.5 = (11 + y)/2$$
$$15 = 11 + y$$
$$4 = y$$

---

14. B Find the area of the entire circle. Then, find $\frac{1}{6}$ of the area since George colored in 1 of the 6 evenly sized wedges.

Area of the circle = πradius^2
Since the diameter is 6 inches, the radius is 3 inches.

Now, find $\frac{1}{6}$ of the area of the circle.

Area = $\pi3^2$
Area = 9π

$\frac{1}{6} \times 9\pi = 1.5\pi$

---

15. D Let's first find the length of the rectangle in terms of w. The length is 4 less than 3 times the width and the width is w.

Length = 4 less than 3 times width
Length = 4 less than $3w$
Length = $3w - 4$

There are four sides on a rectangle, two widths and two lengths. perimeter = width + width + length + length	perimeter = (2 × width) + (2 × length) perimeter = $2w + 2(3w − 4)$ $= 2w + 6w − 8$ $= 8w − 8$

16. A Calculate the area of the circle and the area of the triangle.

Circle: Area of a circle = $\pi \times r^2$. The radius of the circle is half the diameter, therefore the radius = 5.
Area of Circle = $\pi \times 5^2 = 25\pi$

Triangle: Area of a triangle = ½ × base × height. The base of the triangle is 10. The height of the triangle equals the radius of the circle = 5.
Area of Triangle = ½ × 10 × 5 = 25

To find how many times bigger the area of the circle is divide the areas.
Area of circle ÷ Area of triangle = $25\pi \div 25 = \pi$

17. A The volume of a triangular prism is the area of the base × height. We must find the area of the base.

❶ To find the area of the base, you must know the dimensions of the triangle, but unfortunately, not all the dimensions are stated. We know the hypotenuse and one of the sides, so we can use the pythagorean theorem to find the missing side.

❶ $side^2 + 6^2 = 10^2$ $side^2 + 36 = 100$ $side^2 = 64$ $side = 8$

❷ Now, find the area of the base. Area of triangular base.

❷ $= ½ \times 6 \times 8$ $= 24$

❸ Volume = Area of base × Height of Prism

❸ $= 24 \times 12$ $= 288$

18. C The surface area of a triangular prism is the sum of all the areas of the faces. There are 5 faces on a triangular prism. To find the areas of each face, we first need all the dimensions of the shape.

We know the hypotenuse and one of the sides, so we can use the pythagorean theorem to find the missing side. Now, find the area of each face.

$side^2 + 3^2 = 5^2$ $side^2 + 9 = 25$ $side^2 = 16$ $side = 4$

Area of front triangle = ½ × 3 x 4 = 6
Area of back triangle = ½ × 3 x 4 = 6
Area of bottom = 3 × 8 = 24
Area of top = 5 × 8 = 40
Area of left side = 4 × 8 = 32

Surface area = 6 + 6 + 24 + 40 + 32 = 108

19. A Find the volume of each:

A: Cube with sides length 6m³

> Volume = side × side × side
> = 6 × 6 × 6 = 216m³

B: Sphere with diameter 6m
Volume = ⁴⁄₃πradius³

> = ⁴⁄₃π3³
> = 36π = approximately 110m³

C: Cylinder with height 6m and diameter 6m
Volume = πradius² × height

> = π3² × 6
> = 54π = approximately 170m³

D: Rectangular prism with sides length 5m, 6m, 7m

> Volume = length × width × height
> = 5m × 6m × 7m = 210m³

The cube has the largest volume.

---

20. C In the image, you can see the two points have been graphed on the coordinate plane. Then, a right triangle was drawn with the hypotenuse representing the distance between the points.

The vertical side of the right triangle has a length of 8. The horizontal side of the right triangle has a length of 6. Use the Pythagorean theorem to find the length of the hypotenuse.

> $8^2 + 6^2 = hypotenuse^2$
> $64 + 36 = hypotenuse^2$
> $100 = hypotenuse^2$
> $10 = hypotenuse$

Distance between the points is 10.

Chapter 6:
Algebra & Graphing

Lessons

6.1   Slope & Rate of Change

Rate of Change

In the previous module you learned to set up proportions based on the concept of equivalent ratios or rates of change — the relative change in one variable with respect to another. You were able to use the fact that two variables (such as number of pages read by a student and time) interacted in a predictable way to determine what the value of one variable would be for a given value of the other.

Example: How many pages has a student read in one hour if she reads 2 pages per minute?

This information can easily be represented graphically, and the rate of change will be the slope of that graph. $^{2\,pages}/_{1\,min}$
For every minute that she reads, the numbers of pages she has read will increase by 2. The rate of change is 2 pages per minute.

Calculating Slope

The slope of a line is the change in the *y* coordinate divided by the change in the *x*–coordinate. This often referred to as "rise over run".
If you have two points on a graph (x_1, y_1) and (x_2, y_2) then you can use the following formula to find the slope of the straight line that connects them:

$$\text{Slope} = (y_2 - y_1) \div (x_2 - x_1)$$

$(\overset{x_1}{0}, \overset{y_1}{1}) \quad (\overset{x_2}{3}, \overset{y_2}{5})$

The slope between (1,2) and (2,4) is $= {}^{4\text{-}2}/_{2\text{-}1} = {}^2/_1$ To travel between these two points, a line must rise 2 units and run 1 unit to the right.

$$\frac{5-1}{3-0} = \boxed{\frac{4}{3}}$$

Negative Slope

The slope of a line is negative if its *y*–coordinate decreases as you move to the right. In other words, the slope is negative if the rise is negative as the run stays positive. For example, this graph has a slope of $-{}^3/_5$.

Zero Slope

A horizontal line has a slope of 0. There is no rise as you move to the right.

Undefined Slope

A vertical line's slope cannot be defined. It continually rises but has a run of zero, and it is not possible to divide a number by zero.

SLOPE & RATE OF CHANGE PRACTICE

1. What is the slope of the line that passes through points A and B?

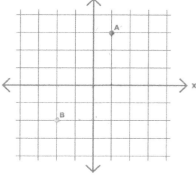

   A. $-\frac{3}{5}$
   B. $-\frac{5}{3}$
   C. $\frac{3}{5}$
   D. $\frac{5}{3}$

2. What is the slope of the line in this graph?

   A. 3
   B. -3
   C. 1
   D. $\frac{1}{3}$

3. What is the slope of the line that passes through the origin and (-3, -4)?

   A. $\frac{4}{3}$
   B. $\frac{3}{4}$
   C. $-\frac{3}{4}$
   D. $-\frac{4}{3}$

4. Which of the following graphs has a variable slope?

A.

B.

C.

D.

5. Choose the best answer to replace the question mark.

The slope from point A to point B **?** The slope from point B to point C.

   A. >
   B. <
   C. =
   D. One slope is undefined, so it can't be determined

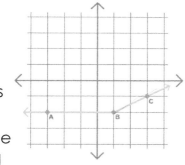

6. If Melissa can type 80 words for every 3 minutes and she needs to finish typing 6 pages with 1000 words on each page, how long will it take her?

   A. 37.5 mins
   B. 1 hour, 15 mins
   C. 3 hours, 45 mins
   D. 4 hours

7. A line with a slope of -12 that passes through the origin has what y value when x is 5?

    A. 60

    B. -60

    C. -7

    D. 17

8. Which of the following lines has an undefined slope?

 A.   B.

C.    D.

9. What is the slope of the line that passes through (-2, 4) and (5, 3)?

$$\frac{y_2 - y_1}{x_2 - x_1}$$

    A. $-\frac{1}{7}$

    B. $\frac{3}{7}$

    C. -7

    D. $-\frac{5}{6}$

$$\frac{3 - 4}{5 - (-2)} = \frac{-1}{7}$$

10. How many times does the slope of the line below change?

    A. 2

    B. 3

    C. 4

    D. 5

SLOPE & RATE OF CHANGE EXPLANATIONS

1. D   Slope is rise over run. From point B to point A, the rise is 5 and the run is 3. Therefore, the slope of that line is $\frac{5}{3}$.

2. C   To determine slope, figure out how much the line rises over how much it runs. In other words, find the change in the y–coordinates and divide by the change in the x–coordinates.

     For this line, let us start at (0, -3) and go to (3,0). From the first point to the second point, the line rises 3 and goes across 3. Therefore, the slope is equal to $\frac{3}{3} = 1$.

3. A   The slope is the rise over run. Therefore, the slope is the change in the y–coordinates over the change in the x–coordinates. Thus, find the change between the following 2 coordinate pairs (0,0) and (-3,-4).

                                              Slope = $\frac{(-4 - 0)}{(-3 - 0)} = \frac{-4}{-3} = \frac{4}{3}$

4. C Any straight line will have a slope that does not change. Answer choice C starts with a positive slope but then it changes to a negative slope.

5. B The slope from point A to point B is zero since it is a horizontal line. The slope from point B to point C is positive since the line is increasing.

Therefore, the slope from point A to B is less than the slope from B to C.

6. C The rate for Melissa is 80 words for 3 minutes. She needs to type 6 pages with 1000 words each, a total of 6000 words. Since we assume that Melissa's rate remains the same, set up a ratio between words and minutes. ❶
❷ Cross multiply and solve.
The answers are in terms of hours and minutes, so convert 225 minutes to hours and minutes.

❶ $80 \text{ words}/3 \text{ mins} = 6000 \text{ words}/y \text{ mins}$

❷
$$80y = 6000(3)$$
$$80y = 18000$$
$$y = 225$$
225 minutes

$$225 \text{ minutes} \times 1 \text{ hour}/60 \text{ mins} = 345/60 \text{ hours} = 3 \text{ hours } 45 \text{ mins}$$

7. B The formula to find slope is:

$$\text{Slope} = \text{change in } y/\text{change in } x$$

Plug in the values you know and solve for y.

$$(y - 0)/(5 - 0) = -12$$
$$y/5 = -12$$
$$y = -60$$

8. D Answer choice A has a positive slope since the line is increasing.
Answer B has a slope of zero since it is a horizontal line.
Answer C has a slope that keeps changing, but it is always defined.
Answer D has an undefined slope since it is a vertical line.

9. A The slope of a line is the rise over the run. Therefore, slope is the change in y over the change in x.

The two points are: (-2, 4) and (5, 3).
The change in y value is $4 - 3 = 1$
The change in x value is $-2 - 5 = -7$

$$\text{Slope}$$
$$= \text{change in } y/\text{change in } x$$
$$= 1/-7$$
$$= -1/7$$

10. B The image has 4 different slopes, therefore the slope changes 3 times. The dots in the image show the places where the slope changes.

6.2   Graphing Equations

Linear Equations

A linear equation is one that results in a straight line when graphed. The equation of a straight line typically takes the form:

$$y = mx + b$$

In this equation, m is the slope and b is the **y–intercept**. The y–intercept is the point at which the line crosses the y–axis — in other words, the y–value when $x = 0$. The x and y represent the x– and y–values of any coordinate pair on the line.

Let's graph the following linear equation: $y = \frac{3}{2} x - 2$

You can see from the equation that the y–intercept is -2. This point is plotted on the graph as (0, -2). The equation also tells us that the slope is $\frac{3}{2}$. Starting at (0, -2), draw a second point up 3 and 2 to the right. Now, connect those points to create the graph of the line.

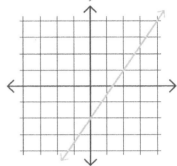

Determining Equations

If you are given two coordinate pairs, you can calculate the slope using the formula you learned in the lesson "Slope & Rate of Change". Once you have the slope, plug in either pair to solve for the y–intercept.

Example:
Find the equation for the line through the two pairs of points (-4, 6) and (-2, -8).

$$\text{Slope} = \frac{(-8 - 6)}{(-2 - -4)} = \frac{-14}{2} = -7$$

Use the slope and one point to calculate the y–intercept:
$$y = mx + b$$
$$y = -7x + b$$
$$6 = -7(-4) + b$$
$$6 = 28 + b$$
$$-22 = b$$
$$y = -7x - 22$$

GRAPHING EQUATIONS PRACTICE

1. **What is the equation of the line in this graph?**

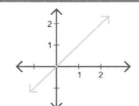

A. $y = \frac{1}{2} x + 1$
B. $y = x$
C. $y = x + 1$
D. $\frac{1}{2} y = x + 1$

$y = mx + b$

yint → set X to 0
Xint → set y to 0

2. What is the slope of the line represented by this equation?

$$\underset{-1}{1} - \tfrac{3}{4}\, y = \tfrac{1}{3}x - 2 \; {-1}$$

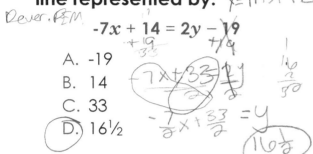

A. ¾

B. ⅓

C. -2

D. -⁴⁄₉

3. What is the y–intercept of the line represented by: $y = mx + b$

Dever. PEM

$$-7x + 14 = 2y - 19$$

A. -19

B. 14

C. 33

D. 16½

4. What is the equation of the line that passes through the points (4, -3) and (2, 7)?

A. $y = 6x + 4$

B. $y = -5x + 17$

C. $y = -\tfrac{1}{5}x - 3$

D. $y = -5x + 4$

5. What is the y–intercept of the following line?

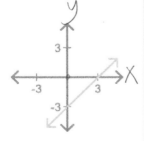

A. 3

B. -3

C. 1

D. -⅓

6. What is the x–intercept of the line $y = 4x - 9$?

A. 4

B. -9

C. ⁹⁄₄

D. ⁴⁄₉

7. What is the equation of the line that passes through (12, 16) and (-4, 8)?

A. $y = -\tfrac{1}{2}x + 22$

B. $y = -2x + 40$

C. $y = 2x - 8$

D. $y = \tfrac{1}{2}x + 10$

8. What is the equation of the line in the graph?

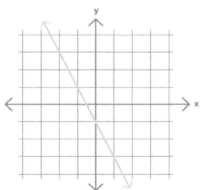

A. $y = -2x - 1$

B. $y = 2x - 1$

C. $y = \tfrac{1}{2}x - 1$

D. $y = -2x + 1$

9. Which of the following equations has a slope of ⅗ and y–intercept of 2?

A. $-3x + 5y = 10$

B. $3x + 5y = 2$

C. $5x + 3y = 2$

D. $-5x - 3y = 10$

10. The slope of a line is (-3). If you
    wanted to find the equation
    of the line, which of these
    pieces of information would be
    enough on their own?

    A. II only
    B. I and II
    C. II and III
    D. I, II, and III

    I. a coordinate pair
       on the line
    II. the y–intercept
    III. the x–intercept

$y = mx + b$

GRAPHING EQUATIONS EXPLANATIONS

1. B   Use the following format of an equation: $y = mx + b$, where m is the slope and b is the y–intercept.

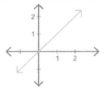

The y–intercept is where the line crosses the y–axis. In this case, the line crosses at 0. Therefore, $b = 0$.

The slope is the rise over the run. In this case, the line goes up 1 every time it goes across 1. Therefore, slope is 1.

$$y = mx + b$$
$$y = 1(x) + 0$$
$$y = x$$

2. D   Manipulate the equation to isolate y and get the equation in the form: $y = mx + b$. Once it is in that form, you can see the coefficient in front of the x, represented by m, will be the slope.

$$1 - \tfrac{3}{4}y = \tfrac{1}{3}x - 2$$
$$-\tfrac{3}{4}y = \tfrac{1}{3}x - 3$$
$$(-\tfrac{4}{3})(-\tfrac{3}{4}y) = (-\tfrac{4}{3})(\tfrac{1}{3}x - 3)$$
$$y = -\tfrac{4}{9}x + 4$$

3. D   Manipulate the equation to isolate y and get the equation in the form: $y = mx + b$, where the b will represent the y–intercept.
The y–intercept is $\tfrac{33}{2} = 16\tfrac{1}{2}$

$$-7x + 14 = 2y - 19$$
$$-7x + 33 = 2y$$
$$-\tfrac{7}{2}x + \tfrac{33}{2} = y$$
$$y = -\tfrac{7}{2}x + \tfrac{33}{2}$$

4. B   Find equation between: (4, -3) and (2, 7).

The form of the equation is $y = mx + b$, where m is the slope and b is the y–intercept.

First, find the slope of the line between those two points. Slope is rise over run, or the change in y over the change in x.

Slope
$= {}^{(-3 - 7)}\!/_{(4 - 2)}$
$= {}^{-10}\!/_2 = -5$

Now, find the y–intercept.
Plug in either point into the equation and solve for b.
Let's use the first point (4, -3).
Equation: $y = -5x + 17$

$$y = -5x + b$$

$$-3 = -5(4) + b$$
$$-3 = -20 + b$$
$$b = 17$$

---

5. B   The y–intercept is where the line crosses the y–axis at $x = 0$.
In the graph, you can see that the line crosses at -3
y–intercept is at -3

---

6. C   The x–intercept is where a line crosses the x–axis. When
something crosses the x–axis, the y value of that point is
$y = 0$. Plug in $y = 0$ and solve for x.

$$y = 4x - 9$$
$$0 = 4x - 9$$
$$9 = 4x$$
$$x = \tfrac{9}{4}$$

---

7. D   To find the equation of the line through the two
coordinate pairs, first find the slope.

The slope is rise over run, so find the difference in y–
coordinates and divide by the difference in x–coordinates. (12, 16) and (-4, 8)
Therefore, the equation, $y = mx + b$, now is $y = \tfrac{1}{2}x + b$

Plug in either coordinate pair to solve for b. ❷

slope $= {}^{8-16}/_{-4-12}$
$= {}^{-8}/_{-16} = \tfrac{1}{2}$

$y = \tfrac{1}{2}x + b$
$16 = \tfrac{1}{2}(12) + b$
$16 = 6 + b$
$b = 10$
$y = \tfrac{1}{2}x + 10$

---

8. A   When finding the equation of a line, find the slope and intercept, to represent $y = mx + b$.
This line crosses the y–axis at -1. Therefore, $b = -1$.
The slope is rise over run, pick any two points on the line and
then figure out how much from one point to the next
the line rises and runs. This line goes down 2 for
every 1 across.

Slope $= {}^{-2}/_1 = -2$
$y = -2x - 1$

---

9. A   There are two methods to solving this problem. The first method involves
rewriting the answer choices in slope–intercept form ($y = mx + b$). The
second method involves writing the problem in slope–intercept form and
then rearranging that equation to match the form of the answer choices.

Method 1: Rearrange each answer choice so that the equations are in
slope–intercept form.

A: $-3x + 5y = 10$	**B:** $3x + 5y = 2$	**C:** $5x + 3y = 2$	**D:** $-5x - 3y = 10$
$5y = 3x + 10$	$5y = -3x + 2$	$3y = -5x + 2$	$-3y = 5x + 10$
$y = \frac{3}{5}x + 2$	$y = -\frac{3}{5}x + \frac{2}{5}$	$y = -\frac{5}{3}x + \frac{2}{3}$	$y = -\frac{5}{3}x - \frac{10}{3}$
Slope $= \frac{3}{5}$,	Slope $= -\frac{3}{5}$,	Slope $= -\frac{5}{3}$,	Slope $= -\frac{5}{3}$,
y–intercept $= 2$	y–intercept $= \frac{2}{5}$	y–intercept $= \frac{2}{3}$	y–intercept $= -\frac{10}{3}$

Answer A is correct

Method 2: First, write the equation in slope, intercept form: $y = mx + b$. Then, you can rearrange the equation to standard form: $ax + by = c$.

In this case, the problem states both the slope and y–intercept. Therefore, immediately plug them into the equation.

$$y = mx + b$$
$$y = \frac{3}{5}x + 2$$

Now, rearrange the equation. First, multiply everything by 5 to get rid of the fraction.

$$5y = 3x + 10$$

Now, bring the x's and y's to the same side of the equation.

$$-3x + 5y = 10$$

---

10. **D** Throughout this lesson, you have seen methods for finding the equation of a line knowing the slope and a coordinate pair. Remember, the y–intercept, is just a coordinate pair with the x–value of 0. Also, the x–intercept is a coordinate pair with the y–value of 0. With a coordinate pair and a slope, you can plug it into the equation: $y = -3x + b$ and solve for b.

I, II, and III

6.3 Qualitative Graphing

Often, it is possible to gather information about an equation or real–life situation by looking at a graph that represents it. When interpreting graphs, notice the slope at various points and any x and y–intercepts.

Slope

When using the slope of a graph to gain information about a situation keep a few things in mind:

1: Is the slope positive or negative? — For example, if given the scenario that sales of a computer have increased significantly, you should pick out the graph with a positive slope. The one circled in the graph right.

2: What is the rate of change? — You should use information about variations in slope to your advantage. For example, if asked which graph represents the temperature for a month that warmed up for the first two weeks and then remained steady for the rest of the month, you should recognize that the circled graph follows this pattern.

Intercepts

The x and y intercepts of word problems can have many different meanings depending on how the problem is set up. You should practice identifying the meaning of intercepts in graphs of real–world situations. Here's an example:

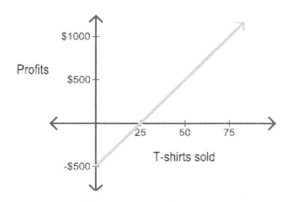

The graph shows the profits on t–shirt sales. As can be seen, the y–intercept is the point at which $x = 0$, or 0 t–shirts are sold. The y–intercept is -$500. Therefore, before any t-shirts are sold, the profit is -$500, which means that the costs are $500. The x–intercept in this case is at 25, so the breakeven point is when 25 t-shirts are sold.

1. Which graph best represents the growth of a plant that took 2 weeks to begin growing and then grew at a steady rate?

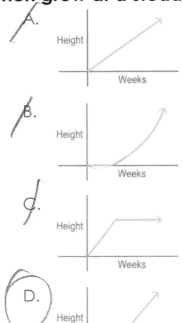

A.
Height
Weeks

B.
Height
Weeks

C.
Height
Weeks

D.
Height
Weeks

2. Which graph shows only a positive slope?

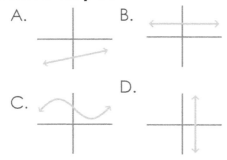

A.

B.

C.

D.

3. What is the initial cost of the candy bars?

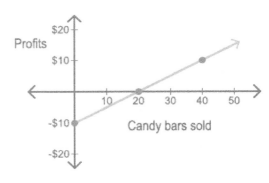

A. $0
B. $1
C. $10
D. -$10

4. Which of the following graphs best represents the x–axis as the length of the side of a square and the y–axis as the area of the square?

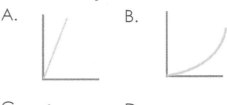

A.   B.

C.   D.

5. How much is being charged per candy bar?

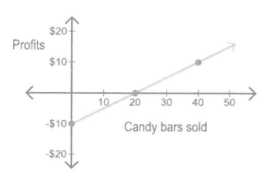

A. 25 cents
B. 50 cents
C. 75 cents
D. $1

6. How many candy bars must be sold to break even?

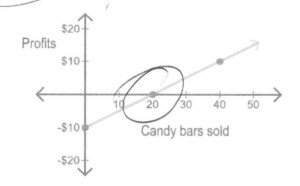

A. 0
B. 10
C. 20
D. 30

7. In the graph below, where is the slope of the line negative?

A. before 2006
B. for part of 2006
C. after 2007
D. up to 2007

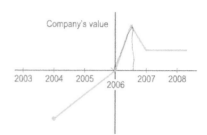

8. When did the value of the company peak based on the graph above?

A. In 2005
B. In 2006
C. In 2007
D. In 2008

9. Based on the information in the graph, which is true?

A. The company started in 2006.

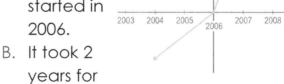

B. It took 2 years for the company to break even.
C. The company's value has increased steadily since it began.
D. The company's value decreased overall between 2006 and 2007.

10. **A stock increases steadily in value over a period of months, before falling quickly and beginning to rebound. Which graph could represent its value over time?**

A.   B.

C.   D.

QUALITATIVE GRAPHING EXPLANATIONS

1. **D**   Since the plant did not begin growing for 2 weeks, there should be a straight line along the x–axis until week 2. Then, the plant grew at a steady rate which would be represented by a straight line with a positive slope. This is seen in the following graph:

2. **A**   Graphs with positive slope increase as you look at them from left to right. The graph in A does that.

3. **C**   The initial cost of the candy bars can be seen at the y–intercept. Where the line crosses the y–axis, means that the number of candy bars sold is 0, so we are dealing with initial costs.

The y–intercept is at -$10, but this shows profit. Therefore, if the profit is -$10, that means that the initial cost was $10.

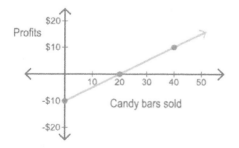

4. B   As the length of the side of a square increases, the area of the square goes up exponentially. For instance, if the side of a square is 2, the area is 4. Side of 3 is area of 9. Side of 4 is area of 16. As you can see, the y values will increase much faster than the x values.

The following graph, answer B, shows this.

5. B   The amount being charged per candy bar is the slope of the line. Slope is rise over run. In this case that would be the profit divided by the number of candy bars sold, which is the price of a candy bar.

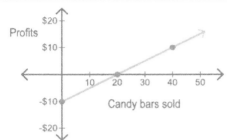

Use any two coordinate pairs to help you find slope. In the graph, you can see the following coordinate pairs, (20 candy bars, $0) and (40 candy bars, $10). Now find the slope:

$$\text{Slope} = \frac{\$10 - \$0}{40 - 20 \ \text{candy}} = \frac{\$10}{20 \ \text{candy}} = \$0.50 \ \text{per candy bar}$$

6. C   The break even point is when the costs = revenue, which means that the profit = $0. The profit is $0 on this graph at the x–intercept. You can see that the line crosses the x–axis at 20 candy bars.

7. B   A negative slope occurs when a line goes down. Slope is rise over run, so a negative slope means that the rise is negative as you move along in the x–direction.
In the graph, there is only one section of the line with a negative slope, and that occurs towards the end of 2006. Therefore, answer B is correct.

Do not be confused by the time before 2006. Even though the company's value is negative, the value is increasing, so the slope is positive.

8. B The point with the highest company value is the point with the greatest y-coordinate.

This occurs in 2006.

9. B Let's examine each answer choice.

   A. The company was started in 2006.
   This is not true. In the graph you can see that the company started in 2004.

   B. It took 2 years for the company to break even.
   This is true. The company started in 2004 and then in 2006 the company's value was at $0, which means the company broke even. This is 2 years.

   C. The company's value has increased steadily since it began.
   This is not true. The company's value decreased in 2006.

   D. The company's value decreased overall between 2006 and 2007.
   This is not true. Even though the value of the company decreased for part of 2006, when 2007 began the company's value was higher than it was when 2006 began.

---

10. D If the stock increases steadily, you want to start with a line with a positive slope. Be careful with answer choice A. The line does increase, but not steadily, since it is not a straight line. Then, the stock falls quickly, you want a line that has a steep negative slope. The stock then begins to rebound, which means you again want a line with a positive slope.

6.4 Systems of Equations

Introduction

A system of equations is a set of equations that can be used to find possible values for multiple variables. Generally, you will be given two equations with two unknowns, and you will solve for the values that make both equations true. Systems of equations can be solved in four ways.

1. Graphing

To find the possible values of a set of variable for two equations, find the point or points where the graphs of the equations intersect. A graph of an equation represents all the points that make the equation true. Therefore, the point where two graphs intersect is the point that makes both equations true.

For example, if you were asked to solve the following system of equations: $y = 2x + 2$ and $y = -3x - 3$, you could graph both equations. The point where they intersect, (-1, 0), represents the solution ($x = -1$, and $y = 0$).

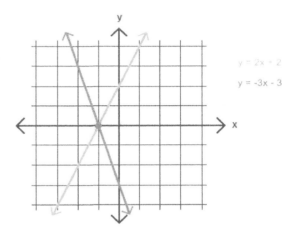

2. Substitution

Another way to solve a system of equations is by substitution. This involves isolating a variable in one equation, and then substituting the value of that variable into the other equation.

Example: $3x + y = -5$, $2x + 3y = -1$

❶ Using the first equation, solve for y.
❷ Now, plug that value for y into the second equation.
❸ Now, plug the value of x back into any equation to solve for y.

Solution: $x = -2$, $y = 1$

❶
$$3x + y = -5$$
$$y = -5 - 3x$$

❷
$$2x + 3(-5 - 3x) = -1$$
$$2x - 15 - 9x = -1$$
$$-7x = 14, \ x = -2$$

❸
$$y = -5 - 3x$$
$$= -5 - 3(-2) = 1$$

3. Elimination

You can also solve a system of equations with elimination. Manipulate the equations so that you can add them to eliminate all but one variable. After solving for that variable, plug it into one of the original equations to solve for the other variable.

Example: $3x + y = -5$, $2x + 3y = -1$.

Choose which variable to eliminate – in this case, let's choose y.
❶ Multiply the first equation by -3:
❷ Now, add the two equations:
  $x = -2$
❸ Now, plug in $x = -2$ to solve for y:
Solution: $x = -2$, $y = 1$

❶
$-9x - 3y = 15$

❷
$-9x - 3y = 15$
$\underline{2x + 3y = -1}$
${-7x = 14}$

❸
$y = -5 - 3x$
$= -5 - 3(-2) = 1$

4. Plugging In

The final option works when you are given a multiple–choice question with a set of possible answers. You can plug each set into the original equations and see which solution makes both equations true.

SYSTEMS OF EQUATIONS PRACTICE

1. **What is the solution to the following system of equations?**

    $$4x + 2y = 6$$
    $$3x - y = 7$$

    A. (-2, 1)
    B. (3, 3)
    C. (2, -1)
    D. (1, -4)

2. **Solve for j in the following system of equations.**

    $$5j + 3 = x - 2$$
    $$j + 45 = x$$

    A. 10
    B. 15
    C. 40
    D. 55

3. **The solution to a system of equations is what?**

    A. Always a coordinate pair
    B. Makes one of the equations true.
    C. Never has the same x and y values.
    D. Is true for all of the equations in the system.

4. What is the solution to the following system of equations?

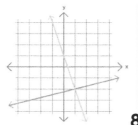

   A. (0, 1)
   B. (1, -2)
   C. (1, 2)
   D. (-2, 1)

5. What is the solution to the system of equations graphed below?

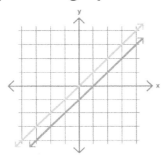

   A. (0, 0)
   B. (1, 0)
   C. (1, 1)
   D. No solution

6. Solve for y in the following equations:

$$2y - 3x = 8 \qquad 2y - 3x + 8$$
$$x = 3y + 2$$

   A. -4
   B. -2
   C. 3
   D. 6

7. Solve for x in the following system of equations:

$$-3x + 2y = -13$$
$$3x = y + 11$$

   A. -2
   B. 3
   C. 9
   D. 11

8. Admission to a baseball game is $2 for general admission and $3.50 for reserved seats. If 12,500 people paid a total of $36,250 to attend the game, how many general admission tickets were sold?

   A. 3500
   B. 5000
   C. 7250
   D. 18125

9. How many solutions does the following system of equations have?

$$4x - 6y = -10$$
$$3y = 5 + 2x$$

   A. 0
   B. 1
   C. 2
   D. infinite

10. You have 16 coins in your pocket that are all pennies and nickels. If the coins are worth 32 cents, how many pennies do you have?

   A. 4
   B. 8
   C. 10
   D. 12

1. C There are multiple ways to solve questions of this type. The easiest method is to plug in each answer in both of the equations, and choose the answer that makes them both true. Another method is to solve using elimination.

$$4x + 2y = 6$$
$$3x - y = 7$$

Option 1: Plugging in
Take each answer and plug in the first value for x and the second value for y.
Answer A (-2,1): $4(-2) + 2(1) = -8 + 2 = -6$; Not true.
Answer B (3,3): $4(3) + 2(3) = 12 + 6 = 18$; Not true.
Answer C (2,-1): $4(2) + 2(-1) = 8 - 2 = 6$. Works in the first equation, now try the second. $3(2) - (-1) = 6 + 1 = 7$. Works in the second equation. This is the answer.

Option 2:
The second method is to use elimination to solve for the variables. Choose a variable to eliminate, in this case, let's eliminate y. Therefore, we want to get the coefficient in front of y to have the same magnitude. Multiply the entire second equation by 2. ❶

❶
$$2(3x - y = 7)$$
$$6x - 2y = 14$$

❷ Now, line up the two equations and add them together to eliminate y.

❷
$$4x + 2y = 6$$
$$6x - 2y = 14$$
$$\overline{10x = 20}$$
$$x = 2$$

❸ Now plug in the value for x into either equation to solve for y.

❸
$$4(2) + 2y = 6$$
$$8 + 2y = 6$$
$$2y = -2$$
$$y = -1$$

2. A Let's use substitution to solve for j in the following equations, since one of the variables is already isolated in one of the equations.

$$5j + 3 = x - 2$$
$$j + 45 = x$$

❶ Substitute $j + 45$ for x in the first equation.
❷ Now solve for j.

❶
$$5j + 3 = x - 2$$
$$5j + 3 = (j + 45) - 2$$

❷
$$5j + 3 = j + 45 - 2$$
$$5j + 3 = j + 43$$
$$4j + 3 = 43$$
$$4j = 40$$
$$j = 10$$

3. D Let's examine each answer choice:

A: Always a coordinate pair
This is not true. There can be any number of solutions to a system of equations. You can have a solution that is a coordinate pair, or you can have no solutions, infinite solutions, etc.

B: Makes one of the equations true.

The solution to a system of equations makes all the equations true, not just one.

C: Never has the same x and y values.

This is also not true. For instance, $x + y = 2$ and $x - y = 0$ has the solution $x = 1$ and $y = 1$.

D: Is true for all of the equations in the system.

This is the definition of a solution to a system of equations.

---

4. B If the equations are already graphed, it is easy to find the solution to the system of equations. You just find the point where the two lines intersect.

The lines intersect at (1, -2).

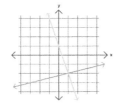

---

5. D The solution to a system of equations that is graphed is where the two lines intersect. In this case, the lines never intersect. Therefore, there is no x–value and y–value pair that makes both lines true. There is no solution to this system of equations.

---

6. B Use substitution to solve this system of equations. Plug in the value for x from the second equation into the first equation.

$$2y - 3x = 8$$
$$x = 3y + 2$$

$$2y - 3(3y + 2) = 8$$
$$2y - 9y - 6 = 8$$
$$-7y - 6 = 8$$
$$-7y = 14$$
$$y = -2$$

---

7. B You can solve the system using substitution or elimination.

***Method 1:* Substitution**
Rearrange the second equation to solve for y. $y = 3x - 11$
❶ Plug in the value for y into the first equation.

$$-3x + 2y = -13$$
$$3x = y + 11$$

❶
$$-3x + 2y = -13$$
$$-3x + 2(3x - 11) = -13$$
$$-3x + 6x - 22 = -13$$
$$3x = 9$$
$$x = 3$$

***Method 2:* Elimination**
❶ Rearrange the equations so that the variables are in the same order and on the same side of the equations.

❷ If you add the equations, you see that the x's will be eliminated.

❸ Now, plug in the value for y into either equation and solve for x.

❶
$$-3x + 2y = -13$$
$$3x - y = 11$$

❷
$$0x + 1y = -2$$
$$y = -2$$

❸
$$3x = y + 11$$
$$3x = -2 + 11$$
$$3x = 9$$
$$x = 3$$

---

8. B There are multiple ways to solve this probem as with any algebra word problem. Here are three different methods:

Method 1: **Using two variables**

Create a variable for each unknown.

g for the number of general admission tickets sold
r for the number of reserved seat tickets sold

❶ Now, set up equataions.
12,500 paid = therefore, 12,500 total tickets were sold.

❷ $36,250 was brought in, $2 for general admission and $3.50 for reserved seats

The amount of money generated for the general admission tickets is: $2g$
Amount of money for reserved tickets: $3.50r$

❶ $g + r = 12{,}500$

❷ $2g + 3.5r = 36{,}250$

❸ $g + r = 12500$,
$r = 12500 - g$

❸ Now solve the system of equations. You can use any method, let's try substitution in this case. Take the first equation and solve for r.

❹ Substitute r into the second equation.
5000 general admission tickets were sold

❹
$2g + 3.5r = 36{,}250$
$2g + 3.5(12500 - g) = 36250$
$2g + 43750 - 3.5g = 36250$
$-1.5g = -7500$
$g = 5000$

Method 2: **Using one variable:** Set up a variable for the unknown you are trying to solve for. In this case, you are being asked to find the number of general admission tickets that were sold. Let's use the variable g to represent this. g = the number of general admission tickets sold. You also don't know the number of reserved seats sold. Instead of making another variable, let's express this in terms of the first variable, g. We know that there were 12,500 people total. Therefore, the number of general admission tickets plus the number of reserved seats must equal 12,500.

general admission + reserved seats
$= 12{,}500$ g + reserved seats
$= 12{,}500$ reserved seats
$= 12{,}500 - g$

Okay, so now we have two pieces of information: g = number of general admission tickets $12500 - g$ = number of reserved seats. Now, let's look at the money. If you multiply the number of tickets by the cost of each ticket, you will get the total amount of money spent on each type of ticket.

$2 \times g + 3.50 (12500 - g) = 36250$
$2g + 43750 - 3.5g = 36250$
$-1.5g = -7500$
$g = 5000$

There were 5000 general admission tickets sold.

Method 3: **Work Backwards:** Try each answer into the problem to see which gives you the correct answer.

For instance, say we tried answer choice B — what would that mean? So, answer choice B says that there were 5000 general admission tickets sold. Therefore, go through the problem and see if that works. If 5000 general admission tickets sold, then that means there were $12{,}500 - 5000 = 7{,}500$ reserved seats sold. Alright, now let's see if the money works. $5000 (2) + 3.50 (7500) = 36250$. It works, this is the right answer.

---

9. D Rearrange the equations so that the x's and y's are on the same side of the equations in the same order. Keep 1st equation in same order and rearrange second equation.

$$3y = 5 + 2x$$
$$-2x + 3y = 5$$

Now, solve using elimination.
Keep the first equation as is. Multiply the second equation by 2 to eliminate a variable. Then add the two equations.

$$4x - 6y = -10$$
$$-2x + 3y = 5$$

Since you get a true statement, that $0 = 0$, it means that any solution to the first equation will be a solution to the second equation. The two equations are the same, just rearranged.

$$4x - 6y = -10 \ (1^{st} \text{ eq})$$
$$-4x + 6y = 10 \ (2^{nd} \text{ eq})$$
$$0 + 0 = 0 \ (\text{sum of equations})$$

Infinite number of solutions to the system of equations. This can also be seen if you graphed the two equations. You would realize that you are graphing the exact same line.

---

10. D There are two unknowns in this equation, set up a variable for each.

p = number of pennies
n = number of nickels

Now, set up equations.

❶ "You have 16 coins" — Therefore, the total number of pennies and nickels will equal 16.

❷ "the coins are worth 32 cents" — Therefore, the total value of the pennies plus the total value of the nickels is worth 32.
Now, solve the system.

❸ Use substitution and isolate a variable in the first equation.

❹ Plug in the value for n into the second equation.

❶ $p + n = 16$

❷ $1p + 5n = 32$

❸ $p + n = 16$
   $n = 16 - p$

❹ $1p + 5n = 32$
   $1p + 5(16 - p) = 32$
   $p + 80 - 5p = 32$
   $-4p + 80 = 32$
   $-4p = -48$
   $p = 12$

6.5　Algebra Word Problems

Translating Word Problems into Equations

Algebraic word problems are similar to the word problems you encountered involving basic operations, and the same strategies are applicable. However, they require you to form an equation containing a variable, and that adds a level of difficulty.

Let's begin with a simple example of translating a given situation into a mathematical expression:

> **Nadine has only red shirts and blue shirts. She has 29 red shirts and 43 shirts total. How many blue shirts does she have?**

Use key words such as "total" to determine the function that needs to be performed. Then, use a variable to represent any unknown quantities.

> **Red shirts + Blue shirts = Total shirts**
> **29 + b = 43**

In the equation above, b represents the number of blue shirts Nadine has. Solve for the variable b by subtracting 29 from both sides:

> **29 + b – 29 = 43 – 29**
> **b = 14**
> **Nadine has 14 blue shirts.**

The most complex algebra word problems involve multiple unknown quantities. Whenever possible, represent all unknown quantities in terms of a single variable. This is easy to do when a specific relationship is given for two or more unknowns.

> **Example: Colleen bought twice as many oranges as apples at the grocery store. If she bought 45 apples and oranges, how many apples did Colleen buy?**

Choose as the variable the quantity the question asks you to find, then define the relationship between that variable and any other unknown quantities.

Let x represent the number of apples Colleen buys. Therefore, the number of oranges is $2x$.

Then, write and solve an equation using only 1 variable: Apples + Oranges = 45

> **x + 2x = 45**
> **3x = 45**
> **x = 15**
> **Colleen buys 15 apples.**

1. Andrew has pennies, dimes and quarters. He has a total of $8.70. There are two times as many pennies as quarters. There are six times as many dimes as quarters. How many dimes does he have?   *solve for d*

    A. 6 $P \cdot \# of = 1P$
    B. 10 $D \# of = 10D$ $D = 10$
    C. 60 $Q = \# of = 25Q$
    D. 87 $P = 2Q$
              $D = 6Q$

2. Find three consecutive odd integers, such that the sum of the third and twice the first is 7 more than twice the third. What is the largest number?

    A. 7
    B. 11
    C. 13
    D. 15

3. An airplane takes 6 hours to fly from San Francisco to Boston and only 5 hours to return. The wind velocity is 50 mph and increases the plane's speed from Boston to San Francisco, but decreases the plane's speed from San Francisco to Boston. What is the average speed of the airplane? (hint: rate × time = distance)

    A. 450 mph
    B. 500 mph
    C. 550 mph
    D. 600 mph

4. At the same moment, two trains leave Chicago and New York. They move towards each other with constant speeds. The train from Chicago is moving at speed of 40 miles per hour, and the train from New York is moving at speed of 60 miles per hour. The distance between Chicago and New York is 1000 miles. How long after their departure will they meet?

    A. 10
    B. 15
    C. 17
    D. 20

5. Christine's father is 3 times her age, and, 4 years ago, he was 4 times older than she was then. How old is Christine now?

    A. 4
    B. 12
    C. 15
    D. 18

6. A woman on a bike and a man in a car leave a restaurant at the same time. The woman heads due East and the man goes due West. If the woman is biking at 15 mph, and the car is traveling at 35 mph, in how many hours will they be 300 miles apart?

    A. 2

    B. 4

    C. 6

    D. 8

7. A door is 3 times as long as it is wide. If the area is 108 square feet when the length and width are each doubled, how wide was the door originally?

    A. 2

    B. 3

    C. 4

    D. 5

8. How much pure water (with no saline) would you need to add to 4 liters (L) of an 80% saline solution to make it a 20% saline solution?

    A. 1L

    B. 8L

    C. 12L

    D. 16L

9. Two trains, A & B, are 540 km apart and travel toward each other on parallel tracks. Train A travels 40 km per hour and train B, 10 km per hour faster than A. In how many hours will they meet?

    A. 6 hours

    B. 7 hours

    C. 8 hours

    D. 9 hours

10. The sum of the digits of a two-digit number is 10. When the digits are reversed, the number decreases by 36. Find the original two-digit number.

    A. 84

    B. 73

    C. 64

    D. 53

ALGEBRA WORD PROBLEMS EXPLANATIONS

1. C You need to assign a variable to one of your unknowns. In this case, let's choose the number of quarters and set that equal to q. Now, relate all the unknowns in terms of that variable:

> Number of quarters: q
> Number of pennies: $2q$
> Number of dimes: $6q$

Now, you must make an equation. Since you know the total amount of money and the value of each coin, you can write the following equation:

$$(0.25)(\text{Number of Quarters}) + (0.10)(\text{Number of dimes}) + (0.01)(\text{Number of pennies}) = \$8.70$$

$$(0.25)(q) + (0.10)(6q) + (0.01)(2q) = \$8.70$$
$$0.25q + 0.6q + 0.02q = \$8.70$$
$$0.87q = 8.70$$
$$q = 10$$

The number of dimes is $6q = 6(10) = 60$

2. D *Method 1:* For algebra word problems, you need to assign a variable to the unknown. You could set the smallest integer to x. Then, we can find out what the other two numbers are in terms of x.

Since we are dealing with consecutive odd integers, the second number will be two more than the first, and the third number will be two more than the second.

Therefore, the three unknowns are: x, $x + 2$, and $x + 4$
Now, we must set up an equation.
The sum of the third and twice the first is 7 more than twice the third

Take each word and translate it into an equation:

Sum = addition, third = $x + 4$, twice = multiply by 2, first = x, more = add

$(x + 4) + 2(x) = 7 + 2(x + 4)$	• Translate words into equation
$x + 4 + 2x = 7 + 2x + 8$	• Distribute
$3x + 4 = 15 + 2x$	• Combine like terms on each side
$3x = 11 + 2x$	• Subtract 4 from each side
$x = 11$	• Subtract $2x$ from each side
Integers are: 11, 13, 15	• You solved for x, the smallest. So find the next 2 consecutive odd integers.

The largest is 15. Answer D.

Method 2: Another method on problems like this is to work backwards and use your answers. They are sitting right there, so why not use them. You want to find the largest number out of 3 consecutive odd integers, such that the sum of the third and twice the first is 7 more than twice the third. Let's try answers. I will just go through the correct answer to illustrate it. If answer D, 15 is correct, that means that 15 is the largest of 3 consecutive odd integers. The integers then would be: 11, 13, and 15. Now, let's check.

Sum of third and twice first is 7 more than twice third. It works, so this is your answer. If you tried any of the other answers, you would not have ended up with a true statement.

$$15 + 2(11) = 7 + 2(15)$$
$$15 + 22 = 7 + 30$$
$$37 = 37$$

3. C   The one formula to remember when dealing with travel problems is that:

$$\text{Distance} = \text{Rate} \times \text{Time}$$

For any algebra word problem, assign a variable to the unknown. In this case, the unknown is the average speed of the airplane, let's assign r to represent this value.

Now, we must set up equations. For the trip from San Francisco to Boston, the airplane was flying at a rate of r, but the wind was going against the plane, thus the rate was $(r - 50)$. The distance the plane flew was then the rate $\times$ time $= (r - 50) \times 6$

For the return trip, the airplane was flying at a rate of r, and the wind was helping the plane go faster, therefore, the rate was $(r + 50)$. The distance the plane flew back was then the rate $\times$ time $= (r + 50) \times 5$

The distances were the same in each case, so we can set the two equations equal to each other.

$(r - 50) \times 6 = (r + 50) \times 5$	• Set distances equal to each other
$6r - 300 = 5r + 250$	• Distribute on both sides
$6r = 5r + 550$	• Add 300 to both sides
$r = 550$	• Subtract $5r$ from both sides

---

4. A   The classic train problem. This is a travel word problem, where the important equation to remember is that distance = rate $\times$ time.

First, let us assign a variable to the unknown. In this case, we want to find out how long after they departed that they meet. So let's assign t to represent this time.

The distance the train that left Chicago travels, is the rate $\times$ time $= 40(t)$

The distance the train that left New York travels, is the rate $\times$ time $= 60(t)$

If the distance between the two cities is 1000 miles, then the total distance the trains travel is 1000. Thus, add the distances and set them equal to 1000.

$$40t + 60t = 1000$$
$$100t = 1000$$
$$t = 10$$

---

5. B   Let's choose the variable c to represent Christine's age now and f to represent Christine's father's age. Now, let's set up equations with the two variables. Translating the words into equations.

❶ Christine's father is 3 times old as her.   ❶ $f = 3c$

❷ 4 years ago, he was 4 times older than she was then.

❷ $f - 4 = 4(c - 4)$

❸ Now we have two equations and can solve. You can use any method you want to solve, here we will use substitution. Substitute $3c$ for f in the second equation.

❸ $f = 3c$
$f - 4 = 4(c - 4)$
$3c - 4 = 4(c - 4)$

❹ Now solve for c.

Christine's age is 12. That makes her father 36.

❹ $3c - 4 = 4(c - 4)$
$3c - 4 = 4c - 16$
$-4 = c - 16$
$c = 12$

---

6. C   Since the man and woman are traveling in exactly opposite directions, the distances they travel can be added together to find out how far apart they are at a given time. The distance a person or thing has traveled can be calculated by multiplying the rate of travel by the time traveled. You know the rate and the total distance that the man and woman need to have traveled, so use a variable such as t to represent the time they have traveled. Since they have both traveled for the same amount of time, you can use one variable for both people.

15 (the speed of the woman on the bike) × t + 35 (the speed of the man on the bike) × t = 300 (the total distance they have gone in opposite directions)

Then solve for time.
$15\,t + 35\,t = 300$
$50\,t = 300$
$t = 6$ hours

---

7. B   The trickiest part of this problem is visualizing the door's dimensions. Draw a diagram to help with this. Label all of the dimensions in terms of the original width because that is the quantity for which you are asked to solve.

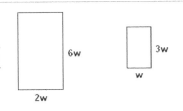

The original width should be labeled with a variable. We'll use w.
The original length is equal to 3 times the width: $3w$.
The new width is doubled: $2w$.
The new length is doubled: $2 \times 3w = 6w$.

The area of a rectangle is determined by length times width, so the formula is: $2w \times 6w = 108$ sq. feet

$12w^2 = 108$ sq. feet
$w^2 = 9$ sq. feet
$w = 3$ feet

---

8. C   You need to solve for the amount of water to add, let's create a variable for this, call it w.

The amount of saline in a solution can be found by multiplying the amount of solution by its concentration. Since adding pure water does not change the amount of saline, you can set up the following equation:

Amount of saline in water + amount of saline in 80% solution = amount of saline in 20% solution.

$$0(w) + (0.80)(4) = (0.20)(4 + w)$$
$$3.2 = 0.8 + 0.2w$$
$$2.4 = 0.2w$$
$$w = 12$$

9. A When solving a traveling problem, keep in mind the three aspects: rate, time, and distance, where rate × time = distance.

Rate:	Time:	Distance:
Train A: 40 km per hour Train B: 10 km per hour faster than Train A = 50 km per hour	This is unknown, but is the same for both trains, so let's create a variable to represent the time, t.	The total distance they travel is 540 km. Train A travels: 40 km per hour × t hours = $40t$ Train B travels: 50 km per hour × t hours = $50t$

Set up an equation to relate the distances.

$$40t + 50t = 540$$
$$90t = 540$$
$$t = 6$$

10. B There are two unknowns in this problem: the digit in the tens place and the digit in the ones place for the two–digit number. Let t represent the digit in the tens place and y represent the digit in the ones place. Now, set up equations.

❶ "The sum of the digits is 10"

❶ $t + y = 10$

"When the digits are reversed, the number decreases by 36."
First, determine the value of the original number in terms of t and y. Since the t is in the tens place and the y in the ones place, the original number equals $10t + y$.

❷ $(10t + y) - (10y + t) = 36$
$9t - 9y = 36$

❸ $t + y = 10$
$t = 10 - y$

❷ Similarly, the number with its digits reversed will have a value of $10y + t$.

❸ Now, you have two equations with 2 unknowns. You can use any method you would like to solve this system of equations. Let's use substitution.

❹ $9t - 9y = 36$
$9(10 - y) - 9y = 36$
$90 - 9y - 9y = 36$
$90 - 18y = 36$
$-18y = -54$
$y = 3$

❹ Substitute the value of t in the second equation.

❺ Plug back in and solve for t.

❺ $t + y = 10$
$t + 3 = 10$
$t = 7$

Original number has a 7 in the tens place and a 3 in the ones place. = 73

6.5   Chapter Review

1. A scientist is growing bacteria in a petri dish. Every minute, the scientist measures how many bacteria are in the dish. He starts with 20, by the end of the first minute there are 60, and at the end of the second minute there are 100. If the scientist represented these results with a graph, what would be the y–intercept?

   A. 20
   B. 40
   C. 60
   D. 100

2. What does y equal in the following system of equations?

   $$3x + 5y = -20$$
   $$-2x - 3y = 11$$

   A. -9
   B. -7
   C. 5
   D. 7

3. A lab assistant has 9 ounces of a 5% acid solution but needs a 10% acid solution. How much pure acid should he add?

   A. 0.5 ounces
   B. 1 ounce
   C. 4.5 ounces
   D. 9 ounces

4. Which graph best represents the perimeter of an equilateral triangle as a function of the length of one side?

   A.
   B.
   C.
   D.

5. The graph of the diagonal line represents which function?

   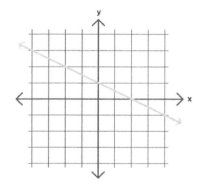

   A. $f(x) = -\frac{1}{2}x + 1$
   B. $f(x) = x - \frac{1}{2}$
   C. $f(x) = -2x + 1$
   D. $f(x) = \frac{1}{2}x + 1$

6. A line with a slope of 7 that passes through (12,44) has what *x*–value when *y* = 100?

    A. -20

    B. -10

    C. 10

    D. 20

7. You have coins in your pocket that are all dimes and quarters. If the number of dimes is four less than 3 times the number of quarters, and the total value of the coins is $1.80, how many quarters do you have?

    A. 2

    B. 4

    C. 6

    D. 8

8. What is the slope of the line between the origin and (-3, 2)?

    A. ⅔

    B. -⅔

    C. 3/2

    D. - 3/2

9. A man leaves on a business trip and at the same time his wife takes their children to visit their grandparents. The cars, traveling in opposite directions, are 360 miles apart at the end of 3 hours. If the man's average speed is 10 mph faster than his wife's, what is her average speed?

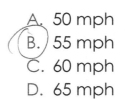

    A. 50 mph

    B. 55 mph

    C. 60 mph

    D. 65 mph

10. Belmont Middle School is headed on a field trip to the museum. Adult tickets are $5 and student tickets are $3. If there are 50 people total who go to the museum and they pay a total of $162, how many adults are on the trip?

    A. 10

    B. 8

    C. 6

    D. 4

11. A line with a slope of -3 that passes through (-2, 4) has what *y*–value when *x* is 3?

    A. -11

    B. -9

    C. 6

    D. 9

12. Which of the following could be an explanation of why some lines have undefined slopes?

    A. Horizontal lines have undefined slopes, since slope is change in *y* over change in *x* and the change in *x* can be any value depending on which two points you pick on the line.

B. Horizontal lines have undefined slopes, since slope is rise over run and there is no rise for horizontal lines.

C. Vertical lines have undefined slopes, since slope is rise over run and you can't determine the rise because you don't know which two points on the vertical line to test.

D. Vertical lines have undefined slopes. Slope is change in y divided by change in x, but any two points on a vertical line have a 0 change in x and dividing by 0 is undefined in math.

13. **You are graphing the number of employees of a startup company versus the year. The graph follows a straight line, where the company started in 2004 (thus had 0 employees at the start of the year) and then in 2006 had 250 employees. Assuming the slope of the line stays the same, how many employees will the company have in 2009?**

   A. 500
   B. 625
   C. 750
   D. 975

14. **Carol is looking to buy a machine for her workshop. Machine Y costs $500 and needs $40 in maintenance and supplies each year. Machine Z costs $400 but needs $50 in maintenance and supplies each year. After how many years will the cost of Machine Y be the same as the cost for Machine Z?**

   A. 4 years
   B. 5 years
   C. 9 years
   D. 10 years

15. **A manufacturer needs 24 tons of a 60% copper alloy. He has tons of 80% copper alloy and 50% copper alloy. How much of the 80% copper alloy does he need to use?**

   A. 8 tons
   B. 12 tons
   C. 16 tons
   D. 20 tons

16. **Which of the following is the graph of the equation: $-2x + y = -3$?**

   A.

   B.

   C.

   D.

17. **What is the y–intercept and x–intercept of the following equation?**

$$-2x + 7y = 14$$

   A. y-int: -2, x-int: -7
   B. y-int: 2, x-int: -7
   C. y-int: 7, x-int: -2
   D. y-int: -7, x-int: 2

18. **An old machine can put 240 caps on bottles every 2 minutes. If the newer model can work at twice the rate of the old machine, how long will it take the new machine to cap 72000 bottles?**

   A. 2.5 hours
   B. 5 hours
   C. 10 hours
   D. 20 hours

19. **Sandra's Sunday afternoon consisted of walking for 15 minutes, running for 30 minutes, and then walking again for 15 minutes. Which graph best illustrates the distance she traveled over the course of her workout?**

A. 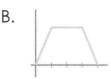 B.

C. 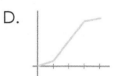 D.

20. **What is the slope of the line between the points (-6, 4) and (8, -12)?**

   A. $\frac{1}{4}$
   B. $-\frac{8}{7}$
   C. 4
   D. $-\frac{7}{8}$

CHAPTER REVIEW EXPLANATIONS

1. A The scientist would graph the data with time on the x–axis and the number of bacteria on the y–axis because time is the independent variable, which is always graphed on the x–axis. The y–intercept on a graph is the point where the line crosses the y–axis. If a point is crossing the y–axis, that means that the x–value is zero.

If the x–value is zero, then we want the value when the scientist started his experiment. He starts with 20, and that is your y–intercept.

2. B   To solve this system of equations, the easiest method is to use elimination. In this case, since the question only asks you to solve for y, eliminate x. Therefore, you have to multiply the equations so that the x's will cancel.

$$\boxed{\begin{array}{l} 3x + 5y = \text{-}20 \\ \text{-}2x \text{ - } 3y = 11 \end{array}}$$

$3x + 5y = \text{-}20$ multiply equation by 2: $6x + 10y = \text{-}40$
$\text{-}2x - 3y = 11$ multiply equation by 3: $\text{-}6x - 9y = 33$

Now, line up the two equations, and add them to eliminate the x's.

$$\boxed{\begin{array}{l} 6x + 10y = \text{-}40 \\ \underline{\text{-}6x - 9y = 33} \\ 0x + y = \text{-}7 \\ y = \text{-}7 \end{array}}$$

---

3. A   The unknown in this problem is how many ounces of acid should the assistant add. Let's call that a.

The total amount of solution will then be the 9 ounces plus the additional a ounces. Total $= 9 + a$.

The total amount of acid in the solutions will be another equation.
The amount of acid in the 5% solution $= 5\% \times 9$ ounces $= .05 \times 9 = .45$
The amount of acid in the pure acid $= 100\% \times a = 1 \times a$
The amount of acid in the final solution $=$
$(9 + a) \times 10\% = 0.1(9 + a)$

$$\boxed{\begin{array}{l} 0.45 + a = 0.1\ (9 + a) \\ 0.45 + a = 0.9 + 0.1a \\ 0.45 + 0.9a = 0.9 \\ 0.9a = 0.45 \\ a = .5 \\ 0.5 \text{ ounces of pure} \\ \text{acid} \end{array}}$$

---

4. A   In this case, the x–axis represents the length of one side of the triangle and the y–axis represents the perimeter. As the length of the side of a triangle increases, the perimeter also increases at a linear rate.

Let's try a few values to see this.
length = 2, perimeter = 6
length = 4, perimeter = 12
length = 6, perimeter = 18

As can be seen by those values, as x increases y also increases. As x goes up by 2, y increases by 6. Therefore, the slope of the line is 3 and the equation of the line is $y = 3x$.

Examining the answer choices, you see that answers B and C do not show straight lines, eliminate both of those answers. Answer D's slope is too low, and therefore, answer A is the correct answer.

---

5. A For a function, you can treat f(x) as y. From the graph, you can see that the y–intercept (where the line crosses the y–axis) is at 1. $b = 1$

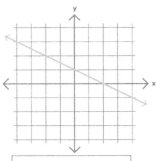

Now, to figure out the graph, pick any two points and determine the rise over the run or the slope. Let's use the points (0,1) and (2,0). From (0,1), the rise is -1 and the run is 2. Therefore, the slope is -½.

Using the slope and y–intercept you can determine the equation of the line.
$y = mx + b$, where m is slope and b is y–intercept.

$$y = -\tfrac{1}{2}x + 1$$
$$f(x) = -\tfrac{1}{2}x + 1$$

---

6. D The slope of a line can be calculated by dividing the change in y by the change in x. The problem stated the slope = 7, one point is (12,44) and y = 100. Therefore, use the slope equation to solve for x.

$$\text{Slope} = \frac{\text{Change in } y}{\text{Change in } x} \qquad 7 = \frac{100 - 44}{x - 12}$$

$$7(x\text{-}12) = 100-44$$
$$7x - 84 = 56$$
$$7x = 140$$
$$x = 20$$

---

7. B You have two unknowns: the number of quarters and the number of dimes. Use variables to represent each.

q = number of quarters
d = number of dimes

Now, set up two equations. The first equation can be set up knowing: "the number of dimes is four less than 3 times the number of quarters"

$$d = 3q - 4$$

The second equation can be set up from: "the total value of the coins is $1.80". Think in terms of cents instead of dollars so that the equation does not have decimals.

$$10d + 25q = 180$$

Now, solve the system of equations. You can use substitution and plug in the value from d in the first equation into the second equation.

$$10(3q - 4) + 25q = 180$$
$$30q - 40 + 25q = 180$$
$$55q - 40 = 180$$
$$55q = 220$$
$$q = 4$$

---

8. B The slope between two points is the rise over the run, or the change in y over the change in x.

(0,0) and (-3,2)

From the first point to the second, y goes up by 2.
From the first point to the second, x goes down by 3.

$$\text{Slope} = \tfrac{2}{-3} = -\tfrac{2}{3}$$

9. B There are two unknowns in this problem. The man's average speed and his wife's average speed. Create variables to represent the two unknowns. ❶

❶ m = man's average speed
w = wife's average speed

Now, let's create two equations.

❷ "the man's average speed is 10 mph faster than his wife's"

❷ $m = w + 10$

"The cars, traveling in opposite directions, are 360 miles apart at the end of 3 hours"

The man's car travels: $3m$, The wife's car: $3w$ ❸

❸ $3m + 3w = 360$

❹ Now, solve the system of equations using any method you like, substitution, elimination, etc. In this case, let's try substitution. Substitute $w + 10$ for m in the second equation.

❹
$3m + 3w = 360$
$3(w + 10) + 3w = 360$
$3w + 30 + 3w = 360$
$6w = 330$
$w = 55$

10. C ❶ Use variables to represent the unknowns:

❶ a = number of adult tickets
s = number of student tickets

Now, set up equations with the variables.
❷ "50 people total who go to the museum"
❸ "they pay a total of $162"

❷ $a + s = 50$

❸ $5a + 3s = 162$

❹ Now, solve the system of equations. In this case, let's use elimination. Multiply the first by -3, so that the s's will cancel.

❹
$a + s = 50$
$-3a - 3s = -150$

❺ Now, add the two equations.

❺
$-3a - 3s = -150$
$5a + 3s = 162$
$2a = 12$
$a = 6$

You could also try plugging in the answer choices.

11. A First, find the equation of the line, then plug in $x = 3$ to solve for y.

❶ $y = -3x + b$

❶ The line has a slope of -3. Therefore, the basic form of an equation is $y=mx+b$. Plug in -3 for m.
❷ Now, plug in the point (-2,4) to solve for b.
Equation: $y = -3x - 2$
❸ Plug in $x = 3$ to solve for y.

❷
$4 = -3(-2) + b$
$4 = 6 + b$
$-2 = b$

❸
$y = -3(3) - 2$
$y = -9 - 2$
$y = -11$

12. D Horizontal lines have a slope of zero, and vertical lines have an undefined slope. Therefore, eliminate answer choices A and B.

Now, let's look at the explanations for answers C and D.

C: Vertical lines have undefined slopes, since slope is rise over run and you can't determine the rise because you don't know which two points on the vertical line to test.

The first part of the statement is true. Vertical lines do have undefined slopes, and slope is rise over run. However, when finding the slope of any straight line, you can pick any two points and you will always find the same slope. Eliminate answer C.

D: Vertical lines have undefined slopes. Slope is change in y divided by change in x, but any two points on a vertical line have a 0 change in x and dividing by 0 is undefined in math.

This is a valid explanation for the fact that vertical lines have undefined slopes. Slope is change in y divided by change in x, and, on a vertical line, the change will always be 0. You can never divide by 0 in math.

---

13. B This problem has given you the coordinate pairs of two points on the line and is asking you to find a third point. As the numbers are large, it will be easier to just represent the year 2004 as 4, 2006 as 6, and 2009 as 9. Using the first two points, find the equation of the line, then plug in the year 9 to find the number of employees. ❶

❷ Slope is change in y divided by change in x
  Equation: $y = mx + b$; $y = 125x + b$
❸ Plug in a point to find b.
❹ Now, plug in $x = 9$ to find the number of employees in the year 2009.
  There will be 625 employees in 2009.

❶ x = year
y = number of employees
Two points: (4, 0) and (6, 250)

❷ Slope = $\frac{250-0}{6-4}$
= $\frac{250}{2}$ = 125

❸ $y = 125x + b$
$0 = 125(4) + b$
$b = -500$
$y = 125x - 500$

❹ $y = 125(9) - 500$
$y = 625$

---

14. D Set up equations to represent the cost of each machine. Let t represent the unknown value, which is in this case is the number of years.

Machine Y costs $500 and needs $40 in maintenance and supplies each year.
Machine Z costs $400 but needs $50 in maintenance and supplies each year.

Cost of Machine Y
= $500 + 40t$

Cost of Machine Z
= $400 + 50t$

Now, set the two costs equal to find after how many years the cost will be the same. Then solve for t.

$$500 + 40t = 400 + 50t$$
$$100 = 10t$$
$$t = 10$$

15. A There are two unknowns in this problem, how many tons of the 80% copper alloy and how many tons of the 50% copper alloy. Let's create variables to represent the unknowns. ❶

❶ a = tons of 80% alloy
b = tons of 50% alloy

Now, let us set up equations with the two unknowns.

❷ The manufacturer needs a total of 24 tons. Therefore, the sum of tons of alloy a and alloy b must equal 24.
Now, with 2 unknowns, you need two equations.

❷ $a + b = 24$

❸ The second equation can come from how much copper the manufacturer needs. The amount of copper in the tons of 80% copper alloy = 80% × a = $0.8a$. The other alloy has $0.5b$. The manufacturer needs 0.6(24).

❸ $0.8a + 0.5b = 0.6(24)$

❹ Now, solve the system of equations.
Multiply the first equation by 10 to remove all the decimals. Multiply the second equation by -5 so that b cancels. Then add the two equations.

❹
$$8a + 5b = 144$$
$$-5a - 5b = -120$$
$$3a = 24$$
$$a = 8$$

You have solved for the unknown a, which represents the number of tons of 80% copper alloy are needed.

16. A Determine the intercept and slope of the equation. Put the equation in the form: $y = mx + b$.
From the equation, you can see the slope is positive 2 and intercept is -3.
Now, let's examine each answer choice.
Answer A has a positive slope and negative intercept.
Answer B has a negative slope and negative intercept.
Answer C has a negative slope and positive intercept.
Answer D has a positive slope and positive intercept.

$$-2x + y = -3$$
$$y = 2x - 3$$

Therefore, answer A is correct. It is the only graph with a positive slope and negative intercept.

17. B The y–intercept is the point on the graph that crosses the y–axis. A point that crosses the y–axis has an x–value of 0. Therefore, plug in $x = 0$ and solve for y.

The x–intercept is the point on the graph that crosses the x–axis. A point that crosses the x–axis has an y–value of 0. Therefore, plug in $y = 0$ and solve for x.

y–int: 2, x–int: -7

$$-2x + 7y = 14$$
$$-2(0) + 7y = 14$$
$$7y = 14$$
$$y = 2$$

$$-2x + 7y = 14$$
$$-2x + 7(0) = 14$$
$$-2x = 14$$
$$x = -7$$

---

18. B The rate of the old machine is 240 caps per 2 minutes, which reduces to 120 caps per minute.
The newer model works at twice the rate of the old machine. Therefore, the newer model can cap 240 caps per minute.

If the newer machine can cap 240 caps per minute and there are 72000 bottles to cap, divide 72000 by 240 to figure out how long it will take this machine.
All the answers are in hours, so convert 300 minutes to hours.

$$72000 \div 240 = 300$$
300 minutes

$$300 \text{ minutes} \times \frac{1 \text{ hour}}{60 \text{ mins}}$$
$$= 5 \text{ hours}$$

---

19. D Sandra walked for 15 minutes — this should be represented by a line with a positive slope.
Sandra ran for 30 minutes — this should be represented by a line with a positive slope greater than the slope of the walking line. In addition, this segment should be twice as long as the walking line since she ran for 30 mins.
Sandra again walked for 15 minutes — this should be represented by the same segment as the first walking segment in terms of slope and length.

The graph in answer D meets these requirements.

---

20. B The slope of a line is the rise over the run. This can also be thought of as the change in y over the change in x.

(-6, 4) and (8, -12)

$$\text{Slope} = \frac{\text{Change in } y}{\text{Change in } x} = \frac{4 - (-12)}{-6 - 8} = \frac{16}{-14} = \frac{-8}{7}$$

Chapter 7:
Geometric Logic

Lessons

7.1 Angles & Parallel Lines

Parallel & Perpendicular Lines

Lines are considered parallel if they have the same slope.

Any line intersecting two parallel lines will create identical sets of angles with each line. The lines LM and NP in the diagram are parallel, and the intersecting line has created equal sets of angles a and b.

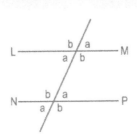

Perpendicular lines intersect to form four 90 degree angles. Lines C and D in the figure to the right are perpendicular.

Slope of Parallel & Perpendicular Lines

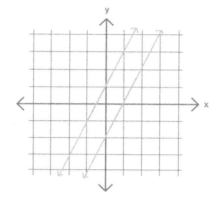

Parallel lines all have the same slope. Let's see this on a coordinate plane.

y = 2x + 1
y = 2x − 2

Both of the equations have a slope of 2. You can see that the graphs of the two lines are parallel, since they have the same slope.

Perpendicular lines have slopes that are negative inverses. Therefore, a line with a slope of 3, will be perpendicular to a line with a slope of -1/3. This can be seen on the graph of the two equations:

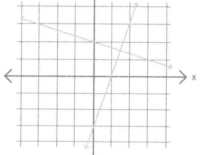

y = 3x − 3
y = -⅓ x + 2

Supplementary Angles

Just as triangles and circles have a set number of degrees that all their angles contain, a straight line always contains 180 degrees. Angles adding to 180 degrees are called supplementary angles.

The picture on the right contains three supplementary angles: a, b, and c. Each of those angles can also be named by referencing the three points that form the angle, for example, Angle c could also be called Angle DAE or EAD. When angles are referenced in this way, the point that forms the vertex of the angle, in this case A, will always be in the middle.

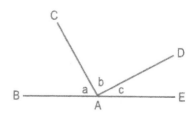

Complementary Angles

Two angles adding to 90 degrees are known as complementary angles.

Angles in Polygons

A triangle contains 180 degrees. To determine the number of degrees in any other polygon, divide the polygon into triangles and multiply the number of triangles by 180°. The chart below shows a few common polygons and the sum of the degree measure of their angles.

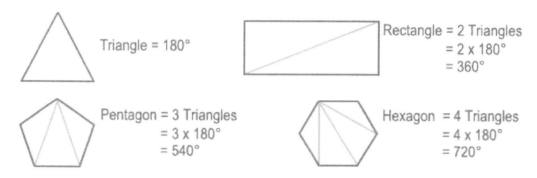

Bisectors

A line that cuts an angle in half is a bisector. Since the bisected angle is cut into halves, each angle created by the line is equal to one–half the measure of the whole angle. In the figure, line LN is bisecting angle MNO:

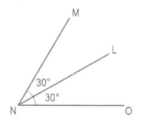

Opposite Angles

Angles adding to 180 degrees are supplementary, so any two intersecting lines create two sets of supplementary angles. In addition, angles on opposite sides of the intersecting lines are equal.

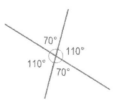

ANGLES & PARALLEL LINES PRACTICE

1. If line LM bisects angle KMN, then what does x equal?

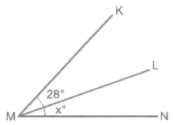

   A. 14
   B. 28
   C. 56
   D. 112

2. In the picture below, y is how many degrees?

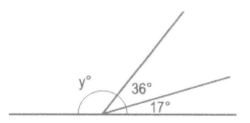

   A. 53
   B. 127
   C. 153
   D. 180

3. In the figure, if line L is parallel to line M, what is the measure of angle c in degrees?

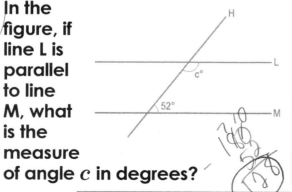

   A. 38
   B. 52
   C. 128
   D. 180

4. Which graphed equation would be parallel to the line in the graph?

   A. $y = 2x + 2$
   B. $y = 1/2\,x - 2$
   C. $y = -2x + 4$
   D. $y = -1/2\,x + 2$

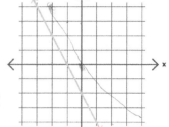

5. Choose the best answer to fill in the blank.

   In a regular hexagon, each angle equals ___ degrees.

   A. 30
   B. 60
   C. 90
   D. 120

6. Which of the angles in the picture is angle ACD?

   A. I
   B. II
   C. III
   D. none of them

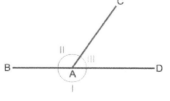

7. Geometric Logic

7. In the figure, which of the other angles is angle a equal to?

A. I and II
B. II only
C. III only
D. II and III

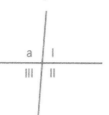

8. If triangle ABC is equilateral, what is the measure of angle BCA?

    A. 45
    B. 60
    C. 90
    D. 180

9. If angle CAB = 65°, what is the measure of angle ACD?

A. 25°
B. 65°
C. 115°
D. 155°

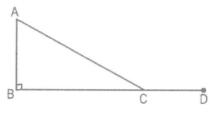

10. In parallelogram ABDC, angle BAC = 70°. What is the measure of angle ACD?

A. 20°
B. 70°
C. 110°
D. 170°

ANGLES & PARALLEL LINES EXPLANATIONS

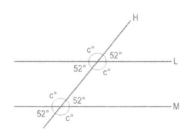

1.B   A line that bisects an angle cuts it in half, creating two equal angles. Since the other half of the angle equals 28 degrees, so does x.

$$x = 28°$$

2. B   There are 180 degrees on each side of a straight line. To find y, add the measures of the two angles and subtract their sum from 180.

$$180 - (36 + 17) = 127 \text{ degrees}$$

3. C   Using what you know about parallel lines and angles, fill in the angles you know. Remember that vertical angles and alternate interior angles are equal.

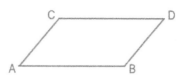

You can see that angle c and 52 degrees make a straight line. Therefore, c plus 52 must equal 180 degrees. c + 52 = 180, c = 128

4. C   To find out which line is parallel to the line in the graph, first calculate the slope of the line, and then find out which equation has a line with the same slope.

To calculate the slope of the line in the graph, take any two points on the line. It doesn't matter which points you choose, the slope will always be the same. Let's choose (0, -2) and (1, -4). Remember, to find the slope, it is the change in y over the change in x.

Slope = (change in y)/(change in x)
= (-2 - -4)/(0 - 1) = (-2 + 4)/(0 - 1) = 2/-1 = -2

Now, let's look at each answer choice to see which has a slope of -2. All the equations are in the form: y = mx + b, where m is the slope. The only equation with a slope of -2 is Answer C. y = -2x + 4

---

5. D   A regular hexagon has six equal sides and six equal angles. A hexagon can be divided into 4 triangles, so it has 4 × 180, or 720 degrees. See tutorial for more information on determining the total measure of interior angles in a polygon.

A hexagon contains a total of 720 degrees for the 6 angles, so divide that number by six to find the measure of each angle. 720° ÷ 6 = 120°

---

6. D   According to the naming scheme discussed in the tutorial, angle I could be named BAD or DAB. Angle II is BAC or CAB. Angle III is CAD or DAC.

To create angle ACD, C would have to be the vertex of the angle. The only way this is possible is to draw a line from point C to point D. The angle created by lines AC and CD would be ACD. In this case, none of the angles in the picture have C as the vertex.

---

7. B   Angle a is equal to II since opposite angles are congruent.
Angle a is supplementary to I. That means that angle a + angle I = 180°. However, they are not equal unless angle a was a right angle.
Angle a is supplementary to III, therefore not equal.

---

8. B   If a triangle is equilateral then all of its sides and angles are equal. Let y represent the measure of angle BCA. Since all the angles are equal, each angle in this triangle will equal y.

The angles in a triangle add up to 180°.
Set up an equation to solve for y.
All angles in the equilateral triangle are equal to 60°.

$$y + y + y = 180$$
$$3y = 180$$
$$y = 60$$

9. D First, calculate angle BCA, the third angle in the triangle. We know two of the angles in the triangle are 65° (given in problem) and 90° (right angle) and we know that all the angles in a triangle add to 180°.

> 90° + 65° + angle BCA = 180°
> 155° + angle BCA = 180°
> angle BCA = 25°

Now, find the measure of angle ACD. We know that angle BCA and angle ACD form a straight line, and the sum of the measures of angles that form a straight line is 180°.

> angle BCA + angle ACD = 180°
> 25° + angle ACD = 180°
> angle ACD = 155°

10. C Since we know that the quadrilateral is a parallelogram, the opposite sides of the polygon are parallel. Therefore, AB is parallel to CD. If you extend line CD, as seen in the diagram, you can see that line segment AC cuts across the parallel lines. Since the lines are parallel, the two angles that are marked in the diagram must be equal. They are both equal to 70°. Angle ACD and the 70° angle form a straight line where the measures add to 180°.

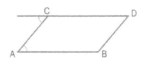

> angle ACD + 70° = 180°
> angle ACD = 110°

7.2   Transformations

Types of Transformations

Transformations are ways of manipulating a line, point, or shape on the coordinate plane. There are four basic types of transformations:

This lesson will cover these basic types of transformations and their effect on the graphs and formulas of equations.

1. Translation (shifting position)

2. Reflection (flipping)

3. Rotation (turning)

4. Dilation (increasing or decreasing scale)

Translation

Imagine translation as picking up a graph and moving it without changing it in any other way. Graphs can be translated up, down, right, left, or some combination.

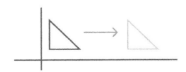

Graphs of equations can be moved up or down by changing the y–intercept.

For example, $y = x + 2$ is up 2 units from $y = x$.

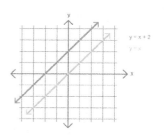

Reflection

You can reflect an object over any straight line, but the most common types of flips are over the x–axis and y–axis. Flipping all the coordinates around an axis is called reflection, since the objects before and after are mirror images of each other.

Rotation

A graph can be rotated by any number of degrees and about any pivot point. The rotation can be clockwise or counter–clockwise. The examples are all rotated clockwise.

Dilation

A graph of an object is dilated by increasing or decreasing all the coordinates of the object proportionately to make the object bigger or smaller on the coordinate system.

Symmetry

Symmetry about a line is the ability to flip an object across the line without changing it.

TRANSFORMATIONS PRACTICE

1. **Which of the following transformations was used on the shape from the image on the left to the image on the right?**

   A. translation
   B. dilation
   C. rotation
   D. reflection

2. Which of the following shapes is symmetric about the x–axis?

A.

B.

C.    D.

Both

3. How many lines of symmetry does the following object have?

A. 0
B. 1
C. 2
D. 3

4. Which of the following transformations has been performed on the shape below?

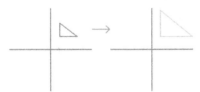

A. translation
B. dilation
C. reflection
D. rotation

5. Which of the following transformations were performed on the object?

I. translation
II. reflection
III. dilation

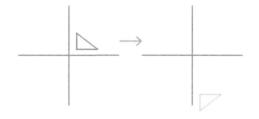

A. I
B. I and II
C. II and III
D. I, II, and III

6. To transform the graph of $y = 3x$ into $y = 3x + 2$, what transformation would you perform?

A. translation
B. rotation
C. reflection
D. dilation

7. By how many degrees and in what direction has the following object been rotated about the origin?

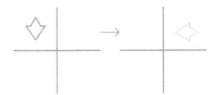

A. 90° clockwise
B. 90° counterclockwise
C. 45° clockwise
D. 180° clockwise

8. If a square with corners at (0,0), (0,4), (4,0), and (4,4) is dilated by a factor of 3, where are its new corners?

    A. (3,3), (3,7), (7,3), (7,7)
    B. (0,0), (0,12), (12,0), (12, 12)
    C. (3,3), (3,12), (12,3), (12, 12)
    D. (0,0), (0,4), (4,0), and (4,4)

9. What transformation(s) was/were performed on the shape below?

    A. reflection
    B. dilation and translation
    C. dilation and rotation
    D. translation and rotation

10. If the length of all the sides of a triangle are tripled, what would happen to its perimeter?

    A. Increase by 3
    B. Triple
    C. Multiply by 6
    D. Multiply by 9

TRANSFORMATIONS EXPLANATIONS

1. A   To translate an object is to move it without changing its shape, size, or orientation. The shape moved down and to the left without any other changes, so the shape was translated. Dilation involves changing the size of a shape. Rotation would have changed the orientation of the shape. Reflection would have also changed the orientation.

2. D   Symmetry about an axis means that you can flip the shape over that axis without changing it.

    Answer A shows a shape symmetric about the y–axis.
    Answer B shows a shape that is symmetric, but not about either axis.
    Answer C also shows a shape symmetric about the y–axis.
    Answer D shows a shape symmetric about the x–axis.

3. A   There are no lines of symmetry in the shape. No matter what lines you draw, you can not flip the object over that line to make it identical.

4. B   An object is dilated by increasing or decreasing all of its x and y values proportionately. In this case, the shape has changed size proportionately, which means dilation was performed.

5. B Multiple transformations were performed on the shape. The object was reflected about the *x*–axis, which means it was flipped over the *x*–axis. In addition, the shape was translated downward. The shape was not dilated since the size of the shape didn't change. I and II, Translation and Reflection.

6. A Both of the equations are graphed. As can be seen, the graph has been translated, or moved by 2 units.

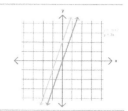

7. A The object has been rotated in a clockwise direction. You can tell that, since it has moved one full quadrant, it has moved 90°. If you draw a line from any point on the object to the origin and then draw a line perpendicular to that, you will see it will touch the same point on the new object. 90° clockwise.

8. B Dilation is a type of transformation where the object is resized. Each coordinate is multiplied by the factor of dilation, in this case, the factor is 3. Therefore, to solve this question, take each original coordinate pair of the corners and multiply the *x*–value and *y*–value by 3.

(0,0) becomes (0,0)
(0,4) becomes (0,12)
(4,0) becomes (12,0)
(4,4) becomes (12,12)

9. C This shape had more than one transformation performed on it. The first one to notice is that the shape is now a different size. The only transformation where the size of an object changes, is dilation.

The next transformation to note is that the shape is now facing the other direction. This shape has been rotated around the origin so that it is now facing the other way. Dilation and Rotation

10. B Let the sides of the original triangle equal X, Y, and Z. Then the sides of the new triangle will equal 3X, 3Y, and 3Z.

Original perimeter = X + Y + Z
New perimeter = 3X + 3Y + 3Z = 3(X + Y + Z) = 3(Original perimeter)

The perimeter triples.

7.3   Similar & Congruent Polygons

Congruent Polygons

Polygons are considered congruent if they have
exactly the same size, shape, and interior angles.
Congruent polygons might consist of a polygon and
various combinations of translations, reflections,
and rotations of itself:

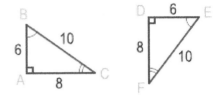

Proving Congruence - Triangles

There are several ways to prove that two triangles are congruent.
Here are a few:

1.	**Side-Angle-Side (SAS)**	A pair of corresponding sides and the angle in between them are the same.
2.	**Side-Side-Side (SSS)**	All the sides of the two triangles are the same length.
3.	**Angle-Side-Angle (ASA)**	A pair of corresponding angles and the side in between them are the same.

Similar Polygons

Similar polygons share the same shape and angles but
have different sizes. In the image, the second triangle
has been rotated, translated, and dilated. It is still the
same shape with the same angles, so the two triangles
are similar, but not congruent.

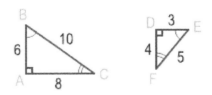

Proportional Sides

Corresponding sides in similar polygons are all proportionate. Another way to
think about this is that there is a scale factor from one polygon to the other, and
this scale factor is the same for every side.

In the image above, you can see that the corresponding sides
have the same proportions:

$$^{AB}\!/_{DE} = {}^6\!/_3 = 2$$
$$^{BC}\!/_{EF} = {}^{10}\!/_5 = 2$$
$$^{CA}\!/_{FD} = {}^8\!/_4 = 2$$

1. Congruent polygons have the same:

    I. size
    II. orientation
    III. shape

    A. III only
    B. II and III
    C. I and III
    D. I, II, and III

2. Similar polygons have the same:

    I. size
    II. orientation
    III. shape

    A. I and III
    B. III only
    C. I only
    D. I, II, and III

3. What is the length of the missing side y in the rectangle below?

    A. 3
    B. 7
    C. 9
    D. don't know

4. Which of the following is similar to this polygon?

    A.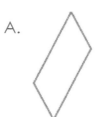

    B.

    C.

    D.

5. Which of the following is true?

    A. All similar polygons are also congruent.
    B. All congruent polygons are also similar.
    C. No similar polygons are also congruent.
    D. No congruent polygons are also similar.

6. What is the length of side a in the figure below if the two triangles are similar?

   A. 6
   B. 12
   C. 13
   D. don't know

7. Which of the following are methods for proving congruence for a pair of triangles?

   I. Side–Angle–Side
   II. Angle–Angle–Angle
   III. Side–Side–Side

   A. I and II
   B. I and III
   C. II and III
   D. I, II, and III

8. In two triangles, all the angles are the same when the two triangles are:

   I. Similar
   II. Congruent
   III. Right triangles

   A. I only
   B. II only
   C. II and III
   D. I and II

9. Triangle ABC is similar to triangle DEF. (angle A = angle D, angle B = angle E, angle C = angle F) If AB = 8, BC = 10, and DE = 12. What is the length of EF?

   A. 10
   B. 14
   C. 15
   D. 16

10. Rectangle ABCD is similar to rectangle EFGH (AB corresponds to EF, BC corresponds to FG, etc.) and the ratio of the perimeter of ABCD to the perimeter of EFGH is 4 to 1. If BC = 16, what is the length of FG?

   A. 2
   B. 4
   C. 16
   D. 32

SIMILAR & CONGRUENT POLYGONS EXPLANATIONS

1. C The definition of congruence is that the polygons are the same size and the same shape. They can be rotated and have different orientations.

2. B The definition of similar polygons is that they have the same shape with all of the same angles. However, similar polygons can have different sizes and orientations.

3. D   Just because the two polygons are rectangles does not mean that they are congruent. Therefore, we can not determine the length of the missing side without more information.

4. B   Similar polygons have the same shape and angles, but not necessarily the same size or orientation.

Answer B is rotated and slightly larger, but it is similar to the original.

5. B   Similar polygons have the same shape.
Congruent polygons have the same size and shape.

Therefore, if polygons are congruent, then they have the same size and shape which means that they are also similar.
All congruent polygons are similar.

6. B   Since the two triangles are similar, their sides are proportional. Therefore, set up a proportion to solve for a. ❶

❷ Multiply both sides by 16 to isolate a.

❶ $a/16 = 9/12$

❷ $a/16 \times 16 = 9/12 \times 16$
$a = 12$

7. B   Having 3 angles the same proves that any two triangles are similar but it does not prove congruence because one triangle can still be a dilation of the other. For example, in the following image, the angles are the same, however the triangles are not congruent.

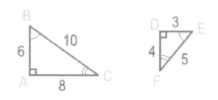

If you review the tutorial, you will see that all 3 sides the same are enough to prove congruence. Also, two sides the same plus the angle in between is also enough for proving congruence.

I and III prove congruence.

8. D Triangles that are similar by definition have the same shape, which means that their angles are all the same. Similar triangles can have sides of different length, but angles the same. I is true.

Triangles that are congruent are the same size and shape. Thus, the angles are definitely the same. Congruent triangles can have a different orientation, but the shapes and sizes are the same. II is true.

Right triangles have one 90° angle in common; however, the other two angles can be different. For instance, you can have one right triangle with the following angles: 30, 60, 90 and another with the angles: 45, 45, 90. III is false. I and II

---

9. C Since the two triangles are similar, their sides are proportional.

$$AB/DE = BC/EF$$
$$8/12 = 10/EF$$

Cross multiply and solve.

$$8\,(EF) = 12\,(10)$$
$$EF = 120 \div 8 = 15$$
$$\text{length of } EF = 15$$

---

10. B The ratio of the perimeters of two similar rectangles will be equal to the ratio of the sides of the rectangles. Therefore, set up a proportion and solve for the missing length.

$$\frac{\text{perim ABCD}}{\text{perim EFGH}} = \frac{BC}{FG} = \frac{4}{1} = \frac{16}{FG}$$

$$4(FG) = 16$$
$$FG = 4$$

7.4   Graphing Inequalities

Graphing Inequalities

You've seen inequalities graphed on a number line, but how would you visually represent an inequality with multiple variables? If you have an inequality with two variables, you can graph it on a coordinate plane. First, you determine the boundary line and graph it. Then, you shade one side of the line.

Boundary Line

To determine the boundary line, treat the inequality as if it were an equation. For example, to graph $y > x + 2$, the boundary line would be the graph of $y = x + 2$. You can graph with whatever method you feel comfortable, such as plugging in points or using slope and intercept.

Next, we have to determine what type of line it is. If the inequality contains the symbols $\geq$ or $\leq$, the boundary line should be included as part of the inequality. This is indicated by drawing a solid line. If the inequality contains the symbols $>$ or $<$. the boundary line is not included and so should be drawn as a dashed line.

Shading

Now you need to shade one side of the line or the other, to represent the range of values that correspond to the inequality. In this case, we want to graph $y > x + 2$, so we shade the part above the boundary line. As you can see, the shaded part of the graph shows all values for y that are greater than $x + 2$.

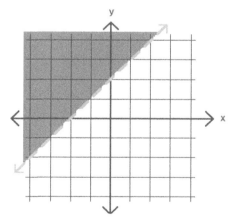

A good way to determine what side of the line to shade is to test a point. Pick any point that is not on the line, usually the origin is the easiest. Then, test that point in the equation. If it holds true, shade the side of the graph that includes that point. If it is not true in the inequality, then shade the opposite side of the line.

For example, in the equation above $y > x + 2$, we can plug in the origin $(0, 0)$. $0 > 0 + 2$ is not true. Therefore, we shade the side of the line that does not contain the origin.

Multiple Inequalities

You may be asked to graph a system of inequalities on the same graph. If so, follow the same steps you would for each inequality, but plot the results on the same coordinate plane. If the system has an "or," then leave everything shaded. If the system of inequalities has an "and," then only shade the region of overlap.

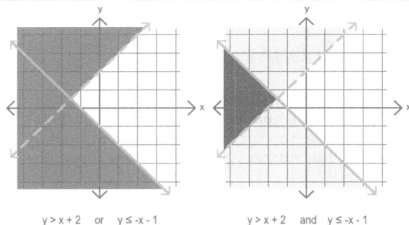

$y > x + 2$ or $y \leq -x - 1$

The entire shaded region is the solution to this set of inequalities.

$y > x + 2$ and $y \leq -x - 1$

The overlapped darker region is the solution to this set of inequalities.

GRAPHING INEQUALITIES PRACTICE

1. $y < 2x$ would be graphed as:

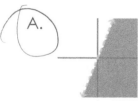

A.

B.

C.

D.

2. The following graph can be represented by what set of expressions?

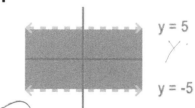

$y = 5$

$y = -5$

A. $y < 5$ and $y > -5$
B. $y < 5$ or $y > -5$
C. $y \leq 5$ and $y \geq -5$
D. $y > 5$ or $y < -5$

3. When graphing inequalities, for which symbols would you use a dashed line?

A. $>$ and $<$
B. $\geq$ and $\leq$
C. $=$
D. absolute value

4. **What is the difference between using a graph and a number line to represent an inequality?**
    A. number line is a simpler way of portraying the same information as a graph
    B. graph shows more detail than a number line
    C. a number line represents single variable inequalities, a graph represents two variables
    D. a graph represents single variable inequalities, a number line represents multiple variables

5. **Which represents the graph of $-x-19 \leq y$?**
    A.
    B.
    C.
    D.

6. **The following is the graph of which inequalities?**

    A. $y \leq -2x$ or $y \geq 4x$
    B. $y \leq -2x$ and $y \geq 4x$
    C. $y \geq -2x$ or $y \leq 4x$
    D. $y \geq -2x$ and $y \leq 4x$

7. **Which area(s) represent the values for which $y > 17$ or $y < 5x$?**

    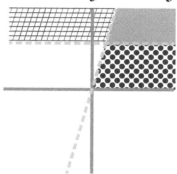

    I. criss-cross
    II. dots
    III. grey

    A. III only
    B. I and II only
    C. II and III only
    D. I, II, and III

8. **How would you graph $y \leq -x + 2$ OR $y \leq -x-3$?**
    A.
    B.
    C.
    D.

9. Which equations does the graph below represent?

A. $y \leq x$ or $y \geq -x$
B. $y \geq x$ or $y \leq -x$
C. $y \leq x$ and $y \geq -x$
D. $y \geq x$ and $y \leq -x$

10. How would you graph: $80 - 20y > -15x + 40$?

A.

B.

C.

D.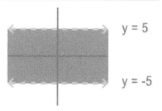

GRAPHING INEQUALITIES EXPLANATIONS

1. A The inequality would be graphed as the area below the dotted line $y = 2x$. The line would be dotted rather than solid to show that the values on the line $y = 2x$ do not fulfill the inequality.

The graph of $y < 2x$ would be:

2. A The area represented on the graph is the set of y values between -5 and 5. The graph does not include $y = 5$ or $y = -5$, so you want to use > or <, not $\geq$ or $\leq$.

The graph represents the values greater than -5 and less than 5 at the same time, so you want to use "and" not "or". $y < 5$ and $y > -5$

3. A Let's go through each answer:

A: > and < :When graphing inequalities with these signs, you would use a dashed line. A dashed line indicates that you do not want to include the line being graphed, and this is true since these signs indicate greater than or less than but not equal to.

B: $\geq$ and $\leq$:These would be graphed with a solid line since you want to include the line.

C: = :This is not an inequality sign. If you were to graph an equation with an equals sign, it would be a solid line.

D: absolute values: Some expressions with absolute values are graphed with solid lines and some are graphed with dashed lines, depending on which inequality symbol is used.

4. C A number line is one dimensional, so it can only represent the range of possible values for one variable. The coordinate plane is two dimensional, and each dimension is a number line. This means that a graph on the coordinate plane can represent the range of possible values for two variables.

5. B First, rewrite the inequality with the y on the left side, since that is the form you are used to seeing.

$$-x - 19 \leq y$$
$$y \geq -x - 19$$

The line should be solid since it is $\geq$ and not just $>$. Then graph the line $y = -x - 19$, and then decide which side of the line to shade.

The graph of the line $y = -x - 19$ has a negative slope, which only happens in answer choices B and C.
Then, you must determine which side of the graph needs to be shaded. You want to graph $y \geq -x - 19$, you can try plugging in a point and in this case you want to graph above the line.

6. B Let's start by looking at the line $y = -2x$. This is the line with the negative slope. The section of the graph that is shaded represents all y values less than $-2x$. Therefore, we want the line $y \leq -2x$, which is in answer choices A and B.

The next thing to look at is whether you want "and" or "or". If you are graphing with "and" then you want just the area of overlap, but, if you are graphing two inequalities with "or" then you want to include all values that both satisfy. In this case, it is clear that only the overlap has been graphed, so look for "and".

7. D For inequalities joined by "or", all of the values that fulfill any of the inequalities are acceptable.
In the above graph, the criss cross and grey portions represent the values that make the equation: $y > 17$ true.
The grey and dots portions represent the values that make the equation: $y < 5x$ true.
Therefore, the criss cross, grey, and dots portions will represent the values that make either equation true. I, II, and III

8. B When graphing inequalities with an OR, you want to shade anything that satisfies either expression. Graph both inequalities, and keep all parts that are shaded for either of them.

The values that satisfy $y \leq -x - 3$ are already included in the graph of the values that satisfy $y \leq -x + 2$. Therefore, answer B shows both lines graphed and the parts below each line shaded in.

9. A First, you can tell that the graph represents an OR statement because all of the areas that satisfy either inequality have been shaded.

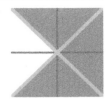

Let's look at the line $y = x$, which has the positive slope. All the points below that are shaded. Therefore, $y \leq x$ has been shaded.

Now, let's look at the line $y = -x$, which has the negative slope. All the points greater than that are shaded. Therefore, $y \geq -x$ has been shaded.

$y \leq x$ OR $y \geq -x$

10. C First, isolate y.

Subtract 80 from both sides.

Divide everything by -20. When dividing by a negative, flip the sign.

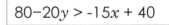

$$80 - 20y > -15x + 40$$

$$-20y > -15x - 40$$

$$y < {}^{-15}\!/_{-20}\,x - {}^{40}\!/_{-20}$$
$$y < \tfrac{3}{4}\,x + 2$$

Now graph the equation. The line should not be solid since the equation is $y <$ not $y \leq$. Finally, shade all the values less than the dashed line.

7.5 Nonlinear Equations

Thus far, you have worked primarily with linear equations and graphs. These can be recognized since linear equations have y's and x's that are not raised to any power. Such as $y = 2x + 3$ and $-4y + 5x = 12$. Linear graphs can be recognized because the graphs have straight lines.

Nonlinear equations

Nonlinear equations that are graphed will not be represented by a straight line. The equations may have variables raised to powers or the roots of variables. For example: $y = 3x^2$, $y = 5x^{-\frac{1}{2}}$

Solving nonlinear equations

The easiest way to solve problems involving nonlinear equations is to plug in x and y values to see which values make which equations true.

FOIL–multiplying expressions

If you need to multiply expressions each with two terms, you can use the FOIL method, which is an extension of the distributive property. FOIL stands for First, Outer, Inner, Last. Multiply the first term in each, the outer terms, the inner terms, and the last terms and then add all the products.

$$(a + b)(c + d) = ac + ad + bc + bd$$
$$\text{Example: } (x + 2)(x - 3) = x^2 - 3x + 2x - 6 = x^2 - x - 6$$

Examples of common nonlinear equations

	x^2, Parabolas	These graphs are shaped like horseshoes. These graphs always have one variable squared.
	x^3	They can have various slopes and intercepts.
	Exponential equations	These are of the form of a number raised to the x power. For example, $y = 2^x$. They will be shaped like the graph to the left.

NONLINEAR EQUATIONS PRACTICE

1. What are all the possible values for x in the quadratic equation $x^2 - 10x + 24 = 0$?

    A. -2, 12

    B. -4, 6

    C. -12, 2

    D. 4, 6

2. Which of the following decreases as x increases, if $x > 2$?

    A. $3x^2 - 2x$

    B. $-3x + x^2$

    C. $2x^2 - x^3$

    D. $x^4 - x^2$

3. Which of the following are solutions to the system of equations, $y = x^2$ and $y = 2x^2 - 1$? They are both graphed below.

    I. (-1,-1)

    II. (-1, 1)

    III. (1,1)

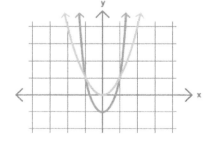

    A. I and II

    B. III only

    C. II and III

    D. I, II, and III

4. What is the product of $(x - 4)(x - 2)$?

    A. $x^2 + 8x + 8$

    B. $x^2 - 6x + 8$

    C. $x^2 + 8x - 6$

    D. $x^2 + 8$

5. Which of the following equations has the largest value when $x = 10$?

    A. $y = x + 10{,}000$

    B. $y = x^5 + 100x^4$

    C. $y = 10^x$

    D. $y = 1000x$

6. In the equation, $y = x^3 - x^2$, what is the change in the y value when x increases from 4 to 5?

    A. 0

    B. 52

    C. 70

    D. 148

7. What equation does this graph represent?

    A. $y = x^3$

    B. $y = (-x)^3$

    C. $y = -3^x$

    D. $y = x^{-3}$

8. If the equation $y = -3x^2 - 7x + 8$ was graphed, what would be the y-intercept?

A. -7
B. -3
C. -2
D. 8

$Y = -3(0)^2 - 7(0) + 8$
$Y = 8$

9. Which of the following equations is represented by the graph below?

A. $y = x^2$
B. $y = 2^x$
C. $y = x^3$
D. $y = 4x$

Bonus Foil

10. What is the value of $(2x - 5)(2x + 5)$?

$4x$

A. $4x^2 + 10x - 25$
B. $2x^2 + 25$
C. $4x^2 - 10x - 25$
D. $4x^2 - 25$

NONLINEAR EQUATIONS EXPLANATIONS

1. D There are many ways to solve this problem.

$x^2 - 10x + 24 = 0$

Method 1: The easiest way to solve this problem is to plug in each answer choice to see which values make the equation true.

A: -2, 12
$(-2)^2 - 10(-2) + 24 = 4 + 20 + 24 = 48$
This does not equal zero.
Eliminate A.

B: -4, 6
$(-4)^2 - 10(-4) + 24 = 16 + 40 + 24 = 80$
This does not equal zero.
Eliminate B.

C: -12, 2
$(-12)^2 - 10(-12) + 24$
$= 144 + 120 + 24 = 288$
This does not equal zero.
Eliminate C.

D: 4, 6
$(4)^2 - 10(4) + 24 = 16 - 40 + 24 = 0$
$(6)^2 - 10(6) + 24 = 36 - 60 + 24 = 0$

Both values for x in this answer choice make the equation true.

Method 2: Another way to solve this problem is to first factor the equation. This can be thought of as reversing the FOIL operation.

Now, we know that if the product of two terms is zero, then one of those terms must equal zero. Set both terms equal to zero to find the possible values for x.

$x^2 - 10x + 24 = 0$
$(x-6)(x-4) = 0$

$x - 6 = 0, x = 6$
$x - 4 = 0, x = 4$
$x = 6$ or 4

---

2. C Let's go through each answer and see what happens as x increases.

A: $3x^2 - 2x$: As x increases, $3x^2$ will increase faster than $2x$. Therefore, the difference will increase. You can also try picking numbers and plugging in to see what happens. $x = 2$, $3(2^2) - 2(2) = 12-4 = 8$ $x = 3$, $3(3^2) - 2(3) = 27-6 = 21$ As x increases, answer choice A increases. Eliminate answer choice A.

B: $-3x + x^2$: As x increases, x^2 will increase faster than $3x$, so the overall expression will increase. Let's pick numbers to see. $x = 2$, $-3(2) + 2^2 =$ $-6 + 4 = -2$ $x = 3$, $-3(3) + 3^2 = -9 + 9 = 0$ As x increases, answer choice B increases. Eliminate answer choice B.

C: $2x^2 - x^3$: As x increases, x^3 will increase faster than $2x^2$. Therefore, the difference will decrease. Let's pick numbers to see. $x = 2$, $2(2^2) - 2^3 =$ $8 - 8 = 0$ $x = 3$, $2(3^2) - 3^3 = 18-27 = -9$ As x increases, answer choice C decreases. Answer choice C is correct.

D: $x^4 - x^2$: As x increases, x^4 increases faster than x^2, and the overall expression will increase. Let's pick numbers to see. $x = 2$, $2^4 - 2^2 =$ $16 - 4 = 12$ $x = 3$, $3^4 - 3^2 = 81 - 9 = 72$ As x increases, answer choice D increases. Eliminate answer choice D.

3. C When solving a system of equations using graphs, the points of intersection are the solutions. In this case, the lines cross twice, once at (-1, 1) and another time at (1,1).

You could have also plugged in each set of points into both equations and see which solutions make them both true. II and III.

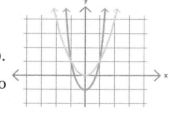

4. B $(x - 4)(x - 2)$ To multiply expressions, remember FOIL: ❶

❷ Now, add the results.

❶ First: $(x)(x) = x^2$
Outer: $(x)(-2) = -2x$
Inner: $(-4)(x) = -4x$
Last: $(-4)(-2) = 8$

❷ $x^2 + -2x + -4x + 8$
$= x^2 - 6x + 8$

5. C For each answer choice, plug in $x = 10$ and solve for y.

A:	B: $y = x^5 + 100x^4$	C:	D:
$y = x + 10{,}000$	$y = 10^5 + 100(10^4)$	$y = 10^x$	$y = 1000x$
$y = 10 + 10{,}000$	$y = 100{,}000 + 100(10{,}000)$	$y = 10^{10}$	$y = 1000(10)$
$= 10{,}010$	$y = 100{,}000 + 1{,}000{,}000$	$y = 10{,}000{,}000{,}000$	$y = 10{,}000$
	$y = 1{,}100{,}000$		

Exponential equations will increase faster than linear equations.

6. B Plug in $x = 4$ into the equation and $x = 5$ into the equation and calculate the difference in the outputs.

Difference in y–values

$$100 - 48 = 52$$

$x = 4$	$x = 5$
$y = x^3 - x^2$	$y = x^3 - x^2$
$y = 4^3 - 4^2$	$y = 5^3 - 5^2$
$y = 64 - 16$	$y = 125 - 25$
$y = 48$	$y = 100$

---

7. B Plug in values from the graph into the equations to see which equation is true. On the graph, when $x = 1$, $y = -1$.

Eliminate answer A. When $x = 1$, $y = x^3 = 1$.
Eliminate answer C. When $x = 1$, $y = -3^1 = -3$.
Eliminate answer D. When $x = 1$, $y = x^{-3} = 1$.

B: When $x = 1$, $y = (-x)^3 = -1$.

---

8. D The y–intercept on a graph is where it crosses the y–axis, and therefore when $x = 0$. Plug in $x = 0$ into the equation and solve for y. y–intercept is 8

$y = -3x^2 - 7x + 8$
$y = -3(0)^2 - 7(0) + 8$
$y = 8$

---

9. B Let's examine each answer choice.

A: $y = x^2$	**B: $y = 2^x$**	**C: $y = x^3$**	**D: $y = 4x$**
The graph of this answer choice looks like a parabola. For instance, as x goes from -1 to -2, y should go from 1 to 4. Eliminate answer A.	This is the correct graph. As x increases, y increases quickly. As x decreases, y gets closer to 0 without ever being negative. Answer B	This can not be the correct equation, since when x is negative, $y = x^3$ is also negative, but this is not the case in the graph.	This is the graph of a straight line with a slope of 4. Eliminate D. 

---

10. D $(2x - 5)(2x + 5)$

❶ To multiply expressions, remember FOIL:

❷ Now, add the results.

❶ First: $(2x)(2x) = 4x^2$
Outer: $(2x)(x) = 10x$
Inner: $(-5)(2x) = -10x$
Last: $(-5)(5) = -25$

❷ 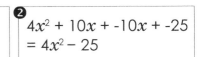 $4x^2 + 10x + -10x + -25$
$= 4x^2 - 25$

7.6   Chapter Review

1. $|2y| \leq 6$ is graphed as?

   A. 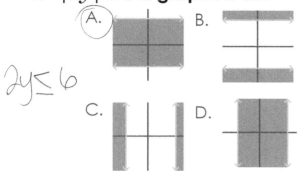 B.

   $2y \leq 6$

   C.   D.

2. If triangle ABC is similar to triangle DEF, what is the length of DE?

   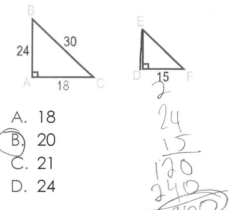

   A. 18
   B. 20
   C. 21
   D. 24

   $\dfrac{2}{24}$
   $\dfrac{15}{120}$
   240
   $\underline{300}$

3. What equations represent the graph below?

   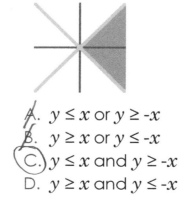

   A. $y \leq x$ or $y \geq -x$
   B. $y \geq x$ or $y \leq -x$
   C. $y \leq x$ and $y \geq -x$
   D. $y \geq x$ and $y \leq -x$

4. If triangles ABC and DEF are similar, what is the sum of x and y?

   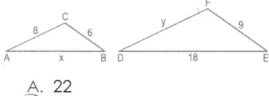

   A. 22
   B. 24
   C. 25
   D. 26

5. In the diagram below, find the measure of angle x.

   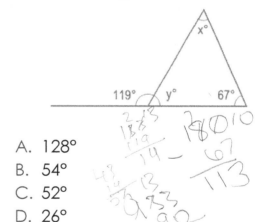

   A. 128°
   B. 54°
   C. 52°
   D. 26°

6. If triangle ABC is isosceles and angle CBA is a right angle, what is the measure of angle BAC?

   A. 45°
   B. 60°
   C. 90°
   D. 180°

7. You have a right triangle
    and you double the length
    of all the sides. How does the
    area change?

    A. Increases by 2
    B. Doubles
    C. Triples
    D. Quadruples

8. If the length of each side of a
    cube is doubled, what happens
    to the volume of the cube?

    A. Doubles
    B. Quadruples
    C. Multiplies by 6
    D. Multiplies by 8

    $\ell = 2$
    $A = 2^2$
    $V = 2^3$

9. If you have two similar
    triangles, which of the
    following transformations could
    have been performed?

    I. Translation
    II. Reflection
    III. Dilation

    A. I only
    B. II and III only
    C. I and II only
    D. I, II, and III

10. If you have two congruent
    triangles, which of the following
    could have been performed on
    one to generate the other?

    I. Translation
    II. Reflection
    III. Dilation

    A. I only
    B. II and III only
    C. I and II only
    D. I, II, and III

11. What is the value of
    $(3x - 8)(2x + 6)$?

    A. $5x^2 + 2x - 14$
    B. $5x^2 - 2x - 2$
    C. $6x^2 + 2x - 48$
    D. $6x^2 - 2x - 48$

12. What are the solutions for x in
    the following equation?

    $$(x - 3)(2x - 1) = 0$$

    A. 3, -½
    B. -3, -2
    C. 3, ½
    D. -3, -1

13. In the figure below, AB = AC
    and angle ABC = 55°. What is
    the measure of angle ACD?

    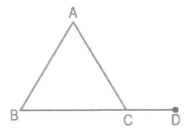

    A. 70°
    B. 110°
    C. 125°
    D. 155°

14. In triangle ABC, angle A = 4x, angle B = 6x − 10, and angle C = 2x + 10. What does x equal?

A. 10
B. 15
C. 20
D. 30

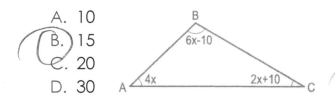

15. When you graph y = -4x^2 + 3x, what is the y–intercept?

A. -4
B. -1
C. 0
D. 3

16. Which inequalities would represent a graph with just quadrant II shaded?

A. $x \leq 0$ or $y \geq 0$
B. $x \leq 0$ and $y \leq 0$
C. $x \geq 0$ or $y \leq 0$
D. $x \leq 0$ and $y \geq 0$

17. What is the measure of each interior angle of a regular pentagon?

A. 90°
B. 108°
C. 120°
D. 540°

18. Which transformation would be performed on the graph of $y = \frac{1}{4}x$ to get the graph of $y = -4x$?

A. translation
B. rotation
C. dilation
D. reflection

19. Bob is buying supplies for his office. He has $60 to spend on pens and pencils. Each pen costs $3 and each pencil costs $1. Which graph represents his buying options?

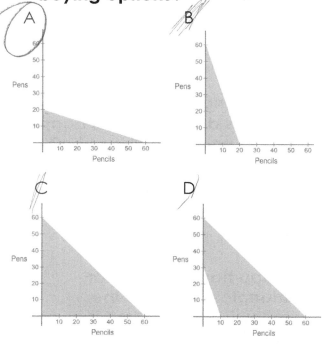

20. Which of the following statements is/are true?

I. All squares are similar.
II. All right triangles are similar.
III. All parallelograms are similar.

A. I only
B. I and II
C. I, II, and III
D. None of the above.

1. A   First, write the absolute value as two separate inequalities connected with and. Then, isolate y in each equation.

$$|2y| \leq 6$$
$$2y \leq 6, \; y \leq 3$$
$$2y \geq -6, \; y \geq -3$$

Now, graph the two boundary lines, and shade the part that overlaps.

$y \leq 3$ is graphed as a horizontal line at $y = 3$, and you should shade the part below the line.

$y \geq -3$ is graphed as a horizontal line at $y = -3$, and you should shade the part above the line.

The shaded part that overlaps is between the two lines.

---

2. B   Since the triangles are similar, set up a proportion.

$$^{AB}/_{DE} = \,^{AC}/_{DF}$$
$$^{24}/_{DE} = \,^{18}/_{15}$$

Cross multiply and solve for DE.

$$(24)(15) = (DE)(18)$$
$$360 = 18(DE)$$
$$DE = 20$$

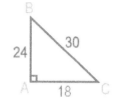

---

3. C   First, you can tell that the graph represents an AND statement since only the overlapped portion is shaded. Or would mean all areas that represent either statement are shaded.

Let's look at the line $y = x$, which has the positive slope. All the points below that are shaded. Therefore, $y \leq x$ has been shaded.

Now, let's look at the line $y = -x$, which has the negative slope. All the points greater than that are shaded. Therefore, $y \geq -x$ has been shaded. $y \leq x$ and $y \geq -x$

---

4. B   Since the triangles are similar, their sides are proportional. Let's first calculate x. Side AB corresponds to Side DE. Side BC corresponds to Side EF.❶

❷ Now cross multiply to solve for x.

❸ To solve for y, follow similar steps.

The sum of x and $y = 12 + 12 = 24$.

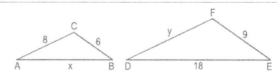

❶
$$^{AB}/_{DE} = \,^{BC}/_{EF}$$
$$^{x}/_{18} = \,^{6}/_{9}$$

❸
$$^{AC}/_{DF} = \,^{BC}/_{EF}$$
$$^{8}/_{y} = \,^{6}/_{9}$$
$$6y = (8)(9)$$
$$6y = 72$$
$$y = 12$$

❷
$$9x = (18)(6)$$
$$9x = 108$$
$$x = 12$$

5. C   Solve for y, which is on a straight line and thus has a supplementary angle of 119 degrees.

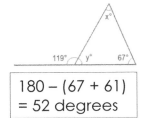

$$180 - 119 = 61 \text{ degrees}$$

Since y equals 61 degrees, you can use the fact that a triangle has 180 degrees to solve for x.

$$180 - (67 + 61)$$
$$= 52 \text{ degrees}$$

6. A   We are told that one angle in the triangle is a right triangle and therefore equals 90°. We know that the sum of all the angles in a triangle are 180°. Subtract to find out the sum of the remaining two angles. The sum of the remaining two angles is $180 - 90 = 90°$

An isosceles triangle has two sides that are equal and two angles that are equal. Therefore, the two remaining angles must be equal. If the two angles are equal and sum to 90°, then each angle must be 45°. Angle BAC = 45°

7. D   The area of a triangle $= \frac{1}{2} \times$ base $\times$ height $= \frac{1}{2}bh$

If you double the length of all the sides, the length of the base and the height will each double. The new area can then be found:

New Area =
$\frac{1}{2}(2b)(2h)$
$= 4\frac{1}{2}bh$
$= 4(\text{original area})$

8. D   Let each side of the original cube = S.
Then, the volume of the original cube $= S \times S \times S = S^3$

Each side of the new cube = 2S
Then, the volume of the new cube $= 2S \times 2S \times 2S = 8S^3 = 8(\text{volume of original cube})$

9. D   Similar triangles have the same shape, but can have different sizes and orientations.

I. Translation	**II. Reflection**	**III. Dilation**
Translation involves moving an object. Moving an object will not change its shape, so this transformation could have been performed.	Reflection involves flipping an object about an axis. Flipping an object will not change its shape, just its orientation, so reflection could have been performed.	Dilation involves changing an object's size. For similar triangles, the sizes can be different, just not the shapes. Therefore, dilation could have been performed.

I, II, and III

10. C Congruent triangles have the same shape and size but can have different orientations.

I. Translation	**II. Reflection**	**III. Dilation**
Translation involves moving an object. Moving an object will not change its shape or size, so this transformation could have been performed.	Reflection involves flipping an object about an axis. Flipping an object will not change its size or shape, just its orientation, so reflection could have been performed.	Dilation involves changing an object's size. For congruent triangles, the sizes cannot be different. Therefore, dilation could not have been performed.

I and II only

---

11. C $(3x - 8)(2x + 6)$

❶ To multiply expressions, remember FOIL:

❷ Now, add the results.

❶
First: $(3x)(2x) = 6x^2$
Outer: $(3x)(6) = 18x$
Inner: $(-8)(2x) = -16x$
Last: $(-8)(6) = -48$

❷
$6x^2 + 18x + -16x + -48$
$= 6x^2 + 2x - 48$

---

12. C In this problem, you have two expressions that multiply to 0. The only way that a product can equal zero is if one of the terms being multiplied equals zero. Therefore, set each expression to zero to find all possible solutions to this equation.

$(x - 3)(2x - 1) = 0$

$x - 3 = 0, x = 3$
$2x - 1 = 0, 2x = 1, x = \frac{1}{2}$
$x = 3$ or $x = \frac{1}{2}$

You can also plug in each answer choice and see which values make the equation true.

---

13. C If AB = AC, that means that the angles opposite the equal sides are equal. Therefore, if angle ABC = 55°, then angle ACB = 55°.

angle ACB and angle ACD form a straight line, and therefore their angles total 180°.

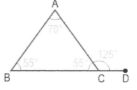

angle ACB + angle ACD = 180°
55° + angle ACD = 180°
angle ACD = 125°

---

14. B In a triangle, all 3 angles add up to 180°. Set up an equation and solve for x.

angle A + angle B + angle C = 180

$4x + 6x - 10 + 2x + 10 = 180$
$12x = 180$
$x = 15$

---

15. C The y–intercept is the point on the graph that crosses the y–axis. The point that crosses the y–axis has an x–coordinate of 0. Plug in $x = 0$ into the equation to solve for y.

$$y = -4x^2 + 3x$$
$$y = -4(0)^2 + 3(0)$$
$$y = 0 + 0$$
$$y = 0$$

---

16. D As can be seen in the graph, quadrant II is in the top left corner.

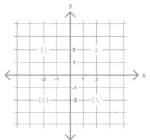

The x–values of any point in quadrant II are negative. Therefore, x is less than or equal to 0. $x \leq 0$

The y–values of any point in quadrant II are positive. Therefore, y is greater than or equal to 0. $y \geq 0$

Since only quadrant II is shaded, we want to use AND to restrict the area to just the overlap of the two equations. $x \leq 0$ and $y \geq 0$

---

17. B The sum of the angles in a triangle is 180°. A pentagon can be divided into 3 triangles, so the sum of the measures of a pentagon is $3 \times 180° = 540°$.

Pentagon = 3 triangles
= 3 x 180°
= 540°

There are 5 interior angles in a pentagon. Since the question asks about a regular polygon, you know that all the angles are equal. Divide 540° by 5 to find the measure of each interior angle.

$$540° \div 5 = 108°$$

---

18. B $y = \frac{1}{4}x$ $\quad$ $y = -4x$
Graph both equations on the coordinate plane.

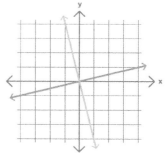

As can be seen in the image above, to get from one graph to the other, you would rotate the line.

Translation moves objects. Dilation changes the size of objects. Reflection flips an object about an axis. None of those transformations were performed on the lines. Rotation

---

19. A First, use the variables x and y to represent the two unknown quantities. Let x = number of pencils Bob purchases.

Let y = number of pens Bob purchases.

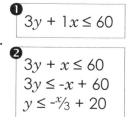

❶ Set up an equation to represent the amount Bob can spend.
Each pen costs $3, so the total cost of pens = $3y$.
Each pencil costs $1, so the total cost of pencils = $1x$.
Bob has only $60 to spend.

❷ Isolate y and then graph.

The graph of that inequality will have a y–intercept of 20 and a slope of $-\frac{1}{3}$. You want to shade below the line. Also, since x and y can not be negative, only shade in quadrant I.

---

20. A Similar polygons have the same shape and same angles. They can be different sizes and in different orientations. To be the same shape, polygons must have sides that are proportionate.

   I.   All squares are similar.
      This statement is true. Squares all have the same angles and shapes. Performing the following transformations will get from one square to another: dilation, rotation, translation, or reflection. All those transformations hold true for similar polygons.

  II. All right triangles are similar.
      This statement is false. Similar polygons have the same angles, but not all right triangles have the same angles. For example, you can have one right triangle with angles 45°, 45°, and 90° and another with angles 30°, 60°, and 90°.

 III. All parallelograms are similar.
      This statement is false. Parallelograms do not necessarily have the same shape or angles. For example, a rectangle is a parallelogram and so is a rhombus, but they are not the same shape.

Only I is true.

Chapter 8:
Statistics & Probability

Lessons

8.1   Gathering & Organizing Data

There are different methods to use when gathering statistical data, some of which are more appropriate than others in certain situations.

Experimental vs Observational Data

One important distinction is the difference between an experiment, in which the experimenter creates artificial conditions for the purpose of drawing a conclusion, and an observational study, in which the observer gathers information without influencing the object of the study. An example of an experiment would be giving one set of plants one type of plant food and another set of plants a second type of plant food and then recording how the different foods impacted their growth. An observational study might involve recording a plant's growth in summer and in winter and comparing the two.

Census

A census involves gathering information from every person in a group. For example, if you wanted to find out how many hours of sleep that seniors at your high school get each night, conducting a census would involve asking every single senior how many hours of sleep they get. This method is generally used for gathering information from small groups of people.

Survey

A survey is generally used to gather information from large groups of people. In a survey, information from a representative sample of the large group is used to make inferences about the entire group. For example, if you wanted to find out how many hours of sleep seniors at your high school get each night, you could survey 50 random seniors and then make an inference about the entire senior class from what those seniors answered.

Representative Sample/Bias

In order for the results of a survey to be meaningful, the sample from which they are drawn needs to be representative of all the variations within the group. A sample that represents one part of the target group more heavily than others is said to include a bias. For example, if a group conducting a survey to determine America's favorite food chose to sample only elementary school students, the results would be biased toward the opinions of younger Americans, most likely toward pizza and fast food. A bias could also be caused in the way the questions were asked. For example, if the same students were surveyed and just had a long lesson on health food and told that they should be healthy and then asked their favorite food, some may be biased to say something healthier than what they normally would have answered.

Random Sample

The best way to ensure a representative sample is to select the sample members randomly from all of the members of the target group. A sample for the amount of sleep that seniors get would not be representative if you only asked seniors who were on sports team. A better random sample would be to ask every 4th person based on the numbers on their student IDs.

Methods of Organizing Data

After collecting data from an experiment or observational study, it is often useful to represent that information graphically to see patterns in the data. There are many different ways to chart or graph data, so only a few will be covered here.

Bar charts

Bar charts are used for comparing values. In a bar chart, rectangular bars are used to proportionately represent data. This chart shows that 20 kids in Ms. Jones' class chose pizza as their favorite food, while 15 chose hamburgers, and only 5 selected chicken nuggets.

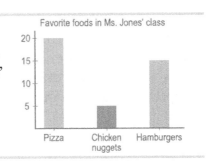

Pie Charts

Another way to show proportionality in data is to use a pie chart. In a pie chart, the circle or pie represents the entire population or whole, and the pie is divided proportionately among the data. The data for Ms. Jones' class can easily be represented in pie chart form. Since there are 40 students in the class and 20 of them chose pizza, pizza takes $\frac{1}{2}$ of the chart. The 5 chicken nugget responses are $\frac{1}{8}$ of the whole, and the 15 hamburger responses are $\frac{3}{8}$.

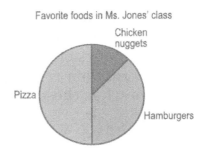

Stem Plot

Another way to show patterns in numerical data is to use a stemplot. In a stemplot, each stem is a number representing a group of ten and is written to the left of the line. The stems are each paired with one or more leaf digits, each of which represents a number in the ones place value, to represent data points. This plot shows 67, 67, 68, 69, and 69 in the 6–stem and 70 and 71 in the 7–stem.

Stem	Leaf
6	7, 7, 8, 9, 9
7	0, 1

Key
Leaf unit: 1
Stem unit: 10

Stem = 10 values
leaf = single

Scatter Plots

Not all data is well represented by a pie or bar chart. Another way to visually illustrate data is by using a scatter plot. Because data in a scatter plot is graphed as a series of coordinate pairs, this method works best with numerical data. For example, this plot shows high temperatures in Menlo Park, CA for a week. On the graph, day 1 represents Sunday, day 2 Monday, and so on.

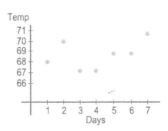

Venn Diagrams

To illustrate how data fits into sets, Venn diagrams can be used. These diagrams can help you see which data elements belong to multiple sets or which data elements belong to just a single set. The diagrams are drawn with overlapping circles, where each circle represents a data set.

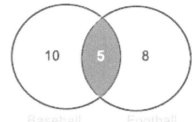

For example, here is an illustration of the after-school activities of a high school class. Ten students play just baseball. Then, you can see that there is a set of 8 students that just play football. There are 5 students in this class that are in the overlapped portion of the Venn diagram and they play both baseball and football.

Line of Best Fit & Independent/Dependent Variables

For data that is best represented by graphing, which is often the case for a large sample, a line of best fit can be used to examine the relationship between the independent and dependent variables. A line of best fit shows the data as a straight line that is drawn to minimize the distances of all the points from that line. In the graph, the month is the independent

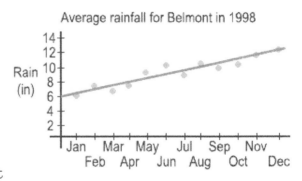

variable, which is always graphed on the x–axis, and the rainfall in inches is the dependent variable. The data points are represented by black dots. The line of best fit on the graph is represented by the diagonal line.

GATHERING & ORGANIZING DATA PRACTICE

1. **A census would be most appropriate for collecting data about which group?**
    A. 18–25 years old in China
    B. senior citizens worldwide
    C. Republican voters in Iowa
    D. employees of the local supermarket

2. A representative sample is:

   I. drawn from the entire population for which data is being collected

   II. is random

   III. is elected by the members of the population

   A. I only

   B. II only

   C. I and II

   D. I, II, and III

3. According to the bar chart below, how many more science textbooks does the store have in stock than reading textbooks?

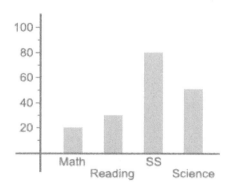

   A. 20

   B. 30

   C. 50

   D. 80

         B.

4. Which pie chart best reflects the data below?

<u>Monthly Finances</u>

Rent $1500   Food $500

Entertainment $1000   Car $500

A.    B.

C.    D.

5. Which stem plot represents the following data? 62, 70, 73, 77, 82, 82, 83, 86, 88, 89, 94, 95, 95

   Test Scores: 77, 86, 95, 62, 94, 82, 73, 70, 95, 89, 88, 82, 82

A.
Stem	Leaf
6	2
7	0, 3, 7
8	2, 2, 2, 6, 8, 9
9	4, 5, 5

B.
Stem	Leaf
6	2
7	0, 3, 7
8	2, 6, 8, 9
9	4, 5

C.
Stem	Leaf
60	2
70	0, 3, 7
80	2, 2, 2, 6, 8, 9
90	4, 5, 5

D.
Stem	Leaf
0	7
2	6, 8, 8, 8
3	7
4	9
5	9, 9
6	8
7	7
8	8
9	8

6. What trend has this company's profits followed?

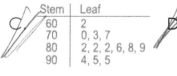

A. Sharp rise followed by sharp drop

B. Steady rise

C. Sharp rise, then drop, then steady rise

D. Steady decline

7. Which would be the best way to represent data from a survey of languages spoken by college students if the goal is to illustrate the proportion of students who speak each language?

A. stem and leaf plot

B. table

C. pie chart

D. scatter plot

8. Which is the independent variable in the graph below?

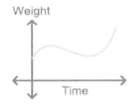

A. time

B. weight

C. neither

D. both

9. Bias may be introduced into a survey by:

I. Over representing a certain portion of the population

II. Under representing a certain portion of the population

III. Phrasing of the questions used in the survey

A. I only

B. II only

C. I and III

D. I, II, and III

10. Which of the following is the line of best fit for the data?

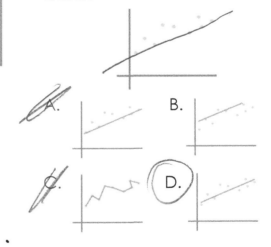

GATHERING & ORGANIZING DATA EXPLANATIONS

1. **D**   Since a census involves collecting data from every member of a population, it is most appropriately used for small groups. In this case, the smallest group is the employees of your local supermarket.

2. C The members that are chosen for the representative sample are chosen by those conducting the experiment, not by the members of the population. A representative sample is useful for drawing inferences about a population without surveying every member of that population. Answer C: I and II

3. A There are 50 science textbooks in stock and 30 reading textbooks. Subtract to find out how many more science textbooks there are.

$$50 - 30 = 20$$

4. A Pie charts should represent the data proportionately. The total amount spent per month is $3500. Rent is slightly less than half of the month spending, therefore, rent should take up slightly less than half the pie. This is only true in answers A and B, therefore eliminate C and D.

Next, we see that entertainment should have twice as large a slice of the pie as both food and car. In answer choice A this is true.

5. A To create a stem plot, take each number, represent the tens place value as the stem and take the ones place value as the leaf. If a number occurs multiple times, such as the 82 in this case, it should be listed multiple times in your stem plot.

6. C The profits of this company rose from 2002–2003, dropped from 03 to 04, and then had a steady rise from 04–07.

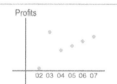

7. C To show proportionality, the best method to choose would be the pie chart. For each of the other plots, it is hard to quickly glance at the illustration of the data to see the proportion of students who speak each language.

8. A Time is graphed on the x–axis which is where the independent variable will be, while the dependent variable will be on the y–axis. Also, common sense tells us that time is not dependent on anything, it will keep going regardless. However, weight is being influenced by or is dependent on the amount of time that has passed.

Independent variable = time

9. D Bias can be introduced into a survey in many ways. If bias is introduced, then the results of the survey won't be reflective of the population.

I. Over representing a certain portion of the population

If some members of a population are more likely or less likely to be included, this is a form of bias. For instance, if you wanted to find out how many high schoolers smoke and you went to the local public school to survey the students, you would have a biased sample that would not include private school or home-schooled students. In this example, public school students would be over represented.

II. Under representing a certain portion of the population

For the same reason as over–representation, under–representation is a form of bias. In the above example, private school students would be under–represented.

III. Phrasing of the questions used in the survey

If questions are not phrased appropriately, then bias may be introduced. For instance, in the above example, if students were asked if they smoked and told that their parents may find out what they said, some students might not answer truthfully.

Bias can be introduced in all three of the ways listed.

---

10. D The line of best fit minimizes the differences between the line and each of the points. You can think of the line of best fit as approximating the average of the data.

In answer A, the line goes through the lower points, not the average.
In B, the line goes through most of the top points, not the average.
In C, there is no line of best fit which needs to be a single line with one slope.
In D, the line goes through the middle of the data. It is the best answer for the line of best fit.

8.2 Central Tendency & Dispersion

Measures of Central Tendency

There are several ways to describe a set of data. One of the most important is to find the "average" or middle value. Generally, when people discuss averages, they are referring to the mean of one or more sets of data. Mathematicians also use other methods of finding the center or describing a set of data: median, mode, and range. In this module, you will learn how to calculate each of these important aspects of data sets.

Mean

In words, the mean value of a set of numbers is equal to the sum of those numbers divided by the number of numbers. For example, to take the mean of 2, 3, 4, 5, and 6, you would add them and divide the sum by 5, because there are 5 numbers being averaged. Their sum is 20 and their mean is 4.

Median

Like the median on a road, the median number in a set is the one located in the middle. To find the median of 29, 113, 1, 4, and 76, order the numbers from least to greatest, and then locate the middle number: 1, 4, 29, 76, and 113. For this set, 29 is in the middle, so it is the median.

For a set containing an even number of numbers, take the average of the two middle numbers. Example: Find the median of 9, 17, 82, and 9. First, order the numbers: 9, 9, 17, and 82. There are two numbers in the middle 9 and 17. Take the average of those two numbers: $(9 + 17) \div 2 = 13$. The median = 13.

Note, the median of a set of numbers can be a number that is not in the original set of numbers.

Mode

The mode of a set of data is the most frequently occurring number or piece of data. If this was your set: 1, 1, 1, 7, 8, 9, 9, 10, 11, 12. Then the mode would be 1, since it occurs the most often. If two or more numbers occur the same number of times within a set, then that set can have multiple modes.

Example:

Find the mode of: 62, 0.9, 0.5, 3.75, 0.5, 0.9, 27
First order the numbers: 0.5, 0.5, 0.9, 0.9, 3.75, 27, 62
Since 0.5 and 0.9 each occur twice, they are the two modes of the set.

Measures of Dispersion

There are also statistical measures that describe how disperse the data is. Range and standard deviation are 2 commonly used measures.

Range

The range of a set of numbers is their spread. To find the range, subtract the smallest number from the largest number.
Example: find the range of 1, 45, 5, 9, 73. The range would be $73 - 1 = 72$.
Example: Find the range of: -27, 32, 58, 96. The range would be $96 - (-27) = 123$

Standard Deviation

The distances of all the data points from a line of best fit are often discussed in terms of standard deviation. The better the line fits the data, meaning the closer all of the points are to the line of best fit, the smaller the standard deviation. If all the data is directly on the line of best fit, the standard deviation is 0.

Box Plots

Box-and-whisker plots are yet another way to show data, which involves calculating median. Here are the steps for creating a box plot:

1. Order your data
2. Find the median
3. Using your median, divide the data into two halves.
4. Find the median of each of those halves.
5. The three points, median of first half of data (called lower quartile or Q1), median of entire data set (Q2), median of second half of data (upper quartile or Q3), divide the data into quarters or quartiles.
6. Draw a box from Q1 to Q3 with a line at Q2.
7. Draw the whiskers from the minimum to the maximum.

Let's try a sample set of data. Data: 11, 5, 16, 23, 30, 3, 0, 47, 50, 10, 14, 2, 20, 40
First, order the data: 0, 2, 3, 5, 10, 11, 14, 16, 20, 23, 30, 40, 47, 50
Then, find the median of the data set, which is 15, the average of 14 and 16.
Next, take the first half of the data, from 0 to 14. Find the median of that set.
First half of data: 0, 2, 3, 5, 10, 11, 14.
Median of first half = lower quartile or Q1 = 5
Find the median for the second half of the data: 16, 20, 23, 30, 40, 47, 50
Median = Upper Quartile = Q3 = 30
Minimum: 0, Maximum: 50
Draw a box from Q1 to Q3 with a line at Q2. Then, add the whiskers from the minimum to the maximum.

CENTRAL TENDENCY & DISPERSION PRACTICE

1. If you have the highest score on a math test, which measure would you need to determine the lowest score on the test?

A. Mean
B. Median
C. Mode
D. Range

2. **Find the mode in the following set:**
square,square,circle,circle,circle
    A. square
    B. circle
    C. 2
    D. 3

3. **This box plot represents which data set?**

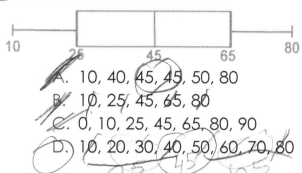

    A. 10, 40, 45, 45, 50, 80
    B. 10, 25, 45, 65, 80
    C. 0, 10, 25, 45, 65, 80, 90
    D. 10, 20, 30, 40, 50, 60, 70, 80

4. **Which is greater, the median or mean of the following set?**
23, 75, 16, 91, 100
    A. Median
    B. Mean
    C. They are equal.
    D. Not enough information.

5. **Find x if the range of the data set is 16.**
x, 2.3, 9.8, 12.9
    A. -2.3
    B. 2.3
    C. -3.1
    D. 3.1

6. **The following is a list of house prices for a given area. What is the best way to describe the average house price to a family interested in purchasing there?**

$750,000	$595,000
$10,000,000	$800,000
$830,000	$840,000

    A. Range
    B. Median
    C. Mean
    D. Mode

7. **For the set: 16, 16, 24, 96, 3 What is 16?**
    I. mean
    II. median
    III. mode
    A. I and II
    B. II and III
    C. III only
    D. I, II, and III

8. **Which set of data has the largest standard deviation?**
    A.
    B.
    C.
    D.

9. **What is the mean of the following set: 5, -4, 0, 3, 16**
    A. 3
    B. 4
    C. 5
    D. 7

10. In America, the gap between the rich and the poor is widening. What impact will that fact most likely have on data concerning average income?
   A. The line of best fit will move up.
   B. The standard deviation will increase.
   C. It will introduce bias.
   D. The standard deviation will decrease.

CENTRAL TENDENCY & DISPERSION EXPLANATIONS

1. D   Let's examine each answer choice.

   A: Mean. The mean is the average of all the numbers. Only knowing the highest score and the mean would not help you find the lowest score. Eliminate A.

   B: Median. This is the middle number if you order the numbers. Therefore, knowing the median would only help you find the middle score not the lowest score. Eliminate B.

   C: Mode. This is the score that appears most often. This can be any score from the highest, to the lowest, to any score in between. This would not help. Eliminate C.

   D: Range. This is the highest score minus the lowest score. Therefore, if you knew the range and the highest score, you could easily find the lowest score. This is the answer.

2. B   The mode is the piece of data that occurs the most often in the set. The word "circle" appears 3 times and the word "square" occurs twice. Therefore, the mode is "circle".

3. D   First, let's analyze the box and whisker plot to get an understanding of the data set it represents. As a box and whisker plot can be the same for different data sets, we will then have to go through each answer choice to see which one matches the plot.
   The first thing to notice on your box plot is the end points. These represent the minimum and maximum of your data set. The minimum is 10 and the maximum is 80.
   Next, in the middle of the box is the median of the data set. The median in this case is 45. The sides of the box are the lower quartile and upper

quartile values. These values are found by dividing your data set into two and finding the median of each half. The lower quartile is 25 and the upper quartile is 65.

Now, let's examine each answer choice.

A. The minimum, maximum, and median all match the box plot. However, let's look at the lower quartile value. If we divide our data set into two, the lower half of the data is 10, 40, and 45. The median of this data set is 40, not 25. Eliminate A.

B. The minimum, maximum, and median all match the box plot. The median divides the data into the upper and lower halves. The lower quartile is found by taking the median of the first half of the data, which is 10 and 25. The median of those two data points is not 25. Eliminate B.

C. The minimum of the data set is 0 and not 10. Eliminate C.

D. The minimum is 10, the maximum is 80, and the median is the average of 40 and 50, which is 45. The data is divided into the lower half: 10, 20, 30, and 40, and the upper half: 50, 60, 70, and 80. The lower quartile is the median of the first half, which is the average of 20 and 30, which is 25. The upper quartile is the median of the second half, which is the average of 60 and 70, or 65.

4. A To answer this question, you must calculate both the median and mean of the set: 23, 75, 16, 91, 100.

Median: First put the numbers in order and then find the middle number: 16, 23, 75, 91, 100. The middle number is 75, so that is the median.

Mean: Add the numbers and divide that sum by 5.

$$23 + 75 + 16 + 91 + 100 = 305$$
$$305 \div 5 = 61$$
$$\text{Mean} = 61$$

Median is greater than the mean for this data set.

5. C To find the range, subtract the largest number from the smallest number.

Range = 12.9 − smallest = 16.

The smallest number that is given in the set, 2.3, is too large to give a range of 16, therefore x must be the smallest number.

$$12.9 - x = 16$$
$$x = -3.1$$

6. B Notice that the data set has an outlier, or a data point whose value is very different than the rest of the sample. The outlier is the $10,000,000 home. Let's see how this affects each of the measures.

Range: The range does not describe the average of a set, only its spread. Therefore, this would not be useful.

Median: The median of this set is $815,000. This would give the family a good indication of the average house price.

Mean: The mean house price is $2,302,500. This is not a good description of the average house price since it was obviously affected greatly by the outlier.

Mode: There is no data point that occurs more than once, eliminating the usefulness of the mode as a descriptor.

The median is the best descriptor in this case. Answer B.

---

7. B I.   **mean:** To calculate the mean, add all the numbers and divide by 5 since there are 5 numbers in the set.
mean = (16 + 16 + 24 + 96 + 3) ÷ 5 = 155 ÷ 5 = 31

II. **median:** To find the median, order the set and find the middle number. 3, 16, 16, 24, 96
The middle number in the set is 16. Therefore, 16 is the median.

III. **mode:** To determine the mode, find the number that appears most often in the set. 16 appears twice and is the only number that appears more than once. Therefore, 16 is the mode.

16 is the median and mode. II and III.

---

8. C The standard deviation measures how far the data varies from the line of best fit. Therefore, the data with the largest standard deviation will have the greatest dispersion, and the data will be farthest from following a pattern. In this case, the graph in answer choice C has the largest standard deviation. In the rest of the answer choices, the data is closer to following a straight line.

---

9. B To calculate the mean of a set, sum the elements in the set and divide by the number of elements in the set.

First, let's add the numbers in our set: 5 + -4 + 0 + 3 + 16 = 20
Now, divide by 5 since there are 5 numbers in the set. 20 ÷ 5 = 4
The mean = 4.

---

10. B Since the rich and the poor are moving in opposite directions, there is no way to determine if the line of best fit will increase or decrease overall. Introducing bias would require that the data on incomes of Americans was being misrepresented.

Now, let's examine the effect on the standard deviation. If the gap is getting wider, then the data points will be farther from the line of best fit, which would thus increase the standard deviation.

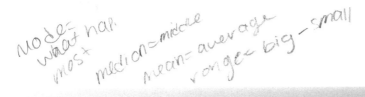

mode= what hap. most
median=middle
mean= average
range big - small

8.3 Sample Space & Simple Probability

Sample Space

A random experiment is one for which the outcome is unknown before the experiment is performed. An example of a random experiment is flipping a fair coin with one side heads and the other tails.

A simple event is one that relies on one independent outcome. For the example of flipping a coin, a simple event would be flipping the coin once. The outcome of that experiment would be whichever side lands face–up: heads or tails.

To calculate the probability (or likelihood of occurrence) for an event, you must first determine the sample space or total number of possible outcomes for that event. For the simple case of flipping a coin once, the sample space includes heads and tails, the only two possible outcomes. For rolling a dice, the sample space includes 1, 2, 3, 4, 5, and 6, the six possible outcomes for the dice.

Counting Principle

Determining sample space by writing out all possible outcomes works for very simple experiments but it can be quite cumbersome for even slightly complex situations.

For example, if a woman is making a sandwich with three types of bread: white, wheat, and rye and four kinds of meat: turkey, ham, roast beef, and pastrami. Listing possibilities will take quite a bit of time:

> White–Turkey, White–Ham, White–Roast Beef, White–Pastrami,
> Wheat–Turkey, Wheat–Ham, Wheat–Roast Beef, Wheat–Pastrami,
> Rye–Turkey, Rye–Ham, Rye–Roast Beef, Rye–Pastrami

Notice that the number of possibilities is 12, which is equal to 3 × 4, the number of outcomes for event A (the type of bread) multiplied by the number of outcomes for event B (the type of meat). This is called the counting principle or multiplication rule.

The set of possible outcomes for n events =
possible outcomes for first event × possible outcomes for second event × possible outcomes for third event × ...
The counting principle works for any number of events.

Theoretical Probability

The theoretical probability that an event will occur is the number of favorable outcomes divided by the total number of outcomes. Finding the probability of rolling a dice and getting an even number, would involve first finding the favorable outcomes: 2, 4, and 6 then finding the total number of outcomes: 1, 2, 3, 4, 5, and 6. There are 3 favorable outcomes and 6 total outcomes, therefore the probability of getting an even number is $\frac{3}{6} = \frac{1}{2} = 0.5$

Experimental Probability

The experimental probability is the number of favorable outcomes divided by the number of times an experiment was performed. For example, if you wanted to calculate the experimental probability of rolling an even number on a die, you could roll a dice a certain number of times and count the number of even outcomes that occur. For example, if you rolled a die 20 times and counted that an even number came up 11 times, then your experimental probability of rolling an even number would be $\frac{11}{20} = 0.55$

The Law of Large Numbers

In the example above, as with many real–life experiences, there is a difference between the theoretical and experimental probabilities for an experiment. The Law of Large Numbers states that as the number of trials for an experiment approaches infinity (grows as large as possible), the experimental probability approaches the value of the theoretical probability. For example, if the experiment of rolling a die was performed thousands and thousands more times, the experimental probability would get closer to 0.5, which is the theoretical probability.

SAMPLE SPACE & SIMPLE PROBABILITY PRACTICE

1. **If you were picking a card from a standard deck, how many elements would there be in the sample space?**
   A. 1
   B. 4
   C. 13
   D. 52

2. **What is a sample space?**
   A. Geographic area over which a survey or experiment is conducted.
   B. A test survey conducted before the actual survey.
   C. Number of favorable outcomes.
   D. Number of possible outcomes.

3. A man has 17 ties, 12 suits, and 3 pairs of shoes. Assuming that he wears 1 tie, 1 suit, and 1 pair of shoes, how many different ways can he get dressed for work?

    A. 51
    B. 204
    C. 612
    D. 1290

4. A student rolls two dice. One die has six faces that are marked with 1, 2, 3, 4, 5, or 6 spots. The other is a special die with eight faces that are marked with A, B, C, D, E, F, G, or H. How many outcomes are in the sample space for this experiment?

    A. 14
    B. 28
    C. 48
    D. 64

5. June has 19 pairs of pants, 30 short sleeved shirts, 20 long sleeved shirts, and 15 dresses in her closet. If she picks a shirt randomly, how many items are in her sample space?

    A. 20
    B. 30
    C. 50
    D. 84

6. At a particular ice cream shop, one flavor of ice cream per month is randomly selected as the "ice cream of the month."

Assuming the shop has a rocky road ice cream, what piece of information is necessary to calculate the probability that rocky road will be selected this month?

    A. Number of days in the month.
    B. how much of each flavor is carried by the shop.
    C. number of flavors carried by the shop
    D. method of selection (drawing flavor from a hat, etc)

7. A journalist is conducting a survey of favorite colors among kindergarten classrooms. In a particular class, there are 19 students, 2 of whom have blue for a favorite color. If the journalist randomly selects one student from this class, what is the probability that the child will give blue as his or her favorite color?

    A. $\frac{1}{2}$
    B. $\frac{1}{19}$
    C. $\frac{19}{2}$
    D. $\frac{2}{19}$

8. For a high school's senior class, the theoretical probability is 60% that a student is taking Honors English. The principal of the school conducted a survey of Mr. Jones' homeroom which had 20 seniors. His results were

16 Honors and 4 not in Honors English. What experimental probability did the principal find for students being in Honors English?

A. 16%
B. 60%
C. 70%
D. 80%

16/20 = ⁷
4/5

9. A boy is pulling marbles out of a bag without putting the marbles back. If the bag contains 7 marbles, 1 of which is blue, 4 of which are green, and 2 of which are red, which of the following could not be a list of his first three draws?

A. green, green, green
B. blue, blue, green
C. blue, red, red
D. blue, green, red

10. Something that is 87% likely should occur how many times for an experiment with an infinite number of trials.

A. 87 times
B. never
C. more than half of the time
D. less than half of the time

SAMPLE SPACE & SIMPLE PROBABILITY EXPLANATIONS

1. D   The sample space is the total number of possible outcomes. If you are picking a card from a standard deck, there are 52 possible cards that you could choose. Therefore, the sample space has 52 elements.

2. D   The sample space of a survey or experiment is the set of all possible outcomes for that experiment.

   For example, for flipping a coin, the sample space is: Heads, Tails. If you roll a die and want to get a 3, the sample space is: 1, 2, 3, 4, 5, and 6, since those are all the possible outcomes.

3. C   Use the multiplication rule to determine the total number of ways he can get dressed.

| Total = # ties × # suits × # shoes |
| = 17 × 12 × 3 |
| = 612 |

4. C To find the number of possible outcomes in a sample space, multiply the number of outcomes for each part of the experiment.

There are 6 outcomes for the first die.
There are 8 outcomes for the second die.

Therefore, the total number of outcomes = 6 x 8 = 48

---

5. C If June is choosing from among the shirts, then the number of shirts is the number of items in her sample space. June has 30 short sleeved shirts and 20 long sleeved shirts for a total of 50 shirts.

---

6. C To calculate the simple probability, create a fraction with the number of favorable outcomes (rocky road = 1 flavor) in the numerator and the number of possible outcomes in the denominator. The number of flavors carried by the shop is the number of possible outcomes.

Number of flavors carried—Answer C

---

7. D The probability of an event happening is the number of favorable outcomes divided by the number of possible outcomes.

The probability that a child will give blue as his or her favorite color is the number of children whose favorite color is blue divided by the number of students in the class.

Probability = # of favorable outcomes ÷ # of possible outcomes
= # of students whose favorite color is blue ÷ # of students = 2/19

---

8. D The experimental probability is the probability that was found during an experiment or survey. Do not be confused by the theoretical probability which is extraneous information.

In this case, the experimental probability has 16 favorable outcomes and 20 possible outcomes. 16/20 = 4/5 = 80%

---

9. B There is only one blue marble in the bag and since the boy is not replacing the marbles, he cannot pull the blue marble out twice. Therefore, his first three draws can not be: blue, blue, green.

---

10. C If something is 87% likely, than it will happen 87 out of every 100 trials. This is more than half of the time.

8.4 Probability of Compound Events

Compound Events

In statistics, the probability that 2 or more events will occur sequentially is referred to as the probability of a compound event. For example, the probability of flipping a fair coin and having it land heads up is $\frac{1}{2}$. How do you calculate the probability of getting heads twice in a row?

One way, which you have already learned, is to list out all of the possible outcomes for flipping two coins.

Heads–Heads, Heads–Tails, Tails–Heads, Tails–Tails

There are 4 possible outcomes, and one is favorable with heads–heads, therefore, the probability is $\frac{1}{4}$.

This method will not work if there are a large number of outcomes and events. For example, finding the probability of getting heads 20 times in a row by this method would be quite tedious.

Determining Probability of Compound Events

To find the probability of independent compound events, multiply the probability of each of the individual events. Independent events are events that do not affect the outcome of each other. For example, flipping a coin that lands heads up does not affect the probability of a heads–up result for the next coin flip. To answer a question that asks for the probability of rolling a die and getting a 3 and flipping a coin that lands heads–up, you should find the product of the probabilities of each event.

Prob of getting a 3 on die × Prob of getting heads $= \frac{1}{6} \times \frac{1}{2} = \frac{1}{12}$

To find the probability of getting 3 heads in a row, multiply the probability of each of the heads $= \frac{1}{2} \times \frac{1}{2} \times \frac{1}{2} = \frac{1}{8}$

Dependent Events

Dependent events are those with outcomes that affect the probability of another. When calculating the probability of a combination of dependent events, you must consider how the sample space of the second is affected by the first event, and so on.

Example: A bag contains 8 marbles, 3 red and 5 blue. What is the probability of pulling a red marble and then a blue marble from the bag if you do not replace the marbles as you take them?

The probability of drawing a red marble from the bag is $\frac{3}{8}$, since there are 3 red marbles and 8 marbles total. After that marble has been removed, there are 2 red marbles and 5 blue marbles remaining. Therefore, the probability of pulling out a blue marble on the second draw is $\frac{5}{7}$. To find the probability of drawing a red and then drawing a blue, multiply the two probabilities.

$$\frac{3}{8} \times \frac{5}{7} = \frac{15}{56}$$

If the marbles were replaced on each round, then these events would be independent and not dependent.

Compound Events with "OR"—use addition rule

To find the probability of one of multiple events occurring, add the probabilities of each event occurring independently and subtract any overlap (double–counting of situations where both events occur).

For example, what is the probability of rolling a 3 or a 4 on a fair die?
Add the probability of rolling a 3, $\frac{1}{6}$, to the probability of rolling a 4, also $\frac{1}{6}$. In this situation there is not a potential for overlap.

Prob of 3 or 4 = Prob 3 + Prob 4 − Prob 3 and 4
$$= \frac{1}{6} + \frac{1}{6} - 0 = \frac{2}{6} = \frac{1}{3}$$

Example with overlap. What is the probability of getting an ace or a club when pulling a card from a deck?
Add the probability of getting an ace, $\frac{4}{52}$, to the probability of getting a club, $\frac{13}{52}$, and subtract the overlap of getting a club and ace, $\frac{1}{52}$.

Prob of Ace or Club = Prob Ace + Prob Club − Prob Ace and Club
$$\frac{4}{52} + \frac{13}{52} - \frac{1}{52} = \frac{16}{52} = \frac{4}{13}$$

PROBABILITY OF COMPOUND EVENTS PRACTICE

1. If there are 120 red marbles and 5 green marbles in a bag of 1200 marbles, what is the probability that a marble drawn from the bag will be red or green?

   A. $\frac{5}{1200}$
   B. $\frac{120}{1200}$
   C. $\frac{125}{1200}$
   D. $\frac{600}{1200}$

2. What is the probability of drawing a red skittle out of a bag of 100 skittles that are 20% red and then rolling a 2 on a fair die?

   A. $\frac{1}{120}$
   B. $\frac{11}{30}$
   C. $\frac{1}{11}$
   D. $\frac{1}{30}$

   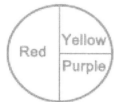
   $\frac{1}{5} \times \frac{1}{6} = \frac{1}{30}$

3. What is the probability of spinning purple 300 times in a row on the spinner below?

   Red | Yellow | Purple

   A. $\frac{1}{1200}$
   B. 1200
   C. $\frac{1}{4}$
   D. $(\frac{1}{4})^{300}$

4. Francisco is trying to guess a letter of the alphabet that has been randomly selected. What is the probability that Francisco will guess the letter correctly on the 2nd try?

   A. $\frac{1}{26}$
   B. $\frac{1}{25}$
   C. $\frac{2}{26}$
   D. $\frac{25}{26}$

5. There are 8 lockers in a school hallway and 5 of them have star stickers on the inside. If the first locker opened does not have stars in it, what is the probability that the 2nd won't either?

   A. $\frac{1}{4}$
   B. $\frac{2}{7}$
   C. $\frac{3}{8}$
   D. $\frac{3}{7}$

   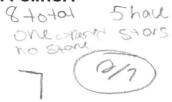
   8 total   5 have
   one opened stars
   no stars
   $\frac{2}{7}$

6. If 20 red, 30 purple, and 40 yellow marbles are in a bag, and marbles are drawn from the bag without replacement, how would you find the probability that a red will be selected on the first random draw, a purple on the second, and a yellow on the third?

   A. $\frac{2}{9} \times \frac{1}{3} \times \frac{4}{9}$
   B. $\frac{2}{9} \times \frac{30}{89} \times \frac{5}{11}$
   C. $\frac{2}{9} + \frac{1}{3} + \frac{4}{9}$
   D. $\frac{2}{9} + \frac{30}{89} + \frac{5}{11}$

7. If 5 marbles are in a bag—2 red and 3 purple, what is the probability that, if you randomly draw 2 marbles out, you will get one red and one purple?

   A. $\frac{3}{5}$
   B. $\frac{3}{10}$
   C. $\frac{3}{20}$
   D. 1

8. If you roll 2 dice, what is the probability that the numbers rolled will have a sum of 10?

    A. $\frac{5}{18}$

    B. $\frac{1}{36}$

    C. $\frac{1}{18}$

    D. $\frac{1}{12}$

9. You have a bag with 100 marbles, only 1 of which is red, and you have to keep picking marbles until you pick the red marble. If you want to minimize your number of draws, should you choose to replace the marbles or not?

    A. Replacement

    B. Without replacement

    C. Doesn't matter — same results

    D. Not enough information

10. A number is selected randomly from between 2 and 19, inclusive. What is the probability that the number will be even or a multiple of 5?

    A. $\frac{2}{3}$

    B. $\frac{13}{18}$

    C. $\frac{11}{18}$

    D. $\frac{1}{2}$

PROBABILITY OF COMPOUND EVENTS EXPLANATIONS

1. **C**   Use the addition rule since you want the probability of red marbles or green marbles. First, find the probability that you will pull a red marble and then the probability that you pull a green marble. Add them together to find probability of drawing one or the other.

    Probability of red marble: $\frac{120}{1200}$

    Probability of green marble: $\frac{5}{1200}$

    Probability of red or green: $\frac{120}{1200} + \frac{5}{1200} = \frac{125}{1200}$

2. **D**   For independent compound events, multiply the probability of each of the events.

    Probability of drawing a red skittle out of 100 skittles that are 20% red = 20% = $\frac{1}{5}$

    Probability of rolling a 2 on a fair die
    = Favorable outcomes ÷ total outcomes = $\frac{1}{6}$

    Probability of both events happening = Probability of drawing a red × Probability of rolling a 2 = $\frac{1}{5} \times \frac{1}{6} = \frac{1}{30}$

3. D   The probability of multiple independent events occurring is the product of the probabilities of the individual events. The probability of spinning purple once is $\frac{1}{4}$ since that is the fraction of the circle that is shaded purple.

This question asks for the probability of spinning a purple 300 times. Therefore, you need to multiply $\frac{1}{4}$ times itself 300 times. You can use exponents to represent this. $(\frac{1}{4})^{300}$

---

4. A   For Francisco to guess it correctly on his 2nd try it means that Francisco did not guess it correctly on his first try. Therefore, we need to find the probability of these two events which can be found by multiplying the probability of each individual event.

Probability of Francisco not guessing correctly on his first try.
= Number of letters he could have guessed ÷ Total number of letters = $25 \div 26 = \frac{25}{26}$

Probability of guessing correctly on 2nd try.
= Number of correct letters ÷ Total number of letters left to guess = $1 \div 25 = \frac{1}{25}$

Multiply the two probability to find the probability that Francisco guesses the letter on his 2nd try. $\frac{25}{26} \times \frac{1}{25} = \frac{1}{26}$

---

5. B   There were originally 5 lockers with stars and 3 lockers without stars. One locker was opened which did not have a star. Therefore, out of the remaining 7 lockers to be opened, 5 have stars and 2 do not.

The question asks for the probability that the 2nd locker won't have a star either. Therefore, the number remaining without stars is 2 and there are a total of 7 lockers remaining to be opened.

$$\text{Probability} = \frac{2}{7}$$

---

6. B   To find the probability of multiple events, multiply the probability of each individual event. Make sure to keep in mind how one event may affect the sample space and probability of the following events.

Probability red is selected first = # of red marbles divided by total marbles = $20 \div 90 = \frac{2}{9}$

Probability purple is selected second
= # of purple marbles divided by total marbles remaining = $\frac{30}{89}$

Probability yellow is selected third = # of yellow marbles divided by total marbles remaining = $40 \div 88 = \frac{5}{11}$

To find the probability of all three events occurring, multiply the probabilities of each event. $= \frac{2}{9} \times \frac{30}{89} \times \frac{5}{11}$

---

7. A   There are two possible ways that you can get a red and a purple, red first and then purple, or purple first and then red. You must first figure out the probability of each way occurring and since you want the probability of one way or the other way, you add the two probabilities.

Probability of red then purple.
= Prob red on first draw × Prob purple on 2nd draw with 4 marbles remaining

$\begin{aligned}&= \frac{2}{5} \times \frac{3}{4} \\ &= \frac{6}{20} = \frac{3}{10}\end{aligned}$

Probability of purple then red.
= Prob purple on first draw × Prob red on 2nd draw with 4 marbles remaining

$\begin{aligned}&= \frac{3}{5} \times \frac{2}{4} \\ &= \frac{6}{20} = \frac{3}{10}\end{aligned}$

Now add the probabilities.

$\begin{aligned}&\frac{3}{10} + \frac{3}{10} \\ &= \frac{6}{10} \\ &= \frac{3}{5}\end{aligned}$

---

8. D   Probability is the number of favorable outcomes divided by the total number of outcomes. We must calculate how many favorable outcomes and how many total outcomes.

The number of favorable outcomes is how many ways you can get a sum of 10 if you roll 2 dice. Let's list out the possible ways:

4 and 6, 5 and 5, 6 and 4
3 possible ways

The number of total outcomes can be found by multiplying how many possible outcomes on the first die multiplied by how many outcomes for the 2nd die. $6 \times 6 = 36$

Probability $= \frac{3}{36} = \frac{1}{12}$

---

9. B   With replacement: Every time you choose a marble that isn't red, you have to throw it back in to the bag. Therefore, your probability of drawing the red marble remains $\frac{1}{100}$ for each draw.

Without replacement: Every time you draw a marble that isn't red, you keep it. Therefore, each time you draw a marble the sample space decreases, increasing your probability of drawing the red marble.

Choosing to draw without replacement will increase the probability of getting the red each round, so it provides your best chance of minimizing the number of draws.

10. C To find the probability of selecting an even number or a multiple of 5, you must first figure out the probability of selecting an even and the probability of selecting a multiple of 5. Then subtract out any overlap—in this case, numbers that are both even and a multiple of 5. In total, there are 18 numbers between 2 and 19, inclusive.

Probability of getting a multiple of 5
The multiples of 5 in that range are: 5, 10, and 15

$$\text{Prob of multiple of 5} = \frac{3}{18} = \frac{1}{6}$$

Probability of getting an even number
The even numbers in that range are: 2, 4, 6, 8, 10, 12, 14, 16, and 18

$$\text{Prob of even number} = \frac{9}{18} = \frac{1}{2}$$

Probability of an even and a multiple of 5
10 is even and a multiple of 5, therefore this one number has been counted twice

$$\text{Prob of even and multiple of 5} = \frac{1}{18}$$

Probability of even or multiple of 5
= Prob of even + Prob of multiple of 5 − Prob even and multiple of 5

$$= \frac{1}{6} + \frac{1}{2} - \frac{1}{18}$$
$$= \frac{11}{18}$$

8.5 Permutations & Combinations

Permutation vs. Combination

Permutations and combinations deal with choosing elements from a larger set of elements. The difference is whether the **order** matters:

- If the order does not matter, you are counting combinations.
- If the order of the elements matters, you are dealing with permutations.

For example, suppose you are awarding 3 medals in a race to the top 3 runners from a group of 9. Figuring out how many groups of 3 could be awarded medals is an example of counting combinations. Now let's say you want to specifically award gold, silver and bronze. Finding the number of ways in which 1st, 2nd, or 3rd can be awarded is an example of a permutation problem. In a problem, identify whether the arrangement or order of the chosen elements is important.

If choosing 2 letters from the alphabet, in combinations AB is the same as BA and therefore would only count as one combination. However, in permutations AB and BA are different as the order or arrangement matters, and therefore choosing those 2 letters actually results in two possible permutations.

Understanding Factorials

Before we go on with permutations and combinations, it's important that you understand how to calculate factorials. The factorial of a positive integer is the product of all positive integers less than or equal to that number. Factorials are denoted by an exclamation mark (!). For example:

$$4! = 4 \times 3 \times 2 \times 1$$
$$6! = 6 \times 5 \times 4 \times 3 \times 2 \times 1$$

When dividing a factorial by a lesser factorial, it is helpful to cancel before multiplying. In the example below, you can cancel the 4, 3, 2, and 1.

$$\frac{7!}{4!} = \frac{7 \times 6 \times 5 \times 4 \times 3 \times 2 \times 1}{4 \times 3 \times 2 \times 1} = 7 \times 6 \times 5 = 210$$

An exception to the factorial definition is that $0! = 1$.

Permutations

For a set of n objects, the factorial of n (or $n!$) gives you the total amount of possible permutations in the set. For example, take a set of three balls of colors red, green, and blue. The possible permutations are **❶**.

Note that there are 6 possible permutations, which equates to the factorial for 3. Or, $3! = 6$.

❶
{red, green, blue}
{red, blue, green}
{green, red, blue}
{green, blue, red}
{red, blue, green}
{red, green, blue}

Now suppose you are trying to figure out how many ordered sequences involving a set of numbers, r, can be made from a larger set of numbers, n. Here, you divide the factorial of n by the different between n and r. The formula is written as **❷**.

❷

$$\text{Permutations} = \frac{n!}{(n - r)!}$$

For example, suppose you want to find the number of different possible selections of 10 people for 4 different lead roles in a play. The order of selection matters because choosing Bob to play Character 1 is different from choosing Bob to play Character 2.

Choosing 4 lead roles from 10 people:

$$\frac{10!}{(10 - 4)!} \times \frac{10!}{6!} = 10 \times 9 \times 8 \times 7 = 5040 \text{ ways to select the lead roles}$$

Another way to think about solving the problem is by figuring out how many possibilities there are for each role. The first role has 10 possiblities. There are then only 9 people for the next role, 8 for the next role, and 7 for the remaining role. Multiply the possibilities: 10x9x8x7 = 5040 ways.

Combinations

A combination is also an arrangement of objects, but this time order is not important. For example, if we wanted to find the number of combinations of pairs of the three balls red, green, and blue, it would be 3 sets: (red, green), (green, blue), (blue, red).

When a certain number of elements are selected from a greater number of elements, various combinations of elements can be selected. The number of ways to choose r elements from n possible elements uses the formula:

$$\frac{n!}{r!(n - r)!}$$

Example: A man chooses 8 of 12 coins in his collection to show at an exhibit. If he chooses the coins at random, how many possible combinations can he choose? There are 12 elements, 8 of which will be selected:

$$\frac{12!}{8!(12-8)!} = \frac{12!}{8!4!} = 495 \text{ combinations}$$

PERMUTATIONS & COMBINATIONS PRACTICE

1. **You have to bring 4 gallons of ice cream home for a party, and the ice cream store has 20 different flavors to choose from. How many different ways can you choose the ice cream flavors?**

    A. $^{20!}/_{4!}$
    B. $^{20!}/_{16!}$
    C. $^{20!}/_{16!4!}$
    D. $^{16!}/_{4!}$

2. **There are 4 girls trying out for pitcher on a softball team and 10 girls trying out for the remaining 3 available positions: short stop, first base, and second base. How many teams could be selected?**

    A. 480
    B. 720
    C. 2880
    D. 4320

3. **How many different ways can you rearrange the letters in MONKEY?**

    A. 30
    B. 360

C. 600
D. 720

4. **How many different ways are there to arrange all 26 letters of the alphabet?**

    A. 26
    B. 13!
    C. 26!
    D. 2626

5. **If you are exhibiting 15 of the 600 pieces of art in a museum's collection, how many ways can you arrange the art?**

    A. 15!
    B. 15! × 600!
    C. $\dfrac{600!}{585!}$
    D. $\dfrac{600!}{15!\,585!}$

6. **If 4 of the letters of ABCDEFGH are arranged in a row, what is the probability that A will be first?**

    A. $^1/_8$
    B. 1680
    C. $^1/_4$
    D. $^1/_{16}$

7. In how many different ways can 10 girls and 10 boys sit alternately in a row of chairs if a boy will be in the first seat? To clarify, the first three seats will be boy, girl, boy, and they will continue to alternate.

    A. 10!

    B. 20!

    C. 10! × 10!

    D. 10! + 10!

8. If a card game involves players being dealt 4 cards, how many different possible hands can you have out of a standard deck?

    A. 4!

    B. 48!

    C. $\dfrac{52!}{4!}$

    D. $\dfrac{52!}{4!\,48!}$

9. How many ways can you rearrange the letters in GUPPIES if the two Ps must stay together?

    A. $6!/_2$

    B. $7!/_2$

    C. 6!

    D. 7!

10. There are 3 bags and 5 different marbles. In how many ways can the marbles be put into the bags?

    A. 30

    B. 120

    C. 243

    D. 360

PERMUTATIONS & COMBINATIONS EXPLANATIONS

1. C   Since the order does not matter, use the formula for combinations to find the number of ways to choose 4 ice cream flavors from 20 different flavors. In this case, $n = 20$ and $r = 4$.

$$\frac{n!}{r!(n-r)!} = \frac{20!}{4!(20-4)!} = \frac{20!}{4!\,16!}$$

2. C   This problem has multiple steps. First, figure out the number of ways to choose the pitcher; then calculate the number of ways to choose people for the remaining positions. Finally, multiply the number of ways to choose a pitcher by the number of permutations for the remaining positions to find the number of possible teams.

Choose the pitcher: There are 4 girls trying out for one position, so there are 4 possible ways to choose the pitcher.

Choose players to fill the 3 remaining positions out of 10 players:
The order matters for the remaining positions, since it makes a difference if someone is chosen for first base or short stop. Therefore, use permutations.

$$\text{Permutations} = \frac{n!}{r!(n-r)} = \frac{10!}{(10-3)!} = \frac{10!}{7!} = 10 \times 9 \times 8 = 720$$

Total number of ways to select the teams: $4 \times 720 = 2880$ ways

Another way to think about it is multiply the number of possibilities for each position.
4 (pitcher) x 10 (first base) x 9 (second base) x 8 (short stop) = 2880 ways

---

3. D There are 6 letters in the word monkey and order matters, so this is a simple permutation where you are choosing 6 elements from 6 elements.

Therefore, the number of ways is $6! = 6 \times 5 \times 4 \times 3 \times 2 \times 1 = 720$. 720 ways

---

4. C In this case, $n = 26$ and $r = 26$ since you are choosing all 26 letters from 26 possible letters.

$$\text{Permutations} = \frac{n!}{r!(n-r)} = \frac{26!}{(26-26)!} = \frac{26!}{0!} = 26!$$

You can also think of how many possibilities are there for each spot. For the first spot, 26 possible letters, next there are 25 left, then 24, etc. Multiply the possibilities. 26x25x24x23x... = 26!

---

5. C The question asks for the number of ways to arrange the art, so order matters. To find the number of ways, use the formula for permutations.

$n = 600$, $r = 15$

$$\text{Permutations} = \frac{n!}{r!(n-r)} = \frac{600!}{(600-15)!} = \frac{600!}{585!}$$

---

6. A There are a few ways to solve this problem.

Method 1: The question asks what is the probability that A will be first. Well, each letter has an equal probability of being selected first and there are 8 possible letters to choose from, and therefore the probability is $\frac{1}{8}$
Method 2: You could also first calculate all the possible permutations. Then, find all the possible permutations where A is first, and divide to find the probability that A is first.

All possible permutations:

$$\frac{8!}{(8-4)!} = \frac{8!}{4!} = 1680$$

Number of possible permutations with A in front = number of ways you can choose 3 from 7 for the remaining 3 spots =

$$\frac{7!}{(7-3)!} = \frac{7!}{4!} = 210$$

$$\text{Probability} = \frac{210}{1680} = \frac{1}{8}$$

---

7. C Think of this problem as two sets of permutations. First, the number of permutations of the 10 girls and then the permutations of the 10 boys. You will then multiply to find the total number of ways since for each permutation of girls , each of the permutations for boys is possible.

> Permutations of Boys: 10!
> Permutations of Girls: 10!
> Total = 10! × 10!

---

8. D The question is asking how many ways can you select 4 cards out of the 52 cards. Since the order of the cards does not matter, use combinations.

Combinations: where n is 52 and r is 4

$$\frac{n!}{r!(n-r)!} = \frac{52!}{4!(52-4)!} = \frac{52!}{4!\,48!}$$

---

9. C Since the two Ps must stay together, you can consider them as a single element. Therefore, you need to find the number of ways to rearrange 6 elements (G, U, PP, I, E, S).

$$\text{\# of ways} = 6!$$

---

10. C Let's think about each marble at a time. The first marble can be put into one of the three bags, so there are 3 ways for that marble. The second marble can also be put into one of three bags, so 3 ways for the 2nd marble. This is the same for each of the 5 marbles.

Therefore, multiply the number of ways for each marble to find the total number of ways: 3 × 3 × 3 × 3 × 3 = 243

8.6   Chapter Review

1. There is a bag with 5 green marbles, 2 red marbles, and 6 yellow marbles. If you reach into the bag and take out two marbles without replacing, what is the probability that both are green?

    A. $^{25}/_{169}$

    B. $^{5}/_{26}$

    C. $^{5}/_{39}$

    D. $^{9}/_{25}$

2. If a card is drawn at random from a standard 52 card deck, what is the probability that it will be a 10 or a spade?

    A. $^{17}/_{52}$

    B. $^{4}/_{13}$

    C. $^{1}/_{13}$

    D. $^{13}/_{52}$

3. Assuming that every order includes one sandwich, one bag of chips, and one drink, how many different combinations of lunch orders are possible for 5 types of sandwiches, 4 types of chips, and 6 different drinks?

    A. 15

    B. 26

    C. 60

    D. 120

4. A store has 1000 pairs of socks. In how many different ways can shoppers choose one left and one right sock?

    A. 1000

    B. 10,000

    C. 100,000

    D. 1,000,000

5. If the range of a set of test scores is 85 and median 75, which of the following could be the set of all test scores?

    A. 50, 85, 75, 80, 55

    B. 75, 10, 95, 55

    C. 75, 15, 85, 90, 75

    D. 85, 70, 20, 80, 5, 90

6. If you own a mutual fund, and the standard deviation of the return increases while the mean stays the same, what happens to the fund's risk? (A return is a measure of how much the mutual fund has increased or decreased in value over any given time period.)

    A. increases

    B. decreases

    C. stays the same

    D. don't know

7. Adding a zero to a set may change which of the following:

      I. median
      II. mean
      III. range

    A. I only
    B. I and III
    C. II and III
    D. I, II, and III

8. Which set of data can be best represented by a straight line of best fit?

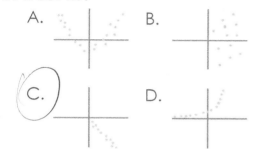

9. How many ways can you rearrange the letters of LESSON, if the two Ss must remain next to each other?

    A. 24
    B. 120
    C. 360
    D. 720

10. Which of the following is/are true?

    I. The median and mean of a data set are always different.

II. The median of a data set is always a member of the set.

III. There can be more than one mode in a data set.

    A. I and II
    B. II and III
    C. III only
    D. None of the above.

11. If the median of the data set is 14, which of the following could be the value of x?

Set: 13, 92, 0, 15, 6, x

    A. -10
    B. 14
    C. 15
    D. 13

12. The probability of occurrence for an event for which the number of favorable outcomes is equal to the number of possible outcomes is:

    A. 0
    B. 1
    C. ½
    D. 100

13. If a scale is off by 5 lbs, what measure changes?

    I. mean
    II. median
    III. mode

A. I and II
B. I only
C. II and III
D. all

14. **Calculate the probability that a woman who randomly picks a number from zero to 10 inclusive will choose an even number.**
    A. ½
    B. ³⁄₅
    C. ⁶⁄₁₁
    D. ⁶⁄₅

15. **If you roll two dice, what is the probability that the sum on them will be 6?**
    A. ¹⁄₆
    B. ¹⁄₃₆
    C. ⁵⁄₃₆
    D. ⁵⁄₆

16. **There are 7 students in a club, and 3 of them need to go the next meeting. In how many ways can these 3 students be chosen?**
    A. 21
    B. 35
    C. 210
    D. 840

17. **There are 20 people playing in a chess tournament, and there will be 3 prizes awarded.**

Which of the following has more possible outcomes?
    A. 3 prizes are different: 1st, 2nd, 3rd place
    B. 3 prizes are the same: order does not matter between winners
    C. Same number of outcomes.
    D. Not enough information.

18. **There are 60 marbles in a bag. The probability of a marble being green or red is ⁵⁄₁₂, and there are 5 green marbles. How many red marbles are in the bag?**
    A. 5
    B. 12
    C. 20
    D. 25

19. **There is a circular dart board with a bulls–eye in the middle. The radius of the board is ten inches, and the radius of the bulls–eye is 2 inches. If a dart thrown randomly hits the board, what is the probability that it hits the bulls–eye?**
    A. ¹⁄₂₅
    B. ⅕
    C. ⅛
    D. ¹⁄₉₆

20. The mean of your 5 test scores for the semester is 82, and you know that your scores for the first four tests were 84, 72, 98, and 86. What did you score on that last test?

A. 68
B. 70
C. 82
D. 85

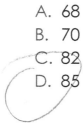

CHAPTER REVIEW EXPLANATIONS

1. C Probability is the number of favorable outcomes over the total number of outcomes. To find the probability of multiple independent events, you multiply the probabilities of each of the individual events.

First, find the probability that the first marble drawn will be green, and then multiply that by the probability that the second marble drawn will be green.

For the first draw, there are 5 green marbles and a total of 13 marbles. The probability of drawing a green marble is $\frac{5}{13}$.

For the second marble, there are only 12 marbles left, 4 of which are green. The probability of drawing a second green marble is $\frac{4}{12}$, which reduces to $\frac{1}{3}$.

The product of the two probabilities is the probability of drawing two green marbles in a row.

$$\frac{5}{13} \times \frac{1}{3} = \frac{5}{39}$$

2. B Use the addition rule, but be sure to account for overlap. First find the probability of drawing a spade, and add that to the probability of drawing a 10. Then subtract the probability of a 10 of spades to avoid counting that card twice.

Probability of 10 or spade = Prob of spade + Prob of 10 − Prob of 10 and spade

Probability of spade: $\frac{13}{52}$
Probability of 10: $\frac{4}{52}$
Probability of 10 and spade: $\frac{1}{52}$

$$= \frac{13}{52} + \frac{4}{52} - \frac{1}{52}$$
$$= \frac{16}{52}$$
$$= \frac{4}{13}$$

3. D The counting principle states that to determine the total number of possible outcomes, multiply the number of ways each event can occur.

In this problem, there are 5 types of sandwiches, 4 types of chips, and 6 different drinks.

To find the number of possible outcomes, multiply $5 \times 4 \times 6 = 120$
There are 120 different lunch combinations.

4. D   Use the multiplication rule to determine the total number of ways to choose one left sock and one right sock.

Total number of ways = # of right socks × # of left socks

| Total = 1000 × 1000 |
| Total = 1,000,000 |

5. D   The range of a set is calculated by subtracting the lowest score from the highest score. The median is the middle number when the scores are put in order from lowest to highest. Below, the set of numbers for each answer choice is ordered from least to greatest and the range and median are given for each.

    A. 50, 55, 75, 80, 85. Range = 85 − 50 = 35. The median is 75.

    B. 10, 55, 75, 95. Range = 95 − 10 = 85. Since there are an even number of numbers, you take the average of the middle numbers. Median = (55 + 75) ÷ 2 = 65

    C. 15, 75, 75, 85, 90. Range = 90 − 15 = 75. Median = 75.

    D. 5, 20, 70, 80, 95, 90. Range = 90 − 5 = 85. Median = (70 + 80) ÷ 2 = 75.

    Answer D has range = 85, median = 75.

6. A   If the mean of the return remains the same, that means the average doesn't change. If the standard deviation increases, that means that the variability in the return increases. Therefore, the risk increases.

7. D   Let's go through each measure to see how adding a zero could affect the value.

    I.   **median:** Adding a zero could change the median since there are now more numbers in the set and the number that used to be in the middle will no longer be there.
Example: The set 2, 4, 6 has a median of 4.
Add a zero to the set: 0, 2, 4, 6, now the median is 3 (average of the 2 middle numbers).
Median changes

    II.   **mean:** Adding a zero to a set could change the mean since the number of elements in the set has now changed.
Example: the set: 3, 4, 5 has a mean = (3 + 4 + 5) ÷ 3 = 4
Add a zero to the set: 0, 3, 4, 5, mean = (0 + 3 + 4 + 5) ÷ 4 = 3
Mean changes

III. range: Adding a zero to the set could change the range since the smallest or largest number may change.
Example: the set 3, 4 , 5 has a range = 5−3 = 2
Add a zero to the set: 0, 3, 4, 5 and the range = 5−0 = 5
Range changes.

I, II, and III could change if a zero is adding to a set.

8. C The data in answer choice C roughly conforms to a straight line. The data in A is most closely parabolic in shape, and the data in D best matches an exponential function. The data in B does not have a pattern.

9. B You want to rearrange the letters of LESSON, but you must keep the two Ss next to each other. Therefore, you are rearranging 5 elements: L, E, SS, O, N

The number of ways to rearrange 5 elements is 5! $\boxed{5 \times 4 \times 3 \times 2 \times 1 = 120}$

10. C I. The median and mean of a data set are always different.
You could have a set where the mean and median are the same value. For example, the set: 2, 3, 4 has a mean of 3 and a median of 3. I−False.

II. The median of a data set is always a member of the set.
If there are an even number of elements in a set, the median may not be a member of the set. For example, the set: 2, 4, 6, 8, the median is the average of the two middle numbers 4 and 6. The median of that set is 5, but 5 is not a member of the set. II−False.

III. There can be more than one mode in a data set.
The mode of a set is the element that appears most often. You could have multiply elements that appear the same number of times, therefore having multiple modes. For example: the set: 1, 2, 2, 3, 4, 4, 5, 6 has two modes: 2 and 4 since they both appear twice. III is true.

III is the only one that is true.

11. C To find the median of a data set, order the elements, and then find the middle element. If there are an even number of elements in a set, then the median is the average of the two middle numbers. In this case, there are 6 elements, so the median must be the average of the two middle values.

First order the set with the values you know: | 0, 6, 13, 15, 92 |

If 14 is the median, it must be the average of the two middle numbers. If 13 and 15 are the two middle numbers, then 14 would be the median. x must be greater than or equal to 15, so that the middle numbers are 13 and 15.

The only answer choice that would make the median equal to 14 is 15.

12. B The probability is equal to the number of favorable outcomes divided by the number of possible outcomes.

If the number of favorable outcomes is equal to the number of possible outcomes, then the probability would be a number divided by itself, which is always equal to 1.

13. D Let's go through each measure and see what would happen.

   I.   **mean:** The mean is the average of the numbers. If each number changes by 5 lbs, the average will also change by 5 lbs.

   II. **median:** The median is the middle value. If each value changes by 5, so does the middle value. Therefore, the median changes.

   III. **mode:** The mode is the value that appears most often. If all values change by 5, so will that value. Therefore, the mode changes.

   Answer D. Mean, Median, and Mode change.

14. C Probability will be the number of favorable outcomes divided by the number of possible outcomes.

Favorable outcomes:
There are 6 favorable outcomes. | 0, 2, 4, 6, 8, 10 |

Possible outcomes:
There are 11 possible outcomes. | 0, 1, 2, 3, 4, 5, 6, 7, 8, 9, 10 |

| Probability = $^6/_{11}$ |

15. C Probability is the number of favorable outcomes divided by the total number of outcomes. We must calculate how many favorable outcomes and how many total outcomes.

The number of favorable outcomes is how many ways can you get a sum of 6 if you roll 2 dice. Let's list out the possible ways: 1 and 5, 2 and 4, 3 and 3, 4 and 2, 5 and 1

| 5 possible ways |

The number of total outcomes can be found by multiplying how many possible outcomes on the first die multiplied by how many outcomes for the 2nd die.

| $6 \times 6 = 36$ |

| Probability = $\frac{5}{36}$ |

16. B The order of the students does not matter, so we are dealing with combinations.

The formula for choosing r elements from n elements where order does not matter is: $\frac{n!}{r!(n-r)!}$

In this case, we are choosing 3 elements from 7 possible elements.

$$\frac{7!}{3!(7-3)!} = \frac{7!}{3!4!} = 35$$

There are 35 ways which these 3 students can be chosen.

17. A We have to figure out how many possible outcomes there are if the prizes are different and how many possible outcomes there are if the prizes are the same.

Different Prizes: 1st, 2nd, 3rd place
In this case, the order of the prizes matters. Therefore, to find the number of outcomes, you would be finding the number of permutations.
Permutations = $\frac{n!}{(n-r)!}$
In this case, $n = 20$ and $r = 3$.

$$\frac{20!}{(20-3)!} = \frac{20!}{17!}$$

Same prizes, order does not matter
In this case, figure out the number of combinations that 3 prizes can be chosen from the 20 people.
Combinations: $\frac{n!}{r!(n-r)!}$

$$\frac{20!}{3!(20-3)!} = \frac{20!}{3!17!}$$

Compare: $\frac{20!}{17!}$ and $\frac{20!}{3!17!}$

The first number is bigger and therefore, there are more possible permutations. Answer A.

In addition, you could have solved this problem by using common sense. For both situations, you have to choose 3 people from the 20. But, if order matters, then for each group of 3 you choose, there are many possible outcomes for how the prizes are awarded. Therefore, there are more ways to choose winners for different prizes.

18. C If there are 60 marbles in a bag and the probability of being green or red is $^5/_{12}$, then you can multiply the probability by the total number to find the number of red or green marbles.

$$\text{Red or Green marbles} = 60 \times {}^5/_{12} = 25$$

The problem also states that there are 5 green marbles. Therefore, the number of red marbles is $25 - 5 = 20$ marbles.

---

19. A To find the probability that the dart hits the bulls-eye, find the area of the bulls-eye, and divide that by the area of the dart board. Remember, the area of a circle is πr^2.

The bulls eye has a radius of 2 inches, the area is $\pi 2^2 = 4\pi$.

The dartboard has a radius of 10 inches, the area is $\pi 10^2 = 100\pi$.

The probability is 4π divided by $100\pi = {}^4/_{100} = {}^1/_{25}$.

---

20. B If the mean or average of the 5 tests is 82, then you can calculate the total number of points that you got on all 5 tests by multiplying.

$$\text{Total number of points on 5 tests} = 5 \times 82 = 410$$

You remember the scores on 4 of your tests, so find the total of those 4 tests.

$$\text{Total number of points on 4 tests} = 84 + 72 + 98 + 86 = 340$$

Find the score on the last test by subtracting your total points on 4 tests from your total points on all the tests.

$$\text{Last test} = 410 - 340 = 70.$$

Open Response

About the Open Response Section

The open response section of the MTEL03 contains one question that accounts for 10% of your math subtest score. The open response section of the test is designed to evaluate not just your deep understanding of mathematical concepts but also your ability to explain and teach those concepts to others. You should allow approximately 30 minutes to complete the open response question on exam day. This lesson provides some strategies for constructing a strong response. The Practice section includes sample answers with explanations of the methods used.

Evaluation Criteria

Open response questions are scored according to a set of standard performance characteristics.

Performance Characteristic	Definition
Purpose	⊙ The extent to which the response achieves the purpose of the assignment
Subject Matter Knowledge	⊙ Accuracy and appropriateness in the application of subject matter knowledge
Support	⊙ Quality and relevance of supporting details
Rationale	⊙ Soundness of argument and degree of understanding of the subject matter

Scoring Scale

Score Point	Definition
4	**Reflects a thorough knowledge and understanding of the subject matter.** ⊙ Purpose of the assignment is fully achieved. ⊙ Substantial and accurate use of subject matter knowledge. ⊙ Supporting evidence is sound with high quality and relevant examples. ⊙ Response reflects an ably reasoned and comprehensive understanding of topic.
3	**Reflects an adequate knowledge and understanding of the subject matter.** ⊙ Purpose of the assignment is largely achieved. ⊙ Generally accurate and appropriate use of subject matter knowledge. ⊙ Supporting evidence is adequate with some acceptable, relevant examples. ⊙ Response reflects an adequately reasoned understanding of topic.
2	**Reflects a limited knowledge and understanding of the subject matter.** ⊙ Purpose of the assignment is partially achieved. ⊙ Limited, possibly inaccurate or inappropriate use of subject matter knowledge. ⊙ Supporting evidence is limited with few relevant examples. ⊙ Response reflects a limited, poorly reasoned understanding of topic.
1	**Reflects a weak knowledge and understanding of the subject matter.** ⊙ Purpose of the assignment is not achieved. ⊙ Little or no appropriate or accurate use of subject matter knowledge. ⊙ Supporting evidence, if present, is weak; there are few or no relevant examples. ⊙ Response reflects little or no reasoning about or understanding of topic.

Constructing a Strong Response

Address All Tasks

The first listed criterion for the open response question is the extent to which the candidate has completed the assignment. That means that your primary goal is to accurately answer all of the questions asked of you in the prompt. Your first step should be to identify your tasks, and your last step should be to make sure that you have completed all of your tasks.

Identify the Skills Required

After reading through the problem, identify the specific skills and concepts you will need to complete it. An open response question consists of a number of tasks. Look for keywords in each part of the problem to help you quickly figure out the methods required. Typically, the question prompt will include some wording to give you guidance (e.g., *"Use your knowledge of quadratic equations to..."*).

Demonstrate Your Understanding

Much of your score will be based on your ability to show understanding of the subject matter. Explain the reasoning behind your approach to each part of the problem. Include relevant information from the problem to support your reasoning, and use charts or visual aids where appropriate. In the same way, discuss the significance of the results of your calculations. This is important, since even if the final calculation is incorrect, you might still be awarded marks for your methods and reasoning.

In a sense, the test graders are using this response to evaluate your potential as a teacher. They want to see that you can explain concepts to elementary school children. This does not mean that you should use child–like language. The grader is an adult and expects to read a well–developed solution written in accurate, academic English. It does mean that strong responses typically discuss the way that a hypothetical student has or would solve the problem and provide as much detail as possible about the steps being carried out.

Write Your Answer Clearly

Two scorers will review your answer, so it needs to be clear and easy to read. Use the free space on your test booklet to work out calculations, make notes, and structure your response. When you are happy with your approach, write it on your answer sheet as a clear and cohesive solution. The response should be structured to match the order of the tasks.

Achieving a strong score for the rationale criterion means explaining your reasoning and method in a detailed way that would help a student develop a deeper understanding of the mathematical concepts involved. Always give a reason for performing a calculation, and discuss the significance of the result of the calculation. Use labels when solving word problems because the graders want to know that you can convey the connection between numbers like 3 and 7 and real–world concepts such as dollars and hours to your students.

Example:

Don't say— "I would solve this problem by multiplying 7 × 3 to get 21."
Do say— "In order to solve this problem, a student would need to successfully use the skill of multiplication. He or she would multiply $7 per hour that the painter is paid by the 3 hours the painter works on the house. This would give $21 as the total that the painter receives for painting the house."

Key differences

1. Use of "a student" instead of "I"
2. Reference to multiplication as a skill (discussed later)
3. Explanation of reasoning behind multiplication
4. Use of labels to give meaning to multipliers and product

Support Answer

Support means providing specific examples from the problem to justify any claims that you make.

Example:

Don't say— "The student was required to multiply to solve this problem."
Do say—"The student had to multiply $7 per hour by 3 hours to find the total amount that the painter earned."

The open response section requires that you demonstrate an understanding of both mathematical skills and concepts needed to solve complex problems. The test refers to computations—applying the four basic operations (addition, subtraction, multiplication, and division) to integers, fractions, decimals, exponents, etc—as skills. The test distinguishes skills from concepts—underlying mathematical principles such as understanding formulas, solving word problems with specific strategies (draw a picture, organize relevant information, break a problem into steps), and comparing like quantities.

You are expected to demonstrate a deep understanding of mathematical skills and concepts in several ways:

1. When analyzing a student's work, identify specific skills and concepts that the student used correctly. Remember to provide specific support for your claims.
2. When analyzing a student's work, identify specific skills and concepts that the student used incorrectly. Don't stop at pointing out an incorrect use of a skill or concept. Explain how the student misapplied the skill or concept, and suggest a way to correct the error.
3. When solving problems, correctly demonstrate the use of as many skills and correctly explain as many concepts as possible. When doing so, try to use multiple, student–friendly methods.

Use multiple, student–friendly methods

While taking this portion of the exam, keep in mind that the test graders and authors are your audience and that they are most interested in your ability to teach elementary school students. Focus on providing methods and analyses that would benefit students by helping them develop a deeper understanding of mathematical concepts. Whenever possible use visual aides such as charts and diagrams. A correctly executed, well–explained alternative solution always strengthens a response.

Examples:

Use a chart to organize information in a word problem. Demonstrate both the lattice and partial product methods to solve a multiplication problem.

Check Your Work

Did you make a computational mistake? Did you leave out a step or not explain a step thoroughly? Did you make a conceptual error? The accuracy of your work contributes directly to your scores for purpose, rationale, and understanding of subject matter. It is crucial that you check your work completely before moving on to the next question. Checking for calculation errors is important, but it's not the only thing you should look for. Check for errors in your logic; reappraise your approach; and make sure you have fully explained each step.

Approach:

Complete Steps 1–7 in the free space on the test booklet. You do not need to write in complete sentences until Step 8.

1. Read the entire exercise, circling or otherwise marking each part of your assignment.
2. Solve the problem, explaining each step in detail. Do this whether or not a student response is provided, and try to use a visual aide or other student–friendly strategy.
3. Identify skills necessary to solve the problem and specific examples of those skills.
4. Identify concepts necessary to understand the problem and specific manifestations of those concepts.
5. If directed, look for an alternate solution to the problem, preferably one that includes a student–friendly strategy. Give a detailed description of this solution. This alternate solution demonstrates your deep understanding of the concepts and allows you to check your answer.
6. If applicable, compare your reasoning and solution with the provided student answer. Identify weaknesses in the skills and concepts used in the student response and suggest methods for correcting the errors and improving the student's understanding of the material.
7. Make sure that your work is accurate and complete (fulfills all tasks).
8. *Complete Step 8 on the answer sheet provided.* Write up your work as a cohesive solution in paragraph form. Try to structure your work to match the order in which the tasks were assigned.

OPEN RESPONSE QUESTION 1

You are in your school's hallway and the wall is lined with one hundred closed lockers numbered 1 through 100. A kid passes by and opens all of them. A second student comes by and closes all the even numbered ones. A third kid passes by and "toggles" every third locker. That is, if a locker is closed, she opens it, but if she finds a locker open, she closes it.

Then, student number 4 toggles every fourth locker and student number 5 toggles every fifth one. And so on until one hundred students have passed through the hallway opening and closing lockers.

A. Which kids will toggle locker number 15? Which kids will toggle locker number 16? Are they open or closed at the end?

B. Which of the first 10 lockers will remain open after all the kids have passed?

C. Which of the 100 lockers will remain open at the end? Why?

Use your knowledge of mathematics to create a response in which you analyze and solve this problem. In your response you should:

⊙ describe two prerequisite mathematical skills necessary for solving this problem;

⊙ identify two mathematical concepts involved in solving this problem; and

⊙ solve the given problem showing your work and justifying the steps you used in arriving at your solution.

OPEN RESPONSE QUESTION 2

Students were asked to solve the following problem.

The nth term of a series can be calculated using the following formula: $f(n) = 1 + 2(n-1)$

A. Write the first 5 terms in this series.

B. Create a new series, Series B, by calculating the sum of each set of terms. For instance, the first term in the new series will be equal to the first term in Series A. The second term will be the sum of the first two terms in Series A. The third term will be the sum of the first three terms in Series A. Write the first 5 terms in Series B.

C. Write a formula which could be used to calculate the nth term in Series B.

Student Response:

Series A	Series B
f(1)=0	f(1)=0
f(2)=3	f(2)=3
f(3)=6	f(3)=9
f(4)=9	f(4)=18
f(5)=12	f(5)=30

Use your knowledge of mathematics to create a response in which you analyze the elementary school student's work and provide a solution to the problem. In your response, you should:

- correct any errors or misconceptions evident in the student's work and explain why the response is not mathematically sound (be sure to provide a correct solution, show your work, and explain your reasoning);
- describe two prerequisite mathematical skills necessary for solving this problem; and
- identify two mathematical concepts involved in solving this problem.

OPEN RESPONSE QUESTION 3

There are 10 shells in a row on a table. Seven of the shells are holding one silver coin each.

A. If a girl picks up a shell at random, what is the percent chance that she will find a coin underneath?

B. If the girl picks up another shell at random (without replacing the first), will she have a better chance of finding a silver coin if she did or did not find a coin under the first shell?

C. What is the probability that the girl will choose 2 shells with coins underneath as her first 2 draws?

Student Response:

A. 700	B.	C.
$\dfrac{\text{Shells with coins}}{\text{Shells}} = \dfrac{7}{10}$ $\frac{7}{10} \times 100\% = 70\%$ *This is correct*	Her probability of choosing a shell with a coin is $\frac{7}{10}$. It does not matter whether she found a coin or not on the first draw. Her probability of finding a coin on the 2nd draw is $\frac{7}{10}$. *wrong* *Probability/Conversion*	$\frac{7}{10} \times \frac{7}{10} = \frac{49}{100}$ $\frac{49}{100} = 49\%$ 49% chance for choosing 2 coins as first 2 draws.

because in order to find the probability of a shell w/coins *Probability and Conversions*   *Multiplication*

Directions:

1. Identify two skills and two concepts necessary to solve this problem.
2. Solve the problem.
3. Analyze the student response.

OPEN RESPONSE QUESTION 4

Use the diagram to answer the questions that follow.

A. What are the angles of the triangle that forms the base of the prism? What are the lengths of its sides?

B. What is the volume of the prism shown above?

C. What is the surface area of the prism shown above?

Use your knowledge of mathematics to create a response in which you analyze and solve this problem. In your response you should:

⊙ identify three mathematical concepts involved in solving this problem; and

⊙ solve the given problem showing your work and justifying the steps you used in arriving at your solution; and

⊙ use this problem to prove that the ratio of side lengths for a right isosceles triangle is $x : x : x \sqrt{2}$.

OPEN RESPONSE QUESTION 5

Use the information below to complete the exercise that follows.

Middle school students were asked to solve the following problem.
Show that $(a + b)(c + d) = ac + ad + bc + bd$.
Please give the reasoning behind the various steps in the proof.

Student Response:

$(a + b)(c + d) = (a + b) c + (a + b)d$ distributive property
$(a + b) c + (a + b)d = ac + bc + ad + bd$ distributive property
$ac + bc + ad + bd$ does not equal $ac + ad + bc + bd$

Use your knowledge of mathematics to create a response in which you analyze the elementary school student's work and provide an alternative solution to the problem. In your response, you should:

⊙ correct any errors or misconceptions evident in the student's work and explain why the response is not mathematically sound (be sure to provide a correct solution, show your work, and explain your reasoning); and

⊙ solve the problem using an alternative method that could enhance the elementary school student's conceptual understanding of the relationship between algebra and geometry in the context of the problem. Use the following diagram in your solution.

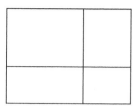

OPEN RESPONSE QUESTION 1 EXPLANATION

Step 1: Circle or otherwise mark your directives.
Solve the problem, justify/explain the steps used to solve it, identify two skills necessary to solve it, and identify two concepts necessary to solve it.

Step 2: Solve the problem; try to use a visual aide or other student–friendly strategy.

A. **Locker Number 15**
The first kid opens all of them. Therefore, he will toggle locker number 15. The second kid only toggles those lockers that are multiples of 2, so he will not touch locker 15.
The third kid toggles every 3rd locker, so he will toggle 15.
The fourth kid only toggles those lockers that are multiples of 4, so he will not touch locker 15.
The fifth kid toggles every 5th locker, so he will toggle 15.
We can see that only students whose position is a factor of 15 will toggle 15. The kids who will toggle 15 are: 1, 3, 5, 15. It starts off closed, then 1 opens it, 3 closes it, 5 opens it, and 15 closes it. It will be closed at the end.
Locker Number 16: The kids who will toggle 16 are: 1, 2, 4, 8, 16. It starts closed, then 1 opens it, 2 closes it, 4 opens it, 8 closes it, and 16 opens it. It will be open at the end.

B. This question asks which of the first 10 lockers will remain open. Let's examine each of the lockers. We know that kids who are factors of the locker number will toggle it. If there are an odd number of toggles, it will be open. If there are an even number of toggles, it will be closed.
Locker 1: Only kid who will toggle it is kid 1. He will open it. Open.
Locker 2: Kids 1 & 2 will toggle it. Two kids touch it, therefore it will be closed.
Locker 3: Kids 1 & 3 will toggle it. Two kids touch it, therefore it will be closed.
Locker 4: Kids 1, 2, & 4. Three kids touch it. Open.
Locker 5: Kids 1 & 5. Two kids touch it, therefore it will be closed.

Locker 6: Kids 1, 2, 3, 6. Four kids touch it, therefore it will be closed.
Locker 7: Kids 1 & 7. Two kids touch it, therefore closed.
Locker 8: Kids 1, 2, 4, & 8. Four kids touch it, therefore closed.
Locker 9: Kids 1, 3, & 9. Three kids touch it. Open.
Locker 10: Kids 1, 2, 5, 10. Four kids touch it, therefore closed.

In order to look for a pattern, it is helpful to organize the information in a chart:

Locker Number	Number of Toggles	Open or Closed
1	1	Open
2	2	Closed
3	2	Closed
4	3	Open
5	2	Closed
6	4	Closed
7	2	Closed
8	4	Closed
9	3	Open
10	4	Closed

Lockers 1, 4, and 9 will be open. The rest of the first ten lockers will be closed.

C. The lockers that will be open will be the ones with an odd number of factors. Those with an even number of factors will be closed.
Now, to determine which numbers have an odd number of factors. As can be seen with the lockers that we already solved, those that are open are 1, 4, 9, and 16. These numbers follow a pattern—they are all perfect squares.
Factors generally come in pairs. Given any number n, if a is a factor of n, then n/a will also be a factor. For instance, for the number 15, since 3 is a factor, $15/3 = 5$ is also a factor.
If a number is a perfect square, like 16, then a and n/a will be equal to each other. In the example of 16, 4 counts twice as a factor. Therefore, perfect squares are the only numbers that have an odd number of factors.
So which lockers will be open at the end? Those numbered: 1, 4, 9, 16, 25, 36, 49, 64, 81, and 100. There are 10 open lockers.

Step 3: Identify skills.

To solve this problem, a student would need to be able to count by multiples. To determine which kids would toggle 15, the student would need to count by 1's, 2's, 3's, 4's, and so on, all the way up to 15's.

To determine which lockers would be left open at the end, the student would need to be able to work with exponents. The student would need to calculate all of the perfect squares (1^2, 2^2, 3^2, 4^2, 5^2...) all the way up to 10^2, which equals 100.

Step 4: Identify concepts.

To solve this problem, a student would need to understand the concept of factors. For example, to find out whether locker 10 would be open or closed at the end, the student would need to determine that the factors of 10 are 1, 2, 5, and 10. This would tell the student that the locker would be toggled an even number of times, so it would end up closed. The student would also need to understand the concept of patterns. It would be an extremely tedious exercise to count by multiples for each of the 100 lockers to see which would be left open, so the student would need to see that only numbers that are perfect squares have an odd number of factors.

Step 5: There is no student response to analyze for this problem

Step 6: The directives do not ask for an alternate solution, so it is not necessary to provide one.

Step 7: Proofread your work for mathematical errors, and make sure that it fulfills all directives.

Step 8: Write your response in paragraph form on the answer sheet provided. Be sure to write from the perspective of a teacher analyzing a student's work and explaining a problem to an adult.

Here is an example of a strong response:

To solve this problem, a student would need to be able to count by multiples. To determine which kids would toggle 15, the student would need to count by 1's, 2's, 3's, 4's, and so on, all the way up to 15's. Also, to determine which lockers would be left open at the end, the student would need to be able to work with exponents. The student would need to calculate all of the perfect squares (1^2, 2^2, 3^2, 4^2, 5^2...) all the way up to 10^2, which equals 100.

A student would need to understand the concept of factors to solve this problem. For example, to find out whether locker 10 would be open or closed at the end, the student would need to determine that the factors of 10 are 1, 2, 5, and 10. This would tell the student that the locker would be toggled an even number of times, so it would end up closed.

The student would also need to understand the concept of patterns. It would be an extremely tedious exercise to count by multiples for each of the 100 lockers to see which would be left open, so the student would need to see that only numbers that are perfect squares have an odd number of factors.

The first part of the problem asks which kids will toggle locker number 15. The first kid opens all of the lockers, so he will toggle locker number 15. The second kid only toggles those lockers that are multiples of 2, so he will not touch locker 15. The third kid toggles every 3rd locker, so he will toggle 15. The fourth kid only toggles those lockers that are multiples of 4. Since 4 is not a factor of 15, he will not toggle it. The fifth kid toggles every 5th locker, so he will toggle 15. Only students whose position is a factor of 15 will toggle 15. The kids who will toggle 15 are: 1, 3, 5, 15. If the locker starts off closed, then 1 opens it, 3 closes it, 5 opens it, and 15 closes it. It will be closed at the end.

The next part of the problem is to determine who toggles locker 16 and whether it ends open or closed. The factors of 16 are: 1, 2, 4, 8, 16, so only the kids in those positions will toggle the locker. It starts closed, then 1 opens it, 2 closes it, 4 opens it, 8 closes it, and 16 opens it. It will be open at the end.

The next question asks which of the first 10 lockers will remain open. Only the kids whose positions are factors of the locker number will toggle it. Lockers 15 and 16 prove that if there are an odd number of toggles, the locker will end up open. If there are an even number of toggles, it will end up closed.

Locker Number	Factors	Number of Toggles	Open or Closed
1	1	1	Open
2	1,2	2	Closed
3	1,3	2	Closed
4	1,2,4	3	Open
5	1,5	2	Closed
6	1,2,3,6	4	Closed
7	1,7	2	Closed
8	1,2,4,8	4	Closed
9	1,3,9	3	Open
10	1,2,5,10	4	Closed

Lockers 1, 4, and 9 will be open. The rest of the first ten lockers will be closed.

The chart right shows a pattern: the lockers that will be open will be the ones with an odd number of factors. Those with an even number of factors will be closed. As can be seen with the lockers that we already solved, those that are open are 1, 4, 9, and 16. These numbers follow a pattern—they are all perfect squares, which means that they each have an odd number of factors. This makes sense because each number is equal to its square root times itself, which only counts as one factor. Factors generally come in pairs. Given any number n, if a is a factor of n, then n/a will also be a factor. For instance, for the number 15, since 3 is a factor, $15/3 = 5$ is also a factor. If a number is a perfect square, like 16, then a and n/a will be equal to each other. For example, four can be multiplied by itself to equal 16, but it only counts once as a factor.

Locker Number	Square
1	1
2	4
3	9
4	16
5	25
6	36
7	49
8	64
9	81
10	100

That is how perfect squares end up with an odd number of factors.

To determine which lockers will be open at the end, it is necessary to calculate all of the perfect squares less than or equal to 100.

OPEN RESPONSE QUESTION 2 EXPLANATION

Step 1: Circle or otherwise mark your directives.
Analyze the student's work and solve parts A, B, and C of the problem. Identify two skills and two concepts needed to solve the problem.

Step 2: Solve the problem; try to use a visual aide or other student– friendly strategy.

A: The first term in the series is generated when $n = 1$. To find the first term of an $f(n)$ function, substitute 1 for n in the formula. Repeat this for terms 2, 3, 4, and 5.

$f(n) = 1 + 2(n-1)$

The first five terms are: 1, 3, 5, 7, and 9

1st term, $n = 1$, $f(1) = 1 + 2(1-1) = 1 + 2(0) = 1$
2nd term, $n = 2$, $f(2) = 1 + 2(2-1) = 1 + 2(1) = 3$
3rd term, $n = 3$, $f(3) = 1 + 2(3-1) = 1 + 2(2) = 5$
4th term, $n = 4$, $f(4) = 1 + 2(4-1) = 1 + 2(3) = 7$
5th term, $n = 5$, $f(5) = 1 + 2(5-1) = 1 + 2(4) = 9$

B: Series B is calculated by finding the sum of the terms in Series A. A sum is the result of an addition problem, so add the terms of Series A to find Series B.

The first five terms of Series B are: 1, 4, 9, 16, 25

1st term: 1
2nd term: $1 + 3 = 4$
3rd term: $1 + 3 + 5 = 9$
4th term: $1 + 3 + 5 + 7 = 16$
5th term: $1 + 3 + 5 + 7 + 9 = 25$

C: The first five numbers of Series B follow a pattern. Each number is equal to the square of what term or position the number is in.

Therefore, to calculate the nth term of series B, you need to square n. $\boldsymbol{g(n) = n^2}$

1st term: $1 = 1^2$
2nd term: $4 = 2^2$
3rd term: $9 = 3^2$
4th term: $16 = 4^2$
5th term: $25 = 5^2$

Step 3: Identify skills.

To solve the problem above, the student needs to be able to solve order of operation problems that use the skills of addition and multiplication. For example, finding the first term of Series A requires simplifying the expression $1 + 2(1 - 1)$ to 1. This involves multiplying 2 and zero and then adding one and zero. In addition, to solve part C, which the student did not do, the student needed to be able to recognize patterns.

Step 4: Identify concepts.

Three concepts that the student needed to solve the problem above were the order of operations, the idea of a function, and the writing of a formula to represent a pattern. To accurately simplify the expression representing the second term in the series, the student would need to substitute the term number for n in the function.

2nd term
$n = 2, f(2) =$
$1 + 2(2-1)$

Then the student would need to perform the operation inside of the parentheses before multiplying and, finally, adding. Then the student needed to take the pattern that they recognized and convert that into a formula.

2nd term
$n = 2, f(2) =$
$1 + 2(2-1)$
$= 1 + 2(1)$
$= 1 + 2$
$= 3$

Step 5: Analyze the student's response. Refer to the skills and concepts identified in steps 3 and 4.

When calculating the terms in Series A, the student understood the concept of a function. He or she appears to have solved for each term by substituting the term number for n, which is correct. The student did not correctly apply the concept of order of operations. The student did not perform the operation inside the parentheses first, nor did the student correctly apply the distributive property.

1st term, $n = 1, f(1) = 1 + 2(1-1)$
2nd term, $n = 2, f(2) = 1 + 2(2-1)$
3rd term, $n = 3, f(3) = 1 + 2(3-1)$
4th term, $n = 4, f(4) = 1 + 2(4-1)$
5th term, $n = 5, f(5) = 1 + 2(5-1)$

This problem could be used to show the student that the reason parentheses are first in the order of operations is because of the distributive property. This could be illustrated by showing the student that

$$1 + 2(4 - 1) = 1 + 2(3) = 7 \quad \text{and} \quad 1 + 2(4 - 1) = 1 + 8 - 2 = 7$$

Since the student made mistakes in parts A and B, the student was unable to complete part C since there was no obvious pattern in the numbers that the student came up with.

Step 6: The directives do not ask for an alternate solution.

Step 7: Proofread your work for mathematical errors, and make sure that it fulfills all directives.

Step 8: Write your response in paragraph form on the answer sheet provided. Be sure to write from the perspective of a teacher analyzing a student's work and explaining a problem to an adult.

Here is an example of a strong response:

A. The first term in the series is generates when $n = 1$. To find the first term of an $f(n)$ function, substitute 1 for n in the formula. Repeat this for terms 2, 3, 4, and 5.

The first five terms of Series A are 1, 3, 5, 7, and 9

$f(n) = 1 + 2(n - 1)$
1st term, $n = 1$, $f(1) = 1 + 2(1 - 1) = 1 + 2(0) = 1$
2nd term, $n = 2$, $f(2) = 1 + 2(2 - 1) = 1 + 2(1) = 3$
3rd term, $n = 3$, $f(3) = 1 + 2(3 - 1) = 1 + 2(2) = 5$
4th term, $n = 4$, $f(4) = 1 + 2(4 - 1) = 1 + 2(3) = 7$
5th term, $n = 5$, $f(5) = 1 + 2(5 - 1) = 1 + 2(4) = 9$

B Series B is calculated by finding the sum of the terms in Series A. A sum is the result of an addition problem, so add the terms of Series A to find Series B.

The first five terms of Series B are: 1, 4, 9, 16, 25

1st term: 1
2nd term: $1 + 3 = 4$
3rd term: $1 + 3 + 5 = 9$
4th term: $1 + 3 + 5 + 7 = 16$
5th term: $1 + 3 + 5 + 7 + 9 = 25$

C. Each term in Series B is the perfect square of the position the number is in. This can be easily represented by a formula since the nth term will be equal to n^2. Using $g(n)$ to represent the formula for calculating the nth term of series B: $g(n) = n^2$

1st term: $1 = 1^2$
2nd term: $4 = 2^2$
3rd term: $9 = 3^2$
4th term: $16 = 4^2$
5th term: $25 = 5^2$

To solve the problem above, a student needs to be able to solve order of operation problems that use the skills of addition and multiplication. For example, finding the first term of Series A requires simplifying the expression $1 + 2(1-1)$ to 1. This involves multiplying 2 and zero and then adding one and zero. Finally, the student needed to be able to recognize patterns to solve part C.

Three concepts that the student needed to solve the problem above were the order of operations, the idea of a function, and the writing of a formula to represent a pattern. To accurately simplify the expression representing the second term in the series, the student would need to substitute the term number for n in the function.

2nd term, $n = 2$, $f(2) = 1 + 2(2 - 1)$

Then the student would need to perform the operation inside of the parentheses before multiplying and, finally, adding.

2nd term, $n = 2$, $f(2) = 1 + 2(2 - 1) = 1 + 2 (1) = 1 + 2 = 3$

Then the student needed to take the pattern that they recognized and convert that into a formula.

When calculating the terms in Series A, the student understood the concept of a function. He or she appears to have solved for each term by substituting the term number for n, which is correct.

For example, for the 4th term, the student appears to have understood to plug in 4 for n.

4th term, $n = 4$, $f(4) = 1 + 2(4 - 1) = 1 + 2(3)$

But, then it appears the student did not correctly apply the concept of order of operations. It appears that the student added before multiplying, getting an answer of 9 for the 4th term which is not correct. The student should be reminded to follow PEMDAS, and multiply before adding.

A: The first term will be when $n = 1$. Therefore, I will substitute 1 for n in the formula to find the first term. I will repeat this for terms 2, 3, 4, and 5.
The first five terms are: 1, 3, 5, 7, and 9

$$f(n) = 1 + 2(n - 1)$$
1st term, $n = 1$, $f(1) = 1 + 2(1-1) = 1 + 2(0) = 1$
2nd term, $n = 2$, $f(2) = 1 + 2(2-1) = 1 + 2(1) = 3$
3rd term, $n = 3$, $f(3) = 1 + 2(3-1) = 1 + 2(2) = 5$
4th term, $n = 4$, $f(4) = 1 + 2(4-1) = 1 + 2(3) = 7$
5th term, $n = 5$, $f(5) = 1 + 2(5-1) = 1 + 2(4) = 9$

B: Series g is calculated by finding the sum of the terms in series f. Sum is the result of an addition problem, therefore, I will add the terms of series f to find series g.
The first five terms of series g are: 1, 4, 9, 16, 25

1st term: 1
2nd term: $1 + 3 = 4$
3rd term: $1 + 3 + 5 = 9$
4th term: $1 + 3 + 5 + 7 = 16$
5th term: $1 + 3 + 5 + 7 + 9 = 25$

C: A pattern can be seen in each term of series g. Each term is a perfect square.

1, 4, 9, 16, 25
$1^2 = 1$, $2^2 = 4$, $3^2 = 9$, $4^2 = 16$, $5^2 = 25$
$g(n) = n^2$

D: To find the 10th term, just plug in $n = 10$ into the formula for g.

$g(10) = 10^2 = 100$
The 10th term is 100.

OPEN RESPONSE QUESTION 3 EXPLANATION

The student needs to use a variety of skills to solve this problem including converting fractions to percents to find the chance, ordering fractions or percents to compare which probability was higher, and multiplication of fractions or percents for calculating the compound probability. In addition, the concepts the student needed to master for this problem included understanding that the probability is the number of favorable outcomes divided by the total number of outcomes, understanding how to find the probability of dependent events, and understanding the probability of compound events.

A. The student was asked to find the chance that the girl will find a coin underneath a randomly chosen shell. To find the chance, calculate the probability and convert it to a percent. The probability is equal to the number of favorable outcomes divided by the total number of outcomes. In this case, the favorable outcome would be picking a shell with a coin underneath, there are 7 of these possibilities. The total number of outcomes is equal to the total number of shells from which the girl can choose, which is 10.

$$\frac{\text{Shells with coins}}{\text{Shells}} = \frac{7}{10}$$

Now, the fraction $\frac{7}{10}$ must be converted to a percent. To convert from a fraction to a percent, first convert from a fraction to a decimal and then multiply by 100%. To convert from a fraction to a decimal, you can divide numerator by the denominator. However, in this case, since the denominator is 10, we know that the fraction is seven tenths, which can easily be written as 0.7. Now, to convert from decimal to a percent, multiply by 100%. $0.7 \times 100\% = 70\%$

There is a 70% chance that she will find a coin underneath. The student was correct and understood probability and converting from a fraction to a percent.

B. The next question asks to determine if there is a better chance of finding a silver coin on the second try if the girl found a coin under the first shell or not. If the first shell did not have a coin underneath, then it is more likely that the girl will find a coin under the second shell because there are more coins for her to find than if she already found one of the coins under the first shell. This can be proven by finding the probability of each situation.

If the first shell had a coin underneath, then to find the probability that the second shell she chooses has a coin, divide the favorable outcomes over the total outcomes. In this case, there are only 6 shells remaining with coins, so 6 favorable outcomes. There are only 9 shells remaining, so 9 total outcomes.

$$\frac{\text{Favorable}}{\text{Total}} = \frac{\text{Shells remaining with coins}}{\text{Shells remaining}} = \frac{6}{9}$$

If the first shell did not have a coin underneath, then the number of favorable outcomes is still 7, since there are still 7 hidden coins. The total number of remaining shells is 9.

$$\frac{\text{Favorable}}{\text{Total}} = \frac{\text{Shells remaining with coins}}{\text{Shells remaining}} = \frac{7}{9}$$

$$\frac{7}{9} > \frac{6}{9}$$

Better chance of finding a coin underneath if the first shell did not have a coin underneath, as predicted. The student did not answer this correctly since the student did not understand the probability of dependent events and the fact that what happened on the first draw would affect what would happen on the second draw.

C. The final part of the problem asks for the probability that the girl will choose 2 shells with coins underneath as her first 2 draws. This question is asking for the probability of 2 events. The probability of compound events is equal to the product of their individual probabilities.

The two events in this problem are: finding a coin on the first draw and finding a coin on the second draw.

The probability of finding a coin on the first draw = $\frac{7}{10}$. (solved in part A)
The probability of finding a coin on the second draw if first had a coin = $\frac{6}{9}$. (solved in part B)

Therefore, to find the probability that the first 2 shells will both have coins, multiply the probabilities of each event.

Probability both will have coins = $\frac{7}{10} \times \frac{6}{9} = \frac{42}{90} = \frac{7}{15}$

The student understood the concept of compound probability equaling the product of each individual event. In addition, the student understood how to correctly multiply fractions.

OPEN RESPONSE QUESTION 4 EXPLANATION

A. The triangular prism has a base that is a right triangle. This can be recognized by the small square in the bottom left hand corner of the triangle. A right triangle forms a 90° angle. The other two angles of the triangular base are marked to indicate that they have the same measure. To solve for this angle, let a represent the unknown value. The angles in a triangle must add to 180°. Therefore, $a + a + 90° = 180°$

$$2a + 90° = 180°$$
$$2a = 90°$$
$$a = 45°$$

Each of the missing angles is 45°. The three angles in the triangular base are 45°, 45°, and 90°.

If a triangle has two angles the same, the sides opposite those angles will also be the same. This is known as an isosceles triangle, and in this case, an isosceles right triangle. Therefore, the two sides of the right triangle will be equal, making them both 5.

To find the hypotenuse of the triangle, use the Pythagorean Theorem, which states that the sum of the squares of the sides of a right triangle will equal the square of the hypotenuse.

$$5^2 + 5^2 = \text{hypotenuse}^2$$
$$25 + 25 = \text{hypotenuse}^2$$
$$50 = \text{hypotenuse}^2$$
$$\text{hypotenuse} = \sqrt{50} = 5\sqrt{2}$$

The sides of the right isosceles triangular base are 5, 5, $5\sqrt{2}$.

For any right isosceles triangle, the sides of the triangle will be the same. In this case, let's use x to

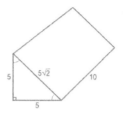

$$x^2 + x^2 = \text{hypotenuse}^2$$
$$2x^2 = \text{hypotenuse}^2$$
$$\text{hypotenuse} = \sqrt{(2x^2)}$$
$$= x\sqrt{2}$$

represent the length of each side. Let's again use the Pythagorean Theorem to find the length of the hypotenuse.

Therefore, any right isosceles triangle will have sides which are in the following proportions: x, x, $x\sqrt{2}$.

B. To find the volume of a triangular prism, find the area of the triangle and multiply by the height of the prism.

The base is a right triangle. The area of a triangle is found by multiplying $\frac{1}{2}$ × base × height.

In this case, since the two sides form a right angle, then the lengths of the sides are equal to the base and height of the triangle.

Area of triangle = $\frac{1}{2}$ × 5 × 5 = 12.5

Volume = Area of triangle × Height = 12.5 × 10 = 125

The volume is 125 units³.

C. The surface area of a prism is equal to the sum of the areas of each face. In this case, the prism has 5 faces.

Face 1: Front triangle: Area = $\frac{1}{2}$ × base × height = $\frac{1}{2}$ × 5 × 5 = 12.5
Face 2: Back triangle: Area = $\frac{1}{2}$ × base × height = $\frac{1}{2}$ × 5 × 5 = 12.5
Face 3: Bottom rectangle: Area = length × width = 10 × 5 = 50
Face 4: Left rectangle: Area = length × width = 5 × 10 = 50
Face 5: Top rectangle: Area = length × width = $5\sqrt{2}$ × 10 = $50\sqrt{2}$
Total surface area = 12.5 + 12.5 + 50 + 50 + 50 = 125 + $50\sqrt{2}$.

To solve this problem, a student needed to understand the concept of an isosceles triangle, the concept of the sum of the angles in a triangle, the Pythagorean theorem, and the formulas for volume and surface area.

OPEN RESPONSE QUESTION 5 EXPLANATION

Step 1: *Circle or otherwise mark your directives.*
Analyze the student's work, provide an alternate solution, and solve the problem using the diagram provided.

Step 2: *Solve the problem; try to use a visual aide or other student–friendly strategy.*
To prove that $(a + b)(c + d) = ac + ad + bc + bd$, break the problem into multiple parts. Beginning by substituting n for $(a + b)$ can help students see the contents of the parentheses as a single quantity ❶.

❶
$$n = a + b$$
$$(a + b)(c + d)$$
$$= n(c + d)$$
$$= nc + nd$$

The distributive property states that you can distribute multiplication over addition, so it is possible to distribute n over $(c + d)$ in the problem above.

❷
$$nc + nd$$
$$= (a + b)c + (a + b)d$$

❷ Next, substitute $a + b$ for n.
❸ Distribute both c and d over $(a + b)$.

❸
$$(a + b)c + (a + b)d$$
$$= ac + bc + ad + bd$$

❹ The commutative property states that you can change the order of an addition problem without changing the sum or result.

❹
$$ac + bc + ad + bd$$
$$= ac + ad + bc + bd$$

Step 3: *Identify skills.*
A skill necessary to solve the problem above was multiplication, which was used when distributing $(a + b)$ over $(c + d)$.

Step 4: *Identify concepts.*
Two concepts that the student needed to understand to solve the problem above were the distributive and commutative properties.
The distributive property was used to prove that $(a + b)c + (a + b)d = ac + bc + ad + bd$, and the commutative property was used to prove that $ac + bc + ad + bd = ac + ad + bc + bd$.

Step 5: *Analyze the student's response.*
Refer to the skills and concepts you identified. The student accurately distributes $(a + b)$ over $(c + d)$ and then c and d over $(a + b)$. This demonstrates mastery of the skill of multiplication and understanding of the concept of the distributive property.
The student does not realize that $ac + bc + ad + bd = ac + ad + bc + bd$, which shows that the student does not understand the commutative property.

Step 6: *Develop an alternate solution that fulfills the directive.*

Describe why the alternate solution is a useful method for teaching the concepts listed above. Make the length of the left rectangle equal a and the length of the right rectangle equal b. Make the width of the top rectangle equal c and the length of the bottom rectangle equal d.

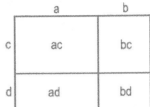

The area of a rectangle can be found by multiplying the length by the width. The area of each of the rectangles is written inside the four rectangles. The sum of the areas of the four rectangles is: $ac + ad + bc + bd$. If the four combined rectangles are thought of as one large rectangle, then the length of the large rectangle is "$a + b$" and the width of the large rectangle is "$c + d$". Therefore, the area of the large rectangle can be found by multiplying length by width.

$$(a + b)\,(c + d)$$

We know that the combined area of the four rectangles must equal the area of the large rectangle. By using a geometric example of $(a + b)(c + d)$, this solution would help students visualize the use of

$$(a + b)(c + d)$$
$$= ac + ad + bc + bd$$

the distributive property in the problem. Also, it would clarify the concept of the commutative property by showing that the order in which the areas of the smaller rectangles are added does not affect the total area of the larger rectangle.

Step 7: Proofread your work for mathematical errors, and make sure that it fulfills all directives.

Step 8: Write your response in paragraph form on the answer sheet provided. Be sure to write from the perspective of a teacher analyzing a student's work and explaining a problem to an adult.

Here is an example of a strong response:

Two concepts that the student needed to understand to solve the problem above were the distributive and commutative properties. The distributive property was used to prove that $(a + b)c + (a + b)d = ac + bc + ad + bd$, and the commutative property was used to prove that $ac + bc + ad + bd = ac + ad + bc + bd$. The student accurately distributes $(a + b)$ over $(c + d)$ and then c and d over $(a + b)$. This demonstrates mastery of the skill of multiplication and understanding of the concept of the distributive property. The student does not realize that $ac + bc + ad + bd = ac + ad + bc + bd$, which shows that the student does not understand the commutative property.

To prove that $(a + b)(c + d) = ac + ad + bc + bd$, break the problem into multiple parts. Beginning by substituting n for $(a + b)$ can help students see the contents of the parentheses as a single quantity.

$$n = a + b$$
$$(a + b)(c + d) = n(c + d) = nc + nd$$

The distributive property states that you can distribute multiplication over addition, so it is possible to distribute n over $(c + d)$ in the problem above.

Next, substitute $a + b$ for n.

$$nc + nd = (a + b)c + (a + b)d$$

Distribute both c and d over $(a + b)$.

$$(a + b)c + (a + b)d = ac + bc + ad + bd$$

The commutative property states that you can change the order of an addition problem without changing the sum or result.

$$ac + bc + ad + bd = ac + ad + bc + bd$$

An alternate solution to this problem would be to make the length of the left rectangle equal a and the length of the right rectangle equal b, and make the width of the top rectangle equal c and the length of the bottom rectangle equal d. Since, the area of a rectangle can be found by multiplying the length by the width. The area of each of the rectangles is written inside the four rectangles. The sum of the areas of the four rectangles is: $ac + ad + bc + bd$.

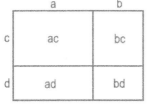

If the four combined rectangles are thought of as one large rectangle, then the length of the large rectangle is "$a + b$" and the width of the large rectangle is "c + d". Therefore, the area of the large rectangle can be found by multiplying length by width. $(a + b)(c + d)$.

Since we know that the combined area of the four rectangles must equal the area of the large rectangle, $(a + b)(c + d) = ac + ad + bc + bd$. By using a geometric example of $(a + b)(c + d)$, this solution would help students visualize the use of the distributive property in the problem. Also, it would clarify the concept of the commutative property by showing that the order in which the areas of the smaller rectangles are added does not affect the total area of the larger rectangle.

Diagnostic Exam

1. Two positive, odd integers and one negative, even integer are multiplied together. Which of the following could be their product?

    A. -60.5
    B. -15
    C. 100
    D. -100

2. Use the diagram below to determine what shape will be the 61st if the pattern continues.

    A. Circle
    B. Triangle
    C. Square
    D. Hexagon

3. If the prime factorization of a number Y is n^2p^3 and the prime factorization of a number Z is n^3p^2. What is the prime factorization of the least common multiple of Z and Y?

    A. np
    B. n^2p^2
    C. n^3p^3
    D. n^5p^5

4. What is the ratio of the area of Triangle T to the area of Triangle S?

    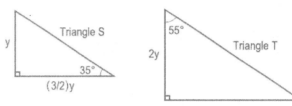

    A. 2
    B. $4y$
    C. ³⁄₂
    D. 4

5. The average number of points you scored in the first 9 basketball games of the season was 23. What do you need in the 10th game to get your average to n?

A. $n - 23$
B. $10n - 207$
C. $9n - 23$
D. $207 - 9n$

A. Associative, Step 1
B. Distributive, Step 1
C. Distributive, Step 3
D. Commutative, Step 3

6. **If $n > r$, what would replace the question mark?**

$n\%$ of r **?** $r\%$ of n

A. >
B. <
C. =
D. Not enough information

7. **If the width of a box is w, the length is ½ the width, and the height is 6 more than the length, what is the volume of the box in terms of w?**

A. $2w + 12$
B. $w^3 + 3\,w^2$
C. $2w^3 + 12w^2$
D. $\frac{1}{4}\,w^3 + 3w^2$

8. **Use the student work sample below to answer the question that follows.**

1. $4(16 + 23) + 36 = 64 + 23 + 36$
2. $64 + 23 + 36 = 64 + 36 + 23$
3. $64 + 36 + 23 = 100 + 23$
4. $100 + 23 = 123$

What property does the student use incorrectly, and in which step?

9. **If n is an odd, prime integer and $10 < n < 19$, which is true about the mean of all possible values of n?**

A. It is greater than the median and greater than the mode.
B. It is greater than the median.
C. It is equal to the median.
D. It is less than the median.

10. **If frequency and wavelength are related by the formula below, then how will the wavelength change for radiation that doubles in frequency?**

frequency = c/wavelength
where c is a constant
equal to the speed of light

A. It will increase by a factor of 2.
B. It will decrease by a factor of 2.
C. It will increase by a factor of c.
D. It will decrease by a factor of c.

11. How many integers between 1 and 1000, inclusive, are divisible by both 5 and 8?

    A. 25

    B. 76

    C. 125

    D. 200

12. If a student wanted to find the equation of a line with a known y–intercept, which of the following would independently provide enough information?

    A. a coordinate pair on the line

    B. the slope

    C. the x–intercept

    D. all of the above

13. Use the table below to answer the question that follows.

Plan	Line fee	Cost per minute
A	$20	$0.05
B	$10	$0.10

How many minutes of talking in one month would cost the same on either phone plan?

    A. 10 minutes

    B. 20 minutes

    C. 100 minutes

    D. 200 minutes

14. Noah is papering one of the walls in his bedroom. He uses 3 rolls of paper to cover 20 square yards of wall space. If the wall is 15 feet high and 18 feet long, how many rolls of paper will he need to purchase?

    A. 2

    B. 3

    C. 4

    D. 5

15. If two cards are drawn at random from a standard 52 card deck with four suits containing 13 cards each, what is the probability that they will both be hearts?

    A. $\frac{1}{16}$

    B. $\frac{1}{8}$

    C. $\frac{1}{4}$

    D. $\frac{1}{17}$

16. Which is a possible ratio of the numbers represented by the 5's in 532.385?

    A. One hundred thousand to one

    B. One hundred to one hundredth

    C. One hundred to one

    D. One to one thousandth

17. At the same moment, two trains leave a station on parallel tracks. Train A travels the 700 miles from Station 1 to Station 3 in the same amount

of time that it takes Train B to travel the 500 miles to Station 2. If the total route is 1500 miles long and both trains travel to the very end before turning around and traveling back to Station 1, which of the following proportions shows the total distance Train A has traveled when Train B reaches the end of the route?

A. $500/700 = x/1000$
B. $500/700 = 1000/x$
C. $500/700 = x/1500$
D. $700/500 = x/1500$

18. If the figure, the distance from B to C is twice the distance from A to B, and the distance from C to D is equal to half the distance from A to C. If the distance from B to C is x, what is the distance from A to D?

A. $\frac{1}{2}x$
B. $\frac{3}{4}x$
C. $2\frac{1}{4}x$
D. $2\frac{1}{2}x$

19. A jet flies from Hong Kong to Mumbai in 4 hours and from Mumbai to Hong Kong in 3 hours 45 minutes. The wind velocity is 14 mph and decreases the plane's speed on the journey from Hong Kong to Mumbai and increases the plane's speed from Mumbai to Hong Kong. If rate × time = distance, which of the following equations could be used to find the average speed s of the jet?

A. $0.25(s - 14) = s$
B. $(4 + 3.75) = (s+14) + (s-14)$
C. $(s - 14)4 = (s + 14)\,3.75$
D. $4(3.75) = (s + 14)(s - 14)$

20. Order the following from least to greatest:

I. the number of fourths in $1\frac{1}{2}$
II. $5 \times \frac{1}{2}$
III. $\frac{3}{2} \div 3$

A. I, II, III
B. III, II, I
C. III, I, II
D. II, III, I

21. The expression $(2^3 \times 4^{-7})$ is equal to which of the following?

A. 2^{-11}
B. 2^{-2}
C. 4^{-11}
D. 8^{-4}

22. If you start with an even number. Then, you add it to an odd number, multiply it by a different odd number, and then subtract the original even number, the result will be:
   A. Even
   B. Odd
   C. Zero
   D. Not enough information.

23. A researcher lost one piece of data from his set. He knows that the median is 83. Which of the following could be the missing element if the rest of the set is: 81, 92, 85, 76, 80?
   A. 78
   B. 82
   C. 84
   D. 90

24. Use the table below to answer the question that follows.

Earnings Plan	Payment Structure
1	$55,000 base salary
2	$25,000 base salary + 15% of sales
3	$35,000 base salary + 1/8 of sales

Ralph has been offered a job, and he can choose from the three earnings plans. If he sells $200,000 worth of merchandise, which plan will give him the highest salary for his first year?
   A. Plan 1
   B. Plan 2
   C. Plan 3
   D. All three plans allow Ralph to earn the same amount in his first year.

25. You have two different types of bacteria in petri dishes. Dish A contains Bacteria A, and Dish B contains Bacteria B. Both start with the same number of bacteria. Bacteria A doubles every 2 days, and Bacteria B triples every 3 days. After 12 days, which petri dish will contain more?
   A. Dish A
   B. Dish B
   C. They will contain equal numbers of bacteria.
   D. The problem does not provide enough information.

26. Use the number line below to answer the question that follows.

What is the distance between A and B on the number line?
   A. 0.14
   B. 0.15
   C. 1.2
   D. 7

27. You have 10L of a 40% saline solution. Which equation would help you calculate how much pure saline (100% saline) you need to add to create a 60% solution?

    A. $40\% (10) + x = 60\% (10 + x)$
    B. $40\% (10 + x) = 60\%(x)$
    C. $40\%x = 60\% (10 + x)$
    D. $40\% (10 + x) = 60\%$

28. If N is a positive integer, which of the following products could be a negative number?

    A. $(N+1)(N-1)$
    B. $(N+1)(N+2)$
    C. $N(N-2)$
    D. $N(N)$

29. In a family, the oldest child is $\frac{7}{3}$ times the sum of the younger children's ages. If the two younger children are twins with an age greater than s and less than t, which of the following inequalities most accurately gives the range of possibilities for the oldest child's age, c?

    A. $s < c < t$
    B. $2s < c < 2t$
    C. $\frac{7}{3} s < c < \frac{7}{3} t$
    D. $\frac{14}{3} s < c < \frac{14}{3} t$

30. Steve reads 80 pages in 2 hours and 40 minutes. If Cassandra reads twice as fast as Steve, how long will it take her to read a 300 page book?

    A. 4 hours 40 minutes
    B. 5 hours
    C. 5 hours 20 minutes
    D. 5 hours 40 minutes

31. Use the diagram below to answer the question that follows.

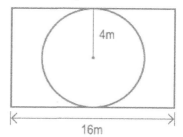

A blacktop has a circle painted inside of it as shown in the diagram above. If a raindrop falls randomly from the sky and lands on the blacktop, what is the probability that it will land inside of the circle?

    A. $\frac{1}{\pi}$
    B. $\frac{\pi}{16}$
    C. $\frac{\pi}{8}$
    D. 16π

32. A student looks at a circle with a circumference of 24 and estimates that the radius is 8. Which most accurately describes the estimate?

    A. The estimate is too low by a factor of 2.
    B. The estimate is too low by a factor of 3.
    C. The estimate is too high by a factor of 2.
    D. The estimate is correct.

33. Everyone in a group is being assigned a secret code of 3 characters. The first character must be a letter and the second and third are numbers which can not be the same. How many possible codes can be made?

    A. 46

    B. 126

    C. 2340

    D. 2600

34. The price of a camera was first increased by $17 and then decreased by 38%. If the final price of the camera was y, what was the original price?

    A. $y/0.62 - \$17$

    B. $0.62(y + \$17)$

    C. $\$17 + (1.38)y$

    D. $0.38(y + \$17)$

35. If **AB = AC and angle BAC = 80°**. What is the measure of angle ACD?

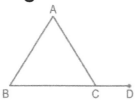

    A. 50°

    B. 100°

    C. 130°

    D. 180°

36. Use the diagram below to answer the question that follows.

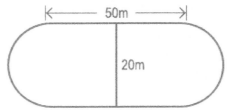

A jogging track is made up of two half circles on either end with a straight line of 50m connecting them. Joaquin jogs at 5km per hour. If his coach estimates that it will take Joaquin a half hour to jog around the track, her estimate is:

    A. Too high by a factor of 15.

    B. Too low by a factor of 15.

    C. Too high by a factor of 6.

    D. Too low by a factor of 6.

37. Use the graph below to answer the question that follows.

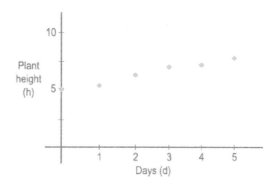

The graph represents that growth of a student's plant over the course of his 7 day science experiment. Which of the following equations best models the relationship between days, d, and plant height in centimeters, h, as shown in the graph above?

    A. $d = \frac{1}{2} h + 5$
    B. $d = 5 h + \frac{1}{2}$
    C. $h = \frac{1}{2} d + 5$
    D. $h = 5 d + \frac{1}{2}$

A.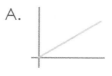
B.
C.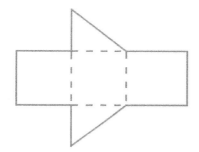
D. None of the above

38. Use the diagram below to answer the question that follows.

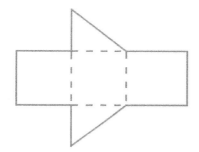

You have a piece of paper shaped like the diagram above. If you fold along the dotted line, what shape have you created?

    A. Pyramid
    B. Tetrahedron
    C. Right triangular prism
    D. Prism with equilateral triangle base

39. A runner starts a race slowly and then picks up speed before sprinting to the finish line. Which graph could represent the position of the runner versus time?

40. Use the diagram to answer the question that follows.

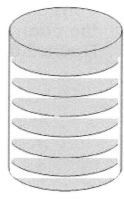

The diagram is used to describe the relationship between the height h, the area of the circular base A, and the volume V of a cylinder. Assuming that the cylinder is sliced into an infinite number of equally–sized sections, which of the following relationships is demonstrated?

    A. $V = \frac{1}{2} Ah$
    B. $V = 2 Ah$
    C. $V = Ah$
    D. $V = \frac{2A}{h}$

41. Use the diagram below to answer the question that follows.

Figure 1   Figure 2

Which of the following transformation or series of transformations best describes the change from Figure 1 to Figure 2 above?

    A. A flip across the y–axis, followed by a flip across the x–axis
    B. A flip across the y–axis, followed by translation
    C. A flip across the x–axis, followed by translation
    D. Rotation

42. Use the incorrect work sample below from a student who was asked to calculate the distance between (5, 5) and (-5, -5) to answer the questions that follow.

    Vertical distance: 5 – -5 = 10
    Horizontal distance: 5 – -5 =10
    Total distance: 10 + 10 = 20

Which of the following strategies would help this student visualize the correct solution to the problem above?

    A. Drawing a square with corners at (0,0), (0,5), (5,0), and (5,5), then rotating the square until it has corners at (0,0), (0, -5), (-5, 0), and (-5,-5).
    B. Drawing a circle with the two points placed along the circumference
    C. Drawing a right triangle with the hypotenuse connecting the two points
    D. Drawing two parallel lines that each have a length of 5 units.

43. Use the graph to answer the question that follows.

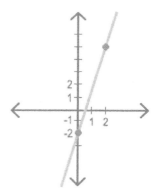

The graph can be represented by the equation $y = Zx - 2$. What is the value of Z?

    A. -2
    B. 2
    C. 3 ½
    D. 4 ½

44. Use the inequality below to answer the question that follows.

$$5\,|y-2| \le 10$$

Which of the following inequalities describes all of the possible values of y and only those values?

    A. $y \ge 0$
    B. $0 \le y \le 4$
    C. $y \le 4$
    D. $-2 \le y \le 0$

45. Which of the following best represents the area of an isosceles right triangle as a function of the length of the sides?

A.   B.

C.   D.

DIAGNOSTIC EXAM EXPLANATIONS

1. D   Let's examine each answer choice.

A: You know that the product of integers is always an integer, so eliminate answer choice A.	**B:** Even × even = even Even × odd = even Odd × odd = odd In this case, we have odd × odd × even = odd × even = even Eliminate answer choice B.	**C:** Positive × positive = positive Positive × negative = negative In this case, we have positive × positive × negative = negative Eliminate answer choice c.	**D:** This is the only answer remaining, so it must be correct. Here is one possible option. Positive Odd × Positive Odd × Negative Even = $25 \times 1 \times \text{-}4 = \text{-}100$

2. A   Extrapolate from the pattern that is given. The pattern is 4 elements (shapes) long.

You are asked to predict the 61st element. The closest multiple of 4 to 61 is 60 (15 × 4). Since the 60th element would complete a repetition of the pattern, the 61st element is the first element of a new repetition—the first element in the pattern.
Therefore, the 61st object will be a circle.

3. C To find the least common multiple of Y and Z, you know you want the smallest possible number that both divide evenly into.

Y must divide evenly into the least common multiple. Therefore, n^2p^3 must divide into the least common multiple.
So far, the least common multiple has a factor of n^2p^3.

Next, let's look at Z.
$Z = n^3p^2$, that does not divide evenly into n^2p^3. There are not enough multiples of n in the least common multiple so you must add another n.

Now, the least common multiple is n^3p^3.

---

4. D There are two ways to solve this problem.

Method 1: Find the length of the missing sides, find the areas of the triangle, and find the ratio. Since the triangles have the same angles, then they are similar. Therefore, their sides are proportional.
The length of the side of triangle T $(2y)$ is twice as much as the corresponding side of triangle S (y). Therefore, the missing base of triangle T is twice as much as the corresponding side.
Missing side = $2\left(\frac{3}{2}y\right) = 3y$.

Area of a triangle = $\frac{1}{2} \times$ base $\times$ height

Triangle T is 4 times as large as Triangle S.
Answer D.

> Area of Triangle S = $\left(\frac{1}{2}\right)(y)\left(\frac{3}{2}y\right) = \frac{3}{4}y^2$
> Area of Triangle T = $\left(\frac{1}{2}\right)(2y)(3y) = 3y^2$

Method 2: If you know the proportionality of the sides in one dimension, you can square that to find the proportionality of the area in 2–dimensions. The sides of Triangle T are twice as much as the lengths of Triangle S. Therefore, square that to find the ratio of the areas.

$$2^2 = 4.$$

---

5. B If the average on the first 9 games was a 23, then the total number of points you scored in those games was:

> $9 \times 23 = 207$

If the average on all 10 games is n, then the total number of points scored in all 10 games must be:

> $10 \times n = 10n$

To find what you need to get in the 10th game, subtract the total number of points in the first 9 games from the total number of points in all 10 games. $10n - 207$ is what is needed in the 10th game.

---

6. C   Let's examine each side of the question mark.

It doesn't matter whether n is bigger than r, both sides of the question mark are equal.

$$n\% \text{ of } r = {}^{n}\!/_{100} \times r = {}^{rn}\!/_{100}$$
$$r\% \text{ of } n = {}^{r}\!/_{100} \times n = {}^{rn}\!/_{100}$$

---

7. D   The volume of a box is found by multiplying the length, width, and height. Let's first put all the dimensions in terms of w.

Width $= w$
Length $= \frac{1}{2} w$
Height $= \frac{1}{2} w + 6$

$$\text{Volume} = w \left(\tfrac{1}{2} w\right) \left(\tfrac{1}{2} w + 6\right)$$
$$= \left(\tfrac{1}{2} w^2\right) \left(\tfrac{1}{2} w + 6\right)$$
$$= \tfrac{1}{4} w^3 + 3 w^2$$

---

8. B   From Step 1 to Step 2, the student attempted to use the distributive property. The distributive property states that $a(b + c) = ab + ac$.

In this case, the correct use of distributive property is:
$$4(16 + 23) + 36 = 4(16) + 4(23) + 36 = 64 + 92 + 36$$

The student forgot to multiply the 4 by the 23.
Answer B. Student incorrectly used distributive property in first step.

---

9. B   The possible values of n are 11, 13, and 17 (15 is not prime).

To find the median, put the numbers in order and take the middle number. 11, 13, 17. Median $= 13$.
Mean is found by adding the numbers and dividing by 3.

$$\frac{(11+13+17)}{3} = \frac{41}{3} = 13\frac{2}{3}$$

Mode is the number that appears the most frequently. However, each number is used exactly once. Mean is greater than the median.

---

10. B   Let the original frequency $= f$ and the wavelength $= w$.

If the frequency doubles to $2f$, plug that in to see what happens to the wavelength.

$$f = {}^{c}\!/_{w}$$
$$\text{Rearrange: } w = {}^{c}\!/_{f}$$

The wavelength went from w to $\frac{1}{2} w$, so it decreased by a factor of 2.

$$\frac{c}{2f} = \frac{1}{2} \frac{c}{f} = \frac{1}{2} w$$

---

11. A If a number is divisible by both 5 and 8, then it must be divisible by 40. Now, we need to find out how many integers between 1 and 1000 are divisible by 40.

$^{1000}/_{40} = 25$. Therefore, there are 25 numbers that are evenly divisible by 1000.

---

12. D There are various ways to find the equation of a line. The y–intercept is one point. Any other point on the line would provide enough information for the student to write the equation of the line. Therefore, answer A which says a coordinate pair would be enough. In addition, the x–intercept is just another point, so answer C would be enough.

Also, using the slope–intercept form of the equation, $y = mx + b$, the slope and y–intercept are the two pieces that are needed to find the equation. Answer B is enough.

Therefore, all would independently provide enough info.

---

13. D Set up a system of equations to solve this word problem. If m equals minutes talked, then the amount paid using each plan can be represented as follows:

> Plan A: Cost = $20 + 0.05m$
> Plan B: Cost = $10 + 0.10m$

To find the number of minutes that would cost the same, set the two equations equal.

> $20 + 0.05m = 10 + 0.10m$
> $0.05m = 10$
> $m = 200$

This problem also could have been solved by working backwards and plugging in each answer choice into each plan until you found an answer where the plans were equal.

---

14. D First, convert from feet to yards. Then find the area of the wall. Finally, determine the number of rolls of paper that are needed.

$$15 \text{ feet} \times \left(^{1 \text{ yd}}/_{3 \text{ feet}}\right) = 5 \text{ yards}$$
$$18 \text{ feet} \times \left(^{1 \text{ yd}}/_{3 \text{ feet}}\right) = 6 \text{ yards}$$
$$\text{Area} = 5 \text{ yards} \times 6 \text{ yards} = 30 \text{ square yards}$$

$$30 \text{ square yards} \times \frac{3 \text{ rolls}}{20 \text{ square yards}} = \frac{90}{20 \text{ rolls}} = 4\frac{1}{2} \text{ rolls}$$

The question asks how many rolls Noah will purchase. If he cannot purchase a part of a roll, then round up.
Answer D. 5

15. D You want to find the probability that both cards will be hearts. To find the probability of compound events, multiply their individual probabilities.

The probability of the first card being a heart is $^{13}\!/_{52} = ¼$
For the second card, there are only 51 cards left and only 12 hearts left.
Probability $= ^{12}\!/_{51}$.

Multiply the probabilities: $¼ \times ^{12}\!/_{51} = ^{3}\!/_{51} = ^{1}\!/_{17}$

---

16. A The 5's in 532.385 represent 500 and 0.005. The possible ratios are:

$$\frac{500}{0.005} \quad \text{which equals} \quad \frac{100{,}000}{1} \quad \text{and} \quad \frac{0.005}{500} \quad \text{which equals} \quad \frac{1}{100{,}000}$$

---

17. D Train A travels 700 miles in the same amount of time that it takes Train B to travel 500. This gives you a rate that you can use to set up a proportion.

The other side of the proportion should be $^{x}\!/_{1500}$ because you are trying to calculate the distance that Train A has traveled in the time that it took Train B to travel the 1500 mile track ❶. Another acceptable proportion would be ❷.

❶
$$\frac{\text{Train A}}{\text{Train B}} : \frac{700}{500} = \frac{x}{1500}$$

❷
$$\frac{\text{Train B}}{\text{Train A}} : \frac{500}{700} = \frac{1500}{x}$$

---

18. C Distance from B to C $= x$
Distance from A to B $= ½\,x$
Distance from A to C $=$ A to B $+$ B to C $= x + ½x = ^{3}\!/_{2}\,x$
Distance from C to D $= ½(^{3}\!/_{2}\,x) = ^{3}\!/_{4}x$
Distance from A to D $=$ A to B $+$ B to C $+$ C to D $= x + ½x + ^{3}\!/_{4}x = 2\,¼\,x$

---

19. C For this problem, and any travel problem, I recommend making a little table. First, set up the rows and columns. The rows will be the things that are traveling. The columns will be rate, time, and distance. Remember, the most important equation on any travel problem is rate × time = distance. Then, fill in the information from the problem into the table.

	Rate	×	Time	=	Distance
HK to Mumbai	$s - 14$		4		
Mumbai to HK	$s + 14$		3.75		

You know that rate × time = distance. So, fill in the last column.

	Rate	×	Time	=	Distance
HK to Mumbai	$s - 14$		4		$4(s - 14)$
Mumbai to HK	$s + 14$		3.75		$3.75(s + 14)$

In this problem, you know the distance is the same. So, set the distance equations equal to each other.

$$4(s - 14) = 3.75(s + 14)$$

20. B Let's examine each answer choice.

I. The number of fourths in $1\frac{1}{2}$. To calculate this, you want to divide $1\frac{1}{2}$ by $\frac{1}{4}$ to see how many there are. $1\frac{1}{2} \div \frac{1}{4} = \frac{3}{2} \div \frac{1}{4} = \frac{3}{2} \times 4 = 6$	**II.** $5 \times \frac{1}{2}$ $= \frac{5}{2}$	**III.** $\frac{3}{2} \div 3$ $= \frac{3}{2} \times \frac{1}{3}$ $= \frac{1}{2}$

$\frac{1}{2} < \frac{5}{2} < 6$ III, II, I.

21. A By scanning the answers, they are all a single number raised to an exponent. Therefore, we want to combine the terms in the expression to something that will match one of the answer choices.

There is not much that can be done with 2^3.
Therefore, let's first focus on 4^{-7}.
You can see that 4 can actually be turned into an expression with an exponential base of 2.

$4 = 2^2$
$4^{-7} = (2^2)^{-7} = 2^{-14}$

Now, multiply. $2^3 \times 4^{-7} = 2^3 \times 2^{-14} = 2^{-11}$.

22. B You start with an even number. Even.
You add it to an odd number. Even + Odd = Odd
Multiply it by an odd number. Odd × Odd = Odd
Subtract even number. Odd − Even = Odd

Result is odd. Answer B.
You can also try this problem by picking numbers and plugging them in as you go through each step.

23. D The data set is missing an element, let's call it n.
Place the rest of the elements in order: 76, 80, 81, 85, 92.

The median is the middle element in a list. If there are an even number of elements in your set, the median is the average of the two middle elements. In this case, when the missing element is included there will be 6 elements, and the median must be the average of the two middle terms.

The median is 83, which is the average of 81 and 85. Therefore, 81 and 85 must remain the middle elements. The only way this can happen is if the missing element is greater than or equal to 85.

Answer D, 90, is the only answer that fits this requirement.

---

24. C Calculate the amount Ralph will make under each plan, then compare.

Earnings Plan	Payment Structure
1	$55,000 base salary
2	$25,000 base salary + 15% of sales
3	$35,000 base salary + $\frac{1}{8}$ of sales

Plan 1: $55,000

Plan 2: First convert the percent to a decimal. 15% = 0.15.
$25,000 + 0.15($200,000)= $25,000 + $30,000 = $55,000

Plan 3: First convert the fraction to a decimal. $\frac{1}{8}$ = 0.125.
$35,000 + 0.125($200,000)= $35,000 + $25,000 = $60,000

---

25. B *Method 1:* The number of bacteria in each dish starts out the same, so call that number x. Dish A doubles every two days and Dish B triples every three days.

> **Dish A:** Day one = x, Day 2 = $2x$, Day 4 = $4x$, Day 6 = $8x$, Day 8 = $16x$, Day 10 = $32x$, Day 12 = $64x$
> **Dish B:** Day one = x, Day 3 = $3x$, Day 6 = $9x$, Day 9 = $27x$, Day 12 = $81x$
> $81x > 64x$

Method 2: Another way you can think of it, is that you know that they start with the same number of bacteria, so let's call that 1. Then, dish A doubles every two days and dish B triples every 3 days. Let's use the variable d to represent the number of days that have passed.

Dish A will double every two days. Therefore, every $\frac{d}{2}$ days, the quantity will double or multiply by 2.

Dish B will triple every three days. Therefore, every $d/3$ days, the quantity will triply or multiply by 3.

Dish A = $2^{(d/2)}$	Dish B = $3^{(d/3)}$
After 12 days, d = 12.	After 12 days, $d = 12$.
Dish A = $2^{(12/2)} = 2^6 = 64$	Dish B = $3^{(12/3)} = 3^4 = 81$

26. A First, determine the value of each space. Between 3.4 and 3.5, there are 5 spaces.

$$3.5 - 3.4 = 0.1$$
$$0.1/5 = 0.02$$

Each space is worth 0.02.

Now, let's determine the values of A and B.

A is one space, or 0.02, below 3.4.	B is one space above 3.5	The distance between A and B.
A = 3.4 − 0.02 = 3.38	B = 3.5 + 0.02 = 3.52	B − A = 3.52 − 3.38 = 0.14

27. A Try setting up a table to help you understand the problem. Use the same structure for any mixture problem and fill in the info from the problem. For the unknown you are solving for, put in a variable. In this case, the unknown is how much liquid of solution 2. Let X represent the unknown, which is the amount of pure saline that must be added.

	Solution 1	Solution 2	TOTAL
Amount of Liquid	10L	X	
Percentage of saline	40%	100%	60%
Amount of saline			

Okay, now that all the information is in your table, fill in the missing spaces.

The total amount of liquid will be solution 1 + solution 2.
The amount of saline, is the percentage of saline times the amount of liquid.

	Solution 1	Solution 2	TOTAL
Amount of Liquid	10L	X	10 + X
Percentage of saline	40%	100%	60%
Amount of saline	40%(10)	100%(X)	60%(10 + X)

So, now make an equation.

The total amount of saline is saline in solution 1 + saline in solution 2.

$$40\%(10) + X = 60\%(10 + X)$$

28. C Let's examine each answer choice.

   A. The smallest positive number for N is 1. Therefore, the smallest that N−1 can be is 0, it can never be negative. N+1 is positive if N is positive, therefore, this answer choice will never be negative.

   B. N+1 and N+2 will both be positive, and a positive times a positive is positive. Eliminate B.

   C. The smallest positive integer is 1.
   If N = 1, then N(N−2) = 1(1−2) = 1(-1) = -1. Answer C.

   D. N is positive, positive times positive= positive. Eliminate D.

---

29. D The lowest possible sum of the two younger children's ages is $2s$, and the highest possible sum is $2t$.
If the oldest child is $\frac{7}{3}$ times the sum of the younger children's ages, then the oldest child is older than $(\frac{7}{3})(2s)$ and younger than $(\frac{7}{3})(2t)$.

$$(\tfrac{7}{3})(2s) < c < (\tfrac{7}{3})(2t)$$
$$\tfrac{14}{3}\,s < c < \tfrac{14}{3}\,t$$

---

30. B First, convert the 2 hours and 40 minutes to minutes.
2 hours and 40 minutes = 160 minutes.
Steve reads 80 pages in 160 minutes.
That's 1 page every 2 minutes.

If Cassandra reads twice as fast, then she reads 1 page per minute. It would take her 300 minutes, or 5 hours, to read a 300 page book.

---

31. C Probability = favorable outcomes ÷ total outcomes
The raindrop has an equal probability of landing on any one point, so the favorable outcomes are represented by the area of the circle, and the total outcomes are represented by the area of the blacktop.

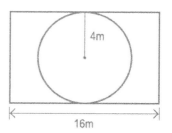

Area of the circle: $\pi r^2 = 16\pi$

Area of the blacktop: length × width
width is equal to the diameter of the circle = 4 × 2 = 8

$$\frac{\text{Area of Circle}}{\text{Area of Blacktop}} : \frac{(16\,\pi)}{(16 \times 8)} = \frac{\pi}{8}$$

32. C Estimate the radius, and then compare your estimate to the student's.

Circumference = $2\pi \times$ radius = 24
π is approximately 3
Substitute that in to the formula

$$\begin{array}{l} 2\pi \times \text{radius} = 24 \\ 2(3) \times \text{radius} \approx 24 \\ 6 \times \text{radius} \approx 24 \\ \text{radius} \approx 4 \end{array}$$

The radius is approximately 4, and the student said the radius was approximately 8.
The estimate is too high by a factor of 2.

---

33. C To find the total number of possibilities, multiply the number of possible characters for each space in the code.

The first character must be a letter, therefore there are 26 possibilities. The second character must be a number, therefore there are 10 possibilities. The third character must be a distinct number, therefore there are 9 possibilities (since one number was already used).

$$\begin{array}{l} \text{Total possibilities} \\ = 26 \times 10 \times 9 \\ = 2340 \end{array}$$

---

34. A Let the original price equal p.
The price was first increased by $17.

$$p + 17$$

This was decreased by 38%.

$$(100\% - 38\%)(p + 17)$$

Now, set this price equal to y and rearrange to isolate the original price p.

$$\begin{array}{l} (100\% - 38\%)(p + 17) = y \\ (62\%)(p + 17) = y \\ p + 17 = {}^{y}\!/_{0.62} \\ p = {}^{y}\!/_{0.62} - 17 \end{array}$$

---

35. C Since AB=AC, you know the triangle is isosceles, and therefore angle ABC=angle ACB.

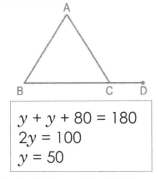

Let angle ACB = y.
The angles in a triangle add up to 180.
angle ABC + angle ACB + angle BAC = 180

$$\begin{array}{l} y + y + 80 = 180 \\ 2y = 100 \\ y = 50 \end{array}$$

The angles on a straight line add up to 180. Angle ACB and angle ACD are along the straight line and therefore add to 180.

$$\begin{array}{l} 50 + \text{angle ACD} = 180 \\ \text{angle ACD} = 130 \end{array}$$

---

36. A Rate $\times$ time = distance
The distance around the track is 50m + 50 m + the total circumference of the two half circles. The two semicircles make one whole circle. The circumference of the circle is $\pi \times$ diameter = 20π.

If you use 3 as an approximation for π, then the circumference is 20π, which is approximately 20(3) = 60.

Distance is approximately: 50 + 50 + 60 = 160m

Joaquin jogs at 5km per hour = 5000 m per hour

Rate × time = distance
5000m per hour × time = 160m
Time = 0.03 hour

The coach estimated 0.5 hours. His estimate is $\frac{0.5}{0.03}$, approximately 16 times too high.

---

37. C The data on the graph is close to a straight line, so it can best be represented by an equation of the form $y = mx + b$ or in this case $h = md + b$, where h is the dependent variable and d is the independent. The y–intercept is 5, so substitute 5 for b.

None of the points are obvious outliers, so you can use any one of them to calculate an approximate slope. The final point appears to be at approximately (5, 7.5). Plugging that point into the equation gives a slope of ½.

$7.5 = m(5)+5$
$2.5 = 5m$
$m = 0.5$
$h = ½d + 5$

---

38. C Let's examine each answer choice.

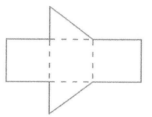

A. Pyramid. All sides other than the base of a pyramid must be triangles. Therefore, you can have one side that is different, but all the rest must be triangles. This is not the case. Eliminate A.

B. Tetrahedron: A tetrahedron has 4 triangular faces. This diagram shows 5 sides. Eliminate B.

C. A right triangular prism would have 2 faces that are right triangles and the remaining faces would be rectangles. In addition, you can see that you can fold up each of the sides, and they would connect to form a prism. Answer Choice C is correct.

D. Prism with equilateral triangle base. There are no equilateral triangles in this diagram. Therefore, this is not the answer. Eliminate D.

---

39. C Since the graph is position versus time and the runner does not stop or turn around, then the graph will never have a negative slope. Eliminate answer B. In addition, it says the runner picks up speed before sprinting to the finish line. Therefore, his graph will not be linear since the slope is not consistent. Eliminate answer A. Graph C correctly shows a graph that could represent position over time. The runner starts slowly, therefore, his position does not change quickly. Towards the end of the race, the runner is sprinting and thus his position will be increasing quickly.

40. C This is actually the simple definition of an integral. However, you don't need to know that to solve this problem. You can either approach it by going through each answer choice and just determining which is a true statement and ignore the diagram, or try to think about how this relates to integrals and what the diagram is showing.

From just looking through the answer choices, the volume of a shape is equal to the area of the base multiplied by the height of an object.

$$V = Ah$$

From examining the diagram, what is happening is that the bases of area A are being repeated all along the height. In other words, you are adding together A's for "h" number of times along the height of the object. Therefore, $A + A + A + \ldots h$ times, is the same as $A \times h$.
Volume $= A \times h = Ah$.

---

41. C The star in figure 1 has one point facing exactly up, while the star in figure 2 has one point facing exactly down. Either rotation or a flip about the x–axis would be necessary to reorient the star in that way, so eliminate answer choice B. The star in figure 2 is much closer to the axes than the star in figure one, so it must have been translated as well. Eliminate answer choices A and D.

---

42. C The student incorrectly assumed that to find the distance between two points you should add the vertical distance to the horizontal distance. However, the shortest distance between two points is the straight line that connects the two points, in this case, as can be seen in the diagram to the right, it is the diagonal line between them.

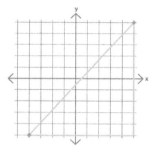

From looking at the diagram, a common way to calculate the distance between two points is to draw a right triangle with the hypotenuse connecting the points. The sides of the right triangle will be the horizontal distance (10 in this problem) and the vertical distance (10 in this problem) and then the hypotenuse or distance between the points can be calculated with the Pythagorean Theorem.

Answer C: Drawing a right triangle with the hypotenuse connecting the two points

43. C In the equation $y = Zx - 2$, Z is the slope of the line. You are given two points on the line: (0, -2) and (2,5). You can calculate the slope either by plugging in one of the points into the equation of the line and solving for Z or by using the formula for calculating slope.

Method 1: Plugging into the equation.
Use the point (2,5) to plug into the equation so that Z does not get multiplied by 0.
Answer C

$$y = Zx - 2$$
$$5 = Z(2) - 2$$
$$2Z = 7$$
$$Z = {}^7\!/_2 = 3\,{}^1\!/_2$$

Method 2: Using both points in the slope formula. (0, -2) & (2, 5)

$$\frac{(y_2 - y_1)}{(x_2 - x_1)} : \frac{(5 - -2)}{(2 - 0)} = \frac{7}{2} = 3\,\frac{1}{2}$$

---

44. B Simplify the inequality by dividing both sides by 5.

Separate the inequality containing an absolute value into two statements joined by "and." Remember to flip the sign when you multiply the inequality by -1. Simplify both statements:
Combine the two statements joined by "and" into one statement.

$$5\,|y - 2| \le 10$$
$$|y - 2| \le 2$$

$$y - 2 \le 2 \text{ and}$$
$$y - 2 \ge -2$$

$$y \le 4 \text{ and } y \ge 0$$

$$0 \le y \le 4$$

---

45. B The area of a triangle is found by multiplying ½ × base × height. For an isosceles triangle, the base and the height are equal.
Therefore, the area = ½ × side × side = ½ side².

Thus, as the length of the side increases, the area will go up as the length squared. For example, if the length triples, the area will increase by $3^2 = 9$.

The graph must show that the increase in the y direction is exponential. Answer B shows this.

Final Exam

1. **Each block = 10 units**

   What is the value of the following?

   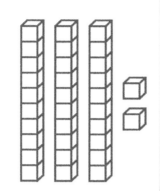

   A. 32
   B. 302
   C. 320
   D. 3020

2. **If the length of one living room is 1.2×10^1 meters and the length of a bacteria is 2×10^{-6} meters, how many times longer is the room?**

   A. 6×10^6
   B. 6×10^8
   C. 2.4×10^{-5}
   D. 2.4×10^7

3. **Which of the following problems could be solved by using the following equation:**

   $$3.5 \div 0.5 \ ?$$

   A. A concert lasts three and a half hours and you missed a half hour. How much of the concert did you see?
   B. The base of a triangle is 0.5cm and the height is 3.5cm, what is the triangle's area?

   C. The length of the wooden plank is three and a half feet and you need pieces that are half a foot long, how many pieces can you get from the plank?
   D. Jimmy's house is 5 miles from Susie's. If Jimmy can run 3.5 miles per hour, how long will it take him to reach Susie's?

4. **A electronics store owner buys products from the manufacturer and then marks them up 20%. For the Labor Day weekend, the store owner has a 10% off sale. What is the percent change from the manufacturer's price to the sales price?**

   A. 8% increase
   B. 10% increase
   C. 12% increase
   D. 18% increase

5. **A scientist has a container with 4.78 million grains of sand. He wants to divide this into 40 cups. He estimates that each cup will have about 12,000 grains of sand. Which describes the reasonableness of his estimate?**

A. The estimate is too high by a factor of 10.
B. The estimate is too low by a factor of 10.
C. The estimate is too low by a factor of 100.
D. The estimate is reasonable.

6. **Which of the following is the farthest from 1?**
    A. $\frac{7}{8}$
    B. 1.12
    C. 0.9^2
    D. $\frac{7}{6}$

7. **What is the value of A on the number line?**

    A. 3.1
    B. 3.5
    C. 3.15
    D. 3.05

8. **Which of the following is/are true?**
    I. The greatest common factor of two numbers can be equal to one of the numbers.
    II. The least common multiple of two numbers can be equal to one of the numbers.
    III. The product of the LCM and GCF of two numbers can equal the product of the two numbers.

A. I only
B. I and II
C. I, II, and III
D. None of the above.

9. **P is divisible by 12 and 30. What is the largest number that we know P is divisible by?**
    A. 30
    B. 60
    C. 120
    D. 360

10. **If the prime factorization of p=2x3³ and the prime factorization of n=2x3x5², then what is the prime factorization of the greatest common factor of p and n?**
    A. 2×3
    B. 2×3^3
    C. $2 \times 3 \times 5$
    D. $2 \times 3^3 \times 5^2$

11. **You are making oatmeal raisin cookies and the recipe calls for ¾ cups of raisins and ⅔ cups of brown sugar. You have 2 cups of brown sugar and decide to increase the recipe in order to use all of your sugar. How many cups of raisins should you use to keep the ratio the same as the original recipe?**
    A. $1\frac{7}{9}$
    B. $2\frac{1}{4}$
    C. $2\frac{5}{6}$
    D. 3

12. An artist created a pattern of shapes: 2 circles, 2 squares, 2 triangles, and 2 rectangles. He can fit 486 shapes in his design. If the pattern continues throughout the design, what will be the last shape?

    A. circle

    B. square

    C. triangle

    D. rectangle

13. Beth can type 40 words per minute, and Vanessa can type 3 words for every 2 that Beth types. If they both start typing at the same time, how many words has Beth typed when Vanessa has finished 4200 words?

    A.   157.5 words

    B.   2800 words

    C.   6300 words

    D.   7000 words

14. You take the square root of a number, multiply it by 3, add 4, and then divide by 2 to get 26. What was the original number?

    A. 4

    B. 32

    C. 256

    D. 2601

15. If the remainder of a number when divided by 7 is 2, what is the remainder when 4 times that number is divided by 7?

    A. 1

    B. 2

    C. 4

    D. 6

16. In the following problem, what properties were used from step 2 to 3 and step 3 to 4, respectively?

1. $73 \times 101 + 200 =$

2. $73(100 + 1) + 200 =$

3. $7300 + 73 + 200 =$

4. $7300 + 200 + 73 =$

5. $7500 + 73 = 7573$

    A. Distributive, Associative

    B. Associative, Commutative

    C. Commutative, Distributive

    D. Distributive, Commutative

17. $|11 - 5| + 12 \div 3^2 \times 6 - 10 =$

    A. -9

    B. 2

    C. 4

    D. 206

18. The ratio of fiction to nonfiction books in a store is 4 to 5. If the store contains 810 books, how many are fiction?

    A. 360

    B. 450

    C. 648

    D. 720

19. A farmer decided to go outside and check on his animals. He passed by the chickens and counted their feet and then he

passed by the pigs and counted their feet. He got a total of 100 feet. He knew he had 8 more chickens than pigs, so he knew the animals were okay. How many chickens did he have?

    A.   14
    B.   22
    C.   23
    D.   44

20. If $^{2n}\!/_3 - 6 = 12$, then what is the value of n?

    A. 9
    B. 12
    C. 24
    D. 27

21. Solve for x in the following inequality. $-4 \le -3x + 2 < 11$

    A. $-3 < x \le 2$
    B. $-3 \le x < 2$
    C. $-2 < x \le 3$
    D. $2 \le x < -3$

22. The formula for converting temperatures in Celsius (°C. to Fahrenheit (°F) is $C = \frac{5}{9}(F-32)$). If the temperature at the beginning of a day was 68°F and it increased by 50% on the Celsius scale, what was the temperature at the end of the day in degree Fahrenheit?

    A. 30° F
    B. 86° F
    C. 98° F
    D. 102° F

23. Solve for y.

$$\frac{(y + 3)}{5} = \frac{(y + 2)}{6}$$

    A. 8
    B. 5
    C. -1
    D. -8

24. Find three consecutive odd integers, such that three times the second is 9 more than twice the third. What is the smallest number?

    A. 9
    B. 11
    C. 12
    D. 15

25. Sonia's brother is 5 less than twice her age. Five years ago, he was 11 less than 3 times her age then. How old is she now?

    A. 6 yrs old
    B. 11 yrs old
    C. 16 yrs old
    D. 27 yrs old

26. y varies directly with x and inversely with z . If $y = 20$, when $x = 10$ and $z = 2$, what does y equal when $x = 15$ and $z = 5$?

    A. 3
    B. 12
    C. 75
    D. 300

27. The graph shows the distance that a car traveled over time. Which of the following graphs shows the same car's speed over time?

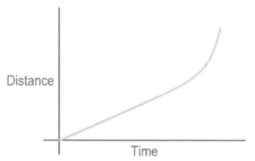

A.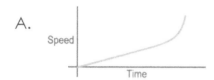

B.

C.

D.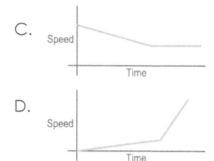

28. What is the y–intercept of the following graph?

$$y = 3x^2 - 8x + 9$$

    A. -8
    B. 3
    C. 4
    D. 9

29. The shaded region in the graph represents what set of inequalities?

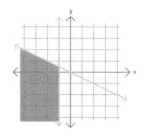

    A. $y \leq -1$ or $y \leq -\frac{1}{2}x$
    B. $y \leq -1$ and $y \leq \frac{1}{2}x$
    C. $x \leq -1$ and $y \leq -\frac{1}{2}x$
    D. $x \leq -1$ and $y \leq -2x$

30. If the area of a circle is A and the circumference is C. what happens to the area and circumference in terms of A and C when you triple the diameter of the circle?

    A. 3A, 3C
    B. 9A, 3C
    C. 9A, 9C
    D. A + 3, C + 3

31. Which of the following is the largest?

    A. 8 square yards
    B. 70 square feet
    C. 10,000 square inches
    D. 5 square yards, 20 square feet, and 500 square inches

32. The outside edges of a picture frame are 8 inches by 12 inches. If the picture that is displayed is 54 sq. inches in area and the picture is 9 inches tall, what is the area of just the frame?

A. 6
B. 7
C. 24
D. 42

A. 2
B. 4
C. 8
D. 9

33. If the volume of a cube is 216 m³, what is its surface area?
   A. 108 m²
   B. 144 m²
   C. 216 m²
   D. 432 m²

34. A man that is 6 feet tall casts a shadow that is 2.5 feet long. If the height of an object and the length of its shadow are proportionate, how tall is a building that casts a shadow 30 feet long?
   A. 12.5 feet
   B. 33.5 feet
   C. 72 feet
   D. 450 feet

35. What is the perimeter of the shape?

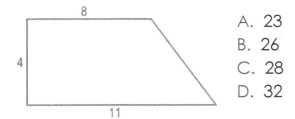

   A. 23
   B. 26
   C. 28
   D. 32

36. What is the area of the square with the coordinates (2,2), (2, -1), (-1, 2), (-1, -1)?

37. In the figure below, angle DCB = 50° and angle BDC = 60°. If AB = BD, find the measure of angle DAB.

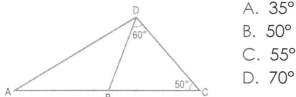

   A. 35°
   B. 50°
   C. 55°
   D. 70°

38. What is the volume of the 3D shape that is made from the following net?

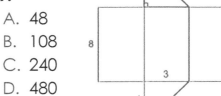

   A. 48
   B. 108
   C. 240
   D. 480

39. Which of the following CANNOT be true of the triangle shown?

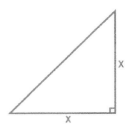

   A. The hypotenuse equals 1000
   B. The side lengths add up to 20.
   C. Two of the angles are equal.
   D. One of the angles measures 60 degrees.

40. You have a circle centered at (-2, -2) and with a diameter of 8. What are the coordinates of the point that is on the circle and has the largest x–coordinate?

    A. (2, -2)
    B. (6, -2)
    C. (8, -2)
    D. (2, 2)

41. Of the following set, which statistical measure is the largest?

7, -3, 11, -4, 8, 2, 9, 2

    A. Mean
    B. Median
    C. Mode
    D. All of the above are equal.

42. If breakdown of favorite sports was consistent across grades, how many 9th graders chose basketball as their favorite?

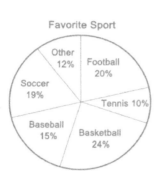

Favorite Sport

Other 12%, Football 20%, Tennis 10%, Basketball 24%, Baseball 15%, Soccer 19%

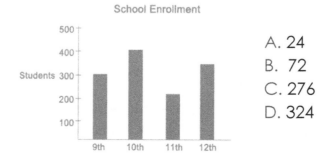

School Enrollment

    A. 24
    B. 72
    C. 276
    D. 324

43. At an amusement park, there is a circular dartboard with radius of 20cm. In the middle of the dartboard, there is a small circle with radius of 4cm. If you have an equal probability of hitting any spot on the dartboard, what is the probability that you will hit the small circle?

    A. $\frac{1}{5}$
    B. $\frac{1}{10}$
    C. $\frac{1}{25}$
    D. $\frac{1}{80}$

44. A game starts by flipping a coin. If you get a heads, then you get to roll a die, and, if you roll a 4, you win the jackpot. If you get a tails, then you must pick a card from a deck, and, if you get a heart, then you win the jackpot. What is the probability of winning the jackpot in this game?

    A. $\frac{5}{12}$
    B. $\frac{1}{8}$
    C. $\frac{5}{24}$
    D. $\frac{1}{96}$

45. You have 70 marbles in a bag that are either yellow, blue, or green. You know that the probability of picking a green marble is 7/10 and you know that there are 39 green marbles in the bag. How many blue marbles are in the bag?

    A. 49
    B. 31
    C. 21
    D. 10

1. C   There are two basic ways to approach this problem. You can start by determining the number of blocks and then multiply by 10.

The number of blocks in each rod is 10. There are three rods, so 30 blocks in the rods. If you add the 30 to the 2 additional blocks, it gives you a total of 32 blocks.

We know that each block is worth 10 units, therefore, 32 blocks is 32x10=320 units.

Otherwise, you can determine the value of each rod. There are 10 blocks in each rod, so 10 x 10 = 100. There are 3 rods, so 100 x 3 = 300. Then, there are two additional blocks, each worth 10. 300 + 10 + 10 = 320.

2. A   ❶ To determine how many times longer the room is, divide the length of the room by the length of the bacteria.

❷ First, divide the numbers. Then, divide the powers of ten by subtracting the exponents.

❸ Convert into proper scientific notation.

❶ $(1.2 \times 10^1) \div (2 \times 10^{-6})$

❷ $1.2 \div 2 = 0.6$
$10^1 \div 10^{-6} = 10^{1-(-6)} = 10^7$
0.6×10^7

❸ 0.6×10^7
$= 6 \times 10^{-1} \times 10^7$
$= 6 \times 10^6$

3. C   Let's examine each answer to see how you would solve it.

A.   A concert lasts three and a half hours and you missed a half hour. How much of the concert did you see? This problem would be solved by using the following equation: 3.5 - 0.5 = 3. Eliminate answer A

B: The base of a triangle is 0.5cm and the height is 3.5cm, what is the triangle's area? The area of a triangle is found by multiplying ½ × base × height. Area = ½ × 0.5 × 3.5. Eliminate answer B

C: The length of the wooden plank is three and a half feet and you need pieces that are half a foot long, how many pieces can you get from the plank? In this case, you want to divide the total plank into pieces. The total plank is 3.5 feet and each piece is 0.5 feet. You must divide to find the total number of pieces. 3.5 ÷ 0.5 = 7. Answer C is correct.

D: Jimmy's house is 5 miles from Susie's. If Jimmy can run 3.5 miles per hour, how long will it take him to reach Susie's?
Distance = rate × time. Therefore, to figure out the time, you divide the distance by the rate. time = 5 miles ÷ 3.5. Eliminate answer D.

4. A The easiest way to solve percent problems is to set the original price of the product to $100 and see how the price changes.

The manufacturer sells the product for $100, and the store owner marks it up 20%. The store sells it for $100 + $20 = $120.

$100 × 20%
= $100 × 0.20 = $20

The store has a 10% off sale. The sale price of $108 is an 8% increase from the manufacturer's price of $100.

$120 × 10%
= $120 × 0.10 = $12
The sale price is
$120 − $12 = $108.

5. B You know you want to estimate and that the total amount of sand will be divided by 40. Therefore, it would make your estimations and calculations easier if you rounded the number to a number divisible by 4. Let's round 4.78 million to 4.8 million.

The next step in solving this problem is to write 4.8 million in a different way. You could either write it with zeros or in scientific notation.

4.8 million
= 4,800,000
= 4.8×10^6

Let's first solve the problem when written in the following form: 4,800,000. Let's divide 4,800,000 by 40. This equals 120,000. Therefore, the estimate was too low by a factor of 10.

You could also use scientific notation.
4.8 million divided by 40
$(4.8 \times 10^6) / (4 \times 10^1)$
$1.2 \times 10^5 = 120,000$
The estimate is too low by a factor of 10.

4.8 million divided by 40
$(4.8 \times 10^6) / (4 \times 10^1)$
$1.2 \times 10^5 = 120,000$

6. C Let's examine each answer choice.

A. $\frac{7}{8}$	B. 1.12	C. 0.9^2	D. $\frac{7}{6}$
Convert the fraction to a decimal by dividing 7 by 8. $\frac{7}{8} = 0.875$. Now, subtract from 1. $1 - 0.875 = 0.125$	$1.12 - 1$ $= 0.12$	0.9^2 $= 0.9 \times 0.9$ $= 0.81$ $1 - 0.81$ $= 0.19$	Convert to a decimal by dividing 7 by 6. $7 \div 6 = 1.1666...$ $1.1666... - 1$ $= 0.1666.$

Answer C has the largest distance from 1.

7. D   Let's determine what the different lines on the number line represent. There is a mark that is halfway between 3 and 3.2. Therefore, this must be 3.1.

Now, we know that A is halfway between 3 and 3.1. If you look at the answers, you can see that answer choice D is the only number that is between 3 and 3.1. But, let's still discuss how to calculate it.

It is sometimes easiest to add trailing zeros to the end of the numbers to help you figure out what is halfway in between. 3 becomes 3.00 and 3.1 becomes 3.10. It is now easier to determine that the number that is halfway between 3.00 and 3.10 is 3.05, as 5 is halfway between 0 and 10.

Another way to figure out what is halfway between two numbers is by finding the average of the numbers. Add the numbers and divide by 2.
$3 + 3.1 = 6.1$
$6.1 \div 2 = 3.05$

---

8. C   Let's examine each option.

| **I.** The greatest common factor of two numbers can be equal to one of the numbers. This is true. If one number divides evenly into the second number, then it would be the greatest common factor of the numbers. Example: the GCF of 8 and 16 is 8. | **II.** The least common multiple of two numbers can be equal to one of the numbers. This is true. If one number divides evenly into the second number, then the second number would be the least common multiple of the numbers. Example: the LCM of 6 and 24 is 24. | **III.** The product of the LCM and GCF of two numbers can equal the product of the two numbers. This is true. If one number divides evenly into the second number, then the smaller is the GCF and the larger is the LCM. Therefore, the product of the two numbers would be equal to the product of the LCM and GCF. Example: 5 and 10. GCF = 5, LCM = 10, product = 50. |

9. B If P is divisible by a number, then the prime factors of that number must also be factors of P. Therefore, we should find the prime factorization of 12 and 30 to determine what are some of the factors of P.

The prime factorization of 12 is: $12 = 2 \times 2 \times 3$
Therefore, factors of P must include 2, 2, and 3.

The prime factorization of 30 is: $30 = 2 \times 3 \times 5$
Therefore, factors of P must include 2, 3, and 5.

We know that the factors of P include 2, 2, 3, and 5.
$2 \times 2 \times 3 \times 5 = 60$
So, the product of some of the factors of P is 60, and P is divisible by 60.

10. A The greatest common factor is the largest factor that both numbers share. Therefore, let's see what factors divide evenly into both numbers.

2 divides evenly into p and n
3 divides evenly into p and n.
There are no additional factors that divide into both numbers.
Therefore, 2×3 is the GCF.

You can also solve for p and n and then find the GCF.
$p = 2 \times 3^3 = 2 \times 27 = 54$
$n = 2 \times 3 \times 5^2 = 150$
GCF of 54 and 150 is 6

11. B Set this problem up as a ratio. The variable y represents the number of cups of raisins that are needed.

$$\frac{\text{Raisins}}{\text{Brown sugar}} = \frac{\frac{3}{4} \text{ cups}}{\frac{2}{3} \text{ cups}} = \frac{y \text{ cups}}{2 \text{ cups}}$$

You can solve for the variable y by cross–multiplying.

❶
$\frac{3}{4} \times 2 = \frac{2}{3} y$
$\frac{3}{2} = \frac{2}{3} y$

❷
$\frac{3}{2} \times \frac{3}{2} = \frac{2}{3} y \times \frac{3}{2}$
$\frac{9}{4} = y$
$2\frac{1}{4} = y$

Multiply both sides by $\frac{3}{2}$ to get y by itself.

12. C There are 8 shapes in the pattern that will continue to repeat. Therefore, every set of 8 shapes will be 2 circles, 2 squares, 2 triangles, and 2 rectangles. The last shape in the pattern is a rectangle. The 8th shape and every multiple of 8 will also be a rectangle. So, we can determine what number close to 486 will be a multiple of 8.

480 is divisible by 8. Therefore, the 480th shape will be a rectangle and then the pattern will continue for the next set. In the next set of shapes, there will only be 6, so the 486th shape will be a triangle.

13. B First, figure out Vanessa's typing rate. "Vanessa can type 3 words for every 2 that Beth types." Therefore, Vanessa can type $\frac{3}{2}$ times faster than Beth.

> Vanessa's rate =
> $\frac{3}{2}$ × Beth's rate
> = $\frac{3}{2}$ × 40 words per minute
> = 60 words per minute

Next, determine the amount of time that Vanessa typed.
Vanessa typed 4200 words, and she can type 60 words per minute.
If you divide the number of words by her rate, you will determine the time it takes.
Time Vanessa typed = # of words ÷ Typing rate = 4200 ÷ 60 = 70 mins

Finally, determine how many words Beth can type in 70 minutes.
Number of words Beth types = Beth's rate × Beth's time
= 40 words per minute x 70 minutes = 2800 words

---

14. C To find the original number, work backwards.
The last step was to divide by 2 to get 26.
Therefore, perform the inverse operation of multiplying by 2.
26 x 2 = 52.

The step before that was to add 4.
Perform the inverse operation of subtracting 4.
52 - 4 = 48.

The step before that was to multiply by 3.
Perform the inverse operation of dividing by 3.
48 ÷ 3 = 16

The step before that was to take the square root of the number.
Perform the inverse operation of squaring the number.
$16^2 = 256$

---

15. A To solve this problem, first pick a number that has a remainder of 2 when divided by 7. There are an infinite number of possible numbers to choose from, including: 2, 9, 16, and 23.

Let's choose 9. Now, the problem asks what is remainder when 4 times that number is divided by 7. Multiply 9 by 4 and divide by 7 to find remainder.
9 x 4 = 36
36 ÷ 7 = 5 remainder 1
Remainder is 1.

---

16. D In the problem, the distributive property was used to help calculate 73×101. The distributive property states that $a(b + c) = ab + ac$.

Then, from steps 3 to 4, the order of the addition problem was changed. The commutative property states that for addition, order does not matter Distributive, Commutative

1. $73 \times 101 + 200 =$
2. $73(100 + 1) + 200 =$
3. $7300 + 73 + 200 =$
4. $7300 + 200 + 73 =$
5. $7500 + 73 = 7573$

---

17. C $|11 - 5| + 12 \div 3^2 \times 6 - 10 =$

❶ Order of Operations is PEMDAS. Parentheses come first. The terms inside an absolute value sign are considered to be in parentheses.

❷ Next, Exponents.
❸ Next, Multiplication and Division from left to right.

❹ Finally, Addition and Subtraction from left to right.

❶ $|6| + 12 \div 3^2 \times 6 - 10$
$= 6 + 12 \div 3^2 \times 6 - 10$

❷ $6 + 12 \div 9 \times 6 - 10 =$

❸ $6 + {}^{12}\!/_9 \times 6 - 10 =$
$6 + {}^4\!/_3 \times 6 - 10 =$
$6 + 8 - 10 =$

❹ $14 - 10 = 4$

---

18. A If the ratio of fiction to nonfiction books is 4 to 5, then the fraction of fiction books in the store is $\frac{4}{9}$.

To determine the number of fiction books, multiply the fraction of fiction books in the store by the total number of books in the store.

$\frac{4}{9} \times 810 = 360$

---

19. B For algebra word problems, you should assign variables to the unknowns. In this case, there are two unknowns: the number of chickens and the number of pigs.

Let c = number of chickens
Let p = number of pigs

Then set up equations by using information in the problem. We know that the farmer had 8 more chickens than pigs.

We know that the total number of feet is 100 and that each chicken has 2 feet and each pig has 4.

$c = p + 8$
$2c + 4p = 100$

Now, solve this system of equations.

You can use the substitution method by substituting for c in the second equation what c equals in the first equation.

$$2c + 4p = 100 \qquad \text{• Second Equation}$$
$$2(p + 8) + 4p = 100 \qquad \text{• Substitute first equation for } c$$
$$2p + 16 + 4p = 100 \qquad \text{• Distribute}$$
$$6p + 16 = 100 \qquad \text{• Combine like terms}$$
$$6p = 84 \qquad \text{• Subtract 16 from both sides}$$
$$p = 14 \qquad \text{• Divide both sides by 6 to solve for } p$$
$$c = p + 8 \qquad \text{• Use first equation to solve for } c$$
$$c = 14 + 8 = 22 \qquad \text{• Plug in value for } p, \text{ and solve for } c$$

---

20. D ❶ To solve equations, you must isolate the variable.

❷ First, since 6 is subtracted from the left side, you must do the opposite, so add 6 to both sides.

❸ Since you are dividing n by 3, perform the opposite operation. Multiply both sides by 3.

❹ Since you are multiplying n by 2, you must divide both sides by 2 to get n alone.

You can plug the 27 back into the original equation to make sure that it works.

❶
$$\tfrac{2n}{3} - 6 = 12$$

❷
$$\tfrac{2n}{3} - 6 + 6 = 12 + 6$$
$$\tfrac{2n}{3} = 18$$

❸
$$\tfrac{2n}{3} \times 3 = 18 \times 3$$
$$2n = 54$$

❹
$$2n = 54$$
$$2n \div 2 = 54 \div 2$$
$$n = 27$$

---

21. A Isolate the variable. Ensure that what you do to one side of the inequality, you do to all sides of the inequality.

Subtract 2.

Divide by -3. When dividing by a negative number, flip the inequality signs.

Rearrange the inequality statement.

$$-4 \le -3x + 2 < 11$$

$$-4 - 2 \le -3x + 2 - 2 < 11 - 2$$
$$-6 \le -3x < 9$$

$$-6 \div -3 \ge -3x \div -3 > 9 \div -3$$
$$2 \ge x > -3$$

$$-3 < x \le 2$$

---

22. B This problem involves many steps.
❶ First, convert the temperature from Fahrenheit to Celsius.
❷ Then, increase the temperature by 50% on the Celsius scale.
❸ Finally, convert the temperature back to Fahrenheit.

❶
$$C = \tfrac{5}{9}(F - 32)$$
$$= \tfrac{5}{9}(68 - 32)$$
$$= \tfrac{5}{9}(36) = 20°C$$

❷
$$20 \times 50\% = 20 \times 0.50 = 10$$
$$20 + 10 = 30$$
$$30° \ C$$

❸
$$C = \tfrac{5}{9}(F - 32)$$
$$30 = \tfrac{5}{9}(F - 32)$$
$$30\left(\tfrac{9}{5}\right) = F - 32$$
$$54 = F - 32$$
$$F = 86 = 86° \ F$$

23. D $\dfrac{(y+3)}{5} = \dfrac{(y+2)}{6}$

❶ First, cross–multiply to remove the fractions.
❷ Use distributive property.
❸ Bring all the variables to one side.
  Subtract 5y from both sides.
❹ Isolate y by subtracting 18 from both sides.

❶ $5(y+2) = 6(y+3)$

❷ $5y + 10 = 6y + 18$

❸ $10 = y + 18$

❹ $-8 = y$
  $y = -8$

---

24. B Use variables to represent the unknown quantities. Let the smallest number = n. Then, the second number would be n+2. The next number would be n+4.

Now, set up an equation and solve for n. Three times the second is 9 more than twice the third.

n, $n + 2$, and $n + 4$

$3(n + 2) = 9 + 2(n + 4)$
$3n + 6 = 9 + 2n + 8$
$3n + 6 = 2n + 17$
$n + 6 = 17$
$n = 11$

---

25. C *Method 1:* There are two unknowns, Sonia's age and her brother's age. Choose variables to represent each of the unknowns. ❶

❷ Now, set up equations. Sonia's brother is 5 less than twice her age.

❸ Five years ago, he was 11 less than 3 times her age then.

❹ Now, solve the system of equations. You can use substitution since they are both solved for b.
  Sonia is 16 years old.

❶ Let s represent Sonia's age.
  Let b represent her brother's age.

❷ $b = 2s - 5$

❸ $b - 5 = 3(s - 5) - 11$
  $b - 5 = 3s - 15 - 11$
  $b - 5 = 3s - 26$
  $b = 3s - 21$

❹ $b = 2s - 5$
  $b = 3s - 21$
  $2s - 5 = 3s - 21$
  $-5 = s - 21$
  $16 = s$

Method 2: You can always plug in answers on algebra word problems, if you ever confused or stuck.

I will demonstrate the steps if you chose to try answer C.

Sonia's age is 16.
Sonia's brother is 5 less than twice her age. Sonia's brother is: 32 - 5 = 27

Okay, what happened 5 years ago. Five years ago, Sonia was 11 and Sonia's brother was 22. Well, let's see if that works.

Five years ago, he was 11 less than 3 times her age then. 22 = 3(11) - 11
This works and is our answer.

26. B First, set up an equation to represent the relationship between the variables.

   ❶ Let k represent the constant of variation between the variables.

   ❷ y varies directly with x and varies inversely with z. Now, plug in the values of the variables to find k.

   ❸ Now, determine what y equals when $x = 15$ and $z = 5$.

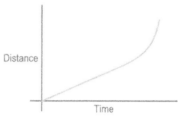

❶ $y = \dfrac{kx}{z}$

❷ $20 = \dfrac{10k}{2}$
$20 = 5k$
$4 = k$
$y = \dfrac{4x}{z}$

❸ $y = \dfrac{4x}{z}$
$y = \dfrac{(4)(15)}{5}$
$y = \dfrac{60}{5}$
$y = 12$

---

27. B As can be seen in the graph, the distance that the car travels increases steadily during the first part of the car's trip. If the distance increases at a steady rate that means the speed for that car is staying the same over that period of time.

During the second part of the trip, the car's distance increases exponentially. Therefore, the car is accelerating, and the speed is increasing.

The graph in answer choice B shows this pattern.

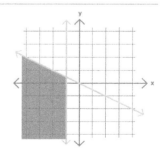

---

28. D The y–intercept of a graph is the point on the graph that crosses the y–axis. If a point is on the y–axis, then its x–value is 0. Therefore, plug in $x = 0$ to find the y–intercept.

$y = 3x^2 - 8x + 9$
$y = 3(0^2) - 8(0) + 9$
$y = 9$

---

29. C Let's first determine the equation of each line.

The vertical line.
The equation for the vertical line is $x = -1$. In this case, the values that are less than -1 are shaded. So, the inequality that represents this is $x \leq -1$.

The diagonal line.
The diagonal line has a y–intercept of 0 and a slope of $-\frac{1}{2}$. Therefore, the equation of the line is $y = -\frac{1}{2}x$. The region below this line is shaded. The inequality that represents this is $y \leq -\frac{1}{2}x$.

Only the overlapped region of the two inequalities is shaded, which is only the areas that make both inequalities true. "AND is used to represent only areas that satisfy the first inequality and the second inequality.

$x \leq -1$ and $y \leq -\frac{1}{2}x$

30. B Let's first examine the area.
The formula for the area of a circle is $\pi \times radius^2$
If the diameter triples, the radius also triples.
Therefore, the new area of the circle is $\pi(3 \times radius)^2 = \pi \times 9 \times radius^2$
$= 9\pi\ radius^2 = 9A$

The formula for the circumference of a circle is $\pi \times diameter$. Therefore, the new circumference $= \pi(3 \times diameter) = 3 \times \pi \times diameter = 3C$

---

31. A Let's convert each answer to square inches, so that you can easily compare the quantities.

   A. 8 square yards
   8 sq yards $\times\ ^{36\ in}\!/_{1\ yard} \times\ ^{36\ in}\!/_{1\ yard} = 10368$ sq. inches

   B. 70 square feet
   70 sq feet $\times\ ^{12\ in}\!/_{1\ foot} \times\ ^{12\ in}\!/_{1\ foot} = 10080$ sq. inches

   C. 10,000 square inches

   D. 5 square yards, 20 square feet, and 500 square inches
   5 sq yards $\times\ ^{36\ in}\!/_{1\ yard} \times\ ^{36\ in}\!/_{1\ yard} = 6480$ sq. inches
   20 sq feet $\times\ ^{12\ in}\!/_{1\ foot} \times\ ^{12\ in}\!/_{1\ foot} = 2880$ sq inches
   $6480 + 2880 + 500 = 9860$ sq inches

---

32. D The key to solving this problem is to focus on relevant pieces of information. the area of the outside of the picture frame, and then subtract the area (54 sq. inches) of the picture inside.

❶ 8 in $\times$ 12 in = 96 sq. in

❷ 96 sq. in – 54 sq. in = 42 sq. in

❶ Area of entire picture including frame.
❷ Area of entire picture – Area of picture displayed.

---

33. C The volume of a cube is found by cubing the length of the side.

Volume = side³
216 = side³
6 = side

The surface area of a cube is found by multiplying the area of each face by the 6 faces.
Surface Area $= 6 \times$ Area of each face $= 6 \times side^2 = 6 \times 6^2 = 216$
Surface Area $= 216\ m^2$

34. C Set up a proportion between the height of the object and the length of the shadow.

$$\frac{\text{height of man}}{\text{shadow of man}} = \frac{\text{height of building}}{\text{shadow of building}}$$

Cross multiply and solve for b.
Building's height = 72 feet

$6/2.5 = b/30$
$6(30) = 2.5(b)$
$180 = 2.5b$
$b = 72$

---

35. C The perimeter of a shape is the distance around its edges. The last side must be found.

Draw a vertical line through the middle of the shape to create a rectangle and a right triangle.

The rectangle has dimensions of 4 by 8. The right triangle's sides are 4 and 3.
❶ To find the missing side, use the Pythagorean Theorem.

❷ To find perimeter, sum the length of all the sides.

❶ $3^2 + 4^2 = \text{hypotenuse}^2$
$9 + 16 = \text{hypotenuse}^2$
$25 = \text{hypotenuse}^2$
$5 = \text{hypotenuse}$

❷ Perimeter
$= 8 + 5 + 11 + 4 = 28$

---

36. D The easiest way to solve this problem is by first graphing the coordinate pairs and then finding the dimensions of the square. The coordinate pairs are graphed.
(2,2), (2, -1), (-1, 2), (-1, -1)
As can be seen in the graph, the square is 3 by 3. Therefore, the area is 9.

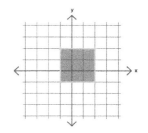

---

37. A First, let's find the measure of angle CBD. In a triangle, the measures of the angles must sum to 180°. In triangle CBD, you know two of the angles, so add them up and subtract the sum from 180 to determine the measure of the third angle.

$180° - (50° + 60°)$
$= 180° - 110° = 70°$
angle CBD = 70°

Now, let's find the measure of angle ABD. You know that angle ABD and angle CBD form a straight angle, which must total 180°. Therefore, angle ABD = 180° − angle CBD.

$180° - 70° = 110°.$
angle ABD = 110°.

The problem stated that AB = BD. That makes triangle ABD an isosceles triangle. The angles opposite equal sides are equal, so angle ADB and angle DAB are equal. We know the third angle in triangle ABD is 110°, so we know the other two angles must sum to 70° so that the total of all three angles is 180°.

Therefore, we know that angle ADB + angle DAB = 70°. We also know that angle ADB = angle DAB, so each of the angles must equal 35°.

38. A The first step to solve this problem is to determine what 3D shape can be made from that net. If you are asked to find the volume, you need a 3D object.

Note that this net has 5 faces - 3 rectangles and 2 triangles. You can think about folding up all the shapes on the outside to form a triangular prism. Here is the shape that is created:

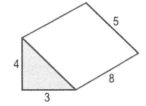

Note, the two triangles are the base of the prism and then you have three rectangles around the prism. Now, we must calculate the volume. To find the volume of a prism, you can note that the triangular base repeats along the entire height of the object. Therefore, find the area of the base and multiply it by the height.

Volume = Area of triangle x Height of Prism
= (½ × 3 × 4) × 8 = 6 × 8 = 48

39. D Let's examine each answer choice to see if can be true.

Answer A. The hypotenuse equals 1000 — This can be true. We know nothing about the lengths of the sides.

Answer B. The side lengths add up to 20. — There is no reason why this could not be true.

Answer C. Two of the angles are equal. — This is definitely true. The triangle has two sides that are the same size; therefore the angles opposite those sides must also be equal.

Answer D. One of the angles measures 60 degrees. — This is false. Since there are two sides that each equal x and one right angle, the triangle is a 45–45–90, or right isosceles triangle. None of the angles can equal 60 degrees.

40. A The easiest way to visualize this problem on a graph. If the diameter of the circle is 8, then the radius is 4. From the center at (-2,-2), go out 4 in each direction, and then draw the circle.

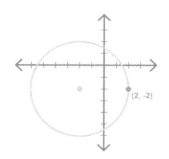

The point on the circle with the largest x–coordinate is going to be 4 points from the center in the positive direction and with the same y–coordinate. 4 points away is at (-2 + 4, -2) = (2,-2)

---

41. B Let's calculate each of the statistical measures of the following set: 7, -3, 11, -4, 8, 2, 9, 2

A. Mean: Mean is the average of the data. It is found by adding all the elements and dividing by the number of elements.

> Mean = (7 + -3 + 11 + -4 + 8 + 2 + 9 + 2) ÷ 8 = 4

B. Median: This is the middle value when the numbers are in order. Order the numbers from smallest to largest. -4, -3, 2, 2, 7, 8, 9, 11 Since this data set has an even number of elements, you must find the average of the two middle numbers, 2 and 7.

> Median = (2 + 7) ÷ 2 = 4.5

C. Mode: The mode is the element that appears most often. In this case, 2 is the only number that appears more than once.

> Mode = 2

Median is the largest.

---

42. B From the pie chart, you can see that 24% of the students chose basketball as their favorite sport. Furthermore, from the bar graph, you can see that there are 300 9th graders in total.

Therefore, to find out the number of 9th graders who chose basketball, we need to multiply.
24% × 300
= $^{24}/_{100}$ × 300
= 72

---

43. C To find the probability, find the area of the small circle and divide that by the area of the total dartboard.

❶ Area of small circle = πradius²
❷ Area of dartboard = πradius²
❸ Probability of getting in the small circle
    = Small Circle Area ÷ Dartboard Area

❶ = π4² = 16π

❷ = π20² = 400π

❸ = 16π ÷ 400π
  = $^{16}\!/_{400}$
  = $^{1}\!/_{25}$

---

44. C You must figure out the probability of winning the jackpot if you flip a heads and then add that to the probability of winning the jackpot if you flip a tails.

Jackpot with Heads	**Jackpot with Tails**	Now, add the two probabilities.
Multiply the probability of getting a heads by the probability of rolling a 4.	Multiply the probability of getting a tails by the probability of picking a heart from a deck.	$^{1}\!/_{12}$ + $^{1}\!/_{8}$ = $^{2}\!/_{24}$ + $^{3}\!/_{24}$ = $^{5}\!/_{24}$
= ½ × ⅙ = $^{1}\!/_{12}$	= ½ × $^{13}\!/_{52}$ = $^{13}\!/_{104}$ = ⅛	

---

45. D If the probability of picking a green or blue marble is 7/10, then you can multiply this probability by the total number of marbles to find out the number of green or blue marbles.
$^{7}\!/_{10}$ × 70 = 49
There are 49 marbles that are either green or blue.

If you know that 39 of those marbles are green, then you can subtract to find the number of blue marbles.
49 − 39 = 10
10 blue marbles

Appendix:
Glossary

Absolute Value:

The magnitude or distance a number is from zero. It is always expressed as a positive number. Example: The absolute value of 7, written as $|\ 7\ |$ is 7. $|\ -3\ | = 3$.

Acute angle:

An angle that has a measure between 0 and 90 degrees.

Area:

The two–dimensional space inside an object.

Associative:

Property that states for problems containing just addition or just multiplication, grouping of numbers does not affect the result.

Bisector:

A line that cuts an angle in half.

Chord:

A line that begins at one point on the circle and ends at another but does not necessarily pass through the center.

Circumference:

The perimeter of a circle which is equal to the product of π and the diameter of the circle.

Combination:

The number of ways a group of elements can be chosen from a larger set of elements when the order of the chosen elements does not matter.

Commutative:
Property that states for problems containing only multiplication or only addition, order does not matter.

Complementary:
Angles that add up to 90 degrees.

Congruent:
Two polygons that are congruent have the same size and shape. All the sides and angles of the shapes will be equal.

Coordinate Plane:
Shows relationship between two variables with a horizontal number line called the x–axis and a vertical number line called the y–axis.

Counting Numbers:
Positive numbers: 1, 2, 3, 4. Also called natural numbers.

Denominator:
The part of a fraction that lies below the line. It serves as the divisor of the numerator.

Diameter:
Any line that begins at one point on a circle, passes through the center, and ends at another point on the circle.

Difference:
The result of a subtraction problem.

Dilation:
A transformation for which an object's coordinates are all increased proportionately.

Direct Variation:
When the value of a variable is equal to a constant multiplied by another variable. $y = kx$

Distributive:
A property indicating a way in which multiplication is applied to addition of two or more numbers. Each term inside a set of parentheses can be multiplied by a factor outside the parentheses. $a(b + c) = ab + ac$

Dividend:
A number to be divided. For example, in the division problem $16 \div 8 = 2$, 16 is the dividend.

Divisor:

The number by which a dividend is divided. For example, in the division problem $16 \div 8 = 2$, 8 is the divisor.

Divisible:

Whether a number is capable of being divided. In other words, if a number is divisible by 3, then 3 is a factor of that number.

Domain:

A description of all the inputs or x–values for which a function has a valid output.

Equilateral:

An equilateral polygon has sides of equal length.

Even Number:

Any integer that is divisible by 2.

Expanded Form:

Writing a number as the sum of the value of each of its digits.
Example: 321 in expanded form $= 300 + 20 + 1$

Factors:

An integer that divides evenly into a number with no remainder.
Example: 4 is a factor of 12.

Factorials:

The factorial of a positive integer is equal to the product of all positive integers less than or equal to that number.

Function:

A specific type of relation for which each independent variable produces exactly one dependent variable.

Greatest Common Factor (GCF):

The GCF of two numbers is the largest factor that they share.
Example: GCF of 18 and 24 is 6.

Identity:

The identity of addition is 0. Therefore, any number plus zero will equal itself. The identity of multiplication is 1. Therefore, any number times 1 will equal itself.

Improper Fraction:

Fractions with numerators that are greater than or equal to the denominator.

Integers:
-3, -2, -1, 0, 1, 2, 3. Integers include negative, zero, and positive numbers. Any number that must be expressed as a fraction or decimal is not an integer.

Indirect Variation:
When the value of a variable is equal to a constant divided by another variable. $y = \frac{k}{x}$. If two variables vary indirectly, then they are inversely proportional.

Irrational Numbers:
Any number that cannot be expressed as a fraction, such as decimals that do not terminate or repeat. The square root of 2 and pi are examples of irrational numbers.

Isosceles Triangle:
A triangle that has exactly two equal sides and exactly two equal angles.

Least Common Denominator:
The least common multiple of all the denominators in an addition or subtraction problem involving fractions.

Least Common Multiple (LCM):
The LCM of two numbers is the smallest non-zero multiple that they both share. Example: LCM of 15 and 20 is 60.

Mean:
The average of a set of numbers which is equal to the sum of the numbers divided by the number of numbers.

Median:
The middle number in a set of numbers.

Mixed Number:
A number containing both a fraction and a whole number.
For example, $3 \frac{4}{5}$ is a mixed number.

Mode:
The most frequently occurring number or piece of data in a set of data.

Multiples:
A multiple of a number is equal to that number times an integer. Example: Multiples of 12 include 12, 24, 36, and 48.

Natural Numbers:
Positive numbers: 1, 2, 3, 4. Also called counting numbers.

Number Line:

A straight line used for representing positive and negative numbers.

Numerator:

The part of a fraction that is above the line. The numerator signifies the number to be divided by the denominator.

Obtuse angle:

An angle that is greater than 90 degrees but less than 180 degrees.

Odd Numbers:

Any integer that is not divisible by 2.

Order of Operations:

Often called PEMDAS. For problems with multiple operations, this is the standardized order in which operations must be carried out. The order is Parentheses, Exponents, Multiplication and Division from left to right, and Addition and Subtraction from left to right.

Parallel Lines:

Lines that never intersect and have the same slope.

Perimeter:

The distance around the edge of an object.

Permutation:

The number of ways a group of elements can be chosen from a larger set of elements when the order of the chosen elements matters.

Perpendicular Lines:

Lines that intersect to form four 90 degree angles.

Pi (π):

Constant that is equal to the ratio of any circle's circumference to its diameter. It is an irrational number but can be approximated as 3.14.

Prime Number:

Any number that has only itself and 1 as its factors. Examples: 2, 7, 23

Probability:

The number of favorable outcomes divided by the number of possible outcomes.

Product:

The result of a multiplication problem.

Pythagorean Theorem:

A relation among the three sides of a right triangle which states that the square of the hypotenuse of a right triangle is equal to the sum of the squares of the other two sides.

Quadrant:

The four areas of the coordinate plane. The quadrant in the upper right is called quadrant I and the quadrants are counted counterclockwise.

Quotient:

The result of a division problem.

Radius:

The distance between the center of a circle and any point on the circle itself.

Range:

Set of y–values or outputs of a function.

Ratio:

A means of comparing one expression containing numbers or variables to another.

Rational Numbers:

Any number that can be expressed as a fraction. This includes decimals that terminate or repeat. Examples: -3.451, ⅓

Real Numbers:

All rational and irrational numbers.

Reflection:

A transformation that involves flipping an object around an axis creating a mirror image of an object.

Relation:

A patterned relationship between two variables.

Remainder:

The portion of the dividend that is not evenly divisible by the divisor. For example, when 13 is divided by 5, the remainder is 3.

Right angle:

An angle that equals 90 degrees.

Rotation:

A transformation that involves turning an object about a pivot point.

Sample Space:

The set of all possible outcomes.

Scalene Triangle:

A triangle with sides of different lengths. In addition, all angles of a scalene triangle will be different.

Scientific Notation:

A way of writing numbers as products consisting of a number between 1 and 10 multiplied by a power of 10.

Similar:

Figures that have the same shape are similar. They can be different sizes and positions as the result of uniform scaling (enlarging or shrinking) or transformations (rotation, reflection, or translation). When two figures are similar, the ratios of the lengths of their corresponding sides are equal.

Slope:

The change in the y–coordinate divided by the change in the x–coordinate for a line. This is often referred to as "rise over run".

Sum:

The result of an addition problem.

Supplementary:

Angles that add up to 180 degrees.

Surface Area:

The sum of the areas of all of the faces of an object.

Tangent:

A line on the outside of a circle that touches the circle at only one point.

Translation:

A transformation that involves the movement of an object without changing it in any other way.

Volume:

The three–dimensional space filled by an object.

Whole Numbers:
0, 1, 2, 3, 4, ... Includes zero and the counting numbers.

x–axis:
The horizontal axis of a two–dimensional coordinate plane.

y–axis:
The vertical axis of a two–dimensional coordinate plane.

y–intercept:
The point at which a line crosses the y–axis.

Made in United States
North Haven, CT
08 February 2022

15892754R00226